India's Transforming Financial Sector

India's Transforming Financial Sector

Edited by
Manoranjan Sharma

ATLANTIC
PUBLISHERS & DISTRIBUTORS (P) LTD

Published by

ATLANTIC

PUBLISHERS & DISTRIBUTORS (P) LTD

B-2, Vishal Enclave, Opp. Rajouri Garden,
New Delhi-110027
Phones : 25413460, 25429987, 25466842

Sales Office
7/22, Ansari Road, Darya Ganj,
New Delhi-110002
Phones : 23273880, 23275880, 23280451
Fax : 91-11-23285873
web : www.atlanticbooks.com
e-mail : info@atlanticbooks.com

ISBN 81-269-0808-4

Printed in India
at Nice Printing Press, Delhi

Preface

An elaborate network of financial institutions and markets forms the edifice of the financial system in India. Pre-reforms, the government regulated the financial sector with administered interest rates and other quantitative restrictions. The process of economic reforms, against the backdrop of severe balance of payments crisis and danger of insolvency in the banking system, liberalised financial sector. Deregulation of interest rates and market-based allocation of resources infused competition in the financial markets and aligned various short-term interest rates, call money and foreign exchange markets. Opening up of current account and progressive capital account liberalisation increased foreign capital inflows and progressively integrated foreign exchange market with the domestic financial system.

India has entered the second stage of financial sector development, where market forces are helping in resources allocation and efficient price discovery process. With the first stage of 'crisis-driven' reforms removing structural bottlenecks in the financial system, the second stage of 'consensus-driven' reforms must enhance stability and efficiency and foster greater market discipline in the financial sector. Public financial institutions need more capital to finance infrastructural projects, social services, global expansion and meeting stringent regulatory requirements. In the ultimate analysis, financial sector reforms must lead to market-driven ownership of public financial institution.

The interaction of real and monetary sectors, a deep, liquid and transparent financial market and greater depth in India's bond market are needed to streamline financial sector. While SEBI and Government of India improved efficiency and transparency in the bond market, removal of 'government's captive market phenomenon' from the debt market and greater participation of insurance and pension funds is imperative.

The harmonisation of regulatory institutions and devising of new financial architecture is necessary to enhance the resilience of India's financial sector and reduce the fragility of some financial institutions. High exposure in government securities, government guaranteed loans, improper valuation of collaterals, vulnerability to interest rate cycle, still high level of NPAs, unsatisfactory corporate governance and disclosures, inadequate surveillance, stock market volatility, risk concentration and policy failure cause concern. This necessitates improving transparency and governance, resolving failure in the industrial and financial sector, de-linking government and private sector, fostering innovation, and improving the supervisory and regulatory infrastructure. Given the debilitating impact of financial sector crisis on the economy, the stability of the financial sector should be the goal of the economy. Corporate governance, accounting disclosures, compliance with international accounting standards and effective offsite surveillance and onsite inspections will help in greater financial stability. Financial stability can be strengthened by improved financial infrastructure, enhanced competition and restructured segments of financial system.

India continues to be predominantly bank-based with a bank intermediation ratio of about 80 per cent. Within the banking sector, Public Sector Banks (PSBs) continue to hold sway. Resource allocation is, therefore, mostly public sector driven. Enhanced financial liberalization through various policy initiatives and calibrated prudential regulatory measures transformed banks and financial services sector. Changes in ownership and capital structure, intensified competition, increased autonomy, technological upgradation, performance measurement and monitoring of banks are reflected in broad indicators of net worth, Net NPA/Net Advances Ratio, Return on Assets (RoA) and Capital to Risk Weighted Asset Ratio (CRAR). Operational excellence and allocational efficiency, corporate governance and corporate social responsibility continue to form the focus of the Indian banking system.

Between 1999-00 and 2005-06, total assets of Scheduled Commercial Banks (SCBs) increased from INR 11054 billion to INR 27879 billion. Current projections suggest that the banking industry in India would continue to grow at a fast clip. Agriculture, SMEs, infrastructure and retail assets would power the growth of Indian Banks.

Sequential reform measures have strengthened balance sheets of commercial banks reflecting the true financial position in accordance with internationally accepted accounting practices. Indian Banks maintained capital adequacy well above the international norm of 8 per cent and adopted 90 days international norm of asset classification. Banks have thus significantly strengthened the quality of their assets portfolio in the last decade.

PSBs expanded their capital base with equity participation. Diversification of ownership has led to greater market accountability and improved efficiency. Institutional and legal reforms in the banking sector include constitution of Board for Financial Supervision (BFS) and Board for Regulation and Supervision of Payment and Settlement Systems (BPSS). Banks are directed to maintain a separate Investment Fluctuation

Reserve (IFR) out of profits towards interest rate risk. Reform measures enhanced efficiency and stability of the banking system in India. Indian banks are well placed compared with their counterparts in developed countries. An effective corporate governance mechanism has been implemented for due diligence and to safeguard the interests of shareholders. Many Indian Banks, including PSBs, adopted US-GAAP in their accounting system. But there are persisting issues of removal of structural barriers to competition, privatisation of banking system, radical restructuring, downsizing of the balance sheet, recapitalisation and eventual privatisation of the financial institutions, withdrawal of quantitative credit controls and directed credit and modernisation of the payment system.

The inexorable process of economic reforms must continue to slash poverty and support sustainable development while strengthening financial institutions. We must work towards a vision of "inclusive" development that promotes not only economic growth but also equity in the sharing of benefits, the reduction of human development disparities in society and sensitivity and pluralistic consciousness in reaching out to the 'teeming millions' of India. This overarching goal of development needs a renewed thrust on financial sector reforms.

I express my deep gratitude to all contributors, who have worked hard to present their papers. While the papers included in this book cover a large ground, all these papers coalesce into the central theme of India's transforming financial sector. It is expected that the book would be useful to a wide cross section of the reading public, including scholars and academics, the government executives, international institutions, business communities, and planners and policymakers. I am grateful to Sri M.B.N. Rao, Chairman and Managing Director, and Sri R.K. Madhukar, General Manager, Canara Bank, Banagalore for their blessings and good wishes, which have been a source of strength and inspiration to me. I am thankful to my friends and colleagues working in the Economic Research Section of Canara Bank for acting as a sounding board and providing help and assistance at all times.

I am deeply thankful to my wife, Archana Choudhary, IRS, for her support to me in all my professional and academic endeavours. I am also thankful to my children Utkarsh and Upasana for bearing with me during this stressful period.

I acknowledge the guidance received from my family members, for whom academic excellence is a way of life. I would particularly like to mention the role of my father, Professor D.D. Sharma (PhD) (Edinburgh), former Pro Vice-Chancellor, Lucknow University and my mother, late Dayamoyee Sharma, for instilling in me a passion for academic pursuits. I am thankful to my parent-in-laws, Professor J.C. Choudhary and Mrs. Usha Choudhary, for their constant encouragement and advice.

MANORANJAN SHARMA

Contents

Introduction

The rolling on of the Indian growth story, the emergence of clear indications that India has come of age is clearly reflected in the fact that the Indian economy is the fourth largest in the world as measured by purchasing power parity (PPP). With a gross domestic product (GDP) of US $4282.204 billion, India is behind only USA, China, and Japan. When measured in USD exchange-rate terms, it is the twelfth largest in the world, with a GDP of US $930.0 billion (2007). India is the second fastest growing major economy in the world, with a GDP growth rate of 9.2 per cent at the end of the second quarter of 2006-2007. However, India's huge population results in a per capita income of $3400 at PPP and $796 at nominal. The World Bank classifies India as a low-income economy.

The global economy continues to expand at about 4 per cent. This global growth has been powered by China, India and Russia. The widely discussed report of Goldman Sachs (*Dreaming with BRICS*) stressed that India would overtake the Japanese economy by 2032 (in terms of US$, not PPP $s). The new BRICS Report released in January 2007 projects that the Indian economy will be even bigger than that of the US before 2050. This is also clearly reflected in indicators across the development spectrum—booming international trade, buoyant bank credit, rising urbanisation, etc. Total factor productivity (TFP) surged from 1.3 per cent per annum in the 1990s to 3.5 per cent during 2003-05. This implies that productivity improvement, which was responsible for around a fourth of the GDP growth in the 1980s and the 1990s, accounted for over 40 per cent of the 2003-05 growth and will continue to account for around 38 per cent of the incremental growth till 2020. Clearly, then, India has come of age and is a global economic power to be reckoned with. This thesis can easily be substantiated by the findings of Merrill Lynch, NCAER (National Council of Applied Economic Research) and so many others. The cover story on the Indian economy in *Time* magazine stressed that over the last three years India has achieved "the second fastest (growth) rate in the world".

The Indian Financial System

The Indian financial system comprises an elaborate network of banks, financial institutions, non-banking financial companies (NBFCs) and a wide range of financial instruments. Ministry of Finance, Government of India, looks after financial sector in India. Finance Ministry every year presents annual budget on February 28 in the Parliament. The annual budget proposes changes in taxes, changes in government policy in various sectors and budgetary and other allocations for all the Ministries of Government of India. The annual budget is passed by the Parliament after debate and takes the shape of law.

Reserve Bank of India (RBI) is the regulator for financial and banking system, formulates monetary policy and prescribes exchange control norms. The Banking Regulation Act, 1949 and the Reserve Bank of India Act, 1934 authorize the RBI to regulate the banking sector in India.

India has commercial banks, co-operative banks and regional rural banks. The commercial banking sector comprises of 27 public sector banks (PSBs), private banks and foreign banks. The public sector banks comprise the 'State Bank of India' and its 7 associate banks and 19 other banks owned by the government and account for almost three-fourth of the banking sector. The Government of India has majority stake in these PSBs.

India has a two-tier structure of financial institutions with 13 all India financial institutions (AIFIs) and 46 institutions at the state level. AIFIs comprise term-lending institutions, specialised institutions and investment institutions, including insurance. State level institutions comprise of State Financial Corporations (SFCs) and State Industrial Development Corporations (SIDCs) providing project finance, equipment leasing, corporate loans, short-term loans and bill discounting facilities to corporate. Government holds majority shares in these financial institutions. Non-banking Financial Companies (NBFCs) provide loans and hire-purchase finance, mostly for retail assets and are regulated by RBI.

Insurance sector in India has been traditionally dominated by state owned Life Insurance Corporation and General Insurance Corporation and its four subsidiaries. With the Government of India allowing FDI in insurance sector up to 26 per cent, several joint venture private companies have entered into life and general insurance sectors and their share in the insurance market is progressively rising. Insurance Development and Regulatory Authority (IRDA) is the regulatory authority in the insurance sector under the Insurance Development and Regulatory Authority Act, 1999.

RBI also regulates foreign exchange under the Foreign Exchange Management Act (FEMA). India has liberalised its foreign exchange controls. Rupee is freely convertible on current account. Rupee is also almost fully convertible on capital account for non-residents. Profits earned, dividends and proceeds out of the sale of investments are fully repatriable for FDI. There are restrictions on capital account for resident Indians for incomes earned in India. Addressing the vulnerabilities associated with the current partial opening up of the capital account and shifting to less market distorting forms of monetary policy and exchange rate policy with greater sensitivity to the goal of orderly markets is necessary to reach the next stage. Real sector reforms are equally significant in creating a vibrant economy with a strong and efficient financial sector.

The elaborate network of financial institutions and markets forms the basis of the financial system in India. Pre-reforms, the government regulated the financial sector with administered interest rates and other quantitative restrictions. A central planning approach with direct government intervention in the process of mobilisation and allocation of resources dominated economic thinking in the aftermath of India's independence. During the initial phase of planned development, government interventions were considered necessary due to conspicuous absence of adequate institutional mechanism. However, over the years, resource mobilisation and allocation became highly complex with administered interest rates, direct lending, cross-subsidisation of interest rates, high statutory pre-emption of lendable resources and the lack of an efficient financial infrastructure. These and other factors constrained the growth momentum.

Banks and financial institutions worked as powerful instruments of social change, particularly since bank nationalisation. Nationalisation led to impressive achievements in terms of rapid branch expansion and channeling of credit according to plan priorities. But the banking system was inefficient in terms of low profitability, high and mounting non-performing assets (NPAs) and relatively low capital base. Accordingly, the reforms attempted to transform the credit institutions into organisationally strong, financially viable and operationally efficient units. The major elements of the financial sector reforms were modifying the policy framework, improving the financial soundness and credibility of banks, creating a competitive environment and strengthening of the institutional framework.

Financial Sector Liberalisation—Move Away from the Precipice

The process of reforms of wide-ranging ramifications was initiated in 1991 because of the severe balance of payments crisis and the imminent danger of insolvency in the banking system. There were also several deeply entrenched problems like financial repression, statutory pre-emption of banking resources, excessive structural regulation and poor prudential regulation. Against this backdrop, financial sector liberalisation was considered a prerequisite for extricating the economy from low-level equilibrium trap through a financial system at once both functional and vibrant. Accordingly, in conformity with the recommendations of Narasimham Committee, sequential financial sector reform measures were initiated to achieve a high and stable rate of growth. Deregulation of interest rates and market-based allocation of resources have infused competition in the financial markets. Deregulation of interest rate has also aligned various short-term interest rates. As a consequence of the reform measures, the call money and foreign exchange markets are intrinsically integrated. The mark-to-market of government securities has further helped in the alignment of various interest rates in the money market. Opening up of the current account and gradual liberalisation of the capital account has led to increase in foreign capital inflows and progressive integration of foreign exchange market with the domestic financial system.

Second Stage of Financial Sector Development

Along with many emerging economies, India has entered the second stage of financial sector development, where market forces are helping in resources allocation and efficient price discovery process. With the first stage of 'crisis-driven' reforms removing structural bottlenecks in the financial system, the second stage of 'consensus-driven' reforms need to address stability, efficiency and foster market discipline in the financial sector. Public financial institutions need more capital to finance large infrastructure projects, social services, global expansion and meeting stringent regulatory requirements. In the ultimate analysis, financial sector reforms must lead to market-driven ownership of public financial institution. Multi-institutional financial system is necessary for financial stability. The Asian financial crisis and recent banking and financial crisis in Latin America and Russia underscored the importance of competitive banking sector and regulatory and supervisory institutions for a strong and stable financial system.

The interaction of real and monetary sectors is crucial for stability of financial system. A deep, liquid, vibrant and transparent financial market is the *sine qua non* for effective dissemination of monetary policy. Despite a heightened consciousness and a greater awareness, there is limited depth in India's bond market because of narrow participation. In recent years, SEBI and Government of India have attempted to improve efficiency and transparency in the Indian bond market. However, there is a need to remove 'government's captive market phenomenon' from the debt market and bring about greater participation of insurance and pension funds.

The harmonisation of regulatory institutions and devising of new financial architecture is necessary to achieve the needs of the present and the expectations of the future. Historically, multiplicity of regulators were considered necessary because of multiple delivery channels and market segmentation. But overlapping of regulatory functions in the sectors of banking, insurance, capital markets, competition and various services sectors, e.g., regulation of commodity derivatives by the Forward Markets Commission (FMC), regulation of equity spot and derivatives, and corporate bonds by SEBI, regulation of government bonds and currency by RBI often provides wrong signals to market. Hence, there emerges a discernible need for a holistic consideration of the supervision of 'Financial Conglomerates' in an emerging market economy like India.

Compared to some Asian countries, India's financial sector, post-reforms, has been greatly resilient. However, in this world of intensified challenges and increased business complexities, an important concern of financial system is the fragility of some of the financial institutions. High exposure in government securities, government guaranteed loans, improper valuation of collaterals, vulnerability to interest rate cycle, still high level of NPAs, unsatisfactory corporate governance and disclosures, inadequate surveillance, stock market volatility, risk concentration and policy failure often distorted the financial system. This necessitates improving transparency and governance, resolving failure in the industrial and financial sector, de-linking government and private sector, fostering innovation, and improving the supervisory and regulatory infrastructure. Given the serious debilitating impact of financial sector crisis on the economy, the stability of the financial sector should be the goal of the economy. Corporate governance, accounting disclosures, compliance with international accounting standards and effective offsite surveillance and onsite inspections will go a long way in establishing financial stability. Financial stability can be strengthened by improved financial infrastructure, enhanced competition and restructured segments of financial system.

Changing Contours of Banking Reforms—The Challenge and the Response

Despite the process of economic reforms for almost two decades, India continues to be predominantly bank based with a bank intermediation ratio of about 80 per cent. Within the banking sector, PSBs continue to hold sway. Resource allocation thus is mostly public sector driven and to those sectors considered important by the government—the majority shareholder.

The sustained growth of the Indian economy has transformed the functions and working of banks in diverse ways. Enhanced financial liberalisation through various policy initiatives and calibrated prudential regulatory measures has resulted in a perceptible welcome transformation of banks and financial services sector. These initiatives had a salutary impact on ownership and capital structure, enhanced competition, increased autonomy, technological upgradation, performance measurement and monitoring of banks. Such changes are reflected in broad indicators of Net Worth, Net NPA/Net Advances Ratio, Return on Assets (RoA) and Capital to Risk Weighted Asset Ratio (CRAR). The twin areas of significance to an emerging economy like India, viz. operational excellence and allocational efficiency, corporate governance and corporate social responsibility continue to be within the focus of the Indian banking system.

Let us now do some number crunching. Between 1999-00 and 2005-06, the total assets of Scheduled Commercial Banks (SCBs) in India increased from INR 11054 billion to INR 27879 billion. Current projections suggest that the banking industry in India would continue to grow at a fast clip. Agriculture, SMEs, infrastructure and retail assets would power the growth of Indian Banks.

The strength of Indian Banks is clearly reflected in their successful implementation of Basel-I norms and improved earnings over the years. Sequential reform measures, in the forms of prudential system of recognition of income, classification of assets and provisioning for bad debts, have strengthened balance sheets of commercial banks reflecting the true financial position in accordance with internationally accepted accounting practices. Indian Banks have been maintaining capital adequacy well above the international norm of 8 per cent. Indian Banks have adopted 90 days international norm of asset classification and in the last ten years banks have significantly strengthened the quality of their assets portfolio.

PSBs have been allowed to expand their capital base with equity participation. Diversification of ownership has led to greater market accountability and improved efficiency. Institutional and legal reforms have been undertaken in relation to the banking sector. Board for Financial Supervision (BFS) has been constituted for supervision of financial system in general and banking sector in particular. As an effective payment system is the pivot of the banking sector, a Board for Regulation and Supervision of Payment and Settlement Systems (BPSS) has also been constituted. Banks are directed to maintain a separate Investment Fluctuation Reserve (IFR) out of profits, towards interest rate risk.

Reform measures have enhanced efficiency and stability of the banking system in India. Indian banks are well placed compared with their counterparts in developed countries. An effective corporate governance mechanism has been put in place for due diligence and to safeguard the interests of shareholders. Many Indian Banks, including Public Sector Banks have adopted US-GAAP in their accounting system. At present, Indian Banks are preparing to migrate to Basel-II norms with an accent on risk management. While all these changes certainly augur well for the future of the banking sector, there are persisting issues of removal of all structural barriers to competition, privatisation of banking system, radical restructuring, downsizing of the balance sheet, recapitalisation and eventual privatisation of the financial institutions, withdrawal of quantitative credit controls and directed credit and modernisation of the payment system.

Adroit Risk Management

Undoubtedly, the Indian financial system has achieved a fair degree of maturity and stability as a consequence of financial sector liberalisation. However, the process of financial alignment has certain macroeconomic implications, particularly, in the formulation of monetary and exchange rate policies. With the financial reforms considerably reducing the distinction between money market and capital market, the movements in the asset prices of both the markets indicate the process of market integration. Volatility of financial prices and consolidation of manufacturing and service sectors poses a new set of challenges for the banking system. Consequently, banks are experiencing an increase in credit risk, interest rate risk as well as exchange rate risks. Hence, management of risks has become an integral element of the growth dynamic of Indian Banks.

While introduction of capital adequacy norms brought credit risk into focus, the issue of guidelines on asset-liability management and risk management systems in banks has enhanced the significance of effective management of interest rate risk. Streamlined risk management, effective governance, market-driven board, faster decision-making process, efficient legal system and adoption of international accounting standards need immediate attention in the present era of technology-intensive and customer-friendly model with an accent on convenience.

Modernisation of the Financial System

A study on the global capital markets (*$118 Trillion and Counting: Taking Stock of the World's Capital Markets*) by the McKinsey Global Institute (MGI) reveals that India's financial stock, defined in terms of the sum of its bank deposits, equity, private-sector debt and government debt, is way behind global benchmarks.

Financial Profile of Major Economies

	World	US	Europe	India	China	Japan	Korea
Financial Stock	118	44	36	0.9	5.1	17.6	1.3
Bank Deposits	30	20	30	45	62	36	36
Government Debt	18	12	21	22	6	35	10
Private Debt	26	36	29	1	5	12	29
Equity	27	33	19	32	27	17	25
Financial Depth	326	329	314	137	323	411	214

Note: Financial stock in $ trillion; data on bank deposits, government debt, private debt and equity in per cent. Financial depth is defined as financial stock divided by nominal GDP.

Source: MGI.

In 2003, India's total financial stock was $0.9 trillion and India's financial depth was 137 per cent. This compared poorly with the financial depth of 326 per cent of the 100 top economies. According to McKinsey, the global financial stock is $118 trillion (of which, India's share is $900 billion), and is likely to exceed $200 trillion by 2010.

While global financial stock was almost equal to global GDP in 1980, today, it is more than three times larger today. A disaggregated analysis shows that bank deposits account for 45 per cent of financial assets in India as against an even higher proportion in China. This could conceivably be explained by inadequate time for China to develop its securities market or the high proportion of non-performing loans (NPLs) the Chinese banks are saddled with. As the above Table clearly brings out, the proportion of the financial stock with banks in US, Europe and Korea is far lower.

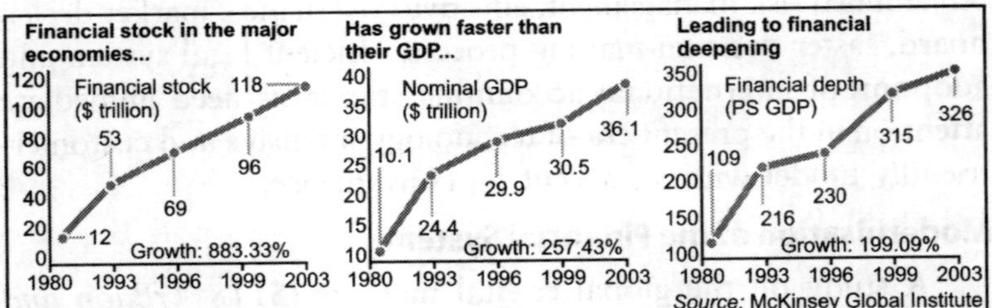

Source: McKinsey Global Institute

India's government debt constitutes 22 per cent of financial stock *vis-à-vis* only 6 per cent in China. True, the proportion of government debt in Europe (with 21 per cent) and Japan (35 per cent) is also unduly high but there is a manifest need on the part of India to slash such a high proportion of government debt.

While India's financial stock growth at 11.9 per cent a year over the past 10 years outstripped the growth in the rest of the world, China performed better with 14.5 per cent. This financial stock growth rate of 11.9 per cent, however, needs to be juxtaposed against the Indian economy's growth rate at a similar rate (in nominal terms) over the past 10 years. In case of several countries, including Britain, their financial stock has also grown at similar rates, despite a lower growth in nominal GDP.

The sustenance of India's high GDP growth trajectory and a less skewed distribution of its benefits require a much more comprehensively market-oriented and efficient financial system. MGI has identified the following three shortcomings of the financial system:

- India's formal financial institutions attract only half of Indian households' savings, and none of the $200 billion locked up in gold.
- India's financial institutions allocate 57 per cent of the capital to the least productive areas of the economy: state-owned enterprises, agriculture, and the unorganised sector (mostly made up of tiny businesses) with the more productive corporations in India's dynamic private sector receiving only 43 per cent of all commercial credit.
- India's financial system is inefficient in both of its main tasks of mobilizing savings and allocating capital leads to borrowers paying more for their capital and depositors receiving less than in comparable economies.

MGI's path-breaking research shows that an integrated program of financial system reforms could add $48 billion to GDP each year thereby raising India's real GDP growth rate to 9.4 per cent per year, way above the current three-year average of roughly 7 per cent.

Capital Market

It is agreed across the development spectrum that stock markets enhance growth, large markets tend to less volatile and internationally integrated markets tend to be less volatile. Cross-country evidence also suggests significant correlation between economic growth and value of stock market trading relative to GDP. This is why healthy development of the capital market has been an area of focus of planners and policy-makers in India, as indeed elsewhere. The Indian capital market comprises of 23 recognized stock exchanges, about 7000 listed companies, 60 million investors and well over 500 foreign institutional investors (FIIs).

The Indian capital market has been characterised by confluence of wide-ranging changes, e.g. establishment of SEBI (1992), introduction of Electronic Trading (1994-95), freedom in pricing of public issues, formulation of Takeover Code (1997) and setting up of Trade/Settlement Guarantee Fund Counterparty Risk (1997). Other important changes aimed at strengthening the financial sector relate to introduction of the depository and share dematerialisation systems, devising of a comprehensive risk management system, replacement of the forward trading mechanism with rolling settlement and launching of the infotech-driven National Stock Exchange (NSE) with a national presence. Corporatisation of stock exchanges, effective functioning of the SEBI as an independent regulator with statutory powers, disclosure and governance, introduction of many new instruments in the markets, including index futures, index options, derivatives and options and futures in select stocks, etc. have not only contributed to the operational efficiency of the market but have also expedited the process of integration of the Indian capital markets with the global financial system.

India is also well-placed in relation to other developing countries in terms of a sophisticated market design of the equity spot and derivatives market, widespread retail participation, resilient liquidity and abundant skills and human capital. Even if financial assets remain at the present level of 12 per cent of the GDP, the actual figure would cross \$120 billion by 2007-08, up from \$ 56 billion in 2000-01. Thus the potential of India's financial sector would more than double in the next few years. With more than 99.5 per cent of the settlements in the NSE & BSE taking place in demat form, the Indian capital markets are as competitive as their Western counterparts. For example, NSE ranks among the best in the world in terms of number of trades, recording on an average 1 lakh trades per hour. Indian markets are also globally competitive even in terms of pricing, efficiency and liquidity. The cumulative impact of mutually reinforcing processes of India's flourishing stock markets, fast-growing mutual funds and capable private banks strongly suggest that the Financial Sector in India has now come of age.

Any attempt to address unsettled issues, emerging challenges, cognisable dilemmas and unfolding scenarios has to be based on a realistic assessment of various factors that go into the making of a healthy capital market. The Indian Capital Market is usually described as an emerging market. But this is an inaccurate description in the sense that the so-called developed world itself continues to be characterised by real and worrisome fault-lines, even in the post-Enron world.

In terms of market capitalisation, the Indian Capital Market is the 14th largest in the world and several so-called developed countries lag far behind India, irrespective of any determinant, size or shape or content of the market, e.g. products, players-individuals and institutions, investors in terms of volume, etc. The Market Capitalisation to GDP ratio in India is presently less than 30 per cent. But with large international players active in the market, this ratio is likely to steadily rise to a level of over 60 per cent as in most other emerging markets.

It is not easy to take a call on the desired number of companies because of inherent complexities. India may have the largest number of listed companies (without even considering the thousand odd companies listed only in the regional stock exchanges) in the world between the NSE & MSE. But half of these companies (listed sometimes between at 1988 and 1992) ought not to have been listed in the first place. Accordingly, unlike the position in other markets, which are preoccupied with the task of increasing the number of listed companies, India needs to drastically prune the number of listed companies to ensure that only companies with traded stocks, reasonable volumes and better price discoveries remain in the market.

There is also a need to regulate around 20,000 registered brokers and sub-brokers in India. The smaller players try and imitate the bigger players, stretch themselves beyond recognition that cause problems to themselves, to the market, to the client and sometimes to the system unless systemic containment measures are put in place. Consolidating these persons, corporatising them, persuading them to get together to get reasonable size, implementing better technological applications, better risk management practices, better margining, is not easy in the Indian Capital Market.

There are diverse players in the Indian market—retail investors, mutual funds and foreign institutional investors (FIIs) including several sub-categories, i.e. pension funds, hedge funds and investment companies. The major challenge for SEBI is the protection of the interests of the investors. But the interests of the Retail Indian investors, mutual funds and the foreign investors in the Indian Market might not always converge causing practical difficulties.

Despite the introduction of the Gold Exchange Traded Fund (GETF), the Real Estate as an asset class based on which there are mutual funds and the reintroduction of Capital Protection Oriented products to bring in more first time investors to the market, the market does not have all the needed products. With changed guidelines for the Indian depository receipts (IDRs), three changes need to be effected by the Ministry of Company Affairs. These changes relate to the following aspects:

(i) Thrust on a track record of profitability instead of a dividend-paying track record. Microsoft did not pay dividend every year because shareholders did not insist on dividend payments but instead wanted their money to be ploughed back into business. They wanted growth; they wanted better value for their shareholders.

(ii) Need to harmonise disclosure standards with global disclosure standards.

(iii) Need to harmonise certain accounting statements with global accounting statements.

While information asymmetry can certainly be reduced by more timely and clearer disclosures and greater transparency, credit ratings transcend credit information. A well-functioning credit market in India requires progressively rising levels of data and information base. These levels relate to the following:

- Basic financial and demographic information about the borrower.
- Information about the track record of the borrower in terms of transactions on the credit market.
- Assessments of failure probability, which typically come from sources such as scoring models, information embedded in the secondary market for debt and equity, or credit rating agencies.

SEBI's efforts at creating a greater awareness of the need for a full disclosure and transparency-based regime have succeeded only partially. There is an imperative need to move towards a National Listing Authority, empowering the investors on the lines of the US class action, using information technology and public disclosure aggressively to improve surveillance, adopting a more aggressive pro-competitive policy, introducing an effective and competitive securities lending system and broad basing the derivative markets.

The SEBI has made it clear that all listed entities must comply with the Clause 49 requirements by December 31, 2006. The proposed Clause 49 of the Listing Agreement stipulates that at least 50 per cent of the board should comprise independent directors. The Government-controlled listed entities (where the Government has a majority stake) in the recent months have been forced to review the composition of their boards on account of the proposed revised Clause 49 and also due to the capital market regulators' stance that the Government nominees on the boards of Government-owned entities cannot be counted as independent directors. Non-compliance with Clause 49 (Corporate Governance) can invite punishment of imprisonment of up to 10 years or a fine of up to Rs. 25 crore or both. Besides, stock exchanges can suspend the dealing or trading of the securities of the company. Clause 49 of the Listing Agreement says that the CEO & the CFO must authenticate statements on the basis of certification systems and control systems in place.

There are other important issues relating to sufficiently representative Board composition, the existence and the role of the Audit Committees, kind of person heading the Audit Committee, functions of the Audit Committee, availability of financially literate people heading the Audit Committees, careful examination of the Audit Reports by the members are also important issues.

Policies and procedures of capital markets in India also underwent significant changes in terms of fair, efficient and transparent markets, investor education, investor protection, reduction of systemic risk, VAR based margining and exposure norms, cumulative margins and rising corporatisation of brokers. These and other wholesome alchemy of measures helped to make the financial markets more efficient, more competitive and more global. However, the inadequate development of the debt markets hampers accurate pricing of current and future assets, retail trading still accounts for over 85 per cent of transactions, participation by institutional players continues to be low and PFs/Pensions are not allowed to invest in equities. The functioning of the stock markets in India continues to be fraught with the dangers of frauds and scandals. While prevention and detection of frauds must rely heavily on market discipline, the regulator must ensure swift prosecution and effective punishment. Market discipline can be enhanced by encouraging hostile takeovers, allowing free short selling, permitting and facilitating class action lawsuits, and promoting competition among rating agencies, auditors, investment bankers, etc.

The process of rapid economic growth requires wide distribution of the ownership of equity both by direct participation in the capital market, and indirectly, through financial institutions, such as mutual funds, pension funds and insurance companies to increase long-term savings and the availability of long-term financing. This necessitates an efficient and transparent price discovery process with high disclosure and regulatory standards and with sound liquidity and risk management in place.

The Indian debt market is poised for rapid growth. The decision to set up a single clearing corporation for money, debt and foreign exchange and the provision to hold securities in dematerialised form will help the debt markets in India to become deeper, broader and more liquid to meet emergent challenges and widen and deepen capital markets. Towards this end, robust development of the insurance sector with a higher capital base and more diverse products would generate the necessary long-term funds for investing in a debt market and make available resources for the investment needs of our country particularly in the vital infrastructure sector.

The convergence with international best practices in respect of clearing and settlement, payment systems and funds transfer, governance, disclosure and transparency is of utmost importance. Given the extremely uneven application of standards across markets, there is a manifest need for uniformity and consistency in various markets. This would facilitate greater integration across the markets and thus accelerate the ongoing process of economic reforms in India. In the ultimate analysis, vibrant capital market is a function of the nature of economic growth, nature of the financial system and nature of the markets.

Litmus Tests of the Financial Sector

In an excellent paper by Ajay Shah et al. on 'New Directions in Indian Financial Sector Policy' five litmus tests about the health of the financial sector have been identified and isolated. These tests are:

1. Is there sound stock market liquidity for the top 1000 firms? By international standards, the top 1000 firms in India should enjoy turnover ratios of roughly 100 per cent. In India today, the turnover ratio drops to roughly 15 per cent for ranks 300 to 1000. This reflects an unhealthy concentration of liquidity in an extremely narrow set of firms.
2. Are C rated bonds being issued and traded actively? In India today, the corporate bond market is primarily accessible to firms with low failure probabilities. A well functioning credit market should offer market

access (at appropriate prices) to a much larger range of firms.

3. Do the stock price for the largest ten banks reflect distress? The stock market is an effective tool for inferring the (unobserved) value of assets of a bank. It can be a valuable early warning tool, signaling banking distress.
4. Do the derivatives markets satisfy no-arbitrage? In India today, the currency and equity derivatives markets suffer from significant unexploited arbitrage opportunities. Measuring and monitoring the extent of market inefficiencies on these markets would be a window on the regulations governing the spot and derivatives markets, and the accumulation of human capital and IT systems amongst participants.
5. How important is the private sector in the assets of banking, insurance and pensions? This is a traditional measure of financial repression.

Clearly, India has still some way to traverse in crossing these litmus tests.

International Standards and Codes

International standards and codes have evoked greater interest because of increasing cross-border flows, upscaling of technology and availability of large institutional funds, such as pension funds and mutual funds. As the significance of these mutually reinforcing forces rapidly increases, the stake rise higher necessitating minimisation of systemic risks by transparent operations and uniform definitions benchmarked against international norms.

The sequencing of the structure of reporting is a function not only of constitutional, legal and institutional mechanisms but also the likely impact on the financial sector soundness and stability. Indian accounting standards lag behind global practices in Consolidation of Accounts, Segment Reporting, Deferred Tax Accounting, International Transactions and Combinations, Joint Ventures and Related Party Transactions.

Despite the categorical recommendations of Malegam and Bhave Committees, India is yet to adopt global benchmarks in respect of derivatives accounting, lease accounting, interest Capitalisation and Accounting, Extraordinary and Non-Operating Income and Expenses, Results from Discontinued Operations and Formatting and Presentation of Accounts. While there are several issues involved here, some of the important issues relate to the valid approach, adequate coverage of issues, symmetrical treatment between participants, linkage between international standards and codes and financial stability and issues of coverage of standards in IMF surveillance. What is basically required is setting of standards domestically with an international character, consultative and participative processes of setting, prioritising, incentivising, monitoring and reorienting and effective implementation.

Without in any way reducing the significance of standards and codes in the emerging landscape, the calibrated Indian approach is predicated on heightened awareness on the part of the official agencies, self-regulating bodies and market participants rather than making it a statutory requirement.

Lessons for India from the East Asian Crisis

It is often maintained that the rapid build-up of external short-term debt increased the vulnerability of exchange rate and the channeling of funds including these external borrowings into speculative activities by an under supervised financial system contributed to the East Asian crisis. The literature on the extensively researched East Asian crisis demonstrates that the crisis was primarily due to a combination of structural as well as proximate factors. The crisis drove home the point that in the absence of a strict adherence to sound prudential regulations by the banking system, the entire financial and economic super structure could crumble. This has significant policy implications for planners, bankers, economists and even those at the helm of affairs in India.

The relationship between finance and development has evoked wide interest in the annals of economic history down through the ages. It has been increasingly realised that a strong and resilient financial system and the orderly evolution of financial markets is central to sustained economic development. The East Asian crisis of 1997 and the nature of the financial markets have important policy prescriptions. Financial reforms and liberalisation of markets are only means to an end and not ends in themselves. In the ultimate analysis, the success of the development strategy rests on a sustained and rising income for all the people and removal of poverty and deprivation within a reasonable period of time.

The international financial architecture needs to be looked at from the standpoint of developing countries. The collapse of the Bretton Wood's model because of its inherent weaknesses and the dramatically altered present-day ground realities necessitates forging of an equal partnership between developed and developing countries with greater representation to developing countries on the boards of the IMF and the IBRD and providing developing countries with a larger voting power.

The issue of Corporate Governance in relation to the banking sector also needs to be seriously considered by planners and policy makers and even those at the helm of affairs to place Indian banking on a sound footing. While professionalism and organisational effectiveness—aspects intrinsic to the firm—would have to be the buzzwords for success in the present differentiated system, which represents social realities through its heterogeneity and variability, the role of the government continues to be important in reducing uncertainty and risk to the investors and savers and in enhancing the investments in physical infrastructure.

Insurance in India

The strategy to be adopted by banking and financial institutions needs to be redefined in the context of changing times. These institutions can no longer afford to exist in cocoon or adopt an ostrich like attitude and need to adopt new practices to adapt themselves. With the opening of the market, foreign and private Indian players are keen to convert untapped market potential into opportunities by providing customised products. The presence of several new players in the sector has resulted in a shift in approach and the launch of innovative products, services and value-added benefits. New players have entered the insurance market and have become aggressive players in both life and non-life areas with their innovative, 'out-of-box' marketing strategies. The market has benefited in terms of superior technology, improved customer servicing and newer products.

At present, there are 15 life insurers and 14 general insurers in India. Hence, some shakeout and exit of some companies is not improbable in the future. As banking and insurance sectors in India are regulated by two different entities, i.e. banking by RBI and insurance by IRDA, bancassurance comes under the jurisdiction of both RBI and IRDA. In line with the recommendations of the R.N. Malhotra Committee on Reforms in the Insurance Sector, the Indian Parliament passed the IRDA Act 1999. The IRDA Act provides for the establishment of an authority to protect the interests of the holders of insurance policies, to regulate, promote and ensure orderly growth of the insurance industry and amend the Insurance Act, 1938, the Life Insurance Act, 1956 and the General Insurance Business (Nationalisation) Act, 1972.

The IRDA Act allows foreign equity stake in domestic private insurance companies to a maximum of 26 per cent of the total paid-up capital and seeks to provide statutory status to the insurance regulator. IRDA progressively attempted to lay down the ground rules. IRDA permits banks to venture into marketing insurance products on a risk participation basis. According to IRDA, a private sector participant has to fulfil the following criteria for entry into insurance sector: (a) minimum paid-up capital of Rs. 100 crores, (b) investment in policyholders' funds only in India, (c) restriction of international companies to minority equity holding of 26 per cent. RBI has prescribed entry guidelines under the following three options for banks wanting to diversify into insurance. The regulator attempts to ensure that only serious players with the necessary financial muscle enter into selling of insurance products. Consequently, certain prerequisites for banks, e.g. minimum Rs. 500 crore of net worth, minimum capital adequacy of 10 per cent, at least three continuous years of profits, net Non-Performing Assets (NPAs) 1 per cent below the industry average and "satisfactory" track record of performance of existing subsidiaries, have been stipulated.

Banks, ineligible for joint ventures (JV), can invest upto 10 per cent of the net worth of the bank or Rs. 50 crores, whichever is lower, in an insurance company for providing infrastructure and service support without any contingent liability, provided they fulfill the requirements of CRAR, NPA and net profit as mentioned above. IRDA guidelines for bancassurance stipulate nomination of a chief insurance executive by each bank selling insurance to handle all insurance activities, all persons involved in selling to undergo mandatory training at an institute accredited by IRDA and pass the examination conducted by the authority, commercial banks, including cooperative banks and regional rural banks, might become corporate agents for one insurance company and banks prohibited to be insurance brokers.

Emerging Role of Venture Capital

The modern world has been characterised by rapid technological changes, blurring of geographical frontiers of countries and revolution of 'rising expectations'. Such changes necessitate fundamentally reoriented development strategies with an accent on technology and knowledge. Given the inherent strength and resilience of the economy reflected in human capital, technical skills, cost competitive workforce, research and entrepreneurship, India is on the cusp of rapid economic growth. The realisation of the immense potential, however, hinges on provision of adequate risk finance and venture capital (VC) funding to leverage innovation, promote technology and harness knowledge based ideas as demonstrated by VC experience across developed and developing countries.

VC, which is sometimes referred to as "business of businesses", is a type of private equity capital typically provided by professional, institutionally-backed outside investors to new grown businesses. Venture capitalists finance innovation and ideas with high growth potential but inherent uncertainties making it a high-risk, high-return investment. Venture capitalists also provide networking, management and marketing support.

VC finance contributed significantly to the industrial and economic growth in Western Europe and the US. The venture capitalist has been responsible for commercialising technology developed in R&D labs of Universities and the industry in semi-conductors, microprocessors, mini-computers, biotechnology, etc. Thus, VC helps in developing the entrepreneurial culture that thrives on the principles of individual and collective risk taking to create new industries and new technologies. This, in turn, increases the productivity of the nation's economic process and of its workers. Attributes such as a solid business plan, a good management team, investment and passion from the founders, a good potential to exit the investment before the end of their funding cycle and targetting of minimum returns in excess of 40 per cent per year make it easier to raise venture capital.

The venture capitalists act as a primary and economical source of equity funding for SMEs, Start-ups and Early stage as they take the risk, pre-screen and validate investment opportunities. The venture capitalist helps in enhancing information flow, transparency, corporate governance and in providing realistic valuations. Early Stage financing comprising Seed Financing, Start-up and Other Early Stage and Expansion Stage Financing comprising Second Stage Financing and Later Stage Financing are needed at various stages of development. The VC investment process is divided into four stages, viz.: (a) Initial evaluation, (b) Due diligence, (c) Deal structuring and (d) Final negotiation and legal aspect.

Pre-investment, VC must create an effective communication channel through information sharing and identifying critical issues, deal structuring to "align interest" by creation of win-win situation, goal congruence and clarification of expectation. Post-investment, involvement without interference requires protecting investor's interest through value creation, quick identification of weakness, anticipation of problems and probable solutions. In other words, VC, which necessitates high level of involvement, building relationship and creation of synergies with complementary role, involves a judicious mix of risk financing and hand holding of entrepreneurs. This creates an environment particularly suitable for knowledge and technology-based enterprises.

Considered in a proper historical and comparative perspective, the history of VC in India can be divided into four phases: Phase I—Formation of TDICI in the 80s and regional funds as GVFL & APIDC in the early 90s; Phase II—Entry of Foreign Venture Capital Funds between 1995-1999; Phase III (2000 onwards)—Emergence of successful India-centric VC firms, and Phase IV—US VCs' increasing appetite to invest in India. This growth has been powered by strong value proposition, scalable business model, new market and surmounting of entry barrier. This also required focused business plan and growth strategy, niche vertical, transparency, growth appetite, building of organisation and systems, undivided attention, openness to constructive suggestions, exit strategy, use of network and resource planning in terms of team building, finance, evolving growth strategy and providing an "outside view".

According to *itbusinessedge.com* $7.46 billion—three times more money than in 2005 according to research firm Venture Intelligence—was invested in India in 2006 with the bigger deals being Idea Cellular by Providence Equity Partners, ChrysCapital, Citigroup and Spinnaker Capital ($950 million) and Kohlberg Kravis Roberts's purchase of Flextronics Software ($900 million). VCs are investing in India in IT and IT-enabled services, Software Products (Mainly Enterprise-focused), Wireless/Telecom/Semiconductor, Banking, PSU Disinvestment, Media/Entertainment, Computer Graphics, Animation, Bio-Technology/Bio-Informatics, Pharmaceuticals, Contract Manufacturing, Retail, etc.

Top destinations for venture capitalists in 2006 were China (around $900 million), London ($800 million) and India ($746 million). According to the 2006 Global Venture Capital Survey, 53 per cent of the respondents intended to expand their global investment focus, with China (30 per cent) and India (25 per cent) identified as the two top foreign countries of interest over the next five years because of cost factors, emerging entrepreneurial culture and high quality deal flow. United States VC respondents cited India as the best country with access to quality entrepreneurs outside the US and China as the best country with access to foreign markets.

There has been a resurgence of VC market in India. VC players operating in India include Government Funds (e.g. SIDBI Venture Capital Limited, Gujarat Venture Fund Limited, RVCF, APIDC, Canbank Venture Capital Fund Limited, IFCI Venture Capital Funds Limited, etc.), non US-based Funds (e.g. Barings, 2iCapital Private Limited, Aavishkaar India, 3i, Chryscapital Management Companies, HSBC Private Equity Management (Mauritius) Limited, IL&FS Investments Managers Limited, Information Technology Venture Enterprises Limited, Indian Direct Equity Advisors Private Limited, Kotak Mahindra Finance Ltd, Merlion India Fund (Standard Chartered Private Equity), Punjab Venture Capital Limited, SICOM Capital Management Limited), Large Company Funds (e.g. Intel, BlueRun Ventures, Motorola, SAP Ventures, Siemens, Acer Technology Ventures, and Cisco), VC Entrants from the US and New Groups Raising Money for Investing in India.

With a VC friendly framework, VC industry crossed learning curve, greater awareness among entrepreneurs/ intermediaries and government, increasing R&D lab-industry linkage, improved environment for creating new start-ups and quality professionals becoming entrepreneurs, India is expected to reach $10 billion in 2007 with an accent on sectors like nanotechnology, biotechnology, RFID, 3G applications, e-governance besides IT and software. Benchmarking domestic projects with global markets/technology, increasing cross border investments, high overseas VC investors interest, stake in companies of US Indians, growth of knowledge based industries and M&A (Mergers and Amalgamations) emerging as an exit option suggest that the Indian boom might not just be a flash in the pan and could justifiably be sustained over the medium-term.

Hubs of the industry have been Bangalore, Mumbai, Chennai, Hyderabad, Delhi (NCR), Pune and Ahmedabad not only in traditional industries but also in service industries, biotechnology and pharmaceuticals, telecommunications, media and entertainment, healthcare and medical tourism; auto-components; travel and tourism; retail; textiles; real estate and infrastructure; entertainment and media; and gems and jewellery and other technology based manufacturing and product development. In line with the Silicon Valley model, most venture capital funds have a fixed life of 10 years, with the possibility of some extensions to allow for private companies still seeking liquidity. The investing cycle for most funds is generally 3-5 years, after which the focus is managing and making follow-on investments in an existing portfolio.

The growth of VC in India received an impetus from the fast growth of knowledge based industries, availability of world class engineers, professionals, entrepreneurs, 2nd largest English speaking population, rapid advance in the 90s catching up with global markets including the US in many sectors, Indian founders of 25 per cent of small IT companies in the US have disproportionately large presence of Indians in the US Software Sector (1 million) and issue of 50 per cent of all H1 visas to Indians.

The Government has spurred growth in technology and knowledge based sectors with strong and supportive legal framework—Information Technology Act, VC norms, ESOPs, copyright, full deregulation of government controlled telecom, one of the most advanced Capital Market systems in Asia and electronic trading through NSE and BSE.

The significance of active VC community for high and sustained growth emanates from innovation (risk capital in a largely regulated, conservative, legacy financial system), job creation (large pool of skilled graduates in the first and second tier cities) and creation of new industry clusters (Media, Retail, Call Centers and Back Office Processing). VC is also a source of patient capital, not prone to sudden flights like FIIs.

Wholesome development of VC industry in India is constrained by targeting of large investments (above US $2 million) and later stage investments by most VC funds, inadequate servicing of high tech, early stage and SMEs, non-availability of Indian Nasdaq type exchange, exit problems, particularly for SMEs, rare exit success stories and moderate valuations of non-IT companies. There are also issues of skewed sector-specific growth of industry, inadequate trained manpower, limited ability of VCs to cut losses, recognise failure, change management, structural issues for VC funds, promoters attempt to hold on to companies, difficulty in fund raising for domestic funds, absence of funds from banks, insurance companies, pension funds, high net worth and private sectors, etc.

VC funds for SMEs come after faith money (friends and associates). Business plan initially submitted requires major changes in fund requirement, projections. Generally high level of handholding is required because of weak organisational structure, marketing/financial/information systems. VC SMEs are characterised by lack of awareness of IPR issues, overseas markets, building brand equity, possessiveness about ownership and profit sharing and unwillingness to dilute for growth. There are problems of phasing out the disbursement, linking to benchmarks, small equity base, problems of structuring and exit. Consequently, the initial cash accruals are low leading to a liquidity crunch. There is also difficulty in raising 2nd round of funds and working capital. Most units tend to reduce their interaction with VC funds leading to increase in problems. VC SMEs need greater flexibility and mindset to modify business plans to adapt to sudden changes. A time horizon of at least 5-7 years is required to make a successful equity exit for successful units. VC exit is generally the last priority for units.

Indian VC is yet to be established as a sustainable asset class among institutional investors. A limited amount of true "risk-capital" impacts entrepreneurial activity. Exit challenges exist mainly due to shallow capital markets and dull M&A environment for small companies. Beyond services, India is yet to create a brand-name for IP-led companies.

Enhanced technological base of the industry requires new initiatives to replace obsolete business, meet changing customers' needs and develop technological capabilities and skills to be competitive. AIFIs and State level financial institutions played a vital role in development of the venture capital industry. A futuristic policy framework and action plan involving governments, financial institution, R&D organisations and other institution needs to address issues of long gestation period of technology-oriented start-up companies, hand-holding and nurturing, evaluation of the new technology, exit problems of small technology-oriented companies, co-investment with other VCFs to reduce risk, system of reward for the promoters, unwillingness on the part of the promoters to dilute their stake, etc.

With progressive economic liberalisation, enlarged business opportunities are certain to emerge. New market niches would also result from transfer of technologies and marketing of ideas tested in the developed countries. As an ideal form of finance enabling dynamic small enterprises to graduate to newer and sophisticated technologies, VC has immense latent potential in India.

Financial Inclusion—Searching Questions, Groping for Answers

In bracing for tomorrow, contextual and socio-economic influences need to be seriously considered to address persisting concerns that banks have been unable to include vast sections of the society, especially the underprivileged ones, into their fold. Despite increased geographic and functional coverage, vast swathes of the rural hinterland are still underdeveloped, with very little safety nets for both employment generation and poverty alleviation. Given the extremely limited access to bank finance by the rural poor because of high default risk, high transaction costs, uncertainty in re-payments, absence of credit information, lack of collateral, etc., issues relating to "inclusive" growth, distributive equity, "banking at the bottom of the pyramid", thrust on the development of agriculture and rural non-farm sector (RNFS) have increasingly come to the fore in spreading institutional finance in rural areas. Hence, the rural economy must be vibrant and resilient to achieve the avowed goal of growth with distributive equity. The reform of the national financial architecture must lead to early and sustained results to deal more effectively with future challenges and to raise general living standards. This necessitates a renewed thrust on lowering the costs of financial intermediation and increasing access to finance for agriculture, small businesses and the poor.

While the thrust on growth in quantitative terms has been sustained, banks in India have not to be impervious to the qualitative aspects of the growth process. Financial inclusion is broadly defined as the provision of affordable financial services, viz. access to payments and remittance facilities, savings, loans, and insurances services by the formal financial system to the vast sections of disadvantaged and low income groups. In other words, the term 'financial inclusion' implies the coexistence of a continuum of financial services outlets that work within their comparative advantage to serve the poor and low-income people. This is why financial inclusion goes beyond broad basing banking and financial services and looks at Financial Inclusion in the broader context of Quality of Physical Life Index (QPLI) and provision of adequate economic opportunities. Both the Government and the banking sector attach immense significance to 'financial inclusion' because of its profound implications for the poor, the deprived and the vulnerable sections of population.

Microfinance

Post-nationalisation, there has been a discernible increase in banking services and institutional credit facilities to rural poor. Despite significant upscaling of access to finance for India's teeming millions, large sections of rural poor still have very limited or even no access to bank finance. High default risk, high transaction costs, uncertainty in re-payments, absence of credit information, lack of collateral, etc., constrained the spread of institutional finance in rural areas. Against this overarching scenario, the bank-linkage with SHGs has transformed the rural credit landscape and has significantly reduced the vulnerability of poor households.

Microfinance has triggered a silent revolution in the rural areas. But the global experience of successful microfinance has evoked widespread debates. Some of the main strands of this debate relate to provision of sustained financial services to the poor, extraordinarily high repayment rates, continuum of microenterprise finance intermediaries, socio-economic transformation, etc. While microfinance in India has made a perceptible difference, there are persisting problems of MF still forming a miniscule proportion of the total bank credit, demand-supply imbalance, rate of interest charged, limited involvement of commercial banks and small size of microfinance institutions (MFIs). This necessitates continued stress on microfinance by linking grassroots borrowers with SHGs and close linkage of microfinance to rural livelihoods.

There are also issues of minuscule outreach of MFIs in terms of the proportion of poor households served, skewed distribution across states, extremely narrow scope of Indian MFIs, further scaling up SHGs, ensuring sustainability of MFIs, overcoming competition with banks now providing similar financial products, limited use of credit ratings and information technology. These and other aspects need synchronised measures to meet the requirements of huge and still growing market. Corporates are evincing keen interest because of the profitability and sustainability of microfinance.

Way Forward

The inexorable process of economic reforms must continue to achieve the goal of reducing poverty and supporting sustainable development while helping to strengthen financial institutions. With a clear break from the 'Hindu growth rate' of the past, we must work toward a vision of a resurgent India that is more prosperous, better governed, more cooperative, and less poor, based on development that cares in particular for the most vulnerable groups of society. We must work toward a vision of "inclusive" development that promotes not only economic growth but also equity in the sharing of benefits, the reduction of human-development disparities in society, and sensitivity and pluralistic consciousness in reaching out to the 'teeming millions' of India. This overarching goal of development needs a renewed thrust on financial sector reforms.

Implications of Global Financial Imbalances for the Emerging Market Economies*

1

Y.V. Reddy

...Although fast growing economies are generally grouped together as EMEs, some of their major macroeconomic indicators present a wide spectrum. While some of the EMEs are running large current account surpluses (such as China, the Russian Federation, South Korea, Venezuela, Malaysia, Taiwan and Brazil), some others are running current account deficits (such as Turkey, Hungary, South Africa, Mexico, India and the Czech Republic) and their current account balances range from a deficit of US$ 20 billion to a surplus of US$ 69 billion. While savings rates for select EMEs range from 9 per cent to 43 per cent of the GDP, in most of the EMEs the rates have increased and overtaken those of the industrial countries, with particularly high savings rates in China, Malaysia and Russia. Likewise, while some of the EMEs have fiscal surplus (Russia), several others have fiscal deficit (Turkey, India, the Philippines, Argentina and several other EMEs). Also, while some of the EMEs such as India are largely domestic-demand driven, some other EMEs, particularly in the East Asia (Malaysia and the Philippines) are largely dependent on exports to sustain their growth and their exports of goods and services range from 15 per cent to over 120 per cent of GDP. It is useful to note that while some of the EMEs are net oil exporters, some others are net oil importers.

Thus, given the diverse nature, macroeconomic conditions and policy regimes of the EMEs, it may be difficult to treat all of them as contributing to global financial imbalances, in the same manner, nor would all the EMEs be identically affected

*Reproduced from Dec. 2005 issue of Reserve Bank of India Bulletin.

by the adjustment of global financial imbalances. It may, therefore, be somewhat difficult to speak about the implications of global financial imbalances for the EMEs as a group. I would, therefore, focus primarily on India, but the analytic framework could perhaps be of some help in appreciating the implications for different EMEs.

It is worthwhile to mention that there are some factors which could adversely impact the EMEs as a group, though with varying intensity. Global developments, particularly those in the world financial markets, have the most direct and serious impact on the financing conditions in the emerging markets. An abrupt and sharp adjustment of the currencies may potentially lead to a significant portfolio rebalancing by the foreign investors, which could cause sharp changes in the long-term yields. This, in turn, could result in volatility in the level and cost of capital flows with direct implications for the EMEs.

Volatility in financial markets could adversely affect the EMEs in many ways, and also in a complex and interrelated fashion. For convenience of analysis, the impact may be classified broadly into: (i) the impact on the financing conditions in which EMEs operate; (ii) impairment of the balance sheets of the banking sector, and (iii) hampering of the growth prospects in the real sector. Even within the same EMEs, the impact could vary across different entities such as the Government, the corporate sector, the households and the financial sector, depending upon the country-specific and institution-specific operating environment, the stage of development and the degree of integration with and exposure to the international financial markets. In view of the diversity of the EMEs and the complexity of impact of any unpredictable unwinding of global imbalances, it is proposed to analyse the possible implications, illustratively, with reference to India.

Recent Macroeconomic Developments in India

There are several noteworthy features of India's recent macroeconomic performance. First, the investment climate has improved and industrial and service sector activity has picked up. Second, buoyant exports have emerged as the driver of demand for a broad spectrum of industries. Third, there has been a modest attempt at and a commitment to achieve fiscal consolidation. Fourth, the trend inflation has declined over the years and inflation expectations stabilised. Fifth, India has been successful in managing liquidity against the backdrop of continuing capital flows. Sixth, India has emerged as a preferred destination for foreign investors and received about a quarter of the global portfolio flows to the EMEs in 2004. Seventh, India's foreign exchange reserves are in excess of the total outstanding external debt of the country. Eighth, the performance of the corporate sector has improved and some corporates are now listed on the international stock exchanges. Ninth, India's financial markets have deepened, widened and become vibrant over the years with a robust institutional framework and market infrastructure in place. Tenth, the profitability and soundness indicators of the banking sector have improved. Finally, India has been adopting international benchmarks for financial standards and best practices with suitable adaptations for Indian conditions.

The Indian economy today is characterised by an environment of confidence, positive business expectations, a renewal of rule-based fiscal consolidation, stable and orderly financial markets and institutions and progressive integration with the global economy. Real GDP growth for 2005-06 (April-March) has been conservatively projected at around 7.0 per cent, and more recently, revised upwards to a range of 7.0 to 7.5 per cent. Despite the sustained strength of export performance, the merchandise trade deficit is expected to be somewhat higher in 2005-06 than in the previous year, mainly on account of substantially higher oil prices and non-oil import demand for investment. For the year as a whole, while invisibles may finance a large part of the enlarged trade deficit, the current account deficit is expected to widen during 2005-06 but to remain within acceptable limits that can be financed by normal capital flows. The headline inflation is expected to lie in the range of 5.0-5.5 per cent. Consolidation of Central Government finances is the goal of fiscal policy at the Centre—the targets are: the gross fiscal deficit (GFD) of 3.0 per cent of GDP and the elimination of the revenue deficit by 2008-09. The fiscal position of State Governments also continues to undergo slight correction in terms of key deficit indicators.

Against this background, it may be useful to analyse the implications of global financial imbalances for India in terms of the likely impact on four separate balance sheets—of the Government, of the Reserve Bank of India, of the corporate sector and of the banking sector.

Impact on the Government

The Government of India does not raise resources from the international capital markets to finance the fiscal deficit, though the bilateral and multilateral sources do provide moderate amount of foreign currency funds. The Government could, therefore, be affected indirectly through the spill-over impact of external developments on domestic interest rates. What is of relevance, *inter alia*, is the nominal international interest rates and domestic interest rates, adjusted for inflation differential. To the extent there is a rise in domestic interest rates, there could be an increase in the cost of government borrowings of the Government. Since most of the outstanding debt is at fixed rates and not on floating rates, the rise in the borrowing cost will be incremental. This situation also provides greater headroom for a flexible monetary policy to adjust policy rates, as and when warranted, without any excessive impact on the fiscal deficit.

Impact on the Reserve Bank's Balance Sheet

The fiscal position of the Government could also be indirectly impacted through the nature of management of foreign exchange reserves held by the Reserve Bank. Volatility in the foreign exchange market exposes foreign exchange reserves to both operational and market risks. Depreciation in the value of any reserve currency *vis-à-vis* the domestic currency would result in an equivalent decline in the value of the reserves held, though the impact may be mitigated to some extent through appreciation of other currencies in which foreign exchange reserves are held. Also, increase in global interest rates would entail capital losses on the corresponding assets, including fixed income securities. Valuation and capital losses could impact the income of the Reserve Bank of India and thus, its surplus transferable to the Government which, in turn, would have fiscal implications. It is pertinent to mention that the Reserve Bank of India, as a matter of prudent practice, follows conservative accounting norms whereby the valuation gains/ losses on foreign exchange reserves and gold are not taken to the profit and loss account, but instead, booked under a separate reserve head.

Impact on the Indian Corporates

As a result of deterioration in global financial market conditions, spreads on corporate debt might widen suddenly due to shift in investor confidence in the global financial markets. Increase in the global interest rates may also have impact on other benchmarks such as LIBOR. A sharp rise in yields may entail an increase in cost of variable-rate debt contracted by the corporates. This, to some extent, could be offset if there is a depreciation of the relevant currency and consequent decline in the value of the existing debt contracted by corporates in that currency.

Indian corporates as also some of the public sector enterprises raise resources from the international capital markets. While a part of their external commercial borrowings is at variable interest rate, a part is at fixed interest rates. In order to avoid any serious impact of changes in the exchange rate on the balance sheet of the corporate sector, Reserve Bank has been advising banks to regularly monitor the unhedged position of the corporates and has also been exhorting corporates to hedge their foreign exchange exposures. Thus, India's corporates could be affected by the deterioration in the financing conditions only to the extent they are not hedged either by foreign-currency cash flows in the normal course of business or through recourse to appropriate hedging products. Corporates would, however, be affected to the extent interest rates firm up in the domestic market, depending on their exposure to debt relative to other liabilities.

Impact on the Banking Sector

Banks in India are dependent mainly on domestic deposits, predominantly at fixed rates, for their resource requirements. They would, therefore, be impacted significantly only if the adverse developments in the international capital markets are particularly severe. Banks, in general, also do not hold stock of securities in foreign currency. Banks in India have, thus, relatively small exposure to the foreign exchange market. Their foreign currency borrowings are subject to the prudential limit of 25 per cent of their Tier-I capital and they are also required to maintain capital against the net open position. Foreign currency borrowings by the banks are permitted beyond this ceiling, which is linked to the net worth, exclusively for the purpose of export finance.

Like many other emerging market economies, credit extended by banks in India has increased sharply in recent times. Credit growth, which was earlier seen largely in housing and retail loans, has now turned quite broad-based with agriculture and industry also joining to drive up the credit demand. The credit growth in some sectors, specially those related to assets which are experiencing price volatilities, is being monitored closely.

Banks are allowed to lend to resident exporters in foreign currency at internationally competitive rates of interest from their foreign currency lines of credit as well as out of funds available in exchange earners' foreign currency accounts, resident foreign currency accounts and foreign currency non-resident (banks) accounts. These loans are intended to finance domestic and imported inputs for export production. Foreign currency loans to exporters are generally hedged against credit risk since they are extended for *bona fide* underlying activity, viz. export production. They are also usually covered for exchange risk since they are denominated in foreign currency. Banks are also allowed to extend loans in foreign currency to non-resident Indians against their FCNRB deposits. Funds in foreign currency deposits can also be utilized for lending to domestic corporates for working capital requirements in India, import financing, purchase of indigenous machinery, repayment of rupee term loans and external commercial borrowings.

Banks have also been extending credit for investment in the asset market. Like many other EMEs, asset prices in India have also risen sharply in the last couple of years. Should there be reversal of capital flows, asset prices may decline sharply exposing the banks' balance sheets to credit risk. There is a risk that rise in interest rates in general could impact housing prices and expose the balance sheet of the households to interest rate risk, leading to some loan losses for banks. The overall banking sector's exposure to housing loans is relatively small and may not have serious systemic implications. Likewise, the equity market has also seen a sustained uptrend. Reversal of capital flows could impact the equity market and some of the advances extended for investments in the equity market might turn non-performing. Again, Indian banks do not have large exposure in the asset market though, in the recent past, it has been increasing. Decline in asset prices could cause loan losses and capital losses, if the decline is significant, though the impact on banks' balance sheets might be muted, given their small exposure to the asset market.

The most significant impact on banks' balance sheet, however, could be felt through their investment portfolio. Banks in India hold substantial investments in Government and other fixed income securities. Such investments amounted to US$ 173 billion, constituting 35.1 per cent of their total assets as on September 16, 2005. To the extent a rise in international interest rates impacts the domestic interest rates, it would entail marked-to-market losses on the investment portfolios.

The banking sector, however, has acquired some added strength to absorb such probable shocks, largely aided by regulatory actions. Apart from having built up a significant capital base reflected in the capital to risk-weighted assets ratio (CRAR) for the sector of 12%, specific steps have been taken to meet the interest rate risk. First, separate provision for capital against market risk has been introduced. Second, a gradual building up of Investment Fluctuation Reserve up to 5% of the marked-to-market portfolio (out of tax-free profits) by

March 2006 has been mandated, and several banks have already achieved the target. Third, an enabling risk management environment has been provided to banks to hedge their risks through vanilla derivative instruments. Fourth, Conservative accounting norms followed did not allow banks to book unrealized gains. Fifth, as a one time measure, banks were allowed to transfer securities to HTM, after booking the MTM losses against these. Thus, banks in India, in general, have the resilience to withstand some rise in interest rates.

Impact on the Real Sector

Readjustment of the currencies would also have implications for the real sector. Significant readjustment of the currencies and rise in interest rates could slow down the global growth. This would entail a reduction in export opportunities and reduction in investment demand for EMEs, in general, many of which depend on export demand to sustain their growth. Rise in interest rates, by slowing down spending, may have a negative impact on the global economic growth. Thus, readjustment of the currencies may affect several EMEs in a significant way.

The impact of any slowdown on India may be assessed with reference to two factors. First, India's economy is largely domestic-demand driven. While India's exports constituted 11.5 per cent of GDP, its share in the world trade is only 0.8 per cent. Second, India's exports basket is fairly diversified.

Some concerns arise with regard to the implications for employment in case of a slowdown in the exports sector, especially with regard to the significant specialisation in BPO/IT Enable Services. Rapid job growth that absorbs the huge supply of agricultural labour into its industrial work force is necessary for socio-economic stability in India. Any negative impact on employment resulting in substantial decrease of real earnings and widening income inequality is likely to reduce overall welfare and increase the cost of structural adjustments required, especially in the absence of meaningful social safety nets.

Monetary and Prudential Measures as Responses

The outlook for output growth in India has improved in the recent months, particularly with the momentum gained in manufacturing sector. However, persistence of global imbalances and high oil prices with a significant permanent component do pose some risks. Furthermore, the credit growth has recently been extremely strong possibly impacting credit quality, while money-supply is over-shooting the anticipated trajectory and strong investment demand coupled with high oil-prices is turning the current account surplus into a deficit, though modest and manageable through normal capital flows. These developments pose new challenges to maintaining price and financial stability while ensuring momentum in growth. Consequently, in the Mid-Term Review of Annual Policy Statement for the year 2005-06, released on October 25, 2005, several measures have been announced to contain and manage the downside risks.

First, the reverse-repo rate (overnight liquidity absorption by Reserve Bank) has been increased by 25 basis points to 5.25 per cent, keeping the spread between reverse repo and repo at 100 basis points. The bank rate, being the signalling rate for medium term, is retained at 6 per cent.

Second, rationalization of limits on banks' exposure to capital market has been announced, restricting it to 40 per cent of a bank's net worth while simplifying the exemptions and coverage.

Third, the general provisioning requirement for standard advances has been enhanced from the present level of 0.25 per cent to 0.40 per cent except in regard to banks' exposures to laggards in credit-growth, namely Agriculture and Small and Medium Industries.

Fourth, a decision had been taken to treat the entire balance under Investment Fluctuation Reserve as Tier I capital, thus providing some head-room to banks to raise Tier II capital in future.

Fifth, revised guidelines are being issued on corporate restructuring mechanisms to be followed by banks in the light of experience gained.

Sixth, having regard to the recent trends in the credit markets, RBI is initiating a supervisory review process with select banks having significant exposure to some sectors, namely real estate, highly leveraged non-banking financial companies, venture capital funds and capital markets. The purpose of such a review is to ensure that effective risk mitigants and sound internal controls are in place for managing such exposures.

Some Reflections

From the above discussion, it is clear that the impact on India would depend on the pace and extent of currency and current account readjustments, and changes in global interest rates. While India by itself hardly contributes to global financial imbalances, any large and rapid adjustments in major currencies and related interest rates or current accounts of trading partners could indirectly impact the Indian economy.

From the case of India, it is also clear that readjustment of the currencies and rise in interest rates would impact different EMEs differently. Despite rise in short-term interest rates, long-term interest rates, instead of rising, have moderated, leading to a further flattening of the global yield curve and narrowing down of credit spreads. EMEs have taken advantage of favourable financial conditions. During the first half of 2005, EMEs focused on operations aimed at meeting domestic and external obligations and lengthening maturities. However, higher global interest rates could contribute to widening of emerging market bond spreads, particularly those with high debt to GDP ratio. In view of expected deceleration in financial conditions, some emerging markets have cushioned by advancing their external financing, taking advantage of current benign financial market conditions. Emerging market economies have, however, continued to improve their debt structures in an effort towards reducing their vulnerability to external shocks. EMEs have carried out active liability management operations aimed at meeting their financial requirements while minimising the cost of debt and its risks. Some countries have taken steps to develop their local markets and have reduced the amount of foreign currency-linked domestic debt, while gradually improving the maturity profile. Some of the EMEs have also reduced the share of domestic debt indexed to the exchange rate.

Compared to the past crises, the EMEs, in general, are now resilient and in a better position to absorb a financial shock. They have developed resilience to shocks by improving their macroeconomic conditions and regulatory frameworks. EMEs have been achieving a healthy growth with more or less stable inflation and have reduced their dependence on external demand. There has also been an improvement in fiscal positions, supported by the development of domestic securities markets. The external debt burden has declined and the composition of financial flows has changed with lower reliance on borrowings from international banks. Several EMEs have addressed the weaknesses that led to the earlier crisis by strengthening prudential regulation and supervision more in line with international best practices. Banks' balance sheets have improved and capital ratios have risen. Corporate governance practices have also improved. To the extent EMEs have introduced flexibility in their exchange rates, their vulnerability to external shocks has declined. All these factors have reduced the vulnerability of EMEs. Large reserves held by EMEs should also enable them to cope with the volatility arising out of a sudden shift in market sentiment.

While macroeconomic fundamentals of several EMEs are strong, placing them in a relatively better position to withstand deterioration in international financing conditions, economic performance of some EMEs has been found to be less robust. The conditions in these economies may get accentuated by adjustment of global financial imbalances and high and volatile oil prices. A possible volatility in the global financial markets emanating from a rise in interest rates could magnify and propagate the problems associated with less than satisfactory performance in some of the EMEs, making them vulnerable to sudden reassessment of country risk. Such threats are real as the default rates of sub-investment grade borrowers could increase. Credit derivatives, which have proliferated in recent years and whose pricing has depended on relatively untested models and default correlation assumptions, may in particular be vulnerable to corrections.

The main challenge for EMEs is to continue to take advantage of the current favourable external financing conditions and at the same time pursue domestic macroeconomic and structural reforms necessary for long-term stability. In fact, some EMEs have well-advanced external financing, in some cases even including prefinancing for 2006. EMEs have made significant gains in terms of healthy growth, stable inflation, large trade surplus, greater exchange rate flexibility and lower debt burden. While EMEs are preparing themselves to face sudden shocks, efforts need to be made by all concerned for an orderly adjustment of global financial imbalances. While co-ordinated policy action would minimise the cost of rebalancing, perhaps, a stress testing by all the concerned regulators in the EMEs to assess the extent of the resilience could be helpful.

The EMEs, despite their diversity, seem to generate expectations of high growth and are generally characterized by less-than-fully developed markets, specially financial markets. Consequently, there are significant cross-border capital flows, with market perception of high risk and high reward in EMEs. It is useful to note that implicit in the word "emerging" in the very title given to the EMEs as a group, is the notion that they are undergoing a rapid change or transition. We must recognize that the transition embraces demographics, political institutions, social dimensions and related attitudes. These all-encompassing changes have an in-built potential for uncertainties, possibly some volatility, but it gets exacerbated by the international capital flows, particularly when the changes in such flows happen to be unrelated to domestic fundamentals. In such a situation, managing the transition turns out to be a critical challenge for policy making, and the management requires a more difficult and dynamic trade off between commitment and flexibility in policy.

Overall, while added risks—both upside and downside—are inevitable with increasing global financial and economic integration, the EMEs may consider strengthening their resilience through not only sound macroeconomic management but also by adopting appropriate prudential measures. Over a period, coordinated efforts, both at regional as well as global levels, could also help EMEs to cushion themselves better against the risks of financial globalisation....

ANNEX

Select Economic Indicators—Select Emerging Market Economies

(US $ billion)

Country	GDP (growth rate)[1]	Inflation rate[1]	Trade Balance[2]	Current Account[2]	Foreign Reserves[3]	External Debt[4]	Overall Budget Balance to GDP[5]	Export of goods and services to GDP@
1	2	3	4	5	6	7	8	9
Argentina	10.1	9.7	11.2	2.8	24.4	166.2	-3.3	24.0
Brazil	3.9	6.0	40.1	12.5	54.6	235.4	-1.5@	22.5
Chile	6.5	3.0	8.7	0.6	15.8	43.2	-0.3	38.0
China	9.5	1.3	93.1	68.7	711.0	193.6	-1.7@	40.2
Colombia	5.3	4.9	1.8	-0.8	14.9	33.0	-	19.1
Czech Republic	5.1	1.7	1.3	-4.1	30.2	34.6	-	-
Egypt	4.7	4.7	-9.5	4.4	18.5	31.4	-	25.5
Hungary	4.1	3.6	-3.4	-9.2	18.0	45.8	-	-
India	7.0	4.1	-34.7	-6.4	133.6	113.5	-4.5@	15.4
Indonesia	5.5	8.3	27.8	7.8	31.0	134.4	-1.2	31.3
Israel	4.8	1.6	-7.7	1.3	27.8	-	-	-
Malaysia	4.1	3.7	23.6	16.7	78.0	49.1	-	121.3
Mexico	3.1	4.0	-9.6	-8.4	66.4	140.0	-0.3@	30.1
Peru	4.9	1.2	4.0	0.4	12.8	-	-1.8	19.6
Philippines	4.8	7.2	-0.7	2.9	15.3	62.7	-4.0	52.0
Poland	2.8	1.6	-3.3	0.3	39.4	95.2	-	22.6
Russia	6.1	12.4	110.6	69.2	146.0	175.3	4.4@	25.6
South Africa	4.5	3.9	-2.3	-8.6	17.2	27.8	-1.0	28.2
South Korea	3.3	2.0	26.0	21.3	206.6	-	-	-
Taiwan	3.0	3.6	1.7	13.3	254.1	-	-	-
Thailand	4.4	5.6	-7.3	-2.2	47.3	51.8	-2.8	-
Turkey	4.2	7.9	-38.9	-20.0	42.9	145.7	-19.6	27.0
Venezuela	11.1	14.8	24.7	17.7	23.1	34.9	-	35.7

1. Percentage change on year ago.
2. Latest 12 months.
3. Excluding gold, except Singapore; IMF definition.
4. Relating to 2003.
5. Relating to 2001.
@ Relating to 2004. - = Not Available.

Note: Indicators are based on latest available data and, therefore, relate to different periods for different countries.

Source: 1. *The Economist*, October 1-7, 2005.
2. *Global Development Finance*, 2005.
3. *World Development Indicators*, World Bank, 2004.

Inclusive Growth: Role of Banks

2

M.B.N. Rao

The approach paper to 11th Five-Year Plan of the country aims at "a faster and more inclusive growth". Indian economy is growing at 8 per cent—highest in any plan period. The percentage of people below poverty line is declining but at a modest pace. With economy growing at 8-9 per cent and population growth at 1.5 per cent per year, doubling of income of average Indian takes almost ten years.

In a recent paper on inclusive growth, a World Bank team finds "the gap between the best and worst placed is growing". This concern is validated by NSSO's latest findings. Unemployment is highest among educated youth in the age group of 15-29 and agriculture with merely 20 per cent of GDP accounts for 67 per cent of rural labour force.

The major challenges for ensuring inclusive growth are:

- Providing essential services for poor—education and health at affordable cost.
- Regaining agricultural dynamism—to ensure 4 per cent annual growth.
- Developing human resources.
- Protecting the environment and reverse environmental losses.
- Increasing the competition of manufacturing sector.
- Improving the rehabilitation and resettlement practices.
- Improving governance.

The above challenges when converted into goals are similar to United Nation's Millennium goals.

In the light of Government's policy making *growth more inclusive*, the strategies of bringing equity are being pushed forward in all the spheres including financial sector. The path of economic development for ultimate poverty reduction imposes responsibilities and creates newer & greater opportunities for the financial system.

C.K. Prahlad in his path-breaking work, *The Fortune At the Bottom of the Pyramid* rightly stressed, "doing more of the same, by refining the solutions of the past is important and has a role to play, but has not redressed the problem of poverty".

Issues for Inclusive Growth

I. Binding constraints—are the obstacles for inclusive growth. Inclusive growth is economic growth plus sharing benefits of growth to reduce poverty—the double bottom line. India's growth has not been shared equally. There is hence a need to equalise accelerators along with growth reforms.

II. Bridging divides (including the excluded)

Different dimensions of divide are:

(a) Between below and above poverty line.

(b) Between rural and urban.

(c) Between those with productive jobs and unemployed/ under employed.

(d) Between states.

(e) Between backward and non-backward districts.

(f) Between members in the same family.

III. Managing the Transition in banking sector—from competition to coordination

(a) From a regulated and controlled environment, to provide financial sector a space for fast growth, deregulation of markets and influence of international finance are on the anvil.

(b) Prudent banking practices have to fit into competitive and market driven framework so that a level playing field and incentives to make all the players to expand the scope and their engagement in inclusive growth.

(c) Right technology solution in design, delivery and distribution of financial products and an efficient process for implementation to cover a wide spectrum of clientele spread over a vast geographical area.

(d) Addressing the shortcomings of yester years' social banking in terms of infrastructure, communication channels and human resources with right attitude and aptitude.

(e) Challenge of converting competition into co-ordination across agencies in areas such as product development, common use of infrastructure, sharing of information, technology transfer, liaisoning with Government, etc., to benefit society at large.

Upscaling the Effort

Inclusive growth requires two types of efforts:

(a) Promoting growth to create employment opportunities.

(b) Helping those disadvantaged to take advantage of these opportunities. These disadvantaged/ excluded population have to reap the economic benefits as partners, suppliers, consumers and beneficiaries.

Over 1.2 billion people of the world still have just a dollar [US($)] a day income. More than half of world population (2.8 billion) in developing countries have an income of only US $ 2/day.

We should aim for "High quality growth"—sustained growth that does not collapse in the face of external shock.

Scaling up has to be viewed from angle of:

(a) How—concepts/ implementation factors.

(b) What to do—the strategic pillars like investment climate and social inclusion.

We have to overcome the shortcomings of earlier top-down non-inclusive approach. The linkage strategy must focus on:

(a) Those excluded/not included.

(b) Address the issue in entirety.

(c) Alliance with all stakeholders.

(d) Response to changes in ever evolving Global arena.

Our effort/strategies should alter the stubborn reality of non-inclusion, especially in rural areas and slums. Our financial services have to:

(a) Stand the test of effectiveness, replicability and sustainability of existing deliverables.

(b) Observe sound market approach and discipline in financial intermediation.

(c) Work to narrow gaps in knowledge about the relation between financial services and poverty. It seems 1 per cent increase in agricultural GDP per capita increases 1.6 per cent per capita income of poorest. Ten per cent increase in crop yields reduce 6-10 per cent in number of poor with a dollar a day income.

Inclusive Growth—What Banks Can Do?

SHG—Bank Linkage programme

- Self help group bank linkage programme have been successful in meeting financial requirements of large sections of people in some regions. Again, there is a regional imbalance in the success with nothing much happening in the lagging states. This has been highlighted in the World Bank's recent development policy review titled "India—Inclusive growth and service delivery: building on India's success."
- Exclusive banks/ institutions have been setup in many countries for micro finance. We are following multi agency model—commercial banks, Regional Rural Banks and cooperatives are undertaking rural development and micro finance. There is a need to have a relook for setting of a specialized national micro finance institution to promote inclusive growth to coordinate these efforts.
- SHG—Bank Linkage programme, the largest in the world, has been done in partnership with NGOs. This alliance requires an upscaling in terms of:

- Making linkage happen across country.
- Entering into other areas—savings, insurance, health, education, income generating activities.
- Providing marketing support to SHG products.
- Graduating SHG members to become direct client of banking system.

- Recent deliverables like no frill accounts, general purpose credit card for rural and semi urban areas, schemes for lending to tenant farmers, etc., would facilitate financial inclusion. Both the models of SHG bank linkage programme and individual approach to financial inclusion are considered by banks as good business propositions.

  Also, the challenge lies in effective harnessing of the network of RRBs and reaching the vast unbanked sections, as a profitable proposition.

- There is a need to outsource some of the simple functions of rural branches to make these branches reach the large population of their command area. RBI has already come out with the business facilitator and correspondent models in this direction. Issues like technology interfaces, legal aspects are to be addressed by public sector banks before adopting these models.

Voluntary Initiatives of Canara Bank

- Bank's Rural Development Trust has been bridging the digital divide, by reviving the traditional arts and crafts and instill confidence in youth for self-employment with a settlement rate of 72 per cent.
- Canara Bank has formulated various schemes, deliverables arising out of voluntarism, towards reaching the excluded and marginalized sections of the society, and beyond mere financial inclusion. To name a few -Rural Service Volunteer Scheme (dedicated utilization of service of employees for rural development), Jalayoga (Providing Potable Water), Rural Development & Self Employment Training

Institutes (RUDSETIs a collaborative effort) for varied target groups of women, rural educated & unemployed, artisans, NGOs & Self Help Groups, etc.

- The bank's inclusive growth initiatives in areas of health and education too can be indicated with pride. The Sevaskshetra Hospital at Bangalore, Rural Clinic Services Scheme and Jubilee Education Fund are such initiatives.
- Through a unique programme, bank has covered nearly 790 villages under its plan of covering 1400 villages across the country for 100 per cent financial inclusion. Bank aims to cover all the villages in the command area of its branches in a phased manner.

Framework for Banks

Jobless growth is a prescription for sociological disaster. Hence, a framework for banking in terms of essentials for inclusive growth is proposed—the "**three A approach**" for a detailed deliberation:

- **Access to resources**—How these client could develop an access to resources such as physical assets, financial services, infrastructure, information, etc.
- **Abilities to perform**—Skills and attitude required for development.
- **Assurances required**—These disadvantaged still require some social services and safety net for possible failures.

The role of banks in inclusive growth has wide ramifications. Hence attempts need to be made to examine and promote:

(a) Efforts to upscale inclusive growth.

(b) SHG—bank linkage—beyond the horizon—key role to be played by banks.

(c) The three 'A' approach in improving Access, Abilities & Assurances.

(d) Voluntarism in banking for inclusive growth.

Various inclusive growth strategies, from the banking system coupled with support structure and framework provided by the State can set the pace of inclusive growth to travel across new frontiers. The success of inclusive growth is to be assessed from touching the double bottomline—financial profitability and social welfare. As C.K. Prahlad succinctly said, "the real source of market power is not the wealthy few in the developing world, or even the emerging middle-income consumers. It is the billion of aspiring poor, who are joining the market economy for the first time". Hence, the discussion is not about "whether" but rather about how fast and when inclusive growth can work as a real engine of jobs and services for the poor.

Law and Finance in India: An Overview

3

Rajesh Chakrabarti

1. Introduction

Economists have long emphasized the pivotal role of laws and institutions in determining the economic destinies of nations. Indeed, the Nobel-prize winning economist Douglass North's explanation of varying economic experiences of societies around the world over centuries centers almost exclusively on institutions. Sanctity and low-cost enforceability of contracts lie at the heart of all economic transactions and hence constitute a basic pillar upholding the economy. Nevertheless, it is only lately that the central role of laws and institutions of governance in determining the evolution and structure of a country's financial system is being probed empirically in a systematic manner. Since the late 1990s, "law and finance" is gaining ground as an important sub-field of finance (and law) and efforts are on to better understand the effects of legal system and the social institutions in determining the financial environment and the financial decisions of individuals and businesses.

Nowhere is this inquiry more relevant than in India today. For a decade and a half India has been shedding its decades-long practice of state-controlled economy in favor of greater market orientation. Liberalisation is breathing new life into financial markets and private enterprise. Wide ranging changes have been brought about in financial and business regulations. Concurrently and arguably as a consequence, the growth rate has more than doubled from the infamous "Hindu rate" of 3.5%. Nevertheless, sustainability of this high growth rate depends on what is often called "second generation reforms" focusing on legal and labor reform. While macroeconomic policies have taken the center-stage in the first decade of reforms, there is widespread consensus that a significant overhauling of the legal system is imperative to sustain the initial impetus and to make growth more inclusive. The pace of the reforms process, as always and everywhere, is dictated by political realities and every single element of the reform process has its anticipated effects as well as unintended consequences. At this juncture it is imperative to have a clear understanding of the economic effects of India's legal system and her socio-economic institutions, particularly their impact on the country's financial system.

Small and Medium Enterprises (SMEs) have played a key role in the recent spurt in India's economic growth. They have mushroomed all over the land, employing millions and accounting for a significant fraction of the national output and exports. The business practices of India's SME sector, however, is far from completely documented and understood. As for all businesses, the choice of the extent and form of external financing for these firms, as well as their corporate governance mechanisms are determined to a large extent by the enforceability of the contracts they enter into. In the case of SMEs, however, business is frequently done through informal contracting with little or no paper trail. Courts of law rarely play a decisive role in settling their business disputes and informal mechanisms and social institutions play a key role resolving such disputes. A clear understanding of the grassroots reality of the SME business is essential to properly amend the legal and judicial system to serve them better.

While the laws themselves are doubtless crucial, poor implementation reduces wise legislation into a complete farce. The institutions of governance, therefore, play an equally important role in determining the development trajectory of the country. An assessment of the legal system therefore remains incomplete without a close look at the different institutions of governance and their impact on the financial environment.

The present paper attempts an overview of the recent contributions in the law, institutions and finance literature, and to connect that literature to the situation in India. The following section provides a selective review of the emerging law and finance literature while the third section discusses the current state of the law and institutions of governance in India particularly relative to other countries and the state of its financial markets. The fourth section concludes with pointers towards future research as well as policy advice for legal and institutional reform.

2. The Law, Institutions and Finance Literature—Major Themes

Legal Origin, Investor Protection and Property Rights

In a series of influential papers, La Porta et al. (LLSV) (1997, 1998, 2000, 2002) established the relationship between the protection granted to investors—shareholders and creditors—in the laws of a country and the nature and evolution of its financial system squarely at the center of the finance research agenda. It is instructive to understand their basic argument.

LLSV argue that difference in the extent to which laws in different countries protect investors explain why firms are financed and owned so differently around the globe, why in some countries banks are more important than markets while the opposite is true in other cases, why firms in different countries have access to external finance to such starkly different degrees and why dispersion of shareholding is so different across countries. They demonstrate this empirically by creating measures of investor protection provided in the laws of different countries and regressing variables that represent the various issues noted above on these measures.

Importantly, they note that countries almost never create a legal system from scratch. The legal structure of a country is, almost always, inherited or imported from some other system—voluntarily or otherwise (through conquest and colonisation). Thus, while laws are unique to countries, legal systems stemming from the same origin are more similar than those that grow from a different foundation. Most countries around the world today have legal systems based on either the British common law or one of the civil law traditions that trace their origin to the Roman civil law coded by emperor Justinian. Among these civil law systems, the important ones are the Napoleonic French civil law and the German civil law written in 1897 after the unification of Germany under Bismarck. The Scandinavian countries seem to follow a third variant different from both these civil law systems. The primary difference between a common law system and a civil law system is that the former allows much greater role to jurisprudence as court decisions on specific cases are used as precedents for later cases, while the civil law system is more explicitly codified with less room for jurisprudence. Not surprisingly, the British common law and French civil law systems have seeded the present-day legal systems in countries that were former colonies of these powers. The German civil law has influenced the legal system of several European countries including Austria, former Czechoslovakia, Greece, Hungary, and former Yugoslavia and Asian countries like Japan, Taiwan and Korea. While these four systems of legal origin were studied in the initial papers, in later works a fifth origin—the socialist origin—was added to capture the legal origin of many formerly Communist countries. It is important to note that while the legal systems of many countries are also shaped in part by religious traditions like Islamic law in Arab countries, Hindu law in India and Jewish law for Israel, typically these influences do not extend to the areas of commercial law and laws of contract and tort, which directly affect legal rights of investors. These latter laws are almost always affected by the "secular" legal origin discussed before.

In order to assess the degree of investor protection in a country's legal system, LLSV define seven binary dummy variables and one continuous variable to capture elements of shareholder protection in the law and four binary dummy variables and one continuous variable to capture those protecting creditor rights. The variables included in shareholder protection are: (1) whether the country follows the "one share—one vote" rule; (2) if shareholders are allowed to mail their proxy to ease voting; (3) if shares are not blocked for a period before a general shareholders' meeting; (4) whether the country allows cumulative voting or proportional representation in the election of directors;

(5) if the law grants a judicial venue for minority shareholders (holding 10% or less shares) to redress their grievances against management or requires company to buyback their shares in case of dissent with regard to some fundamental changes; (6) if the law grants the shareholders first right to new issues of stock; and (7) whether the minimum percentage of shareholding required to call an extraordinary general meeting is less than their sample median of 10%. All except the first of these variables are also summed up as "anti-director rights" and, as the sum of the constituent binary variable values, anti-director rights can range from zero to six. Another variable that LLSV consider in the category of shareholder rights is the proportion of net profit companies need to distribute among shareholders as mandatory dividend (zero in case of no such clause). The "anti-director index" construct of LLSV has been criticised by some for being ad hoc and ambiguous (Pagano and Volpin, 2005; Spamann, 2005). Djankov et al. (DLLS, 2006) have constructed an "anti-self-dealing" index, measuring the extent to which laws of a country regulates dealings between related-party firms, which improved upon the "anti-director rights".

For creditor rights, the binary elements are: (1) if the law imposes restrictions like creditors' consent to file for reorganisation; (2) if there is no automatic stay on secured assets on filing the reorganisation petition; (3) if secured creditors are ranked first in the distribution of proceeds of asset sales of a bankrupt firm; (4) if management is replaced by a representative of the court or creditors during the reorganisation period. The "Creditors' rights" index, the sum of the values of these four binary variables, therefore ranges between zero and four. The continuous variable considered in addition is the minimum percentage of total share capital mandated by law to be held as reserve to avoid dissolution of the firm (zero if no such provision). Together these variables constitute measures of the degree to which investors rights are protected in the laws of a country.

LLSV find that, on average, English common law-origin countries provide best shareholder protection in terms of the "antidirector rights" and the French and German civil law-origin countries the worst. In terms of "creditor rights" too, the English common law-origin countries provide the best protection, on average, while the French civil law-origin countries provide the least protection. The differences are statistically significant.

In addition to the provisions in the laws itself, LLSV examined the efficacy of the *implementation* of laws in the different countries to check if the effect of poorer statutory investor protection in civil law countries is ameliorated through better implementation of the laws. Using country credit rating scores for dimensions like Rule of Law, Efficacy of Judiciary, Corruption, Risks of appropriation and repudiation of contract by government, they find, perhaps unsurprisingly, that the quality of law enforcement is primarily a function of wealth (or income) of a nation. However, after taking into account income, legal systems do have some systematic differences in enforcement with English common-law countries having *best* enforcement and French civil-law countries the worst. The same is true for accounting standards as well.

Armed with this comparative information about investor rights in the books as well as its implementation in different countries, LLSV then demonstrate that the countries with legal origin in systems that provide relatively less shareholder protection actually witness much more concentrated ownership, presumably because only the large shareholders can effectively protect their interests in such legal systems. They also show that such countries have smaller and narrower capital markets—both debt and equity markets—relative to the size of their economy. Legal origin evidently determines the ease of access to external finance in an economy. The difference in protection of shareholders' rights has led to completely different trajectories of financial and economic developments in the different countries. The English-origin systems spawn the largest number of firms per capita (on average 35.45 companies per million citizens as compared to 27.26 for Scandinavian-origin countries and 16.79 and 10.00 for German and French-origin countries respectively). They are also the best performers in mobilising external finance. The ratio of the stock market capitalisation held by minority shareholders (i.e. shareholders other than the three largest shareholders in each company) to the GNP of a country averages a remarkable 0.60 for the English-origin countries, substantially higher than the average ratio for German, Scandinavian and French-origin countries of 0.46, 0.30 and 0.21 respectively.

Finally, LLSV argue that investor protection lies at the heart of corporate governance. Strong investor rights protect the outside investor from expropriation by management and therefore lead to more effective corporate governance and greater investment and growth in the economy. Indeed, Johnson et al. (2000) have demonstrated that corporate governance failure—appropriation by controlling shareholders—lay at the heart of the Asian financial crisis. Corporate valuation (as measured by Tobin's *q*) tends to be higher in countries with better investor protection in the laws, i.e. the English common-law countries. Djankov, McLiesh and Shleifer (forthcoming) use the LLSV creditor rights index to show that countries with better legal protection creditors rights experiences significantly larger credit as a proportion of its GDP. They also emphasise the importance of widely available credit rating information in making credit more available. The presence of public credit registries and private credit bureaus enhance private credit significantly.

While the LLSV papers have established the importance of legal origin in explaining the nature of financial system, there are more than a single theory about the exact mechanism through which laws affect the financial system and financial decision-making. Beck et al. (2003) empirically evaluate two broad theories. The two "transmission channels" they seek to distinguish between are the "political channel" and the "adaptability channel". The former contends that laws of different countries differ in their allocation of rights and power between the state and the private sector. Broadly speaking, the general bias is determined by the legal origin. Typically civil law countries give fewer rights to the private individuals and institutions *vis-à-vis* the state as compared to the common law system. Financial institutions and markets develop best when private property and contracts are assured of freedom from state interference. As a result, civil-law countries lag behind their common-law counterparts in developing effective financial systems. On the other hand, the "adaptability channel" argues that effective functioning of financial markets and financial innovations require flexibility in the legal system to adjudicate over issues that have been unforeseen in past legislation. The common law system is marked by greater flexibility and adaptability to changes and innovations than the civil law systems because it gives more room to jurisprudence. This makes common law countries more suitable for financial development. Comparing the relative importance of these two channels in differentiating the financial development of countries with different legal origin, Beck et al. (2003) conclude in favor of the adaptability channel. It seems legal origin affects financial development and the quality of financial institutions primarily because the legal system of countries with different legal origin are varyingly *adaptable* to changes in socio-economic conditions and technology.

Protection of investor rights essentially implies securing property rights. Demirguc-Kunt and Maksimovic (1998) show that firms use more external funds in countries with better property right protection. Johnson et al. (2002) probe the difficult question of which is more fundamental to private sector investment—secure property rights or better access to external finance. Carrying out a survey of businesses in five transition economies—Russia, Ukraine, Poland, Slovakia and Romania—they establish that between the two variables perceived, property rights security is both necessary and sufficient for higher private sector investment. In other words, private sector reinvestment declines with a perception of poor property rights protection but after controlling for property rights protection, private sector investment is not affected by access to external funds.

Securities Laws, Regulation of Entry and Courts

Apart from the question of legal origin, which in spite of its fundamental insight, has limited policy implications, the law and finance literature has also branched off into investigating, in detail, the specific laws that affect issuance and trading of securities as well as the functioning of the legal institutions including the most important of all legal institutions, the courts themselves. This branch has also investigated the legal steps and processes required for starting a new business in several countries and measured the cost (in monetary terms plus the cost of the necessary delay) of this procedural obstacle and its effects in different countries.

Issuance of new securities is one of the most fundamental areas of securities laws. La Porta et al. (2006) carry out a cross-country comparison of the nature of such laws and the power of the supervising authority in the different countries and connect it to relative stock market development. Securities laws and institutions are compared on broadly two dimensions—the disclosure and liability standards that help bring out the maximum information about the issuer in a cost-efficient manner; and the nature and powers of the public enforcer of securities laws. Disclosure requirements are compared by measuring them using a "disclosure requirement index" which is the sum of six dummy variables. These variables indicate: (1) if a prospectus is required by law; the level of detail in information is required in the prospectus; (2) compensation of individual directors and executives; (3) identity of large shareholders of the issuing company; (4) share ownership by insiders of the company; (5) irregular contracts to which the issuer is a party; and (6) related party transactions involving the issuer. Analogously, a "liability standard index" is constructed as the mean of three multi-level dummies reflecting the procedural difficulty in recovering losses, in a civil liability case, for losses due to misleading statements in the prospectus from: (1) the issuer and its directors; (2) the distributor; and (3) the accountant. Finally the "public enforcement index" is the mean of five measures (indices) of the nature and power of the public enforcer of securities laws or the securities authority of the country. These five indices are: (1) the supervisor characteristics index; (2) the rule-making index; (3) the investigative powers index; (4) the orders index; and (5) the criminal index. The first index, in turn, is the mean of three binary dummies measuring the independence of the supervisor from the government in terms of: (i) appointment, (ii) tenure of its members, and (iii) the separation between supervisors of banks and stock exchanges. The rule-making index measures the power of the supervisor to make rules regarding new issues and listing. The investigative powers index measures the supervisor's power to command: (i) documents and (ii) witness testimony when investigating a violation of securities laws. The orders index measures the "stop" and "do" orders that may be issued, in case of a defective prospectus, against: (1) the issuer; (2) the distributor; and (3) the accountant involved in the issue. Similarly the criminal index measures the criminal sanctions that may be issued, when the prospectus omits material information, against: (1) the issuer; (2) the distributor and (3) the accountant involved in the issue.

La Porta et al. (2006) use these measures for 49 countries to study their effect on seven measures of stock market development: (1) External Capital/GDP (average ratio of stock market capitalisation held by small investors to GDP); (2) Logarithm of the number of listed firms per million people; (3) Average ratio of equity issued in IPOs (in thousand) to GDP (in millions); (4) the Dyck and Zinagles (2004) measure of "block premium" in the share transaction; (5) Survey response of level of agreement of business executives in the country to the statement "Stock markets are open to new firms and medium-sized firms"; (6) Average percentage of shares owned by 3 top shareholders in the 10 largest non-financial, privately owned firms in the country; and (7) Liquidity (average total value of stocks traded between 1996 and 2000 as a percentage of GDP). Their first finding is that securities laws *do* matter. In other words, stock markets prosper significantly more in the presence of securities laws than without them. Among the three aspects of securities laws—disclosure, liability and public enforcement—they find that while disclosure and liability standards have clear and substantial positive impact on stock market development, the effects of public enforcement on the various measures of stock market development are inconsistent. Also, disclosure and liability standards have stronger influence on stock market growth than the "anti-directors rights" index though they are moderately highly correlated. The authors speculate that this may be because these standards are the "true" proxy for the effectiveness of private contracting, or that investor protection through securities and corporate laws both matter but the former is a cleaner measure, or that both of these laws depend on similar rules that ultimately protect private investors from expropriation by corporate insiders.

Another important area, where laws directly affect business growth and economic development is the creation of new businesses. Countries around the world have vastly different levels of regulations for starting new businesses and presumably this has a considerable impact on the flourishing of businesses and economic growth. Hernando de Soto was among the first people to conduct a systematic study of such regulations for a developing country (de Soto, 1990). More recently Djankov et al. (2004) have carried out a cross-country comparison of such regulations and studied their association with economic growth.

In their sample of 85 countries, Djankov et al. (2004) find that the number of procedures necessary to start a new business ranges from 2 (Canada and Australia) to 21 (Dominican Republic). The cost of these procedures range from a low of 1.16% of per capita GDP (Finland) to a high of 463% (Dominican Republic). The time the entire process takes ranges from 2 days (Canada and Australia) to 152 days (Madagascar). Thus, regulations of entry vary considerably from country to country though rich countries (the top quartile in terms of per capita GDP) have relatively less regulations as a group. They find that greater regulations do not improve compliance of a country's standards with international standards. In other words, quality of business does not improve with greater regulations. More regulations is associated with low levels of competition and high corruption and a larger unofficial economy and generally symptomatic of poor governance. The evidence appears to support the "public choice" theory of regulation that holds that regulations are a rent extraction device for politicians and bureaucrats.

Finally recent research has also delved into cross-country comparison of judicial efficiency by focusing on the functioning of the central institutions of law and judicial systems, the courts of law. Djankov et al. (2003) compare the degree of procedural formalism in the courts in 109 countries and study its effect on judicial quality. To facilitate comparison and maintain consistency, they focus on two types of legal proceedings—eviction of a defaulting tenant and collection on a bounced check. In keeping with the approach popularised by them, they develop a measure of procedural formalism—"formalism index"—which is the sum of seven sub-indices: (1) Professional versus laymen nature of court officials; (2) Emphasis on written versus oral elements in the case; (3) Necessity of legal justification of verdict; (4) Degree of statutory regulation of evidence; (5) Control of superior review; (6) Engagement formalities; and (7) Independent procedural actions. Each of these sub-indices is, in turn, created by combining innovatively defined dummy variables capturing various elements of the respective dimension. The data is obtained through a survey of member firms of Lex Mundi, a global association of law firms. The authors next put together data on judicial quality. Data on expected duration of the two disputes in calendar days are obtained from the participating Lex Mundi firms, while information on other variables like enforceability of contracts, access to justice and corruption as well as small firm survey data on fairness, consistency, honesty and other aspects of the legal system are obtained from other sources. Finally, the authors also take into consideration incentives that different legal systems provide for litigants and judges like mandatory time limits for various stages of a case, contingent fee clauses for lawyers and the "loser pays legal costs" rule. The general findings are, perhaps, along expected lines. Rich countries have better functioning courts. Greater procedural formalism is associated with longer time for dispute resolution, lower enforceability of contracts, higher corruption and lower honesty, consistency and fairness of the system. To the extent that the French civil law system is more formalised than the English common law system, the findings also imply that French civil law countries have poorer quality legal system than the English common law. Importantly, they also find no clear evidence that the incentives they consider improve the quality of justice.

The "Doing Business" Studies of the World Bank

Based largely on the works discussed above as well as other works by Andrei Shleifer and his co-authors, the World Bank has been publishing its annual "Doing Business" reports since 2004 (World Bank 2004, 2005, 2006). These reports take a close look at the nature of regulation of economic activities around the world and the effect such regulation has on the growth of businesses and the economy in general. The 2004 report focused on describing the regulations in various countries while the 2005 and 2006 issues focus on legal reforms around the world. The "Doing Business" reports focus on five broad areas of regulation: (1) Starting a business; (2) Employment regulation (hiring and firing workers); (3) Enforcing contracts; (4) Access to credit; and (5) Closing a business. Later they added two new categories: (1) Ease of registering property; and (2) Protection of investors.

Much of the findings of these reports are along the lines of studies mentioned (indeed these academic papers constitute the main background papers for these reports). Employment regulation is an area that stands somewhat apart from the subject of the papers discussed before. It includes laws that regulate: (i) part-time hiring; (ii) number of working hours in a day and annual leave; (iii) minimum wage; and (iv) grounds for dismissal. As in all other categories, there is considerable cross-country variation in employment regulations. The "Doing Business" reports are of the view that more stringent employment regulation limits job creation, reduces workforce flexibility and results in smaller firm size with less-than-efficient scale. More importantly, greater regulation appears to hurt employment and welfare of disadvantaged groups to rise from poverty.

The overall conclusions of the Doing Business reports are: (i) poor countries regulate business the most; (ii) greater regulation is associated with bad socio-economic outcomes; and (iii) there is indeed an "ideal" set of regulations or "best practices" that can be adopted and emulated across the globe with beneficial results. These reports have been a strong votary of legal reforms in countries around the world to bring about better economic effects.

3. Law and Finance in India—A Selective Overview

Investor Protection in Indian Laws: An International Comparison

The Indian legal system is, of course, built on the English common law system. In terms of property rights protection, La Porta et al. (2004) give India a score of 3 on an index ranging from 1 to 5. As for investor protection, the Indian system provides one of the highest levels of investor protection in the world *on paper*. India has a shareholder rights index of 5 (out of a maximum possible of 6), *highest* in the La Porta et al. (1998) sample—equal to that of the USA, UK, Canada, Hong Kong, Pakistan and South Africa (all English-origin-law countries) and better than all the other 42 countries in the study including countries like France, Germany, Japan and Switzerland. Among the constituents of shareholder rights, India does not follow the one share-one vote principle, i.e. it is possible to different classes of shares with varying voting rights. India also does not allow proxy voting by mail. Other than these, shareholder rights are well protected in that shares are not blocked before a general meeting, voting for directors does follow cumulative voting or proportional representation rules, there are laws protecting minority shareholders, existing shareholders do have a preemptive right to new share issues, and the percentage of share capital necessary to call an Extraordinary Shareholder Meeting is 10%—less than the sample average. There is no provision of mandatory dividends in India.

In terms of creditor rights, too, the Indian legal system seems to provide the best protection to creditors in the world according to the La Porta et al. (1998) metric. With no automatic stay on assets in the reorganisation phase, the requirement of secured creditors to be paid first in place, restrictions present for going into reorganisation and the provision of replacing management in reorganisation, India has a creditor rights index of 4 (the maximum possible) better than that in Australia, Canada, Ireland, New Zealand and the USA, not to speak of civil law countries.

The La Porta et al. (1998) enforcement variables, constructed using figures obtained from private country risk rating agencies, however, paint quite a different picture of India. Take for instance the "Rule of Law" index. Most advanced countries have very high scores on this index while developing countries typically have low scores. India has a score of 4.17 on this index—ranking 41st out of 49 countries studied—ahead only of Nigeria, Sri Lanka, Pakistan, Zimbabwe, Colombia, Indonesia, Peru and Philippines. Thus it appears that Indian laws provide great protection of shareholders' rights on paper while the application and enforcement of those laws leave much room for improvement.

The corruption figures are even worse. On this dimension, India has a score of 4.58 as compared to the sample average of 6.90 ranking 44th out of 49 nations—better only than Egypt, Nigeria, Philippines, Pakistan and Indonesia. The risk of expropriation by the state in India has a score of 7.75 slightly worse than the sample average of 8.05. As for the risk of contract repudiation, India ranks 38th with a score of 6.11 as opposed to the sample average of 7.58. In terms of accounting standards, India appears to have the worst accounting standards among the English-origin countries (a score of 57) rated, though several civil law countries fare worse. The sample average on this dimension is 60.93. Somewhat surprisingly for people with experiences of Indian judiciary, India gets a score of 8 out of 10 on the efficiency of judicial system variable, just behind the English-law average of 8.15 and *better* than the overall sample average of 7.67.

Financial/Business Laws and Regulations in India

Red tape and regulations are among the leading deterrents for business and foreign investments in India and much of the economic reforms centers around reducing these obstacles. Perhaps a sense of India's legal restrictions and institutions can be obtained from its latest ranking of 116 out of 155 in World Bank's Ease of Doing Business indicator in 2006 (World Bank, 2006). Table 1 Panel A shows India's ranking on the various aspects of business regulation. India features consistently in the

Table 1: Ease of Doing Business in India

Panel A: India's Rank on different components of the Ease of Doing Business Index

Topics	India's rank (out of 155)
Ease of Doing Business	116
Starting a Business	90
Dealing with Licenses	124
Employing	116
Registering Property	101
Getting Credit	84
Protecting Investors	29
Paying Taxes	103
Trading Across Borders	130
Enforcing Contracts	138
Closing a Business	118

Source: World Bank.

Panel B: Business Realities in India

Indicator	India	South Asia	OECD
Starting a Business (2005)			
Procedures (number)	11	7.9	6.5
Time (days)	71	35.3	19.5
Cost (% of income per capita)	61.7	40.5	6.8
Min. Capital (% of income per capita)	0.0	0.8	41.0
Dealing with Licenses (2005)			
Procedures (number)	20	15.7	14.1
Time (days)	270	195.3	146.9
Cost (% of income per capita)	678.5	385.9	75.1
Employing Workers (2005)			
Difficulty of Hiring Index	56	41.9	30.1
Rigidity of Hours Index	40	35.0	49.6
Difficulty of Firing Index	90	42.5	27.4
Rigidity of Employment Index	62	39.9	35.8
Hiring Cost (% of salary)	12.3	5.1	20.7
Firing Costs (weeks of wages)	79.0	75.0	35.1
Registering Property (2005)			
Procedures (number)	6	6.9	4.7
Time (days)	67	124.0	32.2
Cost (% of property value)	7.9	6.3	4.8

(Contd...)

Indicator	India	South Asia	OECD
Getting Credit (2005)			
Legal Rights Index	5	3.8	6.3
Credit Information Index	2	1.8	5.0
Public Registry Coverage (% adults)	0.0	0.1	7.5
Private Bureau Coverage (% adults)	1.7	0.6	59.0
Protecting Investors (2005)			
Disclosure Index	7	4.1	6.1
Director Liability Index	4	4.6	5.1
Shareholder Suits Index	7	6.4	6.6
Investor Protection Index	6.0	5.0	5.9
Paying Taxes (2005)			
Payments (number)	59	25.8	16.3
Time (hours)	264	331.7	197.2
Total Tax Payable (% gross profit)	43.2	35.3	45.4
Trading Across Borders (2005)			
Documents for Export (number)	10	8.1	5.3
Signatures for Export (number)	22	12.1	3.2
Time for Export (days)	36	33.7	12.6
Documents for Import (number)	15	12.8	6.9
Signatures for Import (number)	27	24.0	3.3
Time for Import (days)	43	46.5	14.0
Enforcing Contracts (2005)			
Procedures (number)	40	29.9	19.5
Time (days)	425	385.5	225.7
Cost (% of debt)	43.1	36.7	10.6
Closing a Business (2005)			
Time (years)	10.0	4.2	1.5
Cost (% of estate)	9	7.3	7.4
Recovery Rate (cents on the dollar)	12.8	19.7	73.8

Source: World Bank.

second half of the sample for all but one aspect, and is out of the top 100 for most aspects. The one outlier aspect, interestingly, is investor protection. Panel B of Table 1 describes the various measures for India that leads to this state of affairs.

Panel B describes the hurdles and time costs in the way of regulation to carrying out various business processes. It is important to keep in mind that the figures reported here are the official costs and time necessary "under normal circumstances" and assuming that all "information is readily available and that all governmental bodies function efficiently and without corruption" (DLLS, 2004). Given that India ranks 88th out of 158 countries surveyed by Transparency International in 2005 in terms of corruption (lower rank, less corruption), these figures are almost certainly gross underestimation of the actual costs and delays on the ground.

Starting a business in India is no easy affair. With close to twice the number of procedures to follow as in OECD countries, about three and a half times the time delay and close to *nine* times the cost (as a proportion of per capita income) (in the "best case" scenario for the last two, assuming no corruption and governmental inefficiency), it indeed subjects an entrepreneur to an ordeal perhaps tougher than the that posed by the actual challenges of business. With delays and costs of dealing with licenses in India in roughly corresponding proportions with their respective OECD values, "License Raj" in India appears to be far from dead even after a decade and a half of reforms.

Hiring and particularly firing people are just as difficult. It is almost twice as hard to hire people in India as in OECD countries and almost three times as hard and costly to fire them. Apparently labour-friendly regulations have proven costly to India in terms of development and growth, ironically, mostly for labor itself. Different Indian states have considerable variations in their labour laws. In an interesting study, Besley and Burgess (2004) show that during the three and half decades before liberalisation began, Indian states that followed more pro-worker policies experienced lower output, investment, employment and productivity in the registered or "formal" sector and higher urban poverty. They have also been marked with an increase in informal sector output, which supports the findings of the cross-country analysis by Botero et al. (2004).

As we noted before, the degree of investor protection in the laws is the strongest suit for India followed by "getting credit". In the latter case, India lags behind not because of creditors' rights (which is close to OECD standards) but because of the paucity of credit quality information through the use of public registry or coverage of private bureaus. However, to get a more realistic picture of India's excellent investor protection provisions in the law, they must be viewed together with her performance in contract enforcement where the number of procedures and time delays are about double that in OECD countries and the costs of contract enforcement over *four* times that in OECD countries.

An important area of investor protection is obviously that of securities markets regulation. Using the framework of La Porta et al. (2006) that focuses on disclosure and liability requirements as well as the quality of public enforcement of the regulations controlling securities markets, India scores 0.92 in the index of disclosure requirements. Only two countries in the La Porta et al. (2006) sample of 49 countries—United States and Singapore—have a higher score. As for liability standard, India's score is 0.66 while the sample mean is 0.47. Only four countries—Canada, USA, Netherlands, and Philippines—have higher scores. In terms of the quality of public enforcement, i.e. the nature and powers of the supervisory authority, the Securities and Exchanges Board of India (SEBI), India scores 0.67, higher than the overall sample mean as well as the English-origin average of 0.52 and 0.62 respectively and ranks 14th in the sample.

In terms of the constituent elements of the La Porta (2006) disclosure index, Indian share offerings do require a mandatory prospectus and the prospectus must list the remuneration of individual directors and the managing director (but not that of other officers), the detailed shareholding of the ten largest shareholders as well as the promoters' (insiders) shareholding in the company, any contract that the company is a party to except for those required for day-to-day functioning of the company, and all related party transactions. As for liability, the directors of the issuing company and the distributor (merchant banker) of the issue are liable for any untrue statements in the prospectus and the offence is punishable with fine and/or imprisonment but the standard of establishment of guilt requires proving that (i) an untrue statement existed in the prospectus; (ii) it led to losses for an investor relying on the statement; (iii) it was not an "honest" mistake. The accountant to the issue is not directly liable to SEBI but is likely to face an inquiry from the Institute of Chartered Accountants of India for a serious omission or untrue statement.

As for the quality of public enforcement, all board members of the supervisor, SEBI, are appointed by the government and hold office largely at the pleasure of the government, so there is virtually no independence of the supervisor. Since SEBI does not supervise banks but only markets, it is focused in its role. It has little independent rule-making power though, since all its rules need to be sanctioned by the Parliament. It does have the investigative powers to command documents and summon witnesses in the course of an investigation. SEBI has the power to issue administrative orders against the issuing company and the distributor if it finds them in violation of its "Disclosure and Investor Protection (D & IP)" guidelines. The accountant does not come under SEBI's purview but under that of the Institute of Chartered Accountants of India.

In comparing the regulatory powers and performance of SEBI with those of the SEC (Securities and Exchanges Commission) in the USA, Bose (2005) concludes that while the scope of Indian securities laws are quite pervasive, there are significant problems in enforcing compliance, particularly in the areas like price manipulation and insider trading. Between 1999 and 2004, Bose finds that SEBI took action in 481 cases as opposed to 2,789 cases for the SEC even though the latter regulates a significantly more mature market. As a ratio of actions taken to the number of companies under their respective jurisdictions, SEBI's figure comes out to be an unimpressive 0.09 while that of SEC is 0.52. Also the ratio for action taken to investigations made is quite low for SEBI (e.g. 1 out of 24 cases of issue related manipulation in 1996-97, 7 out of 27 in the 5 year period 1999-2004). As for appeals before higher authorities—the Securities Appellate Tribunal (SAT) or the Finance Ministry—in 30% to 50% of cases, the decision has gone against SEBI. Though SEBI has had some success prosecuting intermediaries, it has failed to convince the SAT in its proceedings against corporate insiders and major market players. Thus, the quality of public enforcement of securities laws in India can definitely be improved.

Two important recent developments in the area of creditors' rights in India have been the institution of Debt Recovery Tribunals (DRTs) in the early 90's and the passing of the Securitisation and Reconstruction of Financial Assets and Enforcement of Security Interest (SARFAESI) Act in 2002. In spite of the superior creditors' rights in the laws, banks have had very little power against defaulting borrowers largely because of the slowness of the judicial process. The establishment of the DRTs sought to remedy that problem. Visaria (2005) estimates that the establishment of DRTs reduced delinquency in loan repayments by 3% to 10% and enabled lenders to reduce interest rates by 1-2 percentage points. The SARFAESI Act paves the way for the establishment of Asset Reconstruction Companies (ARCs) that can take the Non-Performing Assets (NPAs) off the balance sheets of banks and recover them. Operations of these ARCs would be restricted to asset reconstruction and securitisation only. It also allows banks and financial institutions to directly seize assets of a defaulting borrower who defaults fails to respond within 60 days of a notice. Borrowers can appeal to DRTs only after the assets are seized and the Act allows the sale of seized assets. The SARFAESI Act itself, however, does not provide a final solution to the recovery problems. With the borrower's right to approach the DRT, the DRAT (Debt Recovery Appellate Tribunal) and, in some cases, even a High Court, a case can easily be dragged for three to four years during which time the sale of the seized asset cannot take place. It is perhaps too soon to evaluate its effects on reducing defaults but public sector banks have had some success recovering their loans by seizing and selling assets since the Act came into existence.

The area of the Ease of Doing Business index where India fares worst is undoubtedly that of closing a business. India has the dubious distinction of being among the countries where it takes the *longest time to go through bankruptcy in the world* (10 years on an average). Consequently, recovery rates are very low too—below 13% as opposed to about 74% in OECD countries. Kang and Nayar (2004) point out that there is no single comprehensive and integrated policy on corporate bankruptcy in India in the lines of Chapter 11 or Chapter 7 US bankruptcy code. Overlapping jurisdictions of the High Courts, the Company Law Board, the Board for Industrial and Financial Reconstruction (BIFR) and the Debt Recovery Tribunals (DRTs) contribute to the costs and delays of bankruptcy. The Companies (Second Amendment) Act, 2002 seeks to address these problems by establishing a National Company Law Tribunal and stipulating a time-bound rehabilitation or liquidation process to within less than two years as well as bringing about other positive changes in the bankruptcy code. It is too soon to assess the actual impact of this Act in improving the desperate situation of the Indian bankruptcy code.

Corporate Governance in India

Enforcement of corporate laws remains the soft underbelly of the legal and corporate governance system in India. The World Bank's Reports on the Observance of Standards and Codes (ROSC) publishes a country-by-country analysis of the observance of OECD's corporate governance codes. In its 2004 report on India (World Bank (2004b)), the ROSC found that while India observed or "largely observed" most of the principles, it could do better in certain areas. The contribution of nominee directors from financial institutions to monitoring and supervising management is one such area. Improvements are also necessary in the enforcement of certain laws and regulations like those pertaining to stock listing in major exchanges and insider trading as well as in dealing with violations of the Companies Act—the backbone of corporate governance system in India. Some of the problems arise because of unsettled questions about jurisdiction issues and powers of the SEBI. As an extreme example, there have been cases of outright theft of investors' funds with companies vanishing overnight. The joint efforts of the Department of Company Affairs and SEBI to nail down the culprits have proved to be largely ineffective. As for complaints about transfer of shares and non-receipt of dividends, while the redress rate has been an impressive 95%, there were still over 135,000 complaints pending with the SEBI. Thus, there is considerable room for improvement on the enforcement side of the Indian legal system to help develop the corporate governance mechanism in the country.

Indian Courts—An Assessment

A discussion of the legal situation in a country remains incomplete without an assessment of the functioning of its courts of law. Great laws can be brought to naught by an inefficient judicial system or a corrupt judiciary. Presumably one of the main reasons why Indian laws look better on paper than in practice is the inefficiency of the Indian judicial system.

Djankov et al. (2003) in their analysis of "formalism" in the judicial process around the world, gave India a score of 3.34 on its formalism index, higher than the English-origin average of 2.76 but slightly lower than the average for all countries, 3.53. Among the 42 English-origin countries in their sample, India has the 11th highest level of formalism. The countries with higher levels of formalism are Bahrain, Botswana, Cyprus, Namibia, Pakistan, Sri Lanka, St. Vincent, Swaziland, Tanzania and the UAE. All other countries have lower levels of formalism. Interestingly enough, India has the 16th longest process of evicting a tenant (212 days) among English common law-origin countries (average 199 days). For collection on a bounced check, however, India has the 16th *shortest* duration (106 days) among English common law-origin countries (average 176 days). In both cases India's total duration of the process is significantly shorter than the overall mean duration of all the 109 countries considered (254 for eviction of tenant and 234 for collecting on bounced check). Thus, in spite of its formalism, Indian courts do not seem to perform that poorly (relatively speaking) *on these two types of cases* considered.

The DLLS assurance notwithstanding, things are far from all right in Indian courts. Case arrears and decade-long legal battles are commonplace. In spite of having around 10,000 courts (not counting tribunals and special courts), India has a serious shortfall of judicial service. While the USA has 107 judges per million citizens, Canada over 75, Britain over 50 and Australia over 41, for India the figure is slightly over 10 (Debroy, 1999). In April 2003, for instance, the Supreme Court of India had close to 25,000 cases pending before it (Parekh, 2001). Hazra and Micevska (2004) report that there are about 20 million cases pending in Lower Courts and another 3.2 million cases in High Courts. A termination dispute contested that the way can take up to 20 years for disposal. Writ petitions in High Courts can take between 8 and 20 years for disposal. About 63% of pending civil cases are over a year old and 31% are over 3 years old. Automatic appeals, extensive litigation by the government, underdeveloped alternative mechanisms of dispute resolution like arbitration, the shortfall of judges all contribute to this unenviable state of affairs in Indian courts. Since the same courts try both civil and criminal matters and the latter gets priority, economic disputes suffer even greater delays.

The Indian Financial Sector—A Brief Overview

In a recent analysis of the Indian financial markets, McKinsey & Company point out (McKinsey, 2006, on the findings of which most of this sub-section is based) that even after a decade and a half of economic reforms and notwithstanding India's long history of financial development, India's financial depth as measured by the value of financial assets to GDP remains somewhat on the lower side compared to other fast growing Asian countries. In 2004, India's financial assets accounted for 160% of her GDP as compared to 220% for China and 214% for Thailand. However it was higher than that of Philippines and Indonesia—countries with similar per capita income. Of this, currency and bank deposits accounted for 68% of the GDP, equity (before the phenomenal climb of the Indian markets) 56%, government debt 34% and corporate debt a meager 2%. The first decade of economic reforms saw virtually no financial deepening, though between 2001 and 2004 financial markets deepened at an average annual rate of over 14%, much of it (about 60%) stemming from rising equity values (even before the spectacular rise in 2005). Growth in bank deposits and government debt explained about 20% each, while the corporate debt market has stagnated at 2% since 1991. The household saving rate in India is an impressive 28% but only about a half of it is held in financial assets. Investments in housing, "unorganized sector" enterprises and gold account for the other half.

The banking sector, with a smaller share of GDP in deposits than in most advanced and Asian countries, is marked by a dominance of public sector banks that account for about 75% of the assets (second only to China). At 61% in 2004, the ratio of loans to deposits is smaller than in most advanced and emerging market economies. India also has one of the lowest penetration levels of mortgage and banking products like ATM and debit and credit cards among leading emerging market countries. Banks tend to hold about 30% of their assets in government securities, one of the largest figures among advanced and emerging market economies, mostly because regulations require them to do so. Bank credit is also directed to priority sectors like agriculture and small-scale industry. In 2004, 37% of all loans went to priority sectors, which has a default rate 40% higher than the non-priority sectors. Lending rates have been rather rigid while deposit rates have fallen considerably in recent years. On the positive side, the ratio of non-performing loans to total outstanding loans stand at below 5%, one of the best figures among emerging market countries.

Given the relative paucity of bank credit, particularly in rural areas, informal credit markets are particularly large in India—about a third of the credit from the formal financial system. In recent years, microfinance loans from banks to "self help groups" have also ballooned.

Equity markets have a long tradition in India. Nevertheless, in 2004 equity market size was 56% of GDP, including the non-tradable equity. The tradable equity made up only 33% of GDP. Though the Bombay Stock Exchange itself listed over 5,000 stocks—the second highest number of listed companies in the world—over 40% of these companies are not traded at all. While members of the 30 stock Sensex have world class liquidity, the average Indian stock is highly illiquid. Top 10 companies accounted for 36% market capitalisation in 2004. As late as in the 1990s, the market has been subject to manipulations on more than one occasion. About 56% of shares were held by insiders at the end of 2004, reducing the "free float" to below 45%. Institutional holdings accounted for about 17% of equity. About the same amount was held by the Indian public. Mutual funds make up a tiny part of the market though the sector is witnessing rapid growth in recent years. In general, the share of institutional investors in India is considerably less than that in advanced countries and other emerging markets.

While the government bond market account for 37% of GDP, the corporate bond market is rudimentary and virtually stagnant at 2%. Government bonds are also held mostly by institutions. The privately placed corporate debt is 10 times as large as the publicly traded corporate bond market. Interestingly, the size of international corporate bonds issued by Indian companies is over 50% larger than the publicly tradable corporate bonds in India.

In terms of modern payment systems, while over 70% of large-value payments are now handled electronically, the retail payment system is predominantly cash-based (about 97% of transactions). This is reflected in the relatively large amount of currency in circulation in India, close to 12% of GDP.

In terms of the measures employed by the various La Porta et al. studies (figures relate to mid-to-late 90s), India had 7.79 companies per million citizens in 1994, one of the lowest for English-origin countries but higher than many French-origin countries and even Germany. Nevertheless it is considerably short of the sample average of 21.59. As for the ratio of external capital to GNP, India has a score of 0.31 which puts it at about the middle of the pack of English-origin countries though the ratio is significantly less than the average English-origin figure of 0.6. It is also less than the overall sample average of 0.4. As for companies making IPOs, Indian firms made 1.24 IPOs during 1995-1996 per million citizen, less than the English-origin average of 2.23 but greater than the sample average of 1.02. Ownership concentration in India as measured by the median share of three largest shareholders in a firm,

India had a figure of 43%, in between the English-origin and overall sample averages of 42% and 45% respectively. In terms of debt, Indian firms had an average debt of 47% of sales substantially higher than the English-origin and overall sample averages of 0.26 and 0.27 respectively.

Survey Evidence on Law and Finance from India

An important question that needs to be answered in understanding the connection between law and finance in India concerns the extent to which the formal legal environment directly supports and regulates businesses, particularly small and medium enterprises which form an increasingly important part of the Indian industry. Allen et al. (2006) carries out a survey of over 200 small and medium scale firms in Delhi and Hyderabad probing into the extent and nature of the relationship between the legal system and the functioning of these enterprises. The results are quite instructive. They indicate that the small firms sector operate in a system virtually governed through informal mechanisms based on trust, reciprocity and reputation with little recourse to the legal system and deals with widespread corruption.

Over 80% of the firms surveyed needed a license to start a business, and for about 47% obtaining it was a difficult process. Government officials were most often the problem and was solved usually through payment of bribes (87% of responses) or friends of government officials to negotiate (23%). Clearly, networks and connections are of crucial importance in negotiating the government bureaucracy.

As for conducting day-to-day business, legal concerns are far less important to them than the unwritten codes of the informal networks in which firms operate. In cases of default, the primary concern is loss of reputation, followed closely by loss of property, while in situations of breach of contract, loss of future business opportunities ranks the highest, followed by loss of reputation. Significantly, in both cases, the fear of legal consequences is the least important, concerning lower than even threats to personal safety.

About 50% of the firms surveyed do *not* have a regular legal adviser and less than half of those that do have lawyers in that capacity. The most common reason cited was that lawyers are not necessary as the businessmen knew all their business partners and could deal with them fairly. For mediation in a business dispute or to enforce a contract, the first choice are "mutual friends or business partners," followed closely by "settling out of court with the help of legal advisers". Twenty per cent of the respondents mentioned going to courts as the first option indicating that the legal system, while not as effective as the informal mechanisms, is not altogether absent either. As for the mechanism to ensure payment or repayment, going to court leaving negotiation possibilities open was the most common response followed by better screening of borrowers/ clients. Some respondents actually asserted they would seize the defaulters' personal assets themselves. Clearly, the courts, while not the most popular method of conflict resolution, do have their utility as a negotiating tool.

The informal system, however, is not perfect in resolving disputes and has its costs. Over 48% of the respondents experienced a breach of contract or non-payment with a supplier or major customer in the past three years. 35% of them renegotiated while 43% did nothing but continued the business relationships with the defaulting parties.

In general, the business environment of the SME sector is marked by strong informal mechanisms like family ties, reputation and trust. Legal remedies, though present, are far less important than the rules of the informal networks. Ownership and management are not effectively separated. Burkart, Panunzi, and Shleifer (2003) connect the distance between ownership and control to different legal environments, and show that family-run rather than professionally managed firms will dominate in settings with weak minority shareholder protection. Consistent with this environment, external finance for small firms in India comes mostly from family and friends, followed by trade credits.

4. Conclusions and Future Research

Legal reforms are viewed to be among the most important "second generation" reforms for developing countries embracing the markets economy. The specifics of necessary legal reforms, which would lead to the flourishing of markets, however, are less widely agreed upon. We review the recent literature on law and finance and assess the state of India's legal and judicial system as well as its financial system, particularly relative to the rest of the world.

It appears that Indian laws provide good to excellent protection to investor rights, at least on paper. Implementation of these laws, however, has been less than satisfactory. Public enforcement of securities laws has been weak and courts in India have been extremely slow and overloaded with cases. Even a decade and a half after the beginning of the reforms process, India still suffers from too much business regulation and red-tape; and bureaucracy (not to speak of corruption) pose hurdles on every major aspect of business. Consequently, it is perhaps not surprising that the Indian financial markets have had limited though increasing depth and survey evidence reveals the preponderance of internal financing among India's small and medium sector firms as well as a far greater reliance of small businesses in India on informal networks and institutions like reputation and trust rather than the formal legal system to enforce contracts and settle disputes.

Much still remains unknown. The identification of the specific shortcomings of main legislations and a clear understanding of the mechanism through which they have hindered development of financial markets in India are lacking. This can be done through a careful analysis of past court judgments in cases involving these laws—a focus that cannot be expected in cross-country studies that must, to some extent, sacrifice depth of analysis for the sake of comparability across countries. A sense of the seriousness of the problems identified in terms of value lost or growth rate reduced can be estimated as well using international benchmarks, so as to prioritize the areas for legal reforms. The specific regulations that can be reduced or eliminated for the Special Economic Zones (SEZ) can also be identified through this process. These findings would help set the agenda for legal reforms in India that could spur further growth and development in the Indian financial markets.

REFERENCES

Beck, Thorsten, Asli Demirguc-Kunt and Levine, Ross (2003): "Law and Finance: Why Does Legal Origin Matter?" *Journal of Comparative Economics*, 31(4): 653-676 December.

Besley, Timothy and Burgess, Robin (2004): "Can Labor Regulation Hinder Economic Performance? Evidence from India", *Quarterly Journal of Economics,* 119(1).

Bose, Suchismita (2005): "Securities Markets Regulation: Lessons from US and Indian Experience", *Money and Finance*, Jan-June, 83-124.

Botero, Juan, Simeon Djankov, Rafael La Porta, Florencio Lopez-de-Silanes, and Shleifer, Andrei (2004): "The Regulation of Labor", *Quarterly Journal of Economics* 119 (4): 1339-1382.

Burkart, Mike, Panunzi, Fausto and Shleifer, Andrei (2003): "Family Firms", *Journal of Finance,* 58: 2167-2201.

De Soto, Hernando (1990): *The Other Path*, New York: Harper and Row.

Debroy, Bibek (1999): "Some Issues in Law Reform in India", Jean-Jacques Dethier (Ed.) *Governance, Decentralization, and Reform in China, India, and Russia,* Boston: Kluwer Academic Publishers.

Demirgüç-Kunt, Asli, and Maksimovic, Vojislav (1998): "Law, Finance, and Firm Growth", *Journal of Finance,* 53 (6): 2107-37.

Djankov, Simeon, Rafael La Porta, Florencio Lopez-de-Silanes, and Andrei Shleifer (2002): "The Regulation of Entry", *Quarterly Journal of Economics*, 117 (1): 1-37.

—— (2003): "Courts," *Quarterly Journal of Economics*, 118 (2): 453-517.

—— (2006): "The Law and Economics of Self-Dealing", *Working Paper*, Harvard University.

Dyck, Alexander and Zingales, Luigi (2004): "Private Benefits of Control: An International Comparison", *Journal of Finance* 59: 537-600.

Hazra, Arnab K. and Micevska, Maja (2004): "The Problem of Court Congestion: Evidence from Indian Lower Courts", *Working Paper*, University of Bonn.

Johnson, Simon, McMillan, John and Woodruff, Christopher (2002): "Property Rights and Finance", *American Economic Review*, 92: 1335-1356.

——, Rafael La Porta, Florencio Lopez-de-Silanes, and Shleifer, Andrei (2000): "Tunnelling", *American Economic Review,* (Papers and Proceedings), May.

Kang, Nimrit and Nitin Nayar (2004): "The Evolution of Corporate Bankruptcy Law in India", *Money and Finance*, Oct 03—Mar 04, 37-58.

La Porta, Rafael, Florencio Lopez-de-Silanes, and Shleifer, Andrei (2006): "What Works in Securities Laws?" *Journal of Finance* 61 (1): 1-32.

La Porta, Rafael, Florencio Lopez-de-Silanes, Andrei Shleifer, and Robert Vishny (1997): "Legal Determinants of External Finance", *Journal of Finance*, 52: 1131-1150.

—— (1998): "Law and Finance", *Journal of Political Economy*, 106: 1113-55.

—— (2000): "Investor Protection and Corporate Governance", *Journal of Financial Economics*, 58 (1-2).

—— (2002): "Investor Protection and Corporate Valuation", *Journal of Finance*, 57 (3): 1147-1170.

McKinsey (2006): "Accelerating India's Growth through Financial System Reform", McKinsey Global Institute, San Francisco.

McLiesh, Caralee and Shleifer, Andrei (2006): "Private Credit in 129 Countries", forthcoming, *Journal of Financial Economics*.

Pagano, Marco, and Volpin, Paolo (2005): "The Political Economy of Corporate Governance", *American Economic Review* 95: 1005-1030.

Parekh, Pravin (2001): "Access to Justice" in Souvenir of All India Seminar on "Access to Justice", UNDP, 326-340. http://www.undp.org.in/events/AISAJ/

Spamann, Holger (2005): "Recoding LLSV's Law and Finance", Mimeo, Harvard Law School.

Visaria, Sujata (2005): "Legal Reform and Loan Repayment: The Microeconomic Impact of Debt Recovery Tribunals in India", *Working Paper*, New York: Columbia University.

World Bank (2004a): "Doing Business in 2004: Understanding Regulation", Washington DC: World Bank and Oxford University Press.

World Bank (2004b): "Report on the Observance of Standards and Codes (ROSC), Corporate Governance Country Assessment: India, ROSC", Washington DC: World Bank-IMF.

World Bank (2005): "Doing Business in 2005: Removing Obstacles to Growth", Washington DC: World Bank and Oxford University Press.

World Bank (2006): "Doing Business in 2004: Creating Jobs", Washington DC: World Bank and Oxford University Press.

Social Dimensions of Microfinance

Y.S.P. Thorat

4

The concept of microfinance includes provision of thrift, credit, insurance and money transfer facilities of small amounts to poor to enable them to raise their income levels and thereby their living standards. Since poor have low value assets with more often flimsy title to their assets the banks do not lend them credit because of high-perceived risk associated with such lending. Microfinance providers who are engaged in helping the poor have overcome this barrier of collateral by adopting a unique mechanism of group lending. Therefore, microfinance lending is commonly referred to as group-based lending.

Group based lending involves formation of self-help groups and joint liability groups, in which people come together to save and borrow usually with shared liability. The group mechanism replaces the need for physical collateral (assets) with social collateral (human capital). It may be mentioned here that though the group undertakes only finance related activities, many social benefits emanate from these activities, which help improve the social welfare of the poor. The following paragraphs describe the nature, composition and magnitude of the social benefits emanating from the microfinance programmes undertaken by MF providers in India.

This article is divided into four sections. The first section describes how one should look at the relationship between microfinance and social development and the framework to be adopted for assessing the social outcomes. The second section deals with the impact of microfinance on select social development indicators including poverty alleviation, health, education, gender, political participation and increased bargaining power, etc. The third section raises the issue of whether there is a need for a microfinance organisation to specifically focus on social issues either directly or through partnerships with community based organisations, private sector institutions or with government without deviation from provision of financial services. The fourth section describes some of the recent initiatives taken by the Government of India in this area.

SECTION I

Commercial Microfinance and Social Benefits

Although commercial microfinance implies more of a business activity without special reference to social development, the evidence from many countries shows that microfinance may bring about a certain degree of allround social development. Commercial microfinance as an effective instrument for promoting social development could be attributed to three factors: Firstly, group based microfinance creates a sustainable system of empowerment and a tendency among the borrowers to be self-reliant through efficient recycling of funds which could not be accomplished by direct finance to individuals; secondly, it brings small loan recipients into the formal financial fold without grant or free money. Lastly, microfinance builds the capacity of borrowers to access formal finance on a regular basis at least cost of borrowing. This encourages poor, over a period of time to move to a stage where they are exposed to more choices for availing of finance.

Assessment of Social Benefits

Social benefits emanating from microfinance activity could be studied at three different levels, *viz.* individual, family and community levels. However, this three-level model more often leads to overlapping of benefits. Therefore, it may be appropriate to examine the relationship between microfinance and social benefits under broad categories, namely poverty alleviation and reduction in vulnerability, health, education, gender, political participation and bargaining power in mainstream markets, etc.

Microfinance and Poverty Alleviation

One school of thought believes that there is a direct relationship between commercial microfinance and reduction of poverty. Studies on bank-SHG linkage programmes have shown that provision of financial services tends to reduce the vulnerability of poor over time. A study of SHARE[1] (Society for Helping Awakening Rural Poor through Education) has shown that in addition to increased economic well-being there was a marked shift from irregular, low-paid daily labour to more diversified sources of income, with a strong reliance on small businesses. An interesting conclusion of a study by the South Asian Poverty Alleviation Programme [SAPAP] Research Team[2] is that the number of landless labourers had considerably reduced after participation in microfinance programme as these borrowers had graduated to a higher level of asset holding. By availing of microfinance these borrowers could diversify their activities and could successfully spread risk of failure by generating incomes from different sources. Thus, these clients used microfinance as means of reducing their vulnerability. Another interesting impact of microfinance is on reducing levels of migratory. A study conducted by Professor Gibbons[3] showed that the ill effects of migration could be reduced if microfinance programmes provide credit for productive activities to generate jobs locally for the unemployed and partially unemployed poor.

Although 'literature' in part shows a correlation between microfinance activities social development, some social scientists have raised serious doubts about the claim to direct relationship between the two on the following grounds:

Firstly, social benefits emanating from microfinance activity are complex to understand because the focus of financial services

---

1. Microfinance and MDGs.Id21 Insights: Communicating Development Research. Issue 51.
2. Dev. S. Mahendra, Rural Development & Poverty—District Poverty Initiatives: Andhra Pradesh District Poverty Initiatives Project [APDIP], Baseline Survey Report available at http://www.cess.ac.in/cesshome/research 1 b.htm.
3. Gibbons, S. David and Kasim Sukor, Banking on the Rural Poor, Grameen Bank, Dhaka, 1994.

is to promote economic activities/ incomes general activities and not social development. Secondly, quantification and measurement of social benefits arising from microfinance activity is difficult because social benefits are too "broad" to be captured in entirety. For example, social benefits may arise out of group dynamics (where the SHG and JLG models are used) on the principles of which the whole edifice of microfinance is based and not accessibility due to microfinance perse. Lastly, impact of microfinance is extremely difficult to quantify at the individual level as the feeling of *self worth* at the individual level due to caste or religion rather than individual's capability of taking financial decisions.

There are still others[4] who have argued against community benefits of microfinance. They are of the view that microfinance programmes may empower individuals but do not necessarily increase social welfare. The assertion is that these programmes impact society negatively. Firstly, in microfinance programmes, the interest rates charged by the groups are usurious. Secondly, micro-credit increases indebtedness amongst the poor, particularly women, as they borrow money from moneylenders to pay their savings and loan installments. Thirdly, women often take loans for husbands who don't pay back the same, thus increasing their vulnerability. Lastly, microfinance increases the burden on children, particularly girls, as they have to work for longer hours to assist their mothers. Despite these doubts, there is a consensus among microfinance providers and the social scientists that micro finance in fact has a positive impact on social development which may be difficult to measure but can be easily perceived.

SECTION II

Impact of Microfinance on Social Development

Poverty Alleviation

The impact of microfinance programmes on poverty alleviation through increased income is a well-researched topic.

4. Neera Burra, *Micro-credit, Poverty & Empowerment: Linking the Triad*. Sage Publications, 2005.

Studies indicate that where the poor, particularly women have been effectively targeted, new economic opportunities have been opened up for increasing their income. This has led to a higher confidence level among them. A study of ASA, Tamil Nadu,[5] indicates that about 62 per cent of the women contributed between 75 and 100 per cent of the family income. This interestingly, gave them a control over the household expenditure in varying degrees. In other words, the increase in income has had a dual effect not only in terms of enabling the household to move above the poverty line income but also in empowering the women at the household level.

Literature also indicates that increased income due to microfinance programmes not only led to a reduction in vulnerability but also reduced wasteful consumption expenditure. For example, since the members enjoy health insurance facilities, personal expenditure by them on medical treatment which would either have come through borrowed resources or through distress sale of their assets is obviated.

Health

The access to financial services enables the poor to access better health facilities either on account of increased incomes or because the microfinance providers disseminate health care education and information to their clients. A study on the microfinance clients of SHARE showed that higher incomes due to participation in the microfinance programmes had contributed to better nutrition. There was also an impact on dietary patterns which had changed to include more vegetables and occasional consumption of meat—items unaffordable before joining microfinance programme. Many of the microfinance providers have introduced products which specifically aim at increasing health and nutrition status of their clients. These sometimes include credit for health purposes such as health care or nutrition supplements during pregnancy and post-natal care or health insurance.

Generally the very poor do not have the resources to respond positively to preventive health care measures unless such care is

5. ASA, *The Activist for Social Alternatives*. www.asdev.com/Aboutus.htm.

offered free of cost. Such attitudinal barriers are often overcome through discussion on health care in the meetings of women's group. DHAN Foundation has set up education and health interventions alongwith its Community Banking Programme. The programme leverages the microfinance channel for various development interventions and has been fairly successful. It has also been reported that women are becoming increasingly aware of preventive health care issues, such as, vaccination campaigns at the Primary Health Centres because of constant reiteration from the MFI staff and information dissemination within the group. Further, the group forum was found to be an effective mechanism for delivering health related information, distributing medical kits, etc. Some of the SHG Federations have taken up health issues on their own and are conducting health check ups for their members, distributing medicines and strengthening the government health systems in the area.

Women generally do not access health services unless they are seriously ill. They ignore minor ailments. However, when a woman runs an enterprise or takes on more responsibilities in the family through increased contribution to the family income, she begins to take her health seriously and evaluates sickness in terms of labour and income lost. Such an improvement in the health seeking behaviors of individuals has been noticed especially in group-lending models of microfinance, where women support each other in times of ill health and difficulty.

In regard to major illnesses, the scenario is also worrisome. Such illnesses result in loss of income and further outflow of cash. In the situation of a poor family which is already vulnerable to other risks, there is a clear need for micro insurance and public social safety nets. Informal system do not provide adequate risk coverage; larger formal financial institutions find the costs of insuring the health of the poor too expensive on account of the low-ticket size of premiums, and high volumes. However, microfinance institutions because of their local knowledge, outreach and presence may be able to cater to the health insurance needs of the poor (at least in catastrophic illness and accident cover) in a much more customised way. An NBFC providing microfinance services in Andhra Pradesh, has recently decided to set up pharmacies where free consultations will be provided to clients. This will enable the clients to access both doctor and medicines at the same time. The economies of scale generated at the pharmacy due to the servicing of a larger number of clients are expected to cover the charges of the doctor. Low cost diagnostic centers are also in the pipeline, where the poor would be expected to pay only the cost of the tests rather than the high rates charged by private hospitals.

Education

Studies on the relationship between microfinance and education suggest that microfinance smoothes the fluctuations in a household's income and offers a chance to increase income. Micro-credit programmes have enabled the poor to develop agriculture or other enterprises close to their homes thereby reducing the need to migrate for seasonal work. This has greatly increased the children's chances of attending school.

A study of ASA has shown that 76 per cent of the members were sending their children to Balwadi and had contributed to maintenance of the centre as well. Convergence of the education and nutrition agenda at the Balwadi was bringing the children a double benefit, as a result, client households tended to invest more in education that non-client households.

The secondary school enrollment of the sons of SEWA Bank clients rose by 15 percentage points from 55 per cent to 70 per cent between 1997 and 1999. A UNDP funded study found that Lokadrusti,[6] an MFI, had placed considerable emphasis on the education of the children of their borrowers which resulted in higher level of enrollment of their children in school. This is an example where a microfinance channel is used as means of educating clients about the importance of education, health, etc., without microfinance provider actually providing these services.

---

6. UNDP, Community Based Pro-Poor Initiatives Programme of the Government of India Sub-Programme. Document Summary of UNDP and cost sharing.

   www.undp.org.in/Programme/SubPro/LOKDRUSTI Final.doc.

In addition to the quantitative aspects, children of microfinance clients have in some progammes been observed to achieve higher levels of education than children in a control group. In Tamil Nadu, a study found that the children of MFI clients had higher levels of schooling than did non-clients, with statistically significant higher levels for girls.

Some MFIs have found it useful to combine credit with education particularly for their women clients for rasing their financial status and improving their basic capacity. This combination has reported to have increased the perceived value of education for their children leading to a heightened demand for child education.

Swayam Krishi Sangam (SKS), a microfinance provider in Andhra Pradesh, is an interesting example of direct intervention in education. SKS is keen on finding ways of enhancing the primary education among client's children through setting up alternative education providers, financed through loans from SKS. The idea is to use the resources available in the village, such as persons who have a basic necessary level of education to come together in a group of four or five and provide elementary education to the children in the village. For this purpose, they would require to have hired space and minimal infrastructure such as chalks, blackboard, etc. The loan is given to the group for this purpose. Low affordable fees are charged for the education services provided.

Gender

Some aspects of the gender impacts of microfinance have already been dealt with while discussing health and education. However "gender empowerment" perspective of microfinance assumes particular importance in light of the fact that the majority of microfinance clients in India and the rest of the world are women.

A gender impact study of four microfinance programmes in India concluded that women clients who contributed to household income experienced positive change at a personal level, in the form of increased self worth as well as at the household level, in the form of decreased violence. Relative to non-members, clients experienced greater empowerment in regard to asset ownership, control of productive assets, decision-making and political and legal awareness.

Another important aspect of gender empowerment is whether the "empowered" woman recognises the change in her status and accords herself some importance as a member of the family and as an individual. In the SAPAP team's report all the husbands of women in the programme reported that they perceived that their wives were more confident and independent. Only 21 per cent of non-members husbands reported such a change.

Women Empowerment and its Impact

1. The empowerment through microfinance has a positive impact on the physical mobility of the poor. About 47 per cent of members of ASA (all women) had reported to have visited new places and travelled further than before. About 90 per cent of them had traveled alone to the ration shop and to the hospital after joining the programme.

2. The second aspect of empowerment relates to women's control over their labour. SAPAP Research Team had measured this in terms of how often women have to help their husbands in the male-dominated activities such as agriculture and how much access they had to their husband's labour in the women dominated activities such as looking after livestock. Interestingly, women who were participating in the programme reported a higher degree of access to their husbands labour in women dominated activities than non-members from the same social stratum.

3. About 51 per cent of the members reported that they had made the choice to terminate a pregnancy exclusively, as compared with 30 per cent of non-members. The reproductive choice of a woman is a very important factor indicative of the extent to which they are truly empowered in their homes. While domestic violence was reported among non-members at 74 per cent, it was reported at 45 per cent among members. Dowry harassment had also become less explicit because of the fear that such harassment cannot go unnoticed, especially due to regular meetings of women.

4. The third aspect of empowerment relates to leadership and recognition within the community. The practice among groups of rotating leadership has proved to be a positive factor in building confidence of members. Moreover, the proportion of leaders emerging from the more backward caste groups in the study (dalits and Muslims) was more than their representation in the groups. This is indicative of empowerment of the women from these backward groups on two counts, gender and caste.

5. An important indicator of strategic empowerment is whether the women's organisations are able to make their view heard in matters relating to non-gender specific issues such as caste and class issues. This was clearly evident from the groups' participation in the Gram Sabhas and their articulation of non-gender specific goals, such as, getting access to drinking water, getting a road built, etc.

6. The last aspect of empowerment relates to financial decision-making power among women. For women, money management, greater control over resources and access to knowledge leads to greater choices and a voice in family and community matters. The existing literature on the subject shows that clients had begun to handle the work of making accounts, going to the market to transact at the bank and trading, purchasing and selling produce from the enterprises that they are running. This was an indicator of increased power to take decision within the household. Village poverty profile among SHARE clients have also reportedly changed and many of the widows who would have been reduced to beggary were actually sustaining themselves without having to be dependent on any outside charity or aid. Economic empowerment is accompanied by growth is self-esteem, self-confidence and new opportunities.

Political Empowerment and Microfinance

Although the interaction and group dynamics among women borrowers touched upon while dealing with gender, there are some other aspects to the political empowerment of the microfinance borrower.

1. The first aspect of political empowerment of the microfinance borrower is self-esteem. Self-esteem has been acknowledged as an indirect impact of microfinance programmes because participants, especially women suddenly discover an identity as individuals. Not only are they "individuals" in their own right but are recognised as being capable of taking financial decisions and are considered important part of a group.

2. The second aspect of political empowerment of the microfinance borrower relates to group dynamics. Women's groups in ASA, Tamil Nadu have made their presence felt by taking out non-violent collective marches to bring visibility to their collective effort. As part of the larger socio-economic environments/the groups have been able to bargain collectively for prevention of malpractice's by village institutions and thereby induced changes in the social fabric.

3. The third aspect of political empowerment relates to caste dynamics. Contrary to intuition the Lokadrusti study indicated that homogenous caste groups were not as robust as mixed caste groups, although the homogenous groups had been formed with the idea that they would be much more robust because of the similarity between members in case and economic circumstances. This leads to the hypothesis that diversity in a group could actually be better at keeping them together solely for the sake of their business relationship with each other. This is an important learning from the point of view of encouragement for inter-caste and inter-class diversity in group formation, the social implications of which could be immensely important. However, caste is a very complex phenomenon and much more research needs to be done.

The clients of SHARE microfinance also reported that caste barriers had been levelled at least as far as the programme was concerned, as women from all castes sat together at the meetings and no one was discriminated against at any point. The women also indicated that since they were all helping each other in making more money it was of very little relevance who was from which caste.

Among the groups of KAS Foundation, Orison is a group of eunuchs. This group was specifically formed because they had been begging in the traditional way and although it was profitable for them to do so, it being their only means of livelihood, they had no self-esteem. When they formed the Self Help Group under the auspices of KAS Foundation's microfinance programme, they found an alternative means of earning an income. They have set up micro-enterprises and have completely given up begging.

Swayam Krishi Sangam [SKS] in Andhra Pradesh has 75-80 per cent Dalitbahujan, scheduled caste clientele. This community is scheduled caste, but has become empowered after the SKS intervention as they now have choices in access to finance and are on a similar footing as their superior caste contemporaries in the villages. Furthermore, SKS has piloted smart cards with its clients, exposing them to the latest technology in itself an empowering experience for its profile of clients, for whom even a regular credit card is a remote possibility.

4. Political empowerment encourages participation in elections and other political processes. Among clients of ASA, Tamil Nadu, 90 per cent of the women had voted and 40 per cent of the women said that they decided on their own whom they would like to vote for. Seventy-five per cent of ASA's women members contested elections, having taken a loan from ASA for the required election deposit. About 85 of these women had been elected as ward members, two as councilor's and three as panchayat presidents. In 2002, 103 women clients from Activists for Social Alternatives (ASA) were elected to local councils in India.

The SAPAP study indicated that 95 per cent of the members had exercised their vote during the panchayat elections and 19 per cent of the SHGs reported that they had discussed the pros and cons of each of the candidates during their gatherings. Over 25 per cent of the SHGs and voluntary women organisations reported that they had been invited by the Gram Panchayat to take part in the Gram Sabha meetings. Thirteen per cent of the SHGs invited had publicly taken up the issues of domestic violence and other issues that could not be resolved by them without the intervention of the local authorities. Accountability and transparency were their main concerns. DHAN clients have also stopped malpractices in the Public Distribution System, such as, the pilfering of stocks, distribution to non-poor, etc. This is the direct outcome of the strength in collectives.

5. As regards the bargaining power of collectives, there is very little research. However, some interesting observations on voluntary collective action at the ground level have been reported from BASIX, Andhra Pradesh. Thus, where borrowers had taken up similar activities with their microfinance loans, such as, plantation of fruit bearing trees, they had begun aggregating their produce so as to get a better price. This was done by selling the combined produce of the entire village to a trader and splitting the gains. In this way, the clients got a better price and saved themselves the trouble of transporting their produce individually to the market place (mandi), where they would have had less bargaining power due to the small quantity. This ability to command a good price would not have existed in the absence of the microfinance programme. The same principal is being replicated and used for some commodities such as toor dal, milk, biomass, etc.

The SAPAP research documented collective intervention in market organisations. About 59 per cent of the SHGs in the study had impacted either labour market, commodity market or financial market. About 42 per cent of the SHGs had opened bank accounts and had negotiated for bank loans, while 3 per cent had also approached the moneylenders for reduction in interest rates, asserting that the competition from the bank's low rates would affect his business unless he reduced his rates. Nearly 53 per cent of the SHGs had reported a decline in the number of moneylenders after the microfinance programme; also citing that interest rates charged by the surviving moneylenders had dropped by more than 25 per cent.

In most of the instances where demonstrations and protests had been taken out for increasing wages or equalizing the male female wage rates, the wage had increased, although the increase was limited to only around 25 per cent of the existing wage and was still not equal to the men's wage. Among DHAN clients, some women have set up a chilling plant for milk marketing as many of them have taken up dairy as an activity. This has resulted in better bargaining power as the milk is unspoiled and under ambient conditions to be sold to a larger processing facility.

SECTION III

Microfinance and Community Development

At a certain point of time in its existence, an MFI usually hits a plateau. It is likely to feel that it has come to a slowdown through the provision of financial services alone, and that it needs to do more, either because of its sense of social consciousness or because it feels that in the interest of its own long term sustainability. In other words, when an MFI reaches a particular scale and outreach it finds it necessary to address certain broader community related needs which if ignored could result in road blocks.

A few examples are:

a. *Productivity Challenges*: How can clients repay loans beyond a particular point if the productivity of their income generating activity is low?
b. *Absence of Market Linkages*: In the absence of such linkages there would be no market, and the enterprise or activity of the client would cease to be profitable.
c. *Health Challenges*: As long as clients suffer from ill health, they will continue to be averse to taking additional risks of starting any new activity or enterprise, even if there are chances of its increasing their income.
d. *Education Challenges*: As long as clients are uneducated, their bargaining power will be low; they will have limited options for realizing opportunities and low general awareness.

As a financial institution, the MFI depends on the capacity of its clients or borrowers to repay their loans. If the innate capacity of the client base does not permit this repayment beyond a certain point, the MFI will stagnate. Geographical expansion to new territories and addition of more clients are likely to involve more costs to the MFI and beyond a stage, may become unviable. It is at this point that MFIs must seriously look at what its client base is signaling and decide whether they are in the position to provide these services or not. One strategy for meeting the changing needs of its client base is for the MFI to adapt its products and services to the changing needs of clients. In other words, for example, to incorporate education and health loans, microinsurance, etc., in its profile of purely financial activities. Another strategy could be load a social agenda on to its existing microfinance channel. This channel refers to the Groups created by the MFI or its social infrastructure.

However, this would entail a strategic shift from pure finance-to-finance plus. The downside is that when a financial institution has only one agenda (regular repayment, profitability and sustainability), loading other development agendas onto this channel would mean a change in perception of the clients. These services, if provided free could actually be harmful because they would tend to dilute organisational rigor. It would also entail the issue that as part of some such new programmes is grant funded while the core microfinance activities are commercially refinanced. There is nothing right or wrong with this but it has to be thought thoroughly.

Spandana's tie up with Godrej Agrovet for instance is a direct outcome of the low productivity of milch cattle, which meant that clients would not be able to repay cattle loans with ease. Better productivity would mean better repayment possibilities for the organisation. Godrej Agrovet was glad to get access to a large low-segment customer base through an existing preset marketing channel. The clients were more than happy with the productivity gains. Spandana's foray into health diagnostics and establishment of pharmacy stores come from the same need signaled by its clients.

The same applies to KAS Foundation's mission to install sanitation as soon as it reaches the break-even point. This organisation has set the mandate of using its profits to plough back into the community to fulfill sanitation requirements one of the biggest reasons for waterborne diseases in Orissa, its main state of operation.

BASIX undertakes several livelihood promotion activities and sees itself as more than just a microfinance provider, but as a livelihood organisation. BASIX tries to increase the productivity and the marketability in activities commonly undertaken by its clients.

All these organisations are commercially oriented and have a strong focus on repayment rates and sustainability. However, they have responded to their client needs in the interest of their own long-term sustainability.

As organisations serve more and more clients and their clients grow in size and financial strength, they will no longer be ignored by mainstream markets. These markets will then offer better terms to MFIs reach this new customer base, which has better purchasing power and high absorption capacity. The lure of mainstream marketers will be the ready marketing channel and the established identity of the customer base.

Secondly, it must be recognised that MFIs and their client are interdependent. One cannot survive without the other. As the clients of the MFI grow, the MFI has to grow in response to their needs. Along the way, some of the social needs of these clients may also have to be addressed, through commercial tie-ups, networking, through use of the organisation's strength.

Finally, over the long haul, each MFI will have to strive to catalyze community development, whether directly or indirectly in their areas of operation. Were this to happen, social benefits would cease to be incidental, and would be achieved alongside the commercial goals of the organisation.

SECTION IV

Government & Bankers' Perspective on Microfinance

Encouraged by the tremendous impact the microfinance movement has made in the country since 1990s through SHG-Bank Linkage model and MFI model, the Government has recognized the role that it can play in bridging the gap between demand and supply of financial services to the poor. To quote the Finance Minister, Government of India in his budget speech for the year 2005-06 summarizes both the government and banker's perspectives.

"The programme of linking Self Help Groups (SHGs) with the banking system has emerged as the major microfinance programme in the country. 560 banks including 48 commercial banks, 196 RRBs and 316 cooperative banks are now actively involved in the programme. I propose to enhance the target for credit-linking in the next fiscal from 200,000 SHGs to 250,000 SHGs."

The SHG-Bank Linkage model is the indigenous model of micro-credit evolved in India and has been widely acclaimed as a successful model with a present coverage of over 1.6 million groups involving 24 million families with a cumulative credit flow of $ 1549 million as at the end of March 2005 from the banking system. Being a savings-first model, where credit discipline is inculcated in the group with their own funds, banks have found comfort in lending to such groups as they build up an adequate corpus of their own funds before they approach the bank for credit. In view of availability of social collateral and joint liability, banks have found the repayment experience encouraging enough to actually take charge of this programme. The significant learning from the SHG oriented microfinance movement in India have to been to: (i) discover innovative methods of reducing the costs of intermediation; (ii) leverage peer pressure to mitigate default risks; (iii) use NGOs and Civil Society Organisations for need and capability assessment; (iv) incentivise lending and thrift by forming a pool in which the scales are favourable for internal lending; (v) involve and facilitate NGOs/CSOs to help banks to build up quality portfolios, (vi) ensure proper utilization of funds available to groups which tend to function as self-monitoring units; (vii) graduate from thrift to internal lending to consumption credit to micro-enterprises by using the group approach; (viii) empower through collective decision-making, conflict resolution and other social activities; (ix) help the poor and assetless to receive financial services through collateral substitutes and (x) identify risks that can be managed by involving peer groups NGOs/ CSOs.

Today, most of the banks have a corporate policy to expand their microcredit operations under the SHG-Bank Linkage mode. The RBI and the Central Bank has been creating the appropriate policy environment for bankers to leverage social infrastructure available in the country.

An Introduction to Competition Law in India

5

Amitabh Kumar

Benefits of Free Markets

Competition in markets refers to rivalry amongst producers to attract consumers. Economic theory demonstrates that the presence of large number of buyers and sellers, absence of barriers to entry and exit and homogeneity of products are prerequisites to perfect competition. Given the presence of these three basic elements in any market, products would be available at the cheapest possible price since it would tend to converge to the marginal cost in the long run. In order to compete (by fair means), producers will have to innovate and improve quality of the products on a continuous basis. This brings about Pareto allocative efficiency in competitive markets.

In the absence of large number of competitors, competitive constraints posed by potential competitors may be sufficient to bring benefits of competition. In other words, contestability in the market may be sufficient to ensure best possible deals for the consumers.

Market Failures Necessitate Intervention

Markets do not, however, always work in optimal ways as borne both by a survey of steadily burgeoning literature and empirical cross-country evidences.[1] In common parlance, market failure refers to a situation, wherein markets do not efficiently

1. Berglas, et al., 1981; Chipman, 1970; Flatters, et al., 1974; Dixit, et al., 1977; Berglas, et al., 1981; Mills, et al., 1989; Krugman, 1991; Fujita, et al., 1995; Helpman, 1998; Lagueux, M, 1998; Fujita, et al., 1999; Papageorgiou, et al., 1999; Papageorgiou, et al., 2000; Pines, et al., 2001; World Bank, 2006.

organize production or allocate goods and services to consumers. While there could be several plausible reasons for market failure, these could broadly be grouped into two sets: (a) the inadequate expression of cost and benefits in prices because of externalities in production and consumption, public goods, common property resources, undefined property rights and asymmetrical information and (b) sub-optimal market structures because of imperfect competition and natural monopoly. Market failures provide the basic justification for competition policy and law. There are numerous instances of market failures when the Smithsonian "invisible hands" of market forces are not adequate to safeguard fair competition. Firms acquire market power and charge monopoly profits. Firms with market power also squeeze margins of their suppliers. Entry barriers are created to stop competitors entering the market.

Firms collude to divide markets and increase prices to the detriment of consumers. Between 1997 and 2001, the US Department of Justice had obtained over $1.7 billion in criminal fines, which was many times the total fine imposed since 1890, the year of enactment of the first anti-trust law. The largest fines imposed were $500 million against Hoffmann-La Roch (Vitamin cartel, 1999), $225 million against SGL Carbon AG (graphite electrodes cartel, 1998), $110 million against UCAR International (graphite electrodes cartel, 1998) and $100 million against Archer Daniels Midland Company (lysine and citric acid cartels, 1996).[2] The mobile phone operators were overcharging consumers on termination of call charges by 30 to 40% during 2002-03 until the UK Competition Commission intervened.[3] It is estimated that developing countries imported goods worth between $42.86 billion and $81.1 billion in 1997 from industries that had

2. Presentation by Deputy Assistant Attorney General, Antitrust Division to the 49th Annual Spring Meeting of the American Bar Association, March 28, 2001.

3. The inquiry was conducted by the Competition Commission of UK in 2003. Full text is available on their website www.competition-commission.org.uk/inquiries/completed/2003.

price-fixing arrangements.[4] The Vitamin Cartel overcharged consumers in 9 countries $72 million annually during the period 1989 to 1999.

Such examples could easily be multiplied. But the case for competition policy and law is unassailable across countries, irrespective of their stage of development. "Competition forces work best in markets free from distortions. When markets are not competitive, whether due to policy-induced distortions, technological characteristics, or anticompetitive behaviour on past of market participants, an economy may miss many potential benefits for its citizens."[5]

Competition Policy and Law

Competition policy describes the way in which government attempts to promote competitive market structures and behaviour.[6] Competition policy consists of a number of elements including competition law. Industrial policy, i.e. guidelines regarding entry and exit contained in government directives, is one of the elements of competition policy. Privatization of public sector monopolies is another element of competition policy. Policies regarding Foreign Direct Investment (FDI), policy regarding tariff and non-tariff barriers to cross-border trade are elements of competition policy. Competition law is a manifestation of competition policy in terms of do's and don'ts and incorporates sanctions against unacceptable behaviour in the market. Many countries in the developing world have competition enhancing policies and the number of countries with competition laws is on the rise.

The history of the competition law goes back to the 19th century. In the 1880s, the US Congress was faced with monopolization by various groups of companies, led by the Rockefeller group, which had created trusts to do so. This led to the enactment of the Sherman Act in 1890 and came to be known as the antitrust law, a name which has stuck in the US.

---

4. UNCTAD document TD/B/COM.2/CLP/30 of 23 May 2002.
5. *Asian Development Outlook*, 2005.
6. Jones and Surfin, 2004, p. 1.

A number of developed countries started enacting antitrust laws on the European continent and these came to be known as competition laws.

Spread of Competition Law

The underlying concept of competition law is that there are limitations to the manner in which competition is conducted.[7] Competition law seeks to promote effective and undistorted competition in markets.[8] Consequently, benefits of competition law have come to be widely accepted and many countries even in the developing world adopted such laws. Reportedly, more than 100 countries have competition laws as at the end December 2005. The competition authorities have established the International Competition Network (ICN), which is an association of such authorities worldwide. There are other international organizations set up to provide technical support on competition matters, such as, the Global Forum on Competition of the OECD, the Commonwealth and UNCTAD.

These international bodies specialize in competition matters, provide technical support to new competition authorities and are also probably the first steps towards international cooperation in this regard. The necessity of having international cooperation on competition matters is obvious in an era of globalization and increase in cross-border economic activities.

Monopolies and Restrictive Trade Practices Act

India enacted a competition law in 1969 in the form of Monopolies and Restrictive Trade Practices Act (MRTP). The MRTP Act was brought in at a time when the 'commanding heights' of the economy were under state control. Public sector giants strode the economy. When the process of economic reforms was initiated in 1991, following the financial crisis of 1990, certain provisions of the MRTP Act were found to be

7. Sharpe, 2002, p. 512.
8. Jones and Surfin, 2004, p. 1.

obstructive. Although amendments were made to the MRTP Act, the Government found it necessary to constitute a High Power Committee of experts to suggest a modern competition law for the country. A High Level Committee on Competition Policy and Law (herein after called the Raghavan Committee after its chairman) was appointed in 1999. The Report[9] (2000) of the Committee made several important observations before recommending setting up of a new authority. As the Report broke new ground and made several path breaking recommendations, an attempt is made here to briefly highlight some of contemporary concerns brought to the fore by the Report.

The Raghavan Committee Report

The combination of policies (*Five-Year Plans, Industrial Policy, Foreign Investment Policy, Sick Industrial Companies Act, Trade Policy, Price Controls, etc.)* was found to have spawned a non-competitive and high cost industrial structure. Although significant steps had been taken to increase competition in India since 1991, the Committee felt the need for a competition law authority that will act as a watch-dog for the introduction and maintenance of competition policy. Competition policy and liberal trade policy seek to achieve the same objective, namely economic efficiency; the former by liberalising the domestic market and the latter by removing barriers to trade at the border. Irrespective of the stage of development, the international competitiveness of a country is in part determined by the degree of rivalry among domestic firms and therefore an effective competition policy is essential. Free markets work to provide the desired economic outcomes but only when the process of competition in these markets is protected from abuse.

The Raghavan Committee found that the focus of most competition laws in the world is in three areas: anti-competitive agreements among enterprises; abuse of dominance and mergers,

9. Report of the Raghavan committee is available on the website of the Ministry of Company Affairs www.dca.nic.in/comp/competition.htm.

or more generally, combinations among enterprises. Certain anti-competitive practices are presumed to be illegal. Abuse of dominance is prohibited but needs to be defined appropriately without prescribing any arithmetical figure like percentage of market share. Relevant market is an important factor in determining abuse of dominance. By and large, abuse of dominance and exclusionary practices are dealt with by the adjudicating authority on the basis of *rule of reason.* Mergers are discouraged if they reduce or harm competition. Given the size of Indian companies, the Committee felt that only mergers beyond a threshold limit in terms of assets or turnover require prior notification.

The Committee concluded that MRTP Act is limited in its sweep and hence fails to fulfill the need of competition law in an age of growing liberalisation and globalisation. The Committee felt that MRTP Act lacks provisions to deal with anti-competitive practices that may accompany the operations and implementation of WTO agreements. Introduction of a domestic competition law, it opined, will prevent international cartels from indulging in anti-competitive practices in India. It recommended that the Competition Law Authority (Competition Commission of India) should be governed by the principles of competition in its adjudicatory effort. In other words, primarily its objective will be to act as an effective instrument for engendering and protecting competition in the market in the interest of maximizing national welfare. In general, the *rule of reason* test is required for establishing illegality of an agreement. However, many kinds of agreements are presumed to be illegal, following the US laws, in most modern competition laws. In existing competition laws, there are two kinds of prohibition of abuse of dominant position: actions taken by an incumbent firm to charge higher prices and restrict supply; and actions taken by an incumbent firm to create entry barriers. Assessing dominant position requires determination of the relevant market. The Committee noticed that mergers are typically classified into horizontal and vertical mergers. From the point of view of Competition Policy, horizontal mergers are generally the focus of attention. If a dominant enterprise enters into a vertical merger, there may be cause for concern. The Committee emphasized the importance of quick decision making with regard to mergers.

The Raghavan Committee laid down the following principles as desirable in the design and implementation of a competition law:

(a) A system of checks and balances by ensuring due process of law with provisions for judicial review.

(b) A multi-member body comprised of eminent persons of integrity from the fields of judiciary, economics, law, international trade, commerce, industry, accountancy, public affairs and administration.

(c) An appropriate provision for removal of the members of the competition authority to ensure its independent functioning.

(d) Financial and administrative independence.

(e) Separation of investigative, prosecutorial and adjudicative functions.

(f) Punitive provisions for punishing the offenders.

(g) Trasparent, non-discriminatory and rule-bound proceedings.

(h) A proactive advocacy role in shaping policies affecting competition.

(i) According to the Raghavan Committee, a competition authority should have two basic functions: administration and enforcement of competition law to foster economic efficiency and consumer welfare and involvement in governmental policy formulation to ensure that markets remain fair.

The Committee observed that in many countries enforcement of competition law is entrusted to the judiciary. However, the judiciary in developing countries is inexperienced in dealing with free market problems. Such problems, relating to free and fair trade and relating to restrictive and other prohibited trade practices like abuse of dominance, require a certain level of specialised knowledge in economics, trade and relevant law for adjudication. The Committee felt that even if the judiciary has exposure to commerce and market related matters, competition law administration could be better handled by a specialized agency.

The Committee recommended a new law and a new authority and also made some recommendations regarding the organizational structure and procedure. Investigation and prosecutorial functions were recommended to be separated but under one official. Competition Commission of India, as a quasi-judicial body, should dispense justice through bench system. Each Bench must have a judicial member, who must be sitting or retired or qualified to be a judge. It recommended that CCI should have power to formulate own rules and regulations and review them from time to time to bring them in line with prevalent economic conditions.

As stressed earlier, the MRTP Act was based on command and control regime of the sixties and seventies. Although it is a competition law, competition concepts are not expressly defined. One of the important elements of modern competition laws, i.e. merger control, is virtually absent. The MRTP Act has no advocacy role. Advocacy is an important tool with competition authorities for creating awareness and thereby relying on voluntary compliance. The MRTP Commission is rendered toothless with no power to impose penalties. Prosecution proceedings in lower courts in India can be frustrating as the MRTP Commission learnt. Public sector is outside the purview of the MRTP Act although most large companies are in this sector.

The Competition Act, 2002—Salient Features

The Competition Act, 2002 was enacted in January of 2003. It contains three basic elements, which are found in all modern competition laws, namely: Prohibiting anti-competitive agreements having or likely to have appreciable adverse impact; Prohibiting abuse of dominant position—prevention of enterprise acquiring market power; and Merger control—preventing producers from joining together having potential to have appreciable adverse effect on competition.

The new law has made a serious attempt to overcome some of the deficiencies listed in the MRTP Act by the Raghavan Committee. Competition concepts have been expressly defined resulting in providing major role for economic analysis. Merger control has been expressly included, albeit in a weak form. The new Act explicitly provides for advocacy. Power to impose penalty has been included and this is likely to have a deterrent effect. Government, in its non-sovereign commercial functions, has been brought within the ambit of competition law. Other statutory authorities have been empowered to seek the opinion of the competition authority on competition matters. We will learn more about the new law as we proceed.

Economic Reform and Competition Policy

Do economic reforms and competition policy & law go together? One of the important features of economic reforms in India was the opening up of the economy. The preserve of the ubiquitous public sector was thrown open to private sector and even competition from outside the country. This covered, although gingerly, even the utilities and infrastructure sectors. The latter typically enjoy economies of scale and are natural monopolies. Hence, there is reluctance in government to open up these sectors for fear of creating private monopolies out of erstwhile public monopolies. Stiglitz[10] cogently argues that privatisation without the necessary institutional infrastructure in the transition countries leads to asset stripping rather than wealth creation. Stiglitz maintains that privatised monopolies, without regulation, are more capable of exploiting consumers than the state monopolies. By contrast, privatisation accompanied by regulation, corporate restructuring and strong corporate governance leads to higher growth. There is strong opinion in favour of having regulators in place before the economy is opened up and state monopolies are dismantled.

Sector Specific Regulator and Competition Authority

The obvious question is what kind of regulation is necessary? Let us take the example of India. The liberalization

10. Stiglitz, 2003, p. 220.

of capital market, insurance, telecommunications and electricity have led to sector specific regulatory regimes being put in place. Laws dealing with these sectors sometimes speak of promoting competition explicitly but are mostly silent about it. A new competition law has been enacted but is yet to take off. So what was being done overtly by the government continues covertly through the ostensibly independent regulators.[11] Economic theory tells us that the invisible forces of market are the best guide in a free market. Firms faced with constraints of competition bring about the best possible outcomes both for the consumers (in terms of prices and quality) as well as the society (in terms of allocative efficiency). So do we need sector specific regulators or an omnibus competition regulator?

Markets cannot be relied upon to produce goods that are essentially public in nature, like defence.[12] Economists have analyzed what are the attributes of public goods; they are goods for which the marginal costs of supplying the goods to an additional individual are small or zero, and for which the costs of excluding them from the benefits are large. But capital market, insurance, telecommunications and electricity are not public goods. While there can be a strong argument in favour of a sector specific regulator before opening up a sector providing public goods, it would be wrong to stretch the argument to sectors involving goods and services that are or can be traded commercially.

There is debate raging in many countries on the interrelationship between sector specific regulator and competition regulator.[13] It would suffice for this paper to bring to the fore the current thinking in the EU and some other

---

11. There has much furor in the press in recent days on the perceived attempts of the government to curb the independence of the economic regulators in India. Laws governing the regulators contain provision for the government to issue policy directives with the government being the final arbiter in case of a dispute whether the issue is a policy issue.
12. Sitglitz, 2003, p. 220.
13. Readers can refer to the website www.internationalcompetitionnetwork.org.

countries outside the EU. The move is to shift to a soft regulatory regime[14] after establishment of effective competition in the regulated sectors and finally have a sunset clause in the regulatory laws. Importantly, determination of effective competition is done under competition laws by the competition authority. Some sectors have this kind of arrangement. The national telecom regulators can impose *ex ante* obligations only in the sub sectors where the EU competition authority has determined, applying competition principles, absence of effective competition. Similar regime is prevalent in many sectors in Mexico. In contrast, we hear of more sector specific regulators on the anvil in India.

Competition Law and Economic Growth

The efficacy of competition law in fostering economic growth is well documented. The Australian National Competition Council in its media release of 11 November 1998 states that rail freight fell by 40% and energy rates by 60% in 3 years of implementation of the National Competition Policy. The other examples of benefits of competition cited in the release are 50% fall in gas prices and 17% in conveyancing fees. A study by the Centre for the Advancement of Energy Markets, a US based non-profit think tank, estimated the benefits of competition to the tune of $3 billion in the mid-Atlantic region of US during 2002.[15] Competition is known to have led to increase in GDP in Australia, increase in rate of employment in the New Zealand and UK.[16] It could justifiably be argued that effective enforcement of competition law is necessary to strengthen the 'invisible hands' of market forces and keep a check on market failures. The need for competition law enforcement in transition economies is far more

14. This would be characterized by market forces determining prices with competition oversight.
15. www.caem.org/website/pages/PJM.htm.
16. For more details refer to speeches and articles by Vinod Dhall, Member, Competition Commission of India available on the Commission's website www.competitionommission.gov.in.

pronounced due to legacy of market distortions or even the absence of markets due to non-market based economic policies.

Three Elements of Competition Law

It has been stated earlier that the basic elements of the new competition law are prohibiting anti-competitive agreements, prohibiting abuse of dominant position and merger control. Each of these elements need to be looked at in greater details.

Anti-Competitive Agreements

Agreements in respect of economic activities alone are the subject matter of law but need not be formal or written or enforceable in law. The adverse impact of such an agreement on competition has to be appreciable in order to come under the ambit of law. Law makes a distinction between horizontal agreements and vertical agreements, although these expressions have not been explicitly used by the lawmakers.

Horizontal Agreements

Horizontal agreements are agreements between enterprises engaged in production or trade of identical or similar goods or provision of identical or similar services, for example, agreements between manufacturers of match boxes. The parties to the agreement must agree to determine price or output levels or divide the market. Agreement can also be for collusive bidding or bid rigging in order to pre-determine which enterprise would be successful in the bidding process at a pre-set price. An extreme form of horizontal agreement is a cartel, regarded as the most pernicious form of anti-competitive agreement by competition authorities worldwide. A cartel is defined as a group of sellers of a product who join together to control its production, sale, and price in the hope of obtaining the advantages of monopoly.[17] Horizontal agreements are presumed in the Indian law to have appreciable adverse effect on competition and hence are dealt with under the *per se* rule under which conduct is presumed to be harmful to competition. This closely follows the international norm.

17. Baumol and Blinder, 2000, p. 254.

Vertical Agreements

Vertical agreements are dealt with more leniently than horizontal agreements. Such agreements are between enterprises at different stages or levels of production or supply, for example, agreement between a manufacturer and its distributor or a manufacturer and its supplier. While such agreements can lead to anti-competitive outcomes, the universality of this proposition cannot be accepted without further investigation. Usually, competition authorities would investigate vertical agreements and decide against only on the basis of preponderance of probabilities that this is likely to have an appreciable adverse effect on competition. This process is known as the *rule of reason* test.

The inclusive list of vertical agreements given in the Competition Act is self explaining. A tie-in arrangement, where a product (usually slow moving item) is sold together with another product (usually a fast moving item) can have adverse impact on competition. An exclusive supply or distribution agreement can diminish a competitor's ability to compete effectively and, therefore, raises competition concerns. Although an enterprise's prerogative to deal with another enterprise is widely recognized, arbitrary refusal to deal, usually with existing dealers, is brought under the scanner of competition law to determine its adverse impact on competition. Resale price maintenance refers to a practice of an enterprise accepting a dealer on the condition that the latter cannot sell or supply at a price lower than what is agreed to. Such agreement can deny consumers competitive price in the market.

Abuse of Dominant Position

Abuse of dominant position is prohibited by law. Dominant position is defined in the Act as "means a position of strength, enjoyed by an enterprise, in the relevant market, in India, which enables it to:

(i) operate independently of competitive forces prevailing in the relevant market, or

(ii) affect its competitors or consumers or the relevant market in its favour".

Market Power

There are no threshold limits in terms of market share or the like to determine dominant position. It is based on determination of significant market power in the relevant market. Key concern of competition law is with enterprises which can profitably raise prices above marginal cost.[18] It can happen only when an enterprise can act independently of its competitors and consumers. This is known as market power. Such behaviour results in inefficient allocation of resources, deadweight loss of monopoly and distribution of wealth in favour of the producers. These are the reasons because of which both economists and competition authorities are loathe with abuse of dominance.

An enterprise with market power can raise prices without losing consumers. Its ability to do so depends on many factors, namely, availability of substitutes, presence of competitors who can compete effectively and contestability in the market. Delimitation of the relevant market assumes utmost importance in any abuse of dominance investigation. A market is the set of sellers to which a set of buyers can turn for supplies at existing or slightly higher prices.[19] The Raghavan Committee had observed that there are two dimensions to this—the product market and the geographical market. On the demand side, the relevant product market includes all substitutes that the consumer would switch to if price of the product relevant to the investigation were to increase. On the supply side, this would include all producers who could, with their existing facilities, switch to the production of such substitute goods. The relevant product market, therefore, constitutes of products that are regarded as close substitutes or interchangeable by consumers. The geographical boundaries of the relevant market can be similarly defined. Geographic dimensions involve

18. Jones and Surfin, 2004, p. 46.

19. Goetz and McChesney, 2002, p. 389.

identification of the geographical area within which competition takes place and, given the transportation cost, supplies can be made without loss. The relevant geographical market is a geographical area within which products are available on identical or similar terms and can be distinguished from a neighbouring area.

Determination of Market Power

The first step in determining the relevant product is to find cross elasticities in order to judge substitutability. Paucity of data can often hinder this determination. The way out seems to be to take market share as an approximation for dominance. A significant market share for a considerable length of time is suggestive of dominance[20] since profits earned by incumbents have not attracted competitors. Shipment data indicates the relevant geographical market.

The Hypothetical Monopolist Test (HMT) or the Small but Significant Non-Transitory Increase in Price (SSNIP)[21] test is usually applied by competition authorities in determining market power. The enterprise is assumed to be a hypothetical monopolist and price—quantity data of the recent past is used to test whether it can increase its price by 5% or 10% profitably. This requires product-level dis-aggregated data on price and quantity, which may not be readily available in India. Perhaps, law enforcers will have to rely more on market share and analysis of market structure to judge conduct and performance[22] and barriers to entry in terms of actual entry and exit to/from the sector. These factors could shed light on contestability in the market which may be sufficient to provide competitive constraints. A market is perfectly contestable if entry and exit are costless and unimpeded.[23] Bork says that the concept of barriers to entry is crucial to competition debate; its

20. See Hoffmann-La Roche case(1979)and United Brands case (1978).
21. Readers may refer to Bishop and Walker, 2002.
22. Using the Structure-Conduct-Performance model.
23. Baumol and Blinder, 2000, p. 264.

ubiquity and potency is undeniable.[24] It may not be as precise as the tests evolved in the US and EU over the years and yet may be effective until a veritable data base is built.

Essential Facilities

Many concepts would emerge when the Indian competition law becomes fully functional. These concepts emerged mainly in the US and have been accepted in many jurisdictions. One of these is the *doctrine of essential facilities*. In 1912,[25] the US Supreme Court ordered few railroad operators, owning and operating a railway junction, to provide access to newcomers at reasonable terms since denial of such access reduced competition. This was followed in a number of subsequent judgments. It is accepted that if a dominant player controls an essential facility that cannot be easily replicated but is necessary for effectively competing, third party access must be permitted at reasonable terms if providing access is feasible. Similarly, abuse can be by many enterprises acting in "concert". The enterprises singly may not be in a position to acquire market power but acting together, they can exert joint dominance. Generally, accusations of concentration are not proved only on the basis of parallel behaviour, i.e. when a number of enterprises exhibit similar pricing strategy.

Predatory Pricing

Predatory pricing by a dominant firm is an abuse under the competition law of India. The concept of predatory pricing has undergone many stages of evolution, first in the US and then in the EU. Predatory price means selling below cost of production. The courts and the competition authorities in the US were confronted with determination of cost. In 1975, two economists[26] theorized that predatory pricing means pricing below marginal cost. They were aware of the practical difficulties in calculating marginal cost and hence suggested average cost as a proxy to marginal cost. Soon it came to be

24. Bork, 1993.

25. Terminal Railroad Association case, 1912.

26. Professors Areeda & Turner of Harvard University.

recognized that predatory pricing would mean setting prices below the average variable cost. However, the US Supreme Court, in the case of Matsushita Electronics (1986), put forth an additional condition, namely, recoupment of losses, necessary for deciding whether pricing was predatory in nature. In the EU, however, selling below cost (usually average variable cost) continues to be sufficient to hold charge of predatory behaviour. The Indian law does not define cost but leaves its determination to regulations. However, the selling of the product below its cost must be with the intent of ousting competitors to be labeled predatory behaviour in India.

Merger Control

Merger control is an essential feature of all modern competition laws. In fact, the US competition authority attempted merger control by invoking Sherman Act, 1890, which did not explicitly provide for it. However, the US Courts were reluctant to accept attempted merger control under the Sherman Act, 1890. This led the lawmakers to enact the Clayton Act in 1914 with explicit provisions for merger control.

Merger covers all kinds of joining together of two enterprises including amalgamation, acquisition of control, etc. There are clear overlaps between merger control and provisions dealing with anti-competitive agreements and abuse of dominant position. An explicit provision dealing with mergers, called combinations in the Indian law, is welcome, given the controversy witnessed in the US mentioned earlier.

Threshold Limits

It is not unusual for provisions dealing with merger control in competition laws to have threshold limits. In other words, only mergers above a certain value of assets or turnover or whatever be the threshold limit come under the purview of the competition authorities. In India, the threshold limits are asset value of more than Rs. 1,000 crore or turnover over Rs. 3,000 crore.[27] The threshold limits are rather high by Indian standards

27. There are separate threshold limits for combinations involving companies outside India and group companies in Section 5 of the Competition Act, 2002.

and are, in fact, even higher than the limits prescribed in the UK competition law. It seems the limits were deliberately kept high due to apprehensions of certain stakeholders that the size of the Indian companies is relatively small compared to size of the companies in the developed countries and growth through combinations may get stunted if all combinations were brought under the ambit of the competition law.

Notification by Merging Parties

Almost all countries having competition law prefer compulsory notification regime where all intending merging parties are expected to notify the competition authority prior to the actual merger.[28] Although it would seem to throw up lot of work for the competition authorities, practical experience shows that around 95% of the mergers pass muster and intervention is required only in the remaining 5%. Of these 5% cases where intervention is made, very few are outrightly rejected while the balance cases are approved with modifications. The Indian law has adopted a voluntary notification regime, which entails that even if the merger is above the threshold limit, the merging parties, at their discretion, may notify the Competition Commission. However, there is a rider. The Competition Commission, on its own, can investigate a merger up to one year after it has taken place, which results in the Damocles' sword hanging on the combining parties during that period. Certainly, a better alternative would have been to have a compulsory notification regime with the high threshold limits already prescribed.

Types of Mergers

Mergers can be easily divided into three categories, namely horizontal mergers, vertical mergers and conglomerate mergers. Readers would instantaneously recall similarity with the provisions dealing with anti-competitive agreements. This categorization is mainly on the perceived future impact of mergers on the state of competition.

---

28. Norwegian law is an exception.

Horizontal

Horizontal mergers are mergers between enterprises in the same stage of production or distribution. In other words, if two competitors merge it would be a horizontal merger. It is obvious that such mergers raise serious competition concerns and are more likely to create market power, thus necessitating intervention by competition authorities.

Vertical

Vertical mergers are mergers between enterprises at different stages of production or distribution. For example, mergers between producers and suppliers or between producers and distributors would fall under this category. Usually, such mergers would not raise competition concerns unless the mergers diminish the ability of competitors to effectively compete by virtue of losing out an important source of supplies or an important link for distribution. Competition authorities typically would look at such mergers more leniently than they would look at horizontal mergers.

Conglomerate

Conglomerate mergers are mergers between enterprises in different lines of business. For example, if an automobile manufacturer were to merge with cement manufacturer, it would be a conglomerate merger. This category of mergers is most unlikely to raise competition concerns and would pass muster almost all the time.

Procedure for Merger Control

Merger control procedure provided in the Indian competition law is quite different from procedure provided for dealing with anti-competitive agreements and abuse of dominant position. There is no separate investigative machinery provided for merger control and the Commission is to rely on the facts provided by the merging parties and the public at large, including competitors, from whom information is to be sought in every case. Interestingly, a rather stiff time limit of 90 working days is provided to make a decision on mergers in spite of the absence of investigation support. The Indian law goes to the extent of deeming a merger approved if the Commission is not able to make a decision within the stipulated period of 90 working days. It seems that the Commission would be hard pressed to make decisions so quickly without a support mechanism for investigation such as one that has been provided to it for dealing with anticompetitive agreements and abuse of dominant position. If such a mechanism is provided in law,[29] it may not be difficult to adhere to the time limit as practical experiences of other jurisdictions have shown.[30]

Regulation of mergers fundamentally deals with expected behaviour of the merged enterprises and hence calls for *ex ante* regulation. Intervention is only called for if the merger is expected to have appreciable adverse effect on competition. Post merger, typically, adverse effect on competition, can be expected either out of unilateral action or out of collusive action. If the merged entity is expected to acquire market power, it is likely to have adverse effect on account of unilateral action. In such cases, a competition authority is most likely to intervene and prohibit the merging parties from acquiring market power. Mergers can, sometimes, lead to significant reduction in the number of competitors and thereby facilitate collusive action since collusion between small number of players is easier. Intervention in such cases can also be expected.

It is evident from above that investigation into mergers would essentially involve investigation into whether the agreement for joining together is anti-competitive and/or the combination is likely to change the structure of the market in such a way that its conduct is likely to be unacceptable under any competition regime. Thus, all factors that are relevant for determining abuse of dominant position would have to be looked into by the competition authorities while deciding cases of mergers.

---

29. An Amendment Bill introduced in the Lok Sabha in March, 2006 seeks to provide investigative mechanism to the Commission.
30. In Mexico, for example, most of the merger decisions take around 27 days, although in complex cases, time can be extended (under law) to 180 days.

Competition Advocacy

The Competition Act enjoins the Commission to promote and sustain a competition culture in the economy in the interest of consumers. Advocacy is the fourth important element of the Indian competition law, (the other three being prohibiting anti-competive agreements, prohibiting abuse of dominant position and merger control) and rightly so since we are liberalising the economy and transiting from a phase of public sector dominance to a free market economy. Competition advocacy has played a significant role and continues to do so even in the most developed countries. This enables a competition authority to effectively intervene in policy making that impacts competition. Competition advocacy aims at bringing about consensus among stakeholders on competition issues and this provides a strong argument in its favour. Competition advocacy has been defined as competition law enforcement without intervention.[31] It has been the experience of all enforcement agencies that voluntary compliance is superior to compliance enforced through sanctions. Advocacy, as a tool, is powerful enough to bring about awareness of the law and its benefits so as to promote competition within acceptable limits.

Competition Commission & Competition Policy

A far more significant responsibility lies on the shoulders of the Competition Commission. It can be approached by the Central Government for an opinion on competition policy. This provision in the Indian competition law provides an opportunity to the Competition Commission to influence policy making in favour of competition, competitors and consumers. It is not uncommon for competition authorities in many countries to assume such roles. For example, in the UK, the competition authority, i.e. the Office of Fair Trade (OFT), is empowered to comment on any law or policy of the government and put it in the public domain to which the concerned Ministry must reply within 30 days. This serves as a powerful influence on future changes in policy since

31. Dutz Mark, World Bank.

governments are loathe to ignore advice of an independent market regulator on frivolous grounds.

Competition Act, 2002—Salient Provisions

It is not possible to detail all the provisions of the Competition Act in a short paper. But the enormous significance and range of the Act make it necessary to bring out some salient provisions of the law.

It is often said in India that the government is in the business of business. A number of goods and services are supplied by government departments (excluding public sector enterprises). While the competition law recognizes the sovereign functions of the government, its non-sovereign function, more precisely supply of goods and services by governments departments, is within the ambit of the law. Public sector enterprises are also within its ambit. Unlike the MRTP Act, the Competition Act does not distinguish between suppliers on the basis of ownership.

Statutory authorities can refer any competition issue to the Commission for its opinion, which is statutorily to be given within 60 days. However, the existing provision of law makes such a reference possible only if a competition issue is raised by a party[32] before a statutory authority during pendency of a proceeding. Reference is neither mandatory nor is the opinion binding. Thus the scope of this provision is narrow.

In the era of globalization, cross-border economic transactions are on a rise. The competition law recognizes that even acts taking place outside India can have impact on markets in India. This is known as the *effects doctrine*. There is explicit provision in the law to deal with such situations. This would enable the Commission to deal with cartelization outside India provided this impacts competition in the domestic territory.

As said earlier, the MRTP Commission was rendered toothless since it could not penalize offenders and had to

32. The recently introduced Amendment Bill seeks to empower a statutory authority to refer a competition issue suo motu for an opinion of the Commission.

depend on civil courts. The Competition Commission has been empowered to levy penalties. It can also levy penalties for proven charges of cartelization. The law, as it stands today,[33] even empowers the Commission to send the offenders to civil imprisonment.

Just when competition authorities in the US were veering around to the view that cartels only exist in textbooks of economics, they chose to introduce an Amnesty Program for the members of any cartel who broke the rank and provided information against co-conspirators. The introduction of a leniency programme led to a spurt in the number of leniency applications and also in the detection of hardcore cartels, which had siphoned off billions of dollars in overcharges from unsuspecting consumers. Some of the important cases that came to light were the Vitamins cartel (1999), the Lysine cartel (1996), the Electro-graphite cartel (1998), etc., and the perpetrators were put through criminal sanctions[34] on the basis of information provided by the breakaway member, who received amnesty under their newly introduced law. The Indian lawmakers recognized the pernicious effect of hardcore cartels and introduced a leniency programme in the law to assist in their detection. However, since leniency is restricted to the first person inside the door provided he reaches before investigation has commenced,[35] this programme may not prove as successful as Amnesty and Amnesty Plus Programs of the US.

In line with the international trend, the Competition Commission is, by law, an independent and autonomous body with its own fund,[36] can appoint[37] its own officers and other

---

33. The power of civil imprisonment is sought to vest with courts as per the Amendment Bill.
34. Cartelization is a criminal offence in the US and many other countries but not so in India.
35. This is sought to be extended until receipt of the investigation report in the Amendment Bill.
36. With limited resources the funding can be expected to be largely by way of grants by the Government.
37. Except Director General and certain other employees under Section 16.

employees and is also empowered to make regulations on certain issues. The procedure for appointment of its members is a part of law with a selection panel of eminent people. More importantly, removal of members has been made difficult by prescribing the procedure and the necessary conditions for invoking this provision.[38] The Competition Act permits the government to issue policy directions to the Commission. In case of any dispute where the matter concerns policy, decision of the government will be final. How far the well intentioned independence and autonomy will be guaranteed in practical terms will have to be left to future. Since the history of economic regulators is not very long in India, it will be hard to hazard a guess on this tricky issue. It is, however, clear that the intention to make the regulator independent and autonomous has been clearly laid down in law.

Although the Civil Procedure Code is not required to be followed by the Commission in its procedures, principles of natural justice have to be followed. This would mean sufficient opportunity to the enterprise to raise defence, both on facts and law. Many factors, economic and otherwise, have to be considered by the Commission in reaching a conclusion as to existence of anti-competitive behaviour. Some of these factors would mean economic analysis using IO theory. For example, the relevant market has to be determined before dominance in the market can be established. In order to determine the relevant market, the relevant product and the relevant geographical market need to be determined. Some important elements that the Commission will have to consider for determining the relevant market are the physical attributes of the product, availability of close substitutes, number of players, entry and exit conditions, competition constraints from neighbouring areas as well as imports.

The procedure is based on complaints while the authority can also take up any matter on its own or *suo motu*. The complainant has certain rights in the proceedings. Where a

38. The Commission can also be superceded in exceptional circumstances and it will be reasonable to expect such actions to be rare.

matter has been initiated by the Commission itself, probably the Director General will step into the shoes of the complainant. The intention of the lawmakers seems to have two contesting parties before the Commission to bring out the totality of facts of the case with their help.[39]

This brings us to the investigating mechanism provided in law to assist the Commission. The Government appoints a Director General (DG) to assist the Commission for investigating matters concerning anti-competitive agreements and abuse of dominant position. There is no investigating mechanism provided for matters concerning mergers.[40] The DG has been given limited powers of a civil court as far as compelling attendance of witness and production of documents are concerned. In fact, DG enjoys the same powers as the Commission in these matters. The new law is very different in granting these powers to the DG from the MRTP Act, where the investigating agency had to rely upon that Commission to issue summons.

A number of competition laws enable search and seizure by the authorities. The Indian law provides for search in accordance with the Companies Act.[41] The US authorities do not have such powers but have taken the help of FBI (Lysine cartel, 1996). The EU authority has recently acquired this power and used it in August of 2005 on a complaint against Intel by its rival AMD. Although power to enter somebody's premises seems harsh, it may be necessary in certain kinds of cases, like hardcore cartels, where agreements are hush-hush and documentary evidence hard to find. Apprehensions of misuse must always be weighed against the loss on account of its

39. The Amendment Bill seeks to replace 'complaint' by 'information' and these will not be adverserial proceedings before the Commission if the amendments are approved.

40. The Commission will be able to entrust the DG with investigation in merger cases if the Amendment Bill is approved.

41. Sections 240 and 240A of the Companies Act, 1956 permit search and seizure after obtaining warrant of authorization from the local magistrate.

absence. The recent international trend seems to be in favour of giving competition authority power to search and seize.

There are few deeming provisions in the law. *Per se rule* can be applied in limited types of cases, say, for example, in cases of cartelization. Majority of cases will have to be decided on the basis of *rule of reason*. This will be a real challenge to the Commission. Collection of evidence that cannot be controverted will be essential in declaring behaviour unacceptable. The evidence will have to be weighed on the basis of preponderance of probability to declare it sufficient under the *rule of reason* test.

Working of Competition Law

The Competition Act has not been fully notified yet.[42] The Commission, with its present constitution,[43] can only carry out its mandate of competition advocacy, which is precisely what it is doing. In order to have an insight at the working of competition authority, one will have necessarily to look at the authorities in other countries.

Competition law evolved first in the US. Two authorities deal with competition laws, namely the Anti-trust division of the Department of Justice (DOJ) and the Federal Trade Commission (FTC).[44] Most of the principles evolved by these two agencies, settled by the US courts have found acceptance in other countries. The European Court of Justice (ECJ) also has settled certain principles in competition assessment. A look at a couple of cases will be educative.

---

42. This Act requires each section to be separately notified to become operational. While the Act was notified in January, 2003, only few sections have been notified so far. The main sections dealing with enforcement are yet to be notified.
43. The Commission has only one member since inception. The Chairman and other members (there can be up to 10) are yet to be appointed.
44. The interrelationship has evolved over time and there is some sort of division of labour.

Some Cases

A football club, Hetch, wanting to use the stadium owned by a rival club was denied access and complained to the FTC. The rival club had a facility that was difficult to replicate but could be let out at reasonable terms and there could be no effective competition without access to this facility. The matter was finally decided by the US Supreme Court in 1978 in favour of the club intending to hire the rival's stadium invoking the *doctrine of essential facility*.

Two giants[45] in the office statiɔnary supermarket filed a pre-merger notification. Their combined market share in the office stationary market was a mere 6%, which did not indicate competition concern to start with. The FTC investigated and determined consumable office supplies through super market as the relevant market. Their assessment of the relevant market was based on internal memos of the merging enterprises. In this relevant market, the merged entity was likely to cause substantial lessening of competition since facts showed a high positive correlation between price and number of rival supermarket outlets operating in any area. The District Court[46] (1997) agreed with FTC and granted an interim injunction thus killing the merger.

United Brands is a leading supplier of bananas in Europe with its Chiquita brand having about 46% market share at the relevant time. It stopped supplying to its Danish distributor after the latter participated in a promotion campaign of its rival brand. It was charged with exclusionary practice. The ECJ determined banana to be the relevant market due to special characteristics of the fruit that distinguishes it from other fruits. United's share of 46% in the banana market was much higher than its nearest rival with hardly 22%. The company owned extensive plantations in the Carribean and South America and had its own ships for transportation. It had developed a special chemical for ripening and had come to

45. Staples and Office Depot case (1997).

46. FTC does not power to penalize or prosecute. It has to take matters to the regular courts.

acquire market power. Even loss incurred by the firm in few recent years was not considered a good defence against charge of acquiring market power. The Court (1978) upheld the charge of abuse of dominance.

Hoffmann La Roche is a giant among pharmaceutical companies with about 47% market share which was more than the combined share of its two biggest rivals. It was found to have technological lead over its rivals and had built capacity far exceeding the supply requirements. Thus it was found to have a dominant position which it was abusing by having unassailable technological advantage coupled with putting entry barrier in the form of excess capacity that would deter any potential entrant. ECJ (1979) also found a high market share for a fairly long period as evidence of abuse of dominance since its absence would have surely attracted new entry to this highly profitable business.

Lysine[47] cartel was detected in the US in 1996 and had been in operation for about 5 years. It was led by a US company, ADM and its members were 2 Japanese companies and 2 Korean companies. The price of lysine increased during 1992-1993, dipped for a year perhaps on cheating by some cartel members, and then rose again during 1994-1996. ADM broke ranks and claimed amnesty. FTC used FBI to search the premises of the members and used secretly taped conversations between executives to prove cartelization. All other members were fined heavily[48] and top executives were prosecuted. Fines under American laws depend upon calculation of overcharge made by the cartel members. There was some confusion among economist on the exact methodology to be used to calculate overcharge and finally they came up with 5 different measures. The Court used its discretion to quantify the fines.

Sealink Services was a ferry operator and also owner of port at Holyhead, UK. It gave access to the port to B&I, a rival. But the rival had smaller vessels and the waves made by Sealink vessels made it difficult for them to utilize the facility.

47. Lysine is an amino acid used primarily in animal feed.

48. The largest fine imposed was $46 million.

The European Commission (1992) held Sealink guilty under competition law since it could not provide third party access at terms and conditions that were inferior to what it enjoyed.

Predatory pricing is usually an offence under competition laws although some may argue that it is beneficial for the consumers unless the dominant firm succeeds in ousting competitors and then reap monopoly profit. The simple proposition to declare price predatory if it were less than some benchmark of cost did find acceptance in courts in the US for a while. But in the case of Matsushita Electronics vs. Zenith Radios (1986), the Supreme Court added another element to the sufficiency test. Unless the dominant firm charged with predatory pricing can be shown to have recouped its loss (on account of selling below cost), the charge would fail. The charge was of predation by 21 Japanese firms over a 20 year period in the consumer electronic products, mainly televisions. The length of time involved in this case and the fact that the alleged conspirators failed to dislodge their American rivals may have forced the Court to take this view but it has become the standard now. The European courts do not share this view and continue to apply the simpler cost yardstick.

Competition law has evolved well over a century and is increasingly becoming part of competition policy the world over. It started in Canada and USA and, thereafter in Western Europe. Although many countries did not have such laws until recently, Singh[49] found existence of competition policy in many developing countries. The two emerging countries of Asia are in the process of establishing modern competition regime.[50] Since the overall format remains quite similar to the older and well established laws, the principles already evolved will find ready application in the new regimes. Hence, the importance of these cases and the economic theories that have evolved with them can be understood. It is encouraging to see that the Competition Commission seems to strongly believe in

49. Singh, 2002.

50. India enacted its law in 2003 and China is expecting its bill to be approved soon.

transparency in its proceedings as can be seen from its draft general regulations[51] which provides for all dropped cases to be put on its website along with gist of cases decided against enterprises. Transparency will permit healthy evolution of law.

Another healthy feature is the number of advisory committees of experts[52] that are presently helping the Commission in various professional works. The German competition authority had also relied heavily on economists and legal experts in its initial years.

Acceptance of competition laws across nations calls for its convergence, both in content as well as in enforcement. There may be an international competition authority someday. Until then, move towards gradual convergence is required to deal with cross border economic transactions. It entails giving up sovereignty to some degree and yet must be undertaken for the benefit of consumers. We have a good example in the EU, where the European competition authority has primacy over national authorities. More importantly, the definitional and interpretational aspects are controlled by the pan-national body leading to convergence. The intentions of the Treaty of Rome to create one market within the EU economic area may be responsible for such convergence even at the cost of loss of sovereignty in some sense. Creating a world devoid of barriers of any kind in trade and commerce is the cherished goal of all countries. So can convergence be far away? Economic cooperation must have cooperation on competition matters as an important element. There have been efforts in this direction which has been well chronicled by Koul (2005).

Economic analysis[53] requirements in competition cases need dis-aggregated contemporary data, product-level or at least firm-level data. SSNIP test requires calculation of elasticity and

51. Draft Regulations(General) available on www.competitioncommission.gov.in

52. List of committees is available on the Commission's website.

53. For detailed introduction to various tests, readers may refer to Bishop and Walker (2002). For a brief description for those not familiar with mathematics, refer to Jones and Sufrin (2004).

hence data on price and quantity of a particular product. Similar requirement of data exists for numerous economic tests like price correlation test, tests for delineating the relevant geographical market.[54] In dealing with merger control, concentration ratio or Herfindahl-Hirschman Index need to be calculated on the basis of prevalent market share. Some of these data requirements can be easily met out of regular sources as Centre for Monitoring Indian Economy or CRISIL. Trade associations' data collection is not of much use by a competition authority. The only source of firm-level and product-level data is the Annual Survey of Industry (ASI). Data is collected every year from each manufacturing unit employing more than 100 employees product-wise. There are two problems. The data is not current and is usually available with a lag of at least one year. Competition deals with behaviour and the past is not of great value in competition analysis. The bigger problem is the absence of name of the enterprise from the data. The name of the enterprise is deleted in accordance with the law under which it is collected and there is little one can do about it except hope for an amendment, which can be counter-productive by making firms wary of disclosing their data. The problem of veritable data is likely to continue for sometime forcing the Commission to use tests that have less data requirement or depend on other kinds of evidence.

The issue of confidentiality of data is important in competition laws. Enterprises guard their data zealously and rightly so since commercial information is valuable to a rival. A competition authority must have access to all data to analyze and conclude on an alleged anti-competitive behaviour. Confidentiality of the information collected by the authority might be essential for the survival of the concerned enterprise. Maintaining confidentiality is almost universal, usually statutorily. In fact, Microsoft had to waive the confidentiality clauses to enable the DOJ and the EU competition authority

54. Reference here is to LIFO (little in from outside) and LOFI (little out from inside) tests—there are more complicated tests and data requirements would be more.

to exchange information when trying cases of abuse of dominance against it. It is a generally accepted principle that no information that can harm an enterprise is divulged by a competition authority. Even if such information finds place in the order/judgement, the public version blacks out the portions that can cause damage if made public. The Indian law incorporates all necessary provisions for maintaining confidentiality and the same seems to be further strengthened in the regulations.[55]

In the real world it is not necessary to have large number of producers to ensure effective competition. Perfect competition as well as perfect monopoly exists only in textbooks. Reality lies somewhere in between the two extremes and the present day world is characterised by varying degrees of monopolistic competition. Fair competition can be ensured by having contestability in markets. Contestability, in text books, is defined as costless entry and exit.[56] This can only be true if there are no barriers to entry and sunk costs[57] are zero. Obviously, such conditions are tough to be met. Some degree of contestability should be sufficient to have constraints of competition. As long as potential entrants see profit in the venture, they should be able to set up shop at will and exit with minimal loss (that would have been already factored in the decision to enter). The threat of potential competitors deters enterprises from assuming monopoly power in the long run although they may acquire it in the short run. A pre-merger notification was filed by Boeing and McDonnel Douglas. The US competition authority approved it stating that even two rivals, namely Airbus Industrie and Boeing could provide effective competition.[58] This has proved to be right and we witness intense rivalry between the two.[59] A competition

55. See draft regulations on the Commission's website.

56. Baumol and Blinder, 2000.

57. Sunk costs are costs that a new entrant must incur to enter the market, e.g. putting up the necessary infrastructure.

58. The EU competition authority did not agree with this analysis.

59. The recent purchase/intended purchase by Indian Airlines and Air India are examples.

authority is typically wary of such situations since small number of producers of close substitutes can easily collude.

Technological advantage often leads to market power. In the Hoffmann La Roche case, ECJ (1979) had observed on the entry barrier put by the enterprise by acquiring huge technology lead over its rivals. On the other hand, intellectual property rights (IPRs) are exact opposites since they legally provide monopoly power to the holder. It is argued that no one will innovate in the absence of guarantee of monopoly so as to recover costs. The moot question is whether the legal monopoly is used to recover cost and no more? Restraint would never be self imposed and requires some kind of regulation. Laws dealing with IPRs typically have some kind of restriction to ensure welfare of the people and interventions are permitted in public interest. The competition law in India recognizes IPRs and excludes agreements putting reasonable restrictions. However, abuse of a monopoly created because of IPRs is not exempted.

Export cartels are typically exempted under national competition laws[60] since they do not affect the domestic market. The immunity is limited to the domestic market and are open to investigation and prosecution by the competition authority of the country whose market is affected under the *effects doctrine*. The Indian law has adopted such exemption. One can foresee the possibility of retaliation. If one country's authority imposes sanctions against another country's export association, the other country's authority could retaliate (provided there is an export association in the other country). This brings us back to the need for international cooperation and convergence in competition matters. What is not good for us cannot be good for others. Competition laws across countries need to be harmonized in this respect and blanket exemptions should be removed to conduct international trade fairly.

Two major economies of China and India do not yet have functional modern competition regimes. Both have good intentions to have it soon. The world economic order will improve once all major economies have competition laws. India

60. The EU is an exception since its laws transcend national boundaries.

is certainly ahead in this respect since it has already enacted the Competition Act. But the road ahead is difficult. A massive effort is required to make its implementation effective. Capacity building is the first and foremost requirement. Although capacity building initiatives have begun, these are limited in scope and a lot more is needed to meet the manifold needs of the rapidly evolving circumstances. A modern law requires a modern organization and new skills to deliver. These are not easy due to bureaucratic inertia. Courts will also be required to acquire new skills to deal with complex competition issues involving economic analysis of a high order.[61] Along with capacity building of the staff of the Commission, the judiciary, professionals and business managers too need to provide the wherewithal to deal with competition issues. The present initiatives of the government are in the right direction but the pace of transformation needs to gather momentum, particularly with the basic frame now in place. While building and developing conceptual and operational frameworks, the spectrum of work of the CCI could conceivably encompass development of regulatory policy, market reviews, investigation of anti-competitive behaviour, impact assessments, international activities and strategic development. This is a tall order but attainable.

[The views expressed in the paper are of the author alone and do not represent views of the Competition Commission of India. The author acknowledges the contribution of Mr. Manoranjan Sharma, especially on market failures.]

REFERENCES

Baumol, William J. and Blinder, Allan S. (2000): *Microeconomics: Principles and Policy,* Hartcourt College Publication

Berglas, E. and Pines, D. (1981): "Clubs, Local Public Goods, and Transportation Models: A Synthesis", *Journal of Public Economics*, 15: 141-162.

Bishop, S. and Walker, M. (2002): *The Economics of EC Competition Law,* Sweet & Maxwell.

---

61. Eminent economists presented economic analyses on behalf of Microsoft to the US Courts.

Boadway, R.W. and Wildasin, D.E. (1984): *Public Sector Economics*, Boston: Little Brown and Company.

Bork, Robert H. (1993): *The Antitrust Paradox*, Free Press **B&l v. Sealink** (1992) 5 CMLR 255.

Chipman, J.S. (1970): "External Economies of Scale and Competitive Equilibrium", *Quarterly Journal of Economics*, 84: 347-385.

Competition Act, 2002.

Dixit, A.K. and Stiglitz, J.E. (1977): "Monopolistic Competition and Optimum Product Diversity", *American Economic Review*, 67: 297-308.

Flatters, F., Henderson, V. and Mieszkowski, P. (1974): "Public Good, Efficiency, and Regional Fiscal Equalization", *Journal of Public Economics*, 3: 99-112.

Fujita, M., Krugman, P. (1995): "When the Economy is Monocentric? Von Thunen and Chamberlin Unified", *Regional Science and Urban Economics*, 25: 505-528.

Fujita, M., Krugman, P. and Venables, A.J. (1999): *The Spatial Economy*. Cambridge, Massachusetts: The MIT Press.

Goetz, Charles J. and McChesney, Fred S. (2002): *Antitrust Law: Interpretation and Implementation*, Lexis Nexis.

Helpman, E. (1998): "The Size of Regions", D. Pines, E. Sadka, and I. Zilcha, (Eds.): *Topics in Public Economics*, Cambridge: Cambridge University Press, 33-54.

Hetch v. Pro Footbal Inc. (1978): 436 U.S. 956

Hoffman – La Roche & Co AG v. Commission (1979) case 85/76[1979] ECR 461[1979] 3 (MLR21).

Krugman, P., (1991): "Increasing Returns and Economic Geography", *Journal of Political Economy*, 99: 483-499.

Jones, Alison and Sufrin, Brenda, (2004): *EC Competition Law*, Oxford University Press.

Lagueux, M. (1998): "Learning from the Debate on Externalities", *Economics and Methodology* (R.E. Backhouse, D.M. Houseman, U. Maki and A. Salanti, Eds.), London: MacMillan, 120: 120-147.

Matsuhita Electric Ind. v. Zenith Radio Corporation (1986): 475 US 574.

Mills, E.S. and Hamilton, B.W. (1989): *Urban Economics*, New York: Harper Collins Publishers (Fourth Edition).

Papageorgiou, Y. and Pines, D. (1999): *An Essay on Urban Economic Theory*, Boston: Kluwer Academic Publishers.

Papageorgiou, Y. and Pines, D. (2000): "Externalities, Indivisibility, Non-replicability, and Agglomeration", *Journal of Urban Economics*, 48: 509-535.

Pines, D. and Thisse, J.F. (2001): "Urban System: Market and Efficiency", *Journal of Public Economic Theory*, 3: 7-14.

Report of the High Level on Competition Policy and Law, 2000 (known as the Raghavan Committee Report).

Sharpe, Thomas, (2002): "Predation", *Competition Law (International Library of Essays in Law & Legal Theory)* edited by Rosa Greaves, Ashgate Publishers Ltd.

Stiglitz, Joseph E., (2003): *Globalization and its Discontent*, W.W. Norton & Company.

United Brands Co. and United Brands Continental BV v. Commission (1978) (case 27/76) [1978] ECR 207, [1978] ICMLR 429.

US v. Terminal Railroad Association of St. Louis (1912) 224 Us 383.

World Bank (2006): *World Development Report 2006: Equity and Development*, New York: Oxford University Press.

Human Development and State Finances*

Rakesh Mohan

6

Introduction

...The Reserve Bank of India (RBI) bears a special relationship with the State Governments in its multiple role as the banker, debt manager and fiscal adviser. The interactions between the RBI and the State Governments have been stronger through the interface provided by the bi-annual Finance Secretaries' Conference organised by the Reserve Bank since 1997. This Conference has provided a common platform to discuss all aspects concerned with the fiscal affairs of the States and facilitated the evolution of a consensual approach on various key issues through active participation of State Government officials. Some of the outcomes include setting up of Consolidated Sinking Funds (CSF) for debt servicing, constitution of Guarantee Redemption Funds (GRF) to meet guarantee obligations, setting of Ways & Means Advance (WMA) limits for States, fixing limits for guarantees, and most recently, enactment of the Fiscal Responsibility Legislation (FRL)....

Economic Growth and Human Development

The concept of human development signifies improvement in the quality of life of the people in terms of various health and educational indicators. Through betterment of health, education and skills, human development creates human capabilities that can then lead to productivity enhancement and acceleration in economic growth. In a broader sense, human

---

* Reproduced from Dec. 2005 issue of Reserve Bank of India Bulletin.

development also implies improvements in terms of human rights and participation and freedom of choice. The credit for bringing special focus to human development can mainly be attributed to the noted economist Mahbub Ul Haq. He was instrumental in the evolution of the Human Development Index (HDI), which has emerged as a composite measure of development across the countries. The HDI is an index measuring the basic dimensions of human development, namely long and healthy life, education and decent standard of living. Indian economist and Nobel laureate Amartya Sen has also made valuable contributions towards the formulation of HDI. According to the Human Development Report, 2005, published by the United Nations Development Programme (UNDP), all the countries (177 in total) are categorized into three broad groups, such as (i) High Human Development, (ii) Medium Human Development, and (iii) Low Human Development. India is placed in the group of Medium Human Development countries and ranks at 127 amongst total of 177 countries in 2005.

High economic growth facilitates reduction of poverty. Growth in production of goods and services leads to growth in incomes and, hence, to poverty eradication. As might therefore be expected, acceleration of economic growth in India has led to a marked reduction in poverty in recent decades. Compared to average economic growth rate of close to 3.5 per cent in the first three decades since Independence, the Indian economy moved to a higher growth trajectory experiencing an average growth rate of around 6 per cent during 1980s and 1990s, and in the most recent period, the growth rate has been hovering around 7 per cent. More importantly, per capita income growth has witnessed a spectacular rise to about 5.5 per cent in the recent years as against a rise of around 1-1.3 per cent in the three decades after Independence. Reflecting this there has been significant decline in poverty in India. Between 1977-78 and 1999-2000, the proportion of people living below the poverty line (BPL) came down from 51.3 per cent to 26.1 per cent. In absolute numbers, the reduction has been from about 330 million to 260 million during the comparable period.

It is important to note that with lower economic growth of the first three decades it was not possible to reduce the high levels of poverty that had existed in India for generations. However, the foundations of modern economic growth were laid in that period and we have observed significant growth acceleration since the 1980s. It is being increasingly recognized that eradication of poverty requires achievement of higher growth as it is only higher economic growth that can reduce poverty and provide sustainable economic security. No distribution can take place when there is nothing to distribute.

Human capital enhancement is essential to productivity growth. As higher physical capital investment takes place labour productivity is also enabled to grow. But such productivity can grow even faster with corresponding or even faster growth in human capital investment. Thus, per capita income growth is accelerated significantly by improvement in human development all round. Hence, we have a positive sum game: economic growth enables human development, and human development itself contributes to the acceleration of economic growth. Furthermore, for its own sake, in terms of augmenting people's own potential, human development is important.

Performance in Human Development—An Overview

Key indices of human development relate to measures of health and education. Life expectancy at birth in India has grown from about 32 years in 1951 to 62 years in 1996. In 2003, it was 63 years. The literacy rate in India also witnessed significant improvement since independence from 18 per cent in 1951 to 52 per cent in 1991, and further to 65 per cent in 2001. In 2003, life expectancy index for India at 0.64 was close to the world average of 0.70. The education index at 0.61 and GDP index at 0.56 were however farther away from the world averages of 0.77 and 0.75, respectively.

A perusal of the human development indicators across the States in India reveal that life expectancy does not exhibit significant variation across the States. In 2001-06, life expectancy at birth for males (all India average of around 64 years) varied from 59 years in Assam and Madhya Pradesh to around 70 years in Kerala and Punjab. For most of the States, the life expectancy at birth for males was in the range of 62 to 67 years. For the same period, life expectancy at birth for females (all India average of around 67 years) varied from 58 years in Madhya Pradesh, 60 years in Orissa to 72 years in Punjab and 75 years in Kerala. For most of the States the life expectancy at birth for females was in the range of 64 to 70 years. However, the National Human Development Report (NHDR) has revealed wide disparities in the level of human development across the States. States like Bihar, Uttar Pradesh, Madhya Pradesh, Rajasthan and Orissa had HDI close to just half of that of Kerala in 1981 (Table 1). The situation has improved since then. Besides Kerala, among the major States, Punjab, Tamil Nadu, Maharashtra, and Haryana have done well on HDI. In general, HDI is better in smaller States and Union Territories. In terms of the pace of development, Tamil Nadu, Rajasthan, Madhya Pradesh, West Bengal and Bihar improved their HDI significantly in the 1980s. In the 1990s this momentum was maintained in Rajasthan, Madhya Pradesh and Uttar Pradesh while it appeared to slow down in other less developed States. Nevertheless, state-wise analysis in the NHDR indicated a decline in such regional disparity during the last two decades. Further convergence can take place along with substantial improvement in the national human development index if efforts are focused on those states that have low levels of measured HDI. Strengthened policy measures and improvement in health, education and other aspects of rural development in these states will contribute greatly to the overall improvement in human development in the country.

It must be noted that inequalities across the States on HDI are less than the income inequalities in terms of per capita SDP (Graph 1). At a fundamental level, there is no conflict between economic growth and human development. Economic growth implies an improvement in the material well being of the people including better health, education and sanitation. However, the effect of economic growth on human development may be muted if the growth is not well distributed across all sectors and geographical areas. Even in a particular sector, the distribution of benefits of growth amongst all stakeholders in a just way is also important.

Table 1: Human Development Index for India—Combined

States	1981-Value	1981-Rank	1991-Value	1991-Rank	2001-Value	2001-Rank
Andhra Pradesh	0.298	9	0.377	9	0.416	10
Assam	0.272	10	0.348	10	0.386	14
Bihar	0.237	15	0.308	15	0.367	15
Gujarat	0.360	4	0.431	6	0.479	6
Haryana	0.360	5	0.443	5	0.509	5
Karnataka	0.346	6	0.412	7	0.478	7
Kerala	0.500	1	0.591	1	0.638	1
Madhya Pradesh	0.245	14	0.328	13	0.394	12
Maharastra	0.363	3	0.452	4	0.523	4
Orissa	0.267	11	0.345	12	0.404	11
Punjab	0.411	2	0.475	2	0.537	2
Rajasthan	0.256	12	0.347	11	0.424	9
Tamil Nadu	0.343	7	0.466	3	0.531	3
Uttar Pradesh	0.255	13	0.314	14	0.388	13
West Bengal	0.305	8	0.404	8	0.472	8
All India	**0.302**		**0.381**		**0.472**	

Source: National Human Development Report, 2001, Planning Commission, New Delhi.

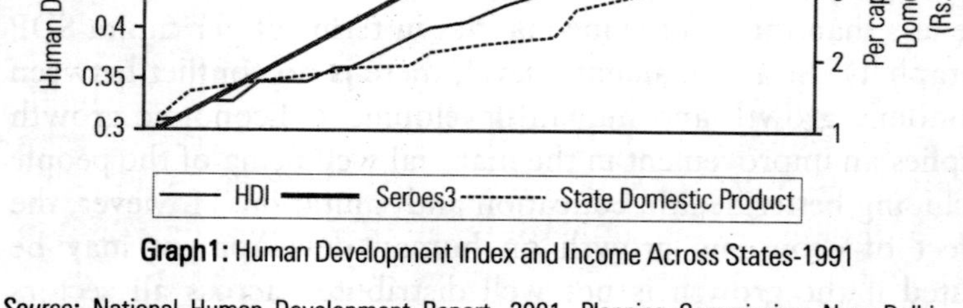

Graph1: Human Development Index and Income Across States-1991

Source: National Human Development Report, 2001, Planning Commission, New Delhi.

It turns out that the economically less developed States are also the ones with low HDI and economically better off States are the ones with relatively better performance on HDI. However, the relation between the HDI and the level of development does not show any correspondence among the middle-income States in the country. In this category of States, some States like Kerala, have high attainments of HDI, at the same time, there are States like Andhra Pradesh, or even West Bengal, where HDI values are not as high.

Finances of State Governments and Social Sector Expenditure

Progress on human development requires adequate provision of funds. State Governments are responsible for most public expenditures for the provision of social services including health and education. Furthermore, the States are responsible for most infrastructure services except for telecommunications, civil aviation, railways and major ports. They are also responsible for law and order. Thus, the ability of the States to spend on social services has important implications for human development.

As widely documented, States have experienced significant fiscal stress since 1998-99 due to a variety of factors. While factors like 5th Pay Commission recommendations, decline in Central transfers, increase in committed expenditure, such as, interest payments and pensions, and low economic growth rate account for the acuteness of the ailment, there are also underlying structural reasons for the persistence of fiscal deterioration. As evident from Table 2, average revenue deficit of all States combined as a percentage of GDP more than doubled from 0.71 during 1990-95 to 1.65 during 1995-2000. It increased further to 2.41 per cent during 2000-04. Similar movement was exhibited by the gross fiscal deficit (GFD) as well. This has had a significant deleterious impact on the States' social expenditures including on education and health. Developmental expenditure as a percentage of GDP had declined from 9.92 per cent during 1990-95 to 8.97 per cent during 1995-2000. Expenditure on social services in general and education and health in particular witnessed a fall as a percentage of GDP during the second half on the 1990s as compared to the first half. The fall in States' expenditure on education and health due to fiscal deterioration impeded their role in promoting human development.

Table 2: Deficit Indicators and Social Expenditure of States

(As Percentage of GDP)

Period	RD	GFD	Developmental expenditure	Social services expenditure	Education expenditure	Health expenditure
1990-95	0.71	2.82	9.92	4.88	2.62	0.81
1995-2000	1.65	3.45	8.97	4.84	2.59	0.75
2000-04	2.41	4.28	9.35	4.98	2.67	0.71
2004-05 RE	1.44	4.00	10.18	5.08	2.47	0.69
2005-06 BE	0.75	3.21	9.35	4.94	2.39	0.70

RE: Revised Estimates; BE: Budget Estimates.

Notes: RD: Revenue Deficit; GFD: Gross Fiscal Deficit; Education includes Sports, Art and Culture; Health includes Family Welfare.

With active initiatives of the States towards fiscal correction and consolidation, some signs of improvements have been visible in state finances in the recent period. The revenue deficit as a percentage of GDP came down to 1.44 in 2004-05 (RE) which is budgeted to further decline to 0.75 per cent in 2005-06. Similarly, GFD as a percentage of GDP was reduced to 4.00 per cent in 2004-05 from the average of 4.28 per cent in 2000-04 and is budgeted to decline further to 3.21 per cent in 2005-06. With improvement in state finances, there is a reversal of the trend of developmental expenditure also. The ratio of developmental expenditure to GDP increased to 10.18 per cent in 2004-05 compared to an average of 9.35 per cent during 2000-04. States' expenditure on social services witnessed similar movement during the comparable period. However, expenditures on health and education as a percentage of GDP, during 2004-05, still remain below the level of the 1990s and early 2000s. In 2005-06, development expenditure and social expenditure of the States as percentage of GDP are budgeted to be lower than the previous year.

New Initiatives

The Union Budget 2005-06 has provided a special focus on enhancing human capital investment in the country in an accelerated manner. Particular emphasis has been given to significant increases in allocations to the flagship schemes of Sarva Shiksha Abhiyan (SSA), National Rural Health Mission (NRHM), Employment Guarantee Scheme (EGS), Rural Electrification, and the like. Sarva Shiksha Abhiyan is the cornerstone of the Government's support in basic education for all children. The allocation for this programme has been enhanced to Rs. 7,156 crore in 2005-06 as against Rs. 3,057 crore in the previous year's budget. A non-lapsable fund called 'Prarambhik Shiksha Kosh' has been created for funding this programme. NRHM envisages strengthening primary health care through grass-root level public health interventions based on community ownership. Total allocations for the Department of Health and the Department of Family Welfare will be enhanced from Rs. 8,420 crore in the current year to Rs. 10,280 crore in the next year when NRHM will be launched. Increase in the funding is envisaged to finance NRHM and its components like training of health volunteers, providing more medicines and strengthening the primary and community health centre system. The allocation for the Integrated Child Development Scheme (ICDS) has also been enhanced significantly.

The Union Budget 2005-06 also proposed launching of a massive rural electrification programme beginning in 2005-06 with the objective of covering 1,25,000 villages in five years with high emphasis on the deficient States. Similarly, higher allocations have been made for provision of drinking water and sanitation facilities in rural habitations. Furthermore, a corpus of Rs. 8,000 crore was provided in the current year for the Rural Infrastructure Development Fund for improving the basic infrastructure in the rural India. The Pradhan Mantri Gram

Sadak Yojana (PMGSY) was launched in December 2000 as a 100 per cent centrally sponsored scheme to provide rural connectivity. It is funded by the diesel cess in the central road fund and through borrowings from domestic financial institutions and multilateral funding agencies. Without appropriate connectivity, it is difficult to bring about the kind of improvements envisaged for human development.

It is also important to note that following the recommendations of the Twelfth Finance Commission (TFC), it has been decided by the Government of India to provide specific grants for education and health to those States which are unable to spend adequately in these sectors because of deficiencies in fiscal capacity. TFC has recommended specific grants amounting to Rs. 10,171 crore to eight States for education and Rs. 5,887 crore to seven States for health over its award period of 2005-10. The grants for both the sectors are an additionality over and above the normal expenditure to be incurred by the States in these sectors. Furthermore, it recommended specific grants to local bodies amounting Rs. 25,000 crore meant to improve basic amenities, viz. water supply, sanitation, solid waste management, etc., which are expected to improve the quality of life both in rural and urban areas.

As regards States' initiatives, many States have embarked upon the path of fiscal correction and consolidation in the recent period. Increase in the Central transfers in the light of TFC recommendation has a comforting impact on State finances. With the debt relief benefits linked to enactment of the Fiscal Responsibility Legislation (FRL) by the TFC, there has been increasing incentive to observe fiscal discipline. As of now, while 15 States have already enacted FRL, 2 States have introduced the Bill and 2 more States have proposed to introduce FRL Bill in their respective Budget for 2005-06. As all the states put into effect fiscal improvement measures, their ability to make focused expenditures on health, education, nutrition and rural infrastructure will increase substantially.

Policy Options

For sustained social sector development, it is important that the high growth rate of the economy is maintained over a sustained period. Similarly, macroeconomic stability in terms of lower inflation is also critically important to protect the poor and vulnerable segment of the population. It is here that the role of the Reserve Bank and Monetary Policy becomes important. In addition, prudent fiscal management through expenditure prioritization and revenue augmentation is also essential. Thus, the recent initiatives by the State Governments to enact FRL is a welcome move.

...widespread and bold imposition of user charges on all non-merit goods is very important for revenue augmentation of the States. The pattern and organization of provision of public services in India has been done in such a way that the public has got used to not paying economic charges for these services. This includes key services, *inter alia*, power, water supply, irrigation and transport. The larger consumers of these services are typically the better off. Thus, appropriate levy of user charges also promotes better income distribution. Moreover, by strengthening the finances of the agencies that supply these services, it also enhances their capacity to improve and expand services and to serve the less well off. According to one estimate, the hidden subsidies on these non-merit goods amount to as much as 10.7 per cent of GDP on an annual basis. The combined fiscal deficit of the Centre and States in recent period is around 2 to 3 percentage points lower than this as a percentage of GDP. This highlights the need for augmenting revenue from user charges. However, it can be noted that with the poor quality of public services provided in India, the public is loath to pay higher charges. Hence, imposition of higher user charges has to be accompanied by perceptible improvements in the quality of services.

Apart from the above, rural connectivity plays a critical role for higher human development index. Evidence suggests that the states like Kerala, Tamil Nadu, Goa, Punjab and

Himachal Pradesh that have invested heavily in the provision of better rural connectivity are also better placed in terms of human development. Thus, better rural infrastructure and connectivity is necessary to accomplish developmental programmes related to human development. The direct benefits of rural development and connectivity in terms of better roads, electrification and communication also enable the doctors, health workers, and teachers to stay in the villages. Such personnel, who have with great effort and difficulty, educated themselves can scarcely be expected to stay in habitations that lack basic infrastructure and connectivity. They obviously have aspirations for their own children and families. Investment in social sectors like health and education is unlikely to be successful unless accompanied by complementary investment in rural infrastructure. The indirect benefits of better communication would be in terms of better dissemination of information on all aspects of agricultural products, particularly that on agricultural prices. Farmers suffer greatly from the large difference between market prices of agricultural products and farm level prices due to large transportation costs and lack of information. Thus, better rural connectivity in terms of both transportation and communication, will promote better price discovery and help in improving farmers' income and, hence, their human development. The extension of institutional credit, be it through banking institutions or microfinance institutions, will also be enabled by better rural connectivity. The improvement in farmers' income from better rural connectivity will itself improve their credit worthiness leading to lower applicable interest rate and further improvements in incomes and human development.

Besides, physical connectivity, economic empowerment of the vast segment of our population who have hitherto remained financially excluded is an important issue for human development. The programme of linking Self Help Groups (SHGs) with the banking system has emerged as the major microfinance programme in the country. At present, micro-finance institutions (MFIs) depend on the banks including commercial banks, Regional Rural Banks (RRBs) and cooperative banks to obtain finance according to the guidelines issued by the RBI. There is an increasing emphasis to promote MFIs which provide small-scale credit and other financial services to low income households and small informal businesses. Empowering MFIs will facilitate their role as intermediary between the lending banks and the beneficiaries. The Union Finance Minister, in his Budget Speech 2005-06, has prescribed that the commercial banks should appoint MFIs as the 'banking correspondents' to provide transaction services on their behalf.

In response, RBI appointed an Internal Group on Rural Credit and Micro-finance to look at the broad aspects of increasing "financial inclusion" and promoting MFIs....

The report has recognised both the supply and demand side constraints and circumstances that has made mass-scale financial inclusion elusive. Pragmatically appreciating that the large-scale expansion of physical infrastructure supported by multifarious policy initiatives could not accelerate the inclusion of a vast majority of rural population into the ambit of formal financial institutions, the report suggested that if "financial inclusion" is to be made a reality, we need to leverage socially active organizations and persons to work with people, particularly those with small means, empower them and bring them closer to financial services provided by the formal financial institutions on the one hand. On the other, these agencies and persons can be harnessed to bring aggregation of quantities so that the constraints of reaching large numbers of dispersed, far-flung and socio-economically disadvantaged clientele is minimized. To translate this into action, the report has suggested that banks may use the services of the "Business Facilitators" to bring people and the banks together without having to handle cash and the "Business Correspondents" who will bring them together and will also handle cash for providing doorstep services. NBFCs, NGO-MFIs, Section 25 Companies, Cooperative societies, corporate entities, post-offices, etc., can be identified as possible correspondents while even informal entities like farmers' clubs, NGOs, cooperatives, rural kiosks, socially conscious individuals, etc., can work as the facilitators....

Hedging and Indian Foreign Exchange Markets*

7

Ashima Goyal

Introduction

Capital markets provide facilities for intermediation of savings, allocation of investment, price discovery, pricing and hedging of risk; but they are subject to information imperfections, deviation from rationality due to psychological factors, excess volatility, and market manipulation, which interfere with the effective utilization of these facilities. Foreign exchange (forex) markets are especially volatile, and many countries have suffered currency crises. Hedging currency risk can both decrease the damage from volatility and make a currency crisis less likely. Yet risk is not covered in many forex transactions.

In this paper we examine hedging currency risk, what it is, why it tends to be incomplete, what regulatory and policy initiatives can improve this aspect of the functioning of financial markets. A common regulatory response to malfunctioning is to impose quantitative restrictions, but this impedes the development of financial markets, their functioning and potential benefits. Alternatively, it is possible for policy to improve incentives for hedging, through appropriate regulation, macroeconomic policy and attention to the psychology of market players. New technology facilitates such policy. The Indian experience with forex market reform illustrates the role of psychological factors, instruments, and inducements to hedge.

---

* I thank the Fulbright Foundation and Claremont Graduate University for hospitality while working on the ideas in this paper. Rijo John provided excellent research assistance and T.S. Ananthi helped with the tables.

Prolonged periods of predictable one-way movement in the rupee led to one-way bets in the market, and made it difficult to relax quantitative controls. As some two-way movement of the rupee started, inadequate hedging caused large losses. This impact, together with availability of more instruments for hedging, may, over time, tilt agents towards covering currency risk and away from making money from rupee movements.

What is Hedging?

Hedging is reducing an existent risk by eliminating exposure to price movements in an asset. Since the asset we focus on is currency, we define hedging to refer to any contract made in order to protect the home currency value of a transaction denominated in a foreign currency. The transaction could be an import or an export of goods or a foreign borrowing, and hedging offsets the exchange risk, or removes the exposure to fluctuation in currency value. Creating exposure in the opposite direction removes the effect on profits of currency movement in any one direction.

Speculation and *arbitrage* are fundamentally distinct from hedging but are often confused with the latter. Speculation is betting on a one-way price movement. Thus speculators aim to profit by taking a position in the market. If they believe a currency is going to depreciate they sell the currency, or take a position using derivative products. It is not linked to any risk from an existing transaction, but is rather "risk-taking attempts to profit from subjective predictions of price movements" (Shiller, 1993). It is sometimes argued that since speculators buy when prices are low and sell when prices are high, rational speculative activity stabilizes markets. But this does not always follow since speculators buy when there is a high probability of price appreciation and sell when the probability is low (Hart and Kreps, 1986), and thus can cause cumulative movements. Hedging, however, stabilizes markets. First, it removes potential shocks to balance sheets that can destabilize the financial system. Second, if hedging is complete at the aggregate level, long and short positions can be matched with less price volatility.

Arbitrageurs make use of riskless profit opportunities across markets. Their activity ensures that such opportunities do not persist, if there are no policy impediments or transaction costs, and thus stabilizes markets and improves their functioning. In forex markets if covered interest parity (the difference between spot and forward prices equals the interest differential) does not hold between any two currencies, arbitrageurs can make riskless profits.

Although there are a number of derivative products available in developed financial markets, hedging can also be accomplished informally, for example if an exporter takes a foreign loan. Then if the home currency depreciates he will gain in export income but lose as the home currency value of his debt rises, so that his net exposure is low. This is an example of portfolio diversification. Or he can enter into an insurance contract in which he pays a certain amount to a foreign party if the home currency appreciates but receives a payment if it depreciates. If the hedging contract is actuarially fair, its expected value is zero so that currency fluctuation has no systematic effect on profit.

A derivative is a financial instrument that derives its value from underlying more basic variables. The spot exchange rate is the basic variable we consider. Among formal instruments

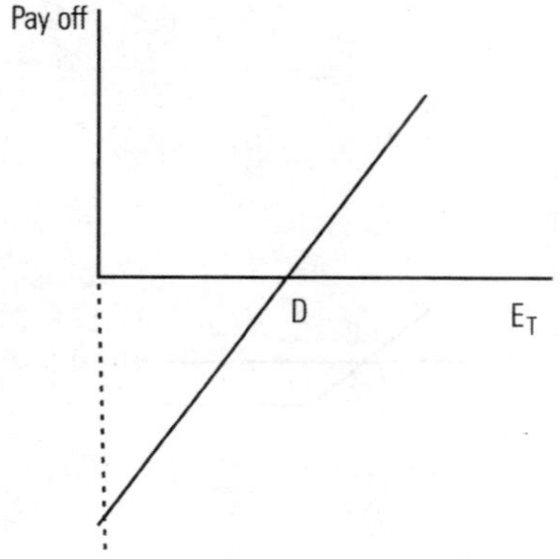

Figure 1 (a): Payoff from a long position in a rupee forward

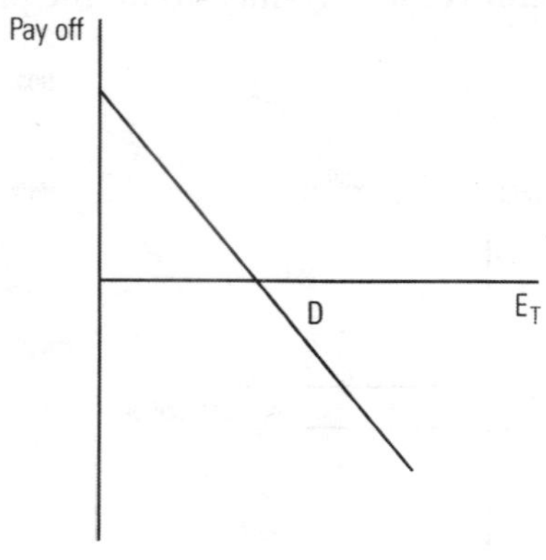

Figure 1 (b): Payoff from a short position in a rupee forward

available for hedging, retail forex traders tend to use foreign currency options, while banks and commercial traders use options, swaps and other complex derivatives that can continually be custom-designed between financial institutions and their clients and then traded in what are called over-the-counter (OTC) markets. Standardized derivatives are traded on exchanges.

Forwards and swaps are commonly used in India. A forward contract is an agreement between two parties to buy or sell a foreign currency at a certain specified *delivery price* and *maturity period*. The one who buys takes a *long position* and the seller is in the *short position*. At initiation the delivery price, D, is chosen to make the value of the forward contract zero to both parties, but if the spot foreign exchange rate, E_T, at the maturity T differs from D, there can be positive or negative payoffs. The payoff to the long position is E_T - D, since after buying foreign exchange at D the investor can sell it at the higher prevailing spot rate. The payoff to the short position is D - E_T, since if the spot rate is lower than the delivery price, the short investor can buy low at E_T and sell the contracted amount at the higher delivery price D.

Figures 1 and 2 show the payoffs from buy and sell positions respectively in rupee forwards. A forward contract removes uncertainty about the price of a future forex transaction

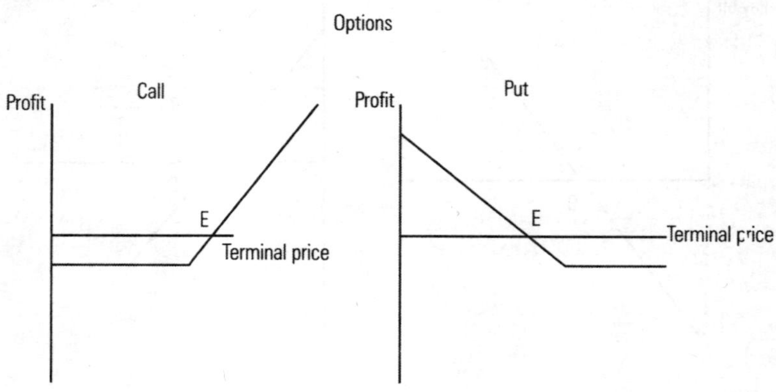

Figure 2(a): Profits from call options

Figure 2(b): Profits from put options

and thus hedges, but it also can be used to speculate on an expected future change in the spot exchange rate. A futures contract is like a forward except that it is normally traded on an exchange and therefore has certain standard features.

Since with forwards money has to be paid only when the actual transaction occurs, it is possible to speculate without current funds. Option leverage funds further, since they confer a right, but not an obligation, to undertake a transaction at a fixed exercise price. But this option comes at a small initial upfront payment the *option price*. Figure 2 (a) shows the profit from a call or buy option. The speculator will buy the currency only if the spot rate appreciates above the exercise price E and could make unlimited profits if it rose further. At a price below E he would choose not to exercise the option and loose the option price paid. The holder of a put or sell option would choose to exercise it only if the rate depreciated below the exercise price E, since he could then buy low and sell high at the fixed exercise price E, thus making profits. But an importer would be covered against having to pay more than E for foreign currency with a call option and an exporter would be sure he would not receive less than E with a put option, therefore hedging currency risk.

A simple currency swap transforms a loan in one currency into another. Both principal and interest payments can be swapped. Thus a swap is basically an agreement between two counterparties to exchange future cash flows according to a prearranged formula. It can be regarded as a portfolio of forward contracts. A swap allows the two counterparties to borrow according to comparative advantage and then realize gains from trade through the swap. Part of these gains may be hedging benefits. The financial institution warehousing the swaps will also monitor its exposure to different currencies and hedge its risks.

Thus the problem is that the same derivative can be used for hedging or for speculation. For example, a forward contract to buy foreign currency at a fixed rate will benefit an importer if the home currency depreciates, and remove a potential gain if the home currency appreciates, thus smoothing his profits.

But a speculator who expects the home currency to appreciate can buy the currency forward at a fixed rate and realize the future gain if it appreciates thus increasing the volatility of his profits, and raising risk. Speculation does contribute to market development, but can be counterproductive if it is the dominant transaction.

Buying and selling currency in the spot market requires an initial cash payment. Forward contracts require no such initial payment, but can lead to a gain or a loss in the future transaction depending on changes in the exchange rate. Therefore, forward markets provide extra leverage to a speculator in comparison to spot markets. Options increase the leverage further since they confer a right but not an obligation to make a transaction. For example, an importer who wants to hedge or a speculator who wants to make profits would exercise a call option to buy a foreign currency only if the currency had appreciated above this fixed rate, otherwise he lets the option expire, incurring a fixed cost, which is much lower than the value of the total transaction. The option has an initial cost but then does not require buying or selling currency either in spot or in the forward market. Therefore it provides even higher leverage, at a price.

Hedging is rarely complete, and this incompleteness adds to the instability of currency markets. The East Asian crisis is a prime example where large unhedged short-term foreign borrowing aggravated the currency crisis as sharp depreciations hurt company balance sheets. Domestic companies speculated on exchange rates remaining constant and borrowed heavily abroad in a context where domestic interest rates exceeded international rates.

Why is Hedging Incomplete?

Why do banks and firms take such risks? Is it irrational behaviour or is it a rational response to incentives arising from the structure of financial markets and government policy? There are psychological factors that undermine rational decisions. But an agent will rationally undertake too much risk under limited liability, when the government, debtors or shareholders absorb bankruptcy costs, while the promoter is able to protect his assets. He will also prefer to speculate rather than hedge if economic structure or policy induces an expected one-way movement in exchange rates. Rather than correct these underlying distortions that induce speculative behaviour, policy makers typically attempt to curb speculation through quantitative controls or restrictions on derivatives, which impede the development of financial markets. We further examine and evaluate these factors below.

The implications of behavioral psychology for inefficiency in financial markets have been studied systemically.[1] They shed light both on why forex risk is left uncovered, and why volatility in such markets exceeds fundamental volatility. One of the early contributions applying psychology to economics was that of Kahneman and Tversky (1979). Their prospect theory showed that people tend to prefer a sure outcome for a gain, but prefer an uncertain outcome with a small probability of a gain to a sure loss. Thus they are willing to undertake more risk when there is a loss involved. This implies a lower demand for hedging products that insure against loss, than is rational. But subsequent work shows the importance of "framing" for the outcome. If the same choice is translated in a way sensitive to psychological attitudes, risk-taking behaviour disappears.

Other psychological traits compound inefficiencies in forex markets. Past trends are expected to persist, leading to overreaction. The tendency towards mean reversion is systematically underrated (Shefrin, 2001). Trend following also occurs because people are trying to guess and follow what other people are going to do, rather than base decisions on fundamentals. Herd behavior is especially prevalent where fundamentals are uncertain as in forex markets. Such markets are subject to irrational bubbles, especially so in emerging market economies where conditions are less settled. The currency of a struggling emerging market economy maybe expected to always depreciate, while that of an economy growing rapidly and attracting large foreign inflows is not expected to depreciate.

1. Shefrin (2002) and Shleifer (2000) provide good recent surveys of this area.

Another frequent psychological factor in financial markets is low error bands; that is, judgments are made with overconfidence. Investors tend to believe in their own evaluations and luck, thus suffering from an "illusion of control" (Shiller, 1993). All this suggests that there may be a rōle for exchange rate policy in focusing market expectations.

Speculation also dominates if there are aspects of the financial structure that encourage taking too much risk, or if policy creates opportunities for speculation or arbitrage. Hedging may shade into speculation for firms when the probability of a one-way currency movement is high or own liability is too low. If firms want to use a hedging instrument to speculate, as they often do, they may enter into only one leg of a forex transaction. Thus, an exporter who expects to gain from a future depreciation of the home currency against a foreign currency when he receives his export proceeds, would not hedge against the expected depreciation, and may speculate further on it by making a forward contract or agreement to buy the foreign currency at a certain future rate for a certain price reflecting current lower prices.

Creditors normally set interest rates to cover expected default under bankruptcy, so that the risk free interest rate is lower. Moreover, bankruptcy imposes costs for the firm. The firm's objective is to minimize cost of borrowing. This is achieved if it is fully hedged so that bankruptcy does not occur. But if government guarantees the loan repayments and it is not required to cover bankruptcy costs[2] the incentive to hedge risks disappears. It then wants to make its residual value as low as possible since that goes to its debtors or to the government. Results are similar if laws make it difficult for creditors to recover loans giving a firm low bankruptcy costs. Limited liability for promoters or managers encourages more risk taking.

---

2. Burnside et al. (2001) demonstrates this rigorously for banks in the context of emerging market economy but the argument is more general and derives from limited liability leading to higher risk taking under asymmetric information.

The opportunity cost of hedging rises if domestic interest rates are much higher than international since borrowing becomes more costly. If an importer holds a dollar deposit as an informal hedge he sacrifices domestic high interest. If he has to borrow in domestic currency, he pays an additional higher interest rate at home. Similar considerations affect banks acting on behalf of retail trade. Banks will not hedge currency risk if exchange rates are fixed, but unless open exposure is strictly limited banks would arbitrage: take dollar deposits and make high interest domestic loans. If zero or low exposure is enforced, banks contribution to developing the forex market and discovering the value of the currency is limited. All this happens just when hedging is required more since expected depreciation also tends to be higher when high interest rates lower activity. The consequence is the overborrowing of unhedged loans abroad[3] as in East Asian countries prior to the crisis.

But why does a gap persist between domestic and foreign interest rates? It may be that foreign lenders are not perfectly informed, or are more optimistic about a country's prospects, and so are willing to lend at lower rates than cautious domestic monetary authorities allow. But unfortunately such an interest differential can provoke the depreciation policy makers fear, as in the Asian crises. Domestic interest rates exceeded international prior to the crisis.

There is the "original sin" argument that foreign creditors are not willing to share currency risk in emerging market economies (EMEs) so EME banks can borrow only limited amounts in domestic currency. They are forced to borrow in foreign currency and bear the currency risk (Hausman et al., 2002). But if original sin is a major factor why did foreign rates not cover default risk in some cases?

---

3. Jeanne (2003) points out that if domestic monetary policy is unstable and domestic interest rates rise very high, firms may borrow abroad to minimize default risk. Default would be certain for the firms after borrowing at high domestic interest rates but conditional on a devaluation occurring if loans are taken abroad.

Moreover, Burnside et al. (2001) presents evidence that markets, instruments and opportunities existed for hedging in East Asian countries prior to the crisis, although there were some restrictions on the use of currency derivatives, for example in Korea. It was possible for those who took foreign loans to lay off the currency risk. These markets certainly existed in a country like Sweden, which also had a twin crises in the early nineties. The failure was more of incentives to hedge. They also present evidence for Asian and European countries that before a twin crises both banks and firms held large net foreign liabilities. Even if banks hedge their own foreign exchange exposure, they are exposed to large indirect credit risk, from their client firms who have borrowed in foreign currency.

Individual hedging is incomplete also because hedging instruments offer incomplete cover. For example, hedging using future contracts is subject to basis risk because of unforeseen divergence between spot and futures prices, and the absence of a perfect match in timing between the hedge contract and the underlying transaction. The optimal hedge ratio, which minimizes the variance in the value of the hedged position, is less than one[4].

Finally, it is very expensive for markets to price and cover Peso risk, which is the small chance of a very large change in the exchange rate. Therefore financial institutions and firms normally leave it uncovered. They take a chance that since everyone would be adversely affected in a systemic crisis, governments and international institutions will come up with a rescue package.

4. It can be shown to equal the product of the correlation coefficient between the change in spot and the change in future prices with the ratio of the standard deviation of the change in spot price to the standard deviation of the change in future price during the life of the hedge (Chance, 1989).

Policy Responses

One reason regulatory authorities put restrictions on hedging is to curb speculation.[5] But with today's technology it is possible to distinguish between forex transactions that are for hedging and those whose aim is speculation. Hedging transactions are charged lower margins on modern exchanges and their tax treatment also differs. Margin requirements reduce the leverage that allows speculation to make markets volatile. Margins are marked daily and can be adjusted in times of excess volatility. Limits are also used in such conditions, thus preventing bubbles. These abilities imply regulators can focus on monitoring the use of derivatives, especially in times when markets are unstable, and not on banning certain derivatives. The latter prevents markets from developing and reduces potential instruments for hedging. Opportunities for profit lead to innovation so putting obstacles on the development of customized OTC hedging products should be avoided. Moreover, such obstacles are not very effective. Markets find ways around them. Miller (1986) points out that tax laws have often functioned as the bit of sand in the oyster producing the pearl of financial innovation.

Derivatives based on exchange rates are not subject to moral hazard since the latter are independent of the insider manipulation that can affect stock prices. But there is a basic inequity in forex markets and that is the superior information with the Central Bank (CB) and its dominance as a trader. Therefore for well-behaved forex markets credibility of CB policy is essential.

This credibility has a number of aspects. First, macroeconomic policy must not create instability; monetary

---

5. Authorities had a blanket suspicion of destabilizing speculative activity in Indian financial markets. They did not distinguish between types of transactions and times of excess volatility. These attitudes blacklisted traders and certain communities that specialize in trade. Politicians made speeches equating foodgrains traders to rats who eat grains and deserve to be shot. See Hardgrove (2004) for a study of the Indian Marwari community and the impact on their self-understanding and sense of identity. They were said to be gamblers but for example, the traditional gambling on the rains actually served to hedge against income loss.

policy has to be balanced and suited to the needs of the domestic cycle, with appropriate support from fiscal policy. Second, exchange rate policy must allow the exchange rate to track fundamentals. Most emerging market economies have some kind of managed floating, but whatever the regime, it must not prevent the nominal exchange rate from adjusting for inflation and productivity differentials with the rest of the world. Although fundamentals cannot be known with precision, an indicator that the real exchange rate is near its equilibrium value is if the current account deficit of the balance of payments does not exceed an amount that can be financed by stable, sustainable, long-term capital inflows. A short-term market indicator of equilibrium rates is the approximate equality of buyer-initiated and seller-initiated orders. Third, the tendency of CBs to create surprise inflation must be restrained. One way to do this is through a transparent inflation target. Since in low per capita income democracies the majority of voters dislike inflation, these pressures are sufficient to keep inflation low even with a less rigid medium-term inflation target.

If monetary policy is loose, the currency is expected to depreciate, and a capital outflow occurs; but if it is too tight also high interest rates harm activity and a capital outflow can provoke the depreciation it fears.[6] A limited two-way volatility of the exchange rate gives more freedom in adjusting interest rates to the needs of the domestic cycle, and can be consistent with trend depreciation if it is required. It can also help meet the inflation target if appreciation accompanies a temporary negative supply shock. The latter category of shocks, which include oil shocks and natural calamities, is common in emerging market economies.

Such an exchange rate regime decreases risk for banks by creating incentives for them and their customers to reduce currency exposure. It lowers the effect of exchange rate volatility on balance sheets and on cumulative spillovers. It reduces the

---

6. The latter set of circumstances occurs especially in emerging market economies, for example in Latin America in the eighties and East Asia in the nineties. But it is also at work in Europe with an overvalued Euro.

number of transactors who are affected by a change in the nominal exchange rate. Agents that have high exposure to currency fluctuations fall into three classes—exporters, importers, and banks and others such as foreign institutional investors (FIIs) who have borrowed or lent abroad. Exporters gain from a home currency depreciation and lose from an appreciation; therefore they would want to hedge against an appreciation and gain from a possible depreciation. With importers it is exactly the reverse. Debtors lose from home currency depreciation, since they require more of the home currency to cover their loan. They gain from an appreciation under which they can repay their loan with less home currency. Banks would hedge against depreciation of the local currency insofar as they are net borrowers from abroad. Their currency exposure also depends on the net exposure of their clients. FIIS stand to gain from local currency depreciation before they enter, and lose from it after. Therefore, even if any one class of agent does not want to completely insulate his income stream from currency fluctuations, and hedges only his downside risk, if regular two-way currency movements are expected, agents with opposite exposure would each hedge their downside risk. The aggregate market exposure would then be low. Even if hedging contracts are incomplete at the individual level, the aggregate level would have more complete hedging, making currency markets more stable.

Exchange rate announcements alone can affect exchange rates because of the CBs dominant position in the forex market, and the markets aversion to uncertainty and ambiguity, provided macroeconomic policy is credible. Ultimately a policy that strengthens fundamentals is credible. With such a policy, the CB can function as a natural social leader, minimizing volatility of exchange rates but creating sufficient volatility to sustain contracts. When the CB influences and limits exchange rate expectations, entry of noise traders is lowered. These are traders without knowledge of fundamentals and who base valuations on others actions. Such traders tend to gain from higher exchange rate volatility so their entry is lowered when this volatility is limited (Jeanne and Rose, 2002). Markets in derivative contracts require the presence of well-informed institutional actors and there are many of those in forex markets. Limited volatility is sufficient to encourage their activity.

The CB may be able to achieve its target nominal exchange rate just through the market if its announcement is credible. Initial intervention with the wind may enhance credibility. The intervention would be destabilizing, since the CB would buy the rupee when it signals a further appreciation and sell it when it wants it to depreciate. Since it would lose money if the opposite movement occurred, the intervention would be a credible signal of its intention. Market players would follow the signal since they would make speculative profits, for example as they sold a depreciating currency. They would not overreact because of the CB commitment to limiting the volatility. Noise traders or those bound by contracts or current requirements would lose. They would be providing the net rupee demand on the opposite side of the market. Since rupee supply would far exceed demand, the required depreciation would soon occur. A reversal of the CBs stance, switching from selling the rupee to buying it, for example, may be required if depreciation begins to exceed the required amount. This against the wind intervention implies the CB buys when low. Since it would also sell when high, in the opposite case if it wanted to stop rupee appreciation, it makes money across the two types of transactions. Since the time of intervention and its direction is random, following random supply shocks, there are incentives to hedge. Since the intervention is sterilized it implies money supply is not tied to the exchange rate and remains free to respond to the domestic cycle. CB buying or selling of the rupee, or its announcement of an expected direction of movement can alone initiate the change even without any change in the money supply. Since in an EME receiving large capital inflows the CB is always intervening or buying the currency to accumulate foreign exchange reserves and prevent a large appreciation only, some modification of this intervention is required to affect the required changes. On other occasions market driven movements in the exchange rate will continue to occur due to shocks to fundamentals or news from foreign markets; here stabilizing intervention may be required. But hedging encouraged by two-way volatility together with credible bounds on volatility will make markets more stable and reduce the extent of intervention required.

Exchange rate fluctuations affect each forex transaction and therefore the cash flow and value of a firm. Firms book profits within a year and these are reported in their balance sheets and affect market valuation, so they would respond by hedging more if two-way variations occurred within a year. Correct framing of hedging making it clear that it is not about reducing profit income but about eliminating risk and preserving wealth, would reinforce improved incentives for hedging[7] (Shiller, 1993). An opaque frame obscures the advantages of lower risk, while highlighting loss in expected profit. The frame should make it clear what is happening. Shefrin (2002) advocates the use of certain "magic words" in what he calls "hedonic editing". For example, while people may not want to reduce risk, they will be willing to "eliminate" risk. Psychology is required to defeat psychology!

A large loss can have such a traumatic effect that it leads to a permanent change in behavior. This is "anchoring" or "salience" when a particular event acquires looms large in mental landscapes and affects future decisions. The East Asian currency and banking crisis, where foreign borrowing without hedging had such drastic consequences, may have made agents more willing to hedge. "Social learning" also occurs from such

7. These matters are currently very imperfectly understood. Thus the finance director of a multinational reported to his board that we do not use hedging derivatives since the exchange rate is not our business, we want to focus on our core areas. But it is not covering exchange rate risk that will allow the exchange rate to affect their profitability. When the Indian rupee began showing some two-way movement, there were news reports that major software firms such as Infosys and Wipro would not be able to gain from depreciation because of the forward cover they had taken. The point is precisely that with hedging they can stop worrying about the impact of the rupee on their profits, and trying to make money from rupee movements. Instead, they can focus on their key activity, producing better software.

situations. People learn from each other or from social leaders and new habits of behavior get established.

Special characteristics of the forex market is the very large share of transactions due to dealers acting on behalf of the original transactors and intermediaries such as banks who may borrow abroad in order to lend in the home country. Dealers tend to acquire large positions, which they unwind slowly, leading to multiple transactions. There are large temporary inventory imbalances. The market is also decentralized, with no publicly announced price, so that expectations are heterogeneous. These features have led to analysis of the role of the market microstructure in determining exchange rates. Lyons (2001) argues that prices do not convey sufficient information about market conditions and the order flow is also a major indicator variable.

But rapid changes are occurring because of electronic exchanges and new institutions such as Continuous Linked Settlement (CLS), which started in 2002. CLS is a real-time settlement system, which functions as a central clearing house. It replaces the traditional mode of settling foreign currency trades in disparate modes over different time zones. By 2004, 11 currencies were eligible to be traded over CLS and it was well accepted in the inter-bank market. Although fixed costs of entering such a system are high, there is a large drop in funding requirements as volumes rise, suggesting that it will become more dominant over time. These changes tend to reduce the importance of order flow information, and will over time reduce the excessive size of forex transactions compared to those required by real trade or capital flows.

Figure 3 contrasts the relative size of forex markets in an EME and a developed country in 2000.[8] The percentage share of average daily global forex market turnover for typical EMEs ranged from 1 to 0.1 (out of 200 per cent) compared to

---

8. Calculated from BIS 2001, IFS 1995 & May 2002. Foreign inflows are measured as the current account deficit plus reserve gains. Merchandise trade is calculated as exports plus imports of goods and services (absolute values).

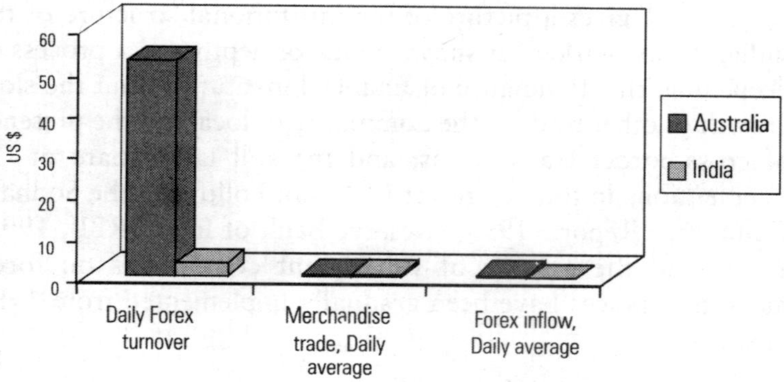

Figure 3: Forex Turnover Compared to Other Sources of Currency Transaction (2000-01)

90.4 per cent for the US in April 2001. In India daily forex turnover has grown from $2 billion to $3 billion over 1998-2001, and now compares favourably with many middle-income developing countries, although it is far below the figure for Australia (Figure 3).

Fund managers, who are becoming more active in forex markets, also tend to take positions on more fundamentals-based information, lessening the importance of noise traders who take decisions based on what others are doing (Gehrig and Menkhoff, 2005). A reduction in noisy trading will reduce excessive market volatility and turnover. All this will make CB intervention or announcements more effective.

Indian Forex Markets

Innovation is changing forex markets worldwide, but EMEs, many of which are emerging from closed regimes and repressed markets, have unique problems and opportunities. They have to decide the kind of market they want, and the shortest transition path. It takes time to develop market institutions but it is also possible, in some aspects, to leap to best practices. CBs have more leverage in thin markets. Development of Indian forex markets illustrates these arguments, and can offer valuable lessons for China, for whom moving to the more flexible exchange rate regime being essential for stability of the global payment system, is conditional on deeper forex markets.

Table 1 gives a picture of the institutional structure of the Indian forex market.[9] It shows a lack of depth and a process of deepening; the dominance of financial institutions but the slow growth of other traders; the dominance of local but the presence of cross-border transactions; and the still large share of CB interventions in total turnover (8-16%). Following the Sodhani Committee Report (1995) (Reserve Bank of India (RBI), 1995-2002, and the reports of subsequent committees on forex markets, changes have been gradually implemented from 1996 onwards.

Table 1: Aspects of the Indian Forex Market

Sl.No.	US $ Million FCY/INR1*	1998-99	2001-2002
1	Total spot turnover (sales + purchases)	333746	450157
2	Total CB intervention (sales + purchases)	55650	38580.8
3	2 as % of 1	16.67	8.57
4	Share of 1 due to interbank (%)	66.17	64.75
5	Share of 1 due to merchant (%)	33.83	35.25
6	Total forward as % of total spot	27.3	20.82
7	Total swap as % of total spot3*	97.04	149.63
8	Total spot (For April, 2001)2*	13946	30381.9
9	Share due to RDs (from CB survey) (%)	63.99	68.15
10	Share due to other financial institutions (%)	12.17	5.76
11	Share of non-financial institutions (%)	23.84	26.09
12	Share in total spot of local transactions (%)	90.4	95.98
13	Share in total spot of cross border transactions (%)	9.6	4.02
14	Total forex derivatives as % of total spot	—	0.06

Notes: (1) to (7) was calculated from RBI bulletins. The data were collected for all the months in the given years and summed up. Each year is taken from July to June.

(8) to (14) are figures for the month of April as is available in the Central Bank Surveys (BIS).

(9) to (14) are as percentage to (8); (14) which comprises OTC currency swaps and options was negligible for the year 1998-99.

1* All transactions involve exposure to more than one currency.

2* Excluding "tomorrow/next day" transactions.

3* A swap is considered to be a single transaction in that the two legs are not counted separately. Including "tomorrow/next day" transactions.

FCY: Foreign currency.

INR: Indian rupees.

RDs: Reporting dealers.

Liberalized regulations for forex derivatives were put together in the Foreign Exchange Management (Foreign Exchange Derivative Contracts) Regulations, 2000, and were

9. The material in this section is based on parts of Goyal (2005).

further amended in 2003. Although residents, non-residents and foreign institutional investors are all allowed to hedge, there are still restraints. Hedging is only allowed for genuine permissible forex transactions where there is no net receipt of premiums. RBI approval is required to hedge foreign currency loans or bonds. Commodity price risk can be hedged but oil and petroleum products are excluded (Regulation 6).[10] It is proposed to allow covered options. The RBI wants convergence in accounting standards for rupee and foreign currency derivatives and between on-balance sheet and off-balance sheet items. Such clarity will make it possible to distinguish between hedge and trade transactions and remove restrictions on the former (Gopinath, 2005).

New technology has been used to offer an efficient trading platform that mitigates risk, and offers netting and operational benefits. The Clearing Corporation of India (CCIL) launched a transparent forex dealing system, FX-Clear, for inter-bank trade through order matching and negotiation mode in August 2003. Although it has not been able to displace the favorite but much more expensive Reuters, maximum daily traded volume increased from USD 24 million on August 11, 2003 to 16,088 million on April 30, 2004. Even in the initial periods netting factors higher than 80 per cent have been achieved. This multilateral offsetting slashed individual member fund obligations. It is proposed to extend settlement guarantees for rupee dollar forward transactions from the trade date which will lower the risk due to large outstanding forward positions. Thus market developments continue.

Incentives for Hedging

Indian exchange rates depreciated steadily from the mid-90s to March 2002. This gave way to steady appreciation until March 2004. Some two-way movement occurred in the

---

10. The ban on this and on hedging indirect forex exposure is a constraint. The rise in oil prices has benefited firms which were hedged against the rise. Southwest Airlines made profits in 2004-05, when most American airlines were making losses. One major reason was that hedges had capped oil prices at around $30 for the airlines.

following year, although expectations were of trend appreciation. Therefore, forex transactions should have changing effects on firms and financial institutions in this time window. Foreign exchange fluctuations impact on a firm in different ways. Cash inflows due to future foreign currency receivables, or cash outflows due to future payables, give rise to transaction exposure. Collectively these, together with a changing economic environment, add up to the economic exposure. It measures how changes in the exchange rate affect the value of the firm (the discounted present value of all future expected cash flows). Hedging individual transactions helps to manage economic exposure, but the latter involves other more general strategic decisions such as location decisions. The affect of exchange rate fluctuations on the consolidated financial statements/ accounts is known as accounting or translation exposure. It is not the same as economic exposure which captures the direct effect on cash flows. Moreover, accounting exposure can differ with different translation methods. However, since in our current exercise we only want to get an idea of the size of the impact of exchange rate fluctuations and for any systematic change in the effect in this period, looking at accounting exposure is an adequate first step. We ask if the exchange rate reversals affected the profit and loss and cash flow accounts of firms and banks in India,[11] or did inducements to hedge currency risk match the relaxation in forex regulations?

---

11. There is some variation in accounting practices, but the Tata Motors Annual Report 2004-05, gives typical practices for firms: "Transactions in foreign currencies are recorded at the exchange rates prevailing on the date of the transaction. Foreign currency monetary assets and liabilities are translated at year end exchange rates. Exchange difference arising on settlement...are recognized as income or expense in the year in which they arise," (Tata Motors, 2005, p.74). There are exceptions in the treatment of acquisition of fixed assets. The Bank of Maharashtra (2005) records balances in Nostro Accounts, Outstanding Forward Exchange Contracts, Foreign Currency Deposits, etc., at market related notional rates which are translated into the official exchange rate at the Balance Sheet date and the effect shown in the "Profit and Loss Account" for some categories and in "Other Liabilities/Other Assets Account" for others. While the accounting standard AS-11 requires

Tables 2 and 3 show the effects on a small sample of net importer and exporter IT firms, Indian private, public and foreign banks. Net income from foreign exchange transactions was higher for net exporting software firms in 2002 when the rupee was depreciating while hardware companies, who are net importers, benefited more when the rupee was appreciating. Loss on forex transactions was zero for all companies in all the years considered,[12] but there were losses reported in the cash flow account. Annual reports for 2005, which give results for 2004, the year of two-way movement in exchange rates, were not available for most of the companies in the Tables. A few companies, for which the results were there, reported either smaller gains or losses.[13] Thus even if companies have not begun to hedge, these higher losses may induce them to hedge. There were reports that companies had created unhedged dollar liabilities of about 30 billion dollars to benefit from expected rupee appreciation through synthetic derivative contracts with banks. There was fear of a panic rush to cover their positions in the forward market as the rupee continued to depreciate in the latter half of 2005. But such a reversal from expected movements will help shift firms from speculation to hedging.

Banks are also foreign exchange dealers and therefore regularly earn income from providing forex services. They can borrow abroad within limits to lend in the domestic market. Table 3 shows that forex earnings remained high through the

---

exchange rate effects to be reported in the profit and loss account Schedule VI of the Companies Act requires these effects to be accounted only through the balance sheet. These anomalies need to be resolved to allow more consistent and continuous assessment and disclosure of currency risk.

12. Very few of these companies had any foreign borrowing, but this is changing. Blue chips began to borrow abroad in the nineties, but now even mid-cap companies are following. As tightening Indian interest rates implied foreign loans continued to be cheaper, 2006 saw a spurt in borrowings aboard through instruments such as Foreign Currency Convertible Bonds (FCCBs).

13. These companies include Infosys, Grasim, Raymond, and Tata Motors. The relationships can be tested econometrically once a larger sample is available.

period both in the period of trend depreciation and trend appreciation. The foreign banks aggressively use derivatives while Indian banks are just beginning—although their forex business is rising steeply. The Table shows income from forex to be rising steeply for Indian banks while it actually fell for the smaller foreign banks. It maybe that the latter's facility with the speculative use of derivatives backfired when an unexpected reversal occurred in the exchange rate.

Table 2: Effect of Exchange Rate Fluctuations on Net Importers and Net Exporters in India

	Net income from forex (Profit and Loss Account) as percentage of Profit after tax			Foreign exchange gain/loss (Cash Flow Account) as percentage of profit after tax		
	March-2002	March-2003	March-2004	March-2002	March-2003	March-2004
Exchange rate, appreciation(+), depreciation (-)	-4.6	2.6	8.5			
Software companies (net importers)						
I-Flex Solutions Ltd.	5.5	0.0	0.0	-2.1	0.7	-6.2
Infosys Technologies Ltd.	1.6	1.8	1.6	-1.6	-0.1	0.5
Larsen & Toubro Infotech Ltd.	0.0	0.0	0.0	-3.4	4.2	15.4
Polaris Software Lab Ltd.	6.9	0.0	0.0	-1.6	-0.4	0.2
Satyam Computer Services Ltd.	11.5	0.0	0.0	0.0	5.1	3.3
Siemens Information Systems Ltd.	10.6	0.0	6.3	0.1	3.3	-3.8
Syntel Ltd.	0.0	0.0	0.0	0.0	1.2	5.3
Tata Sons Ltd.	0.0	0.0	3.4	-0.2	-0.2	-1.0
Wipro Ltd.	2.5	3.4	2.5	-1.3	-3.4	-1.5
Hardware companies (net exporters)						
CMS Computers Ltd.	0.0	0.0	0.0	0.0	0.0	0.0
HCL Infosystems Ltd.	0.0	0.0	9.6	1.5	4.2	-3.2
International Electron Devices Ltd.	0.0	0.0	Na	0.0	0.0	Na
Lipi Data Systems Ltd.	0.8	0.0	Na	0.0	0.0	Na
PCS Technology Ltd.	0.0	3.1	37.7	0.0	0.0	0.0
Redington (India) Ltd.	10.5	12.8	Na	0.0	0.0	Na
Savex Computers Ltd.	0.8	0.8	2.3	0.0	0.0	0.0
Spice Net Ltd.	0.0	0.0	25.7	0.0	-2.9	-0.7
TVS Electronics Ltd.	0.0	0.0	0.0	0.0	0.0	0.0
VXL Instruments Ltd.	46.9	0.0	0.0	0.0	0.0	0.0

Source: Calculated from CMIE Prowess Data Base, 2005, for company data, and www.rbi.org.in for exchange rate data.

Table 3: Effect of Exchange Rate Fluctuations on Banks in India

Banks in India	Income from forex (Rupees crores)		
	March-2002	March-2003	March-2004
ABN-Amro Bank N.V.	59.24	103.12	131.47
American Express Bank Ltd.	40.36	36.18	25.63
Bank Muscat SAOG	1.36	1.67	NA
Bank of America National Trust & Savings Association	31.83	13.4	19.45
Bank of Bahrain & Kuwait BSC	2.6	2.04	1.06
Citibank NA.	124.24	142.4	212.73
ICICI Bank Ltd.	129.33	199	303.69
State Bank of India	37.3	10.24	192.63
Bank of India	407.64	463.57	503.04

Source: CMIE Prowess Data Base, 2005.
Note: The first six banks are private foreign banks, the seventh a private bank, and the last two public sector banks.

Table 3 reports absolute levels of income from forex transactions, but the average ratio of these to profits after tax was 71 per cent, far higher than for firms. But profits are only a fraction of forward exchange contracts.[14] There were arbitrage opportunities because of gaps between domestic and foreign interest rates. The RBI relies on exposure limits to control arbitrage but these are not very effective because of the leverage the modern derivatives provide. Therefore, unexpected changes in exchange rates and removal of interest differentials may help induce banks to hedge more fully. They will aid the required change in mindsets.

Conclusion

We have examined what hedging of currency risk is, how it differs from speculation or arbitrage, how it is done, and why it tends to be incomplete. The reasons for the latter are incentives due to exchange and interest rate policy, and

14. Losses on forex transactions were zero for all years for all banks in Table 3, except Bank Muscat SAOG which made a loss of Rs. 0.25 crores in 2002. State Bank of India had a loss on the cash flow account of Rs. 6 crores. Bank of Maharashtra's profit on exchange transactions (profit and loss account) rose in 2004 compared to 2003. In the latter year it had made a minor loss of Rs. 544,000 on exchange transactions compared to profit which exceeded 20 crores, and its liabilities on account of outstanding forward exchange contracts rose over the two years. These profits were only about 0.3 per cent of the outstanding liabilities.

regulations; psychological attitudes; special features of forex markets including uncertainty in fundamentals and a tendency to overreact. But policy responses that have tried to stifle markets have not worked. We argue that a better feasible mix would combine better incentives for hedging through appropriate interest and exchange rate policy with market microstructure reform to improve hedging avenues, and discourage speculation. Credible Central Banks would be able to focus market expectations, and work with markets.

The issue is especially important for EMEs since they are the more vulnerable to currency crises. Indian experience in reform of forex markets shows the greater availability of instruments for hedging, and more incentives to hedge due to the exchange rate policy followed. But these changes are too recent to affect the psychological propensity to profit from an expected one-way trend in the exchange rate. Firms caught with large synthetic dollar liabilities as the rupee begins an unexpected depreciation will help to drive home the lesson should begin to sink home that short-term changes in the rupee can be sudden, unexpected, and in a direction opposite to the long-term trend.

Therefore, the wise businessman will cover his currency exposure and become immune to rupee surprises. Markets will remain incomplete but a combination of appropriate monetary policy and financial deepening can "reduce" risks as agents become willing to "eliminate" risk.

REFERENCES

Burnside, C., Eichenbaum, M. and Rebelo, S. (2001): "Hedging and Financial Fragility in Fixed Exchange Rate Regimes", *European Economic Review* 45: 1151-1193.

Chance, D. (1989): *An Introduction to Options and Futures*, Orlando, Fla.: Dryden Press.

Gehrig, T. and Menkhoff, L. (2005): "The Rise of Fund Managers in Foreign Exchange: Will Fundamentals Ultimately Dominate?", *The World Economy*, 28 (4): 519-540.

Gopinath, S. (2005): "Recent Developments in Forex, Money and G-sec Markets: Account and Outlook", address at the 16th National Forex Assembly at Kochi, August 13, 2005, available at www.rbi.org.in.

Goyal, A. (2005): "Reducing Endogenous Amplification of Shocks from Capital Flows in Developing Countries", report as part of project on *Macroeconomic Policy Challenges of Low Income Countries* available at http://www.gdnet.org/pdf2/gdn library/global research projects/macro low income/Goyal.pdf.

Hardgrove, A. (2004): *Community and Public Culture*, New Delhi: Oxford University Press.

Hart, O.D. and Kreps, D.M. (1986): "Price Destabilising Speculation", *Journal of Political Economy,* 94 (5): 927-952.

Hausman, R., Eichengreen, B. and Panizza, U. (2002): "Original Sin: The Pain, the Mystery and the Road to Redemption", mimeo, November, 2002.

Jeanne, O. (2003): "Why do Emerging Market Economies Borrow in Foreign Currency?" *IMF Working Paper,* WP/03/177.

Jeanne, O. and Rose, A.K. (2002): "Noise Trading and Exchange Rate Regimes", *The Quarterly Journal of Economics*, CXVII (469): 537-570.

Lyons, R.K. (2001): *The Microstructure Approach to Exchange Rates*, Cambridge, MA: MIT Press.

Miller, M. (1986): "Financial Innovation: The Last Twenty Years and the Next", *Journal of Financial and Quantitative Analysis* 21: 459-471.

Shefrin, H. (2002): *Beyond Greed and Fear: Understanding Behavioral Finance and the Psychology of Investing*, Oxford: Oxford University Press.

Shiller, R.J. (1993): *Creating Institutions for Managing Society's Largest Economic Risks*, Clarendon Lectures in Economics, Clarendon Press: Oxford.

Data Sources:

Annual Reports of Bank of Maharashtra (2005), Grasim (2005), Raymond (2005), Tata Motors (2005); BIS, Central Bank Surveys; IFS (IMF); CMIE Prowess and Capitaline Data Base (2005); RBI (Reserve Bank of India) Bulletins, Reports and website www.ri.org.in.

Is Indian Stock Market More Volatile in Reform Period?: Evidence from E-GARCH Model*

Ranjan Kumar Dash

INTRODUCTION

Stock market is considered as most efficient in allocating scarced capital to its highest-value users. Theoretically, it is proved that stock market helps to increase savings and investment in an economy, which is vital for economic growth. It is also pointed out that stock markets help to reduce risk by diversifying risk across a variety of assets. Thus, it has direct implication in reducing cost of capital which in turn spurns investment in the economy. In order to serve these purposes, stock markets need to be deep, efficient and stable. Hence, volatility and efficiency are very important aspects of stock markets which ultimately determine the effectiveness of the stock market in economic development.

Volatility is considered as a very important indicator of stock market development because, it has implications for investment, corporate financing and financial stability in the economy. For example, excess volatility weakens investor's confidence which, results in reduction in investment. Lessons from financial crisis reveal that financial asset price variability has the potential to undermine financial stability of an economy. As volatility increases, risk also increases simultaneously. So understanding volatility and its magnitude is central to risk management in the economy. Romar (1990) suggested that increased uncertainty associated with financial distress was one

* I am grateful to my supervisors Dr. N. Shanta and Dr. K. Pushpangadan, for their comments and suggestion. Author can be contacted via e-mail-rkumardash@yahoo.com

of the driving forces behind great depressions. Empirical literature also shows that volatility affects corporate financing. Schill (2003) examining the relationship between volatility and corporate financing for US, found that during the period of above normal market volatility, results in 21 per cent decline in the number of IPO dollar raised. So increased market volatility generates greater underwriting fees and hence results in IPO underpricing. Relationship between volatility and economic variables are shown below.

Excess volatility → Economic uncertainty → Market risk ↑→ Financial instability ↑→ Cost of capital ↑→ Reduction in investment → Economic growth↓.

So the objective of this paper is to estimate time varying volatility and its persistence in Indian stock market both in pre- and post-liberalisation period. Basically, we have two questions to address:

(1) Does Indian Stock Market volatility change through time and particularly, is it more volatile in liberalisation period?

(2) Is it possible to find a relationship between changes in stock market volatility and stock market reforms?

In the asset pricing literature volatility refers to asset price variability. Stock price changes following new information hitting the market. It should however, be noted that discontinuity in price movements in order to reach a new equilibrium price warranted by new information is a feature of information efficient market.[1] But excessive volatility or "noise" trading undermines the usefulness of stock prices as a signal about the true intrinsic value of firm. It has large consequences, which we have already discussed.

1. A distinction is made between: (a) weak efficiency, where the market price includes all the information contained in historical prices; (b) semi-strong efficiency, where the market price includes, in addition to information in historical prices, other public information; and (c) strong efficiency, where the market price reveals both public and private information.

The layout of the paper is as follows: section II provides the theoretical background. Section III outlines literature review. Section IV presents methodology and data source. Results and conclusion are reported in Section V.

SECTION II

Theoretical Background

If integration with the world markets makes the equilibrium process more efficient for stocks in emerging markets, it is reasonable to expect a drop in stock market volatility and a concomitant drop in expected returns. It is argued that foreign investors are quick to react to changes in short-term economic outlook in emerging economies, making unrestricted capital flows very volatile. This volatility of capital flows may increase the volatility of the stock market. According to finance theory, stock market volatility could increase or decrease when markets are opened up (see for example Bekaert and Harvey, 1997, 2002 and 2003). Markets may become informationally more efficient leading to higher volatility as price quickly reacts to relevant information; also speculative capital may induce excess volatility. On the other hand, in the pre-liberalisation process, there may be large swings from fundamental values leading to higher volatility. After liberalisation, the gradual development and diversification of the markets could lead to lower volatility. So there are conflicting reports about the impact of financial liberalisation on volatility.

A model was proposed by Tauchen and Pitts (1983) and subsequently used by Kwan and Reyes (1997), which could explain the impact of financial liberalisation on stock market volatility. The model was follows:

Assume that there are J active traders in the market. Within the day, the market passes through a sequence of distinct Walrasian equilibria. The movement from the (i-1)st to the ith equilibrium in a given day is caused by the arrival of new information to the market. The desired net position, Q_{ij} of trader j at the time of the ith equilibrium is assumed to be a linear function of the following form:

$$Qij = \alpha\ [P^*_{ij}-P_i]\ (J= 1, 2....J) \tag{1}$$

Where $\alpha > 0$ – Constant

P^*_{ij} = jth trader's reservation price

P_i = current market price

A positive value for Q_{ij} represents a desired long position in a contact while negative value represents a desired short position. Equilibrium requires that the following holds true:

This implies that the average of the reservation price clears the market:

The price change can then be written as:

$$\sum_{J=1}^{j} Q_{ij} = 0 \tag{2}$$

$$Pi = 1/J \sum_{i=1}^{j} P^*_{ij} \tag{3}$$

$$\Delta P = 1/J \sum_{J=1}^{j} \Delta P^*_{ij} \tag{4}$$

Where $P^*_{ij} = P^*_{ij} - P^*_{i-1}$, j is the increment to the jth trader's reservation price.

Assuming a variance—component model with an information component that is common to all traders, φ_i, and one that is specific to the jth trader, ψ_{ij}, Equation (4) can be written as:

$$\Delta Pi = \Phi_i + 1/J \sum_{J=1}^{j} \varphi_{ij} \tag{5}$$

The first two components of the price change are then derived as the following:

$$E\ [\Delta p_i] = 0 \tag{6}$$

Equation (7) tells us that other things being equal, an increase in the number of traders (J) tends to

$$Var\ [\Delta p_i] = \sigma^2_{\varphi} + \sigma_2/J \tag{7}$$

reduce the stock price variance. On the other hand increase in the variance of information sets ($\sigma^2\phi$) available to traders tends to raise the stock price variance. The number of traders (like FIIs) increases in the stock market following opening of a stock market. At the same time information set available to traders also increases.[2] So, when number of traders increase, it reduces the volatility of stock price whereas when information set available to traders increase, it raises the stock price volatility. The final outcome depends on relative strength.

SECTION III

Literature Review

Considerable research has focused on stock market liberalisation and stock market volatility (e.g. Bekaert and Harvey 1997, 2000, Bekaert et al. 2002a, De Santis and Imrohoroglu 1997, Huang and Yang 1999, Aggarwal et al. 1999, Kim and Singal 2000, Kaminsky and Schmickler 2003 and Edwards et al. 2003). For example, De Santis and Imrohoroglu (1997) study the behaviour of volatility in some emerging countries and the effect of liberalisation of financial markets. They find significant evidence for time-varying volatility and different effect of liberalisation on volatility across countries. Especially, they find that volatility decreased after liberalisation.

Huang and Yang (1999) analyse the impact of financial liberalisation on stock price volatility in ten emerging markets. Taking as reference the dates of financial market liberalisation from De Santis and Imrohoroglu (1997), they show that the unconditional volatility of the stock markets in three of the countries (South Korea, Mexico and Turkey) increased after liberalisation, whereas it significantly decreased in another four countries (Argentina, Chile, Malaysia and the Philippines). However, the conditional volatility of the markets of Brazil, Korea, Thailand and Turkey experienced a significant increase while that of the remaining six countries experienced a decrease

2. Financial liberalisation allows domestic stock market to integrate with other stock markets. So, volatility of domestic markets affected through the transmission effect and contagion effects of financial crisis.

after liberalisation. In a recent paper, Kim and Singal (2000) analyse changes in the level and volatility of stock returns around the opening to international capital markets. The result reveals that opening of the markets is good for domestic investors. Stock price rise while the volatility tends not to increase.

Financial liberalisation hypothesis predicts a decrease in volatility in asset price in the post-reform period. But the empirical findings in this regard suggest a mix conclusion. Singh (1993), Grabel (1995), Levine and Zervos (1998), Kamminsky and Schumkur (2001, 2002), Nilson (2002), and Edwards et al. (2003) found that financial liberalisation increases stock market volatility. Studies, which do not find any significant impact of financial liberalisation on volatility, are De Santis and Imorohoroglu (1994), Kim and Singal (1997), Richards (1996), and Bekaert and Harvey (2000). In Indian context, early studies by Samal (1997) and Pal (1998) found that FIIs investment in Indian stock market is the major source of volatility. Another study by Batra (2004) suggests that stock market volatility is actually marginally lower in liberalised period.

While the predictions of theoretical models that analayse the impact of financial liberalisation on volatility is at best ambiguous, considerable literature exists that highlights the significant increase in volatility following reforms. Our study gives additional empirical support to the financial liberalisation and volatility hypothesis. So the objective of the paper is to estimate time varying volatility in pre- and post-liberalisation period.

SECTION IV

Methodology

Beginning with the mean variance analysis of portfolio and asset returns, volatility has become central to much of modern finance theory. In recent times, empirical studies involving high-frequency financial time series data have focused on volatility of asset returns. It has been observed that the asset returns exhibit changes, which are not independent over time. Rather, large changes tend to be followed by large changes of either sign and small changes tend to be followed by small changes (Mandelbrot 1965, Fama 1965 and French et al. 1987).

It is now a well-established fact that stock market volatility is a non-constant stochastic process with a non-negligible degree of persistence—if stock market volatility is high today, it tends to be high also during near feature. This observation has received much attention from the financial profession due to its implication for asset pricing and portfolio management. The changing volatility and, particularly, its persistence have macroeconomic implication, as we have discussed in the beginning of this paper.

The main objective of modeling temporal variation in variance of return distributions has been drawn from the time varying second order moments. The basis for this has been the fact that a series may be stationary when unconditional variance is constant, but when the variance conditional upon the information set changes over the time, the series becomes non-stationary. For example, if security price follows an Autoregressive (AR) process, the long-run variance is constant but the variance at time t depends on the variance at time t-1. Exploiting the idea of time varying variances, a class of models charactersing such conditional variance has emerged. The first such model was introduced by Engel (1982), known as Autoregressive Conditional Heteroscedasticity (ARCH). A typical ARCH model allows the conditional variance of the error term to vary over time, in contrast to the standard time series regression models which assume a constant variance. So the ARCH model allows the conditional variance to depend on the past squared residuals in that variance period t and is modeled as a constant plus a distributed lag on the squared residual terms from previous period. Consider following AR (1) model,

$$R_t = \delta + \psi R_{t-1} + u_t \quad (1)$$

Where, R_t = return at period t

R_{t-1} = return at period t-1

u_t = error term.

Equation 1 tells us that return in period t depends on its one period past value. The key idea of ARCH is that the variance of u_t at time t (σ^2) depends on the size of the squared error term at time t-1, that is on u^2_{t-1}. So

$$Var(u_t) = \sigma^2 = \gamma_0 + \gamma_1 u^2_{t-1} + v_t \tag{2}$$

Where, v_t is a white nose process. If the value of γ_1 is equal to zero, the variance is simply constant γ_0. Equation (2) is called an ARCH (1) process. But by generalising it we can write for ARCH (p) process. Thus, an ARCH (p) process can be written as

$$Var(u_t) = \sigma^2 = \gamma_0 + \gamma_1 u^2_{t-1} + \gamma_2 u^2_{t-2} + \ldots\ldots + \gamma_q u^2_{t-q} \tag{3}$$

If the values of $\gamma_{1,}\ \gamma_{2,....}\ \gamma_q$ is equal to zero, the variance is simply constant γ_0. Otherwise, the conditional variance of u_t evolves according to the autoregressive process given by equation (3).

The ARCH formulations have several extensions. The most prominent of them has been the genaralised ARCH or GARCH model (Bollerslev 1986), which explains variance by two distributed lags, one on past squared residuals and the second on lagged values of variance itself to capture long-term influences. That is conditional variance is an ARMA process. Now let the error process be such that

$$u_t = e_t h_t^{1/2} \tag{4}$$

Where, $e_t \sim (0, 1)$

$$h_t = \sigma^2_t = \omega + \alpha e^2_{t-1} + \beta h_{t-1} \tag{5}$$

$$h_t = \omega + \sum_{i=1}^{q} a_i e^2_{t-i} + \sum_{i=1}^{p} \beta i h_{t-1} \tag{6}$$

Equation (5) represents GARCH (1, 1) process and equation (6) represents GARCH (p, q) process. Now h_t is the conditional variance, which follows an ARMA process. Now equation (5) allows us to capture various dynamic structures of conditional variance. The size and significance of α indicates the magnitude of the effect imposed by the error term (u_{t-1}) on the conditional variance (h_t). In other words, the size and significance of α implies the presence of ARCH process in the error term. This is called volatility clustering. The significance of β is that it has information about the market structure in general as well as the information influencing the stock prices. The sum of $\alpha + \beta$ represents the change in the response function of shocks to volatility per period. If $\alpha + \beta = 1$, a current shock persists indefinitely in conditioning the future variance. If $\alpha + \beta > 1$, then the response function of volatility increases with time. If $\alpha + \beta < 1$, this means that shocks decay with time, and the closer to unity unit value of persistence measure, the slower is the decay rate.

The economic interpretation of the ARCH effect in stock markets has been provided within both micro and macro frameworks. According to Bollerslev et al. (1992) and other studies, the ARCH effect in stock returns could be due to clustering of trade volumes, nominal interest rates, dividend yields, money supply, oil price index, etc. The GARCH models have been found to be valuable in modeling the time series behaviour of stock returns (French et al. 1987; Chou 1988; Akgiray 1989; Ballie and Degennaro 1990; Koutmos 1992; Kim and Kon 1994; and Tunaru 2002).

The GARCH models have important limitations. For example, researchers beginning with Black (1976) have found evidence that stock returns are negatively correlated with changes in return volatility—i.e. volatility tends to rise in response to "bad news" and fall in response to "good news."[3]

GARCH models, however, assume that only the magnitude and not the positivity and negativity of unanticipated excess returns determine future variance. If the distribution of u_t is symmetric, the change in variance tomorrow is conditionally uncorrelated with excess return today. In equation (5), σ^2_t is a function of lagged σ^2_t and lagged e_t^2, and so is invariant to changes in algebraic sign of the e_t's, i.e. only the size, not the

3. The economic reasons for this are unclear. As Black (1976) and Christie (1982) note, both financial and operating leverage play a role, but are not able to explain the extent of the asymmetric response of volatility to positive and negative returns shocks. Schwartz (1989 a, b) presents evidence that stock volatility is higher during recession and financial crisis.

sign of lagged residuals determines conditional variance. So, this suggests that a model in which σ^2_t responds asymmetrically to positive and negative residuals might be preferable for asset pricing applications.

The second limitation of GARCH model results from the non-negativity constraints on ω and the α_i in (eq. 6), which are imposed to ensure that σ^2_t remains non-negative. These constraints imply that increasing e_t^2 in any period increases σ^2_{t+m} for all m ≥1, ruling out random oscillatory behaviour in the σ^2_t process. Furthermore, these non-negativity constraints can create difficulties in estimating GARCH models.

A third drawback of GARCH modeling concerns the interpretation of the "persistence" of shocks to conditional variance. In many studies of the time series behaviour of asset volatility (e.g., Poterba and Summers (1986), French, Schwert, and Stambugh (1987), and Eangle and Bollerslev (1986a)), the central question has been how long shocks to conditional variance persist. If volatility shocks persist indefinitely, they may move the whole term structure of risk premia, and are therefore likely to have significant impact on investment in long-lived capital goods (Poterba and Summers 1986). According to Nelson (1991), his E-GARCH model overcomes some of the limitations of GARCH family of models. The specification of E-GARCH model follows as below,

$$R_t = d + y\, R_{t-1} + u_{t.\,...}\ ....\text{(As eq.1)}$$

Where, $u_t = e_t h_t^{1/2}$ ......(As eq. 4)

$e_t \sim (0, 1)$

and,

$$\ln h_t = \omega + \beta \ln h_{t-1} + \alpha 1/e_{t-1}/\sigma_{t-1}/+\alpha_2\, e_{t-1}/\sigma_{t-1} \qquad (7)$$

In this model β is the GARCH term that measures the impact of last period's forecast variance. A positive β implies volatility clustering indicating that positive return are associated with further positive changes in stock return and vice versa. α_1 is the ARCH term that measures the effect of news about volatility from the previous period on current period volatility. α_2 measures the leverage effect. If the coefficient of α_2 is significant then the positive shocks and negative shocks have different impact on volatility. Ideally α_2 is expected to be negative indicating "bad news" has higher impact on volatility than "good news" of the same magnitude. The sum of the ARCH-GARCH coefficients indicates the extent to which a volatility shock is persistent over the time.

Data Source

We use two stock market indices—the BSE Sensex indices and the international financial corporation published IFC Global (IFCG) index. Both daily and monthly return series is used in our analysis. Sensex is the most popular market index and widely used by researchers in India. For daily data, our period of analysis is from 1985 to 2004. We have divided this period into two sub-periods such as pre-liberalisation (1985-92) and post liberalisation period (1993-2004). For monthly data, the period of analysis is from 1976-04 for IFCG Data and 1979-2005 for BSE Sensex. The data have been collected from prowess database of CMIE as well from Emerging Stock Market Fact books of S&P. For carrying out empirical analysis, the price series are converted to return series in the following way:

$$R_t = \ln (P_t - P_{t-1})$$

Where, R_t is the logarithmic return on security at time t, and P_t, P_{t-1} closing value of stock price of Sensex at time t and t-1.

SECTION V

Summary Statistics of Sensex Daily and Monthly Return

It is clear from Table 1 is that the return series is not normal. Skewness in both the period is not zero. It is positively skewed in the pre-liberalisation period and negatively skewed in post-liberalisation period as well as for full sample. The kurtosis for all the period is greater than 3, thereby indicating leptokurtic distribution. Mean returns for pre-liberalisation period is higher than that of post-liberalisation period for both daily return as well as monthly returns. The standard deviation in returns is higher in pre-liberalisation period for daily series, indicating stock return is more volatile in pre-liberalisation.

Table 1: Summary Statistics for Daily and Monthly Return

Period	Mean	Max.	Min.	S.D.	Skewness	Excess Kurtosis
1985-1992	0.052	12.6	-13.01	1.44	0.22	201.55
1993-2004	0.010	0.07	-11.08	0.71	-0.23	5.17
1985-2004	0.020	12.6	-13.01	0.98	-5.87	200.1
1991-1992	0.059	8.73	-13.02	1.51	-7.17	77.53
			Monthly Return			
1979-1992	0.68	19.13	-11.14	3.41	1.07	5.33
1992-2005	0.29	8.25	-7.48	3.28	-0.43	1.58
1979-2005	0.48	19.13	-11.14	3.35	0.52	2.81

Standard deviation for sub-period (1991-1992) is higher than any other period, indicating this period is most volatile. Similarly, for monthly series, standard deviation for pre-liberalisation period is higher indicating market is more volatile in pre-liberalisation period.

Table 2: Diagnostic Checking of Daily Return Series

Period	BJ[a]	LB[b]	ADF[c]	LM[d]
1985-1992	35678.74	42.42	-36.16	372.66
	(0.00)	(0.02)	(0.02)	(0.00)
1993-2004	552.97	39.29	-36.07	164.85
	(0.00)	(0.03)	(0.01)	(0.00)
1985-2004	30326	39.45	-49.81	356.00
	(0.00)	(0.03)	(0.01)	(0.00)
1991-92	2786	22.18	-31.23	21.21
	(0.00)	(0.00)	(0.03)	(0.00)
		Monthly Series		
1979-1992	227.34	18.45	-10.55	13.56
	(0.00)	(0.03)	(0.04)	(0.06)
1993-2005	12.96	14.38	-12.29	12.34
	(0.001)	(0.06)	(0.05)	(0.06)
1979-2005	122.47	18.67	-12.53	17.45
	(0.00)	(0.03)	(0.04)	(0.03)

(a) Bera Jarqua Statistics approximately distributed as central Chi-square (2) under the null hypothesis of normally in the underlying distribution of returns. (b) Ljung – Box Statistics to test autocorrelation among residuals of returns (c) Lagarange Multiple Test Statistics to test null hypothesis of no ARCH effect against alternative of ARCH effect, critical values of Chi-square at 1%, 5% and 10% are 15.08, 11.07 and 9.23 respectively.

Before estimating ARCH/GARCH/E-GARCH models to capture volatility, necessary diagnostic statistics are computed and presented in Table 2. Here we assume that daily return follows a first order autoregressive [AR (1)] process. The Bera-Jarqua (BJ) statistics, which exceeds critical chi-square value with 2 degree of freedom in all cases, rejects the normality of the underlying distribution. In order to analyse the behaviour of stock returns, Ljung-Box (LB) statistics are obtained to trace the presence of autocorrelation among residuals of the return. It is clear from the Table 2 that in all the cases the presence of autocorrelation is significant. The Augmented Dickey-Fuller (ADF) test statistics indicate that return series are stationary in nature. LM statistics also indicates the presence of ARCH disturbances in the squared residuals. Here, we have considered the order of the ARCH is to be 5. Because, according to the test procedure, the TR^2 statistics (where T is the sample size and R^2 is the coefficient of determination) follows asymptotically a chi-squared distribution with degree of freedom 5.

It follows from the above analysis that stock returns are not identically and independently distributed. This may lead us to conclude that return variance process is time varying and heteroscedastic in nature and hence ARCH formulation would be appropriate. The result obtained from AR (1) model with disturbance term following ARCH (5) structure is reported in Table 3. The constant term α_0 is found to be insignificant for pre- and post-liberalisation period as well as for the whole sample. It is significant indicating that return process has a drift element. The coefficients of the α_1 are found to be significant and less than one, thereby indicating stability in returns. Further, the coefficients of α_1 exhibit daily serial autocorrelation and in this regard the result indicates that there exit positive daily autocorrelations.

The ARCH (5) models have been estimated by maximising the log likelihood function using an iterative procedure based on the method of BHHH. For given values of past realised returns, α_0 and α_i (i = 1....5) are estimated for total return in the market. The constant term α_0 for whole sample is found to be positive and significant, which indicates that volatility could increase even in the absence of any influence. The summation of α_1 s is more than one for pre-liberalisation period as well as for whole sample, indicating that the estimated variance is not finite. The lagged coefficients are significant at lags 1,2,3,4, and 5. The coefficients from the market point of view may be interpreted as follows: The volatility of previous trading day is carried over to the current period and persisting over a period of four days.

Table 3: Estimation of ARCH (5) Process with AR (1) Model for Daily Returns

Period	A_0	A_1	α_0	α_1	α_2	α_3	α_4	α_5
1985-92	0.023	0.30	0.50	1.50	0.27	-0.01	0.05	-0.001
	(1.71)	(13.1)	(24.7)	(22.08)	(15.05)	(-8.85)	(1.99)	(-0.26)
1993-04	0.032	0.137	0.191	0.228	0.132	0.111	0.089	0.086
	(2.41)	(6.81)	(16.1)	(9.54)	(5.57)	(6.1)	(4.43)	(4.67)
1985-04	0.006	0.118	0.27	0.24	0.14	0.048	0.64	-0.003
	(0.83)	(10.59)	(37.53)	(10.69)	(5.08)	(4.19)	(52.40)	(-1.39)

Figures in parentheses represent t-ratios.

Another important point that may be noted here is that ARCH error structure and autoregressive parameter of the R_t process interact with each other so that volatility of R_t is increasing in α_i and α_1. The explanation is like this: Any large shock in u_t will be associated with a persistently large variance; the larger is α_i the larger is the persistence. Furthermore, the greater the parameter α_1, the more persistent is the volatility.

In addition to the ARCH (5) models, GARCH (1, 1) model has been estimated. The result is reported in Table 4.

Table 4: Estimation of AR (1) Model with GARCH (1, 1) Process

Period	A_0	A_1	ω	α	β	MEAN (%)
1985-92	0.026	0.097	0.11	0.128	0.765	0.052
	(1.17)	(12.77)	(9.96)	(31.87)	(64.95)	
1993-04	0.033	0.134	0.02	0.03	0.83	0.015
	(2.55)	(6.46)	(6.71)	(10.06)	(72.98)	
1985-04	0.036	0.18	0.067	0.146	0.769	0.027
	(2.84)	(11.18)	(22.8)	(20.96)	(83.05)	
1991-92	0.037	0.151	0.093	0.135	0.84	0.081
	(0.74)	(2.52)	(2.09)	(3.00)	(23.72)	
GARCH (1,1) model for Monthly Series						
1979-92	0.45	-0.02	0.35	0.062	0.91	0.44
	(2.13)	(-0.34)	(0.72)	(2.38)	(6.57)	
1993-05	0.23	0.05	0.06	0.08	0.95	0.53
	(1.67)	(2.24)	(2.01)	(3.45)	(18.45)	
1979-05	0.297	0.015	0.143	0.051	0.94	0.49
	(1.63)	(0.27)	(1.17)	(2.56)	(39.62)	

Figures in parentheses represent t-ratios.

The results in Table 4 suggest that GARCH (1, 1) coefficients are found to be significant and positive, thus implying that volatility is captured by GARCH (1,1) model. The significance of a coefficient in the model indicates the tendency of the shocks to persist. The sum of the coefficients of lagged squared disturbance (a) and that of past variance (b) is less than one indicating shocks die with time. The sum is marginally higher in pre-liberalisation (0.89) period than post-liberalisation (0.86) period, thus indicating a marginal higher volatility in pre-liberalisation. The mean volatility also indicates the similar pattern. It was 0.052 % in pre-liberalisation period and came down to 0.015% in post-liberalisation period. In June 1991, India declared Structural Adjustment Programme (SAP) following BOP crisis and then a series of economic as well as financial reform measures were announced. So, we have sub-periods from June 1991 to the end of 1992. This period is highly volatile compared to other periods. Mean volatility is also very high in this period (0.081) compared to other periods. The sum of all coefficients are more than the other periods.

For monthly data, volatility persistent is significantly evident for the whole period as well as for sub-periods. The sum of the coefficients is less than one for pre-liberalisation and for full sample. It is more than one in post-liberalisation. The mean volatility is marginally higher in post-liberalisation (0.53%) period than pre-liberalisation (0.44%) period, indicating market is more volatile in post-liberalisation period. This is just opposite to that of daily series.

We have already discussed that GARCH models take only magnitude not the sign of lagged residuals. Hence it ignores the leverage effect. Nelson's E-GARCH model overcomes this problem. So, we have estimated E-GARCH (1, 1) model for the sample period. The results are reported in Table 5. The Leverage effect is significant for all periods except for sub-period (1991-92). As expected the coefficient of leverage is negative indicating bad news have higher impact than good news. The coefficient of β is positive and significant indicating volatility clustering. In other words, positive stock price changes are associated with further positive changes. The coefficient of ARCH term α_1 is positive and significant. The sum of the ARCH-GARCH coefficients is more than one for the whole sample, pre- and post-liberalisation period, indicating that volatility increases with time. The sum of the ARCH- GARCH coefficients is higher in pre-liberalisation period (1.16) than in post-liberalisation period (1.14), indicating marginal decrease in volatility in post-liberalisation period. This result is just similar to GARCH (1, 1) model for daily data.

For monthly data the result is similar to GARCH (1, 1) model. The mean volatility is higher for post-liberalisation period although marginal. Although the leverage coefficient is significant but the sign is positive. So from daily data it is found that volatility is higher in pre-liberalisation period but from monthly data we found that a marginal increase in volatility in post-liberalisation period. But generally daily data is suffered by "noise' content. Noise plays a big role in high frequency volatility persistence. At less frequent observation, the noise content dies away. Monthly data series is ideal for the volatility analysis. Now the task is to relate whether the marginal increase in volatility is due to reforms as general or due to reform in stock market. The next section takes up this issue.

Table 5: Estimation of AR (1) Model with E-GARCH (1, 1) Process

Period	Mean (%)	ω	β	α_1 (ARCH Term)	α_2 (Leverage)
1985-92	0.052	-0.02 (-6.4)	0.891 (215.09)	0.27 (13.73)	-0.013 (-2.95)
1993-04	0.015	-0.271 (-15.71)	0.93 (97.55)	0.21 (14.72)	-0.068 (-7.95)
1985-04	0.026	0.013 (40.22)	0.92 (265.06)	0.21 (22.36)	-0.036 (-8.91)
1991-92	0.081	-0.0126 (-4.08)	0.975 (31.05)	0.17 (4.44)	0.106 (8.29)
		E-GARCH Model with Monthly Series			
1979-92	0.44	1.00 (1.60)	0.94 (52.34)	0.005 (0.44)	0.016 (3.35)
1992-05	0.53	-0.13 (-13.87)	0.98 (54.67)	0.07 (11.23)	0.08 (5.28)
1979-05	0.48	-0.03 (-1.39)	0.99 (151.33)	0.004 (2.32)	0.08 (11.82)

Figures in parentheses represent t-ratios.

Structural Breaks in Stock Market Volatility

We are interested now in detecting the events that may have led to changes in the volatility of stock market. Some recent contribution have looked for structural changes in the behaviour of emerging stock market, and detecting the causes of these changes, making special reference to episodes of financial liberalisation and economic policy decisions [Aggrawal et al. (1999)].

The location of endogenous structural breaks in time series has been a matter of intense research in the last few years (e.g., Banerjee et al. 1992, Ghysels et al. 1997, and Bai et al. 1998). The issue of estimation of the number and location of multiple endogenous structural breaks as also being an active field of research (See for e.g., Andrews et al. 1996, Gracia and Perron 1996, Bai 1997, 1999, Lumsdaine and Papell 1997 or Bai and Perron 1998, 2003 a, b). Most of the techniques in the above papers have been developed for estimation and location of endogenous breaks in the mean parameters of trend models. However, as Bai and Perron (1998) mention, they can also accommodate changes in the variance. We use the general framework in Bai and Perron (1998 and 2003) and their procedure of sequentially locating the breaks with its associated critical values.

As a first step we detect the shift in unconditional volatility. For this purpose we estimate 12-month rolling variance as well 90-days rolling variance. Figures 1 and 2 represent 90-days and 12-month rolling variance. The annualised rolling variance is calculated as follows:

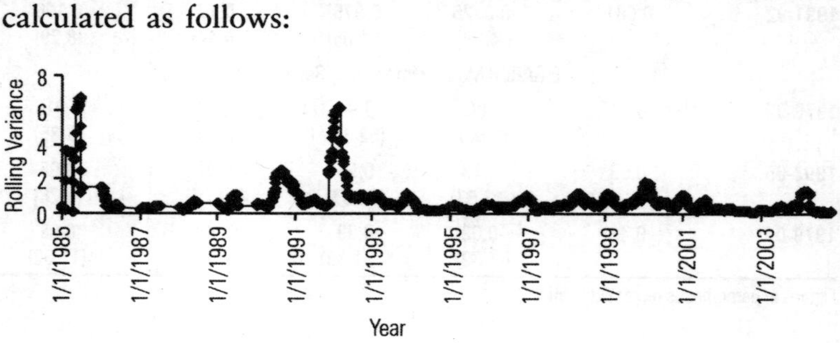

Figure 1: 90-days Rolling Variance.

Where μ_{12} is the sample mean over 12 month window. The 12 before the formula is just a way of annualising the variance.

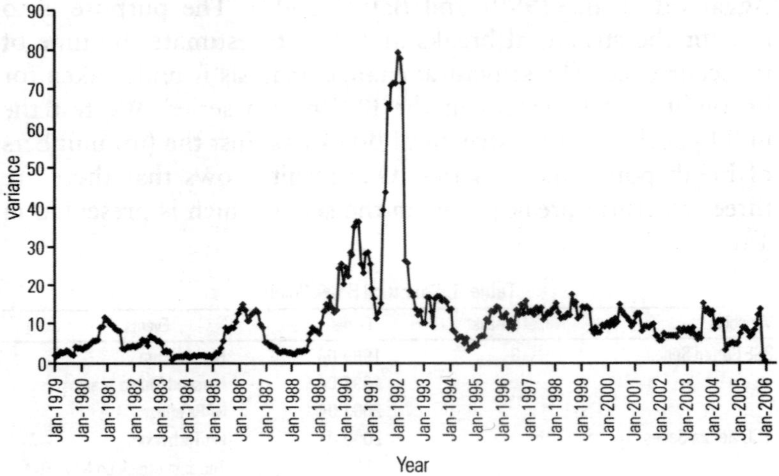

Figure 2: Annualised Rolling Variance.

From Figure 1 it is clear that there is shift in unconditional volatility around the period 1991-93 during which most the liberalisation measures took place. Since then, the volatility follows a downward trend till 2003. From daily return series it is also clear that the rolling variance shows a continuos increase in volatility until 1991-92, when it reaches its highest level. Since then the volatility shows a downward trend. So the period 1991-93 is the most volatile period.

Though standard GARCH models are able to capture times varying nature of volatility but they fail to capture structural breaks in the series that are caused by low probability events such as a crash and/or political/economic event. The GARCH model as discussed above can be modified to include sudden changes in the variance. Lastrapes (1989) and Lamoureux and Lastrapes (1990) have shown that when ARCH/GARCH models are applied to data that include sudden change in variance then the conditional variance may be found to strongly persist over time. According to them, high volatility persistence in GARCH models could be on account of structural changes in the variance process.

We follow the methodology of a combined GARCH as given by Lamoureux and Lastrapes (1990) and followed by Aggarwal et al. (1999) and Batra (2004). The purpose is to test for the structural breaks and then to estimate the time of its occurrence. The structural change analysis is undertaken for unconditional variances in the BSE return series. We test the null hypothesis of no structural breaks against the (m) numbers of break points in the series. Our result shows that there are three structural break points in the series which is presented in Table 6.

Table 6: Structural Break Points

Variables	No. of Breaks*	Dates	Events
BSE Return Series	3	1989:08	Bofors scam
		1992:04	Harshad Mehta scam
		2003:04	SARs effect
IFCG Return Series	3	2000:01	InfoTech boom
		2001:08	Terrorist attack on New York
		2003:04	SARs effect
FII Purchase	2	2003:06	
		2004:10	
FII Sale	2	1999:09	General Election
		2003:12	
Market Cap	2	1993:12	
		2003:10	
Turnover	2	1999:06	
		2001:02	Ketan Parekh scam

*According to BIC, criteria all the break dates are significant.

It is clear that there is no break point around liberalisation period which is associated with stock market reform per se. At the same time there is no structural change that is related to the entry or buying or selling by FIIs. So FIIs is not the source of volatility persistent. Rather, economic reform in general and some political events lead to structural shift in volatility as it is found from the break dates. In most of the cases we found that scams and international factors that led to structural breaks. Financial liberalisation and particularly, stock market reforms do not lead to a structural break in India.

The E-GARCH model discussed in Section IV could be reformulated to take into account the structural change by adding dummy variables. The equation (6) can be rewritten as:

$$\ln h_t = \omega + \beta \ln h_{t-1} + \alpha_1 \left| e_{t-1}/\sigma_{t-1} \right| + \alpha_2 e_{t-1}/\sigma_{t-1} + \delta_1 d_1 + \delta_2 d_2 \ldots + \delta_n d_n \quad (9)$$

Where d_1, d_2 and dn are the dummy variables taking the value of one from each point of sudden change of variance onwards and zero elsewhere. We then compare the implied persistence of the model as in equation (9) using the restricted specification to that of the unrestricted specification in (7). Monthly return series is used for break point test. The results are presented in Table 7.

Table 7: Volatility with Structural Break Point

Period	Mean (%)	ω	α	β	d_1	d_2	d_3
1979-05	0.41	0.125	0.071	0.712	1.44	-1.30	0.697
		(0.48)	(2.38)	(14.5)	(2.98)	(-1.87)	(3.13)
1979-92	0.51	0.20	0.11	0.38	1.11	-0.34	—
		(0.69)	(2.86)	(4.62)	(2.77)	(-1.68)	
1993-05	0.47	0.13	0.06	-0.54	—	—	1.23
		(0.48)	(1.67)	(-2.05)			(2.11)

Out of three dummies, two dummies have a positive impact on volatility. The first dummy (1989: 08) has a positive impact on volatility, and second dummy (1992:04) has negative impact. The third dummy (2003:04) has positive impact on volatility. The result also shows that there is significant reduction in ARCH effect when large shocks are controlled for. But volatility is still persistent even after controlling large shocks. The sum of the ARCH coefficients has come down considerably (from 1.07 to 0.71) for the full sample. In pre-liberalisation period the sum of the ARCH coefficients has come down from 0.96 to 0.38 and for post-liberalisation period declined from 1.13 to -0.54. There is also marginal decrease in mean volatility for all the period.

Conclusion

The objective of this paper is that to estimate time varying volatility and compare pre- with post-liberalisation period. Basically we have addressed two issues: (1) is Indian stock market more volatile in post-liberalisation period? (2) Can we relate the volatility with stock market reforms?

The character of stock returns shows that it is not normal and ARCH effect is present. In the presence of autocorrelation and ARCH effect, unconditional variance is not appropriate measure for volatility. The classes of GARCH family models have been found to be valuable in modeling the time series behaviour of stock returns. Our period of analysis is from 1985-2004 for daily returns and 1976-2004 for monthly returns. Our findings indicate that GARCH models are appropriate measure of volatility. Following conclusions are drawn from our analysis:

(1) Volatility persistent is high for all the periods. From daily return we find that pre-liberalisation period is more volatile. But from monthly data it found that post-liberalisation period is marginally higher volatile.

(2) The period June 1991 to 1992 is the most volatile period because of the announcement of SAP programme along with several reforms in several fields of the economy.

(3) From E-GARCH model it is found that leverage effect is present and significant for all the sample period. However, for monthly data, it not significant. In fact, for pre-liberalisation period the leverage effect is positive which contrast to the model.

(4) From structural break analysis we found that there are four break dates and its relation to economic and political events. None of the break dates is related to stock market liberalisation events. Rather it is related to economic policy change/regime shift.

(5) When large shocks in stock returns are controlled, there is significant reduction in ARCH effect; however the volatility is still persistent.

(6) Buying or selling by FIIs does not coincide with change in stock market volatility.

(7) There is not much change in the level of volatility in pre- and post-liberalisation period.

REFERENCES

Aggarwal, R., Inclan, C. and Leal, R. (1999): "Volatility in Emerging Stock Markets", *Journal of Financial and Quantitative Analysis* 34: 35-55.

Aksiray, V. (1989): "Conditional Hetroscedasticity in Time Series Stock Returns: Evidence and Forecasts", *Journal of Business*, 62: 55-80.

Andreou, E. and Ghysels, E. (2002): "Multiple Breaks in Financial Market Volatility Dynamics", *Journal of Applied Econometrics*, 17: 579-600.

Bai, J. (1997): "Estimating Multiple Breaks One at a Time", *Econometric Theory*, 13: 315-332.

Bai, J. and Perron, P. (1998): "Estimation and Testing Linear Models with Multiple Structural Changes", *Econometrica*, 66: 47-78.

Bai, J. and Perron, P. (2003b): "Computation and Analysis of Multiple Structural Change Models", *Journal of Applied Econometrics*, 18: 1-22.

Banerjee, A., Lumsdaine, R.L. and Stock, J.S. (1992): "Recursive and Sequential Test of the Unit Root and Trend-breaks Hypothesis: Theory and International Evidence", *Journal of Business and Economic Statistics*, 10: 271-287.

Batra, A. (2004): "Stock Return Volatility Patterns in India", *Working Paper*, ICRIER.

Bekaert, G. and Harvey, C.R. (1997): "Emerging Equity Market Volatility", *Journal of Financial Economics*, 43: 29-78.

Bekaert, G. and Harvey, C.R. (2000): "Foreign Speculators and Emerging Equity markets", *Journal of Finance*, 55: 565-613.

Bekaert, G. and Harvey, C.R. (2002): "Research in Emerging Markets Finance: Looking to the Future", *Emerging Market Review*, 3: 429-448.

Bekaert, G. and Harvey, C.R. (2003): "Emerging Markets Finance", *Journal of Empirical Financial*, 10: 3-55.

Bekaert, G., Harvey, C.R. and Lumsdaine (2002): "Dating the Integration of World's Capital Markets", *Journal of Financial Economics*, 65: 203-249.

Black, F. (1976): "Studies in Stock Price Volatility Changes", *Proceedings of American Statistical Association*, 171-181.

Bolloerslev, Tim (1986): "Generalised Autoregressive Conditional Hetroscedasticity", *Journal of Econometrics*, 31: 307-27.

Chou, R.Y. (1988): "Volatility Persistent and Stock Valuations: Some Empirical Evidence Using GARCH", *Journal of Applied Econometrics*, 3: 279-294.

De Santis, G. and Imrohoroglu, S. (1997): "Stock Returns and Volatility in Emerging Financial Markets", *Journal of International Money and Finance*, 16: 561-579.

Edwards, S., Gomez, Biscarri, J. and Perez, de Gracia F. (2003): "Stock Market Cycles, Financial Liberalisation and Volatility", *Journal of International Money and Finance*, 22: 925-955.

Engle, R.F. (1982): "Autoregressive Conditional Heteroscedasticity with Estimates of the Variance of UK Inflation," *Econometrica*, 50: 987-1008.

Engle, R.F. and Bollereslev, T. (1986a): "Modeling the Persistence of Conditional Variances", *Econometric Reviews*, 5: 1-50.

Fama, E.F. (1965): "The Behaviour of Stock Market Prices", *Journal of Business*, 38: 34-105.

French, K.R., Schwert, G.W. and Stambaugh, R.F. (1987): "Expected Stock returns and Volatility", *Journal of Financial Economics*, 19: 3-30.

Grabel, Ilene (1995): "Assessing the impact of Financial Liberalisation on Stock Market Volatility in Selected Developing Countries", *Journal of Developing Studies*, 31: 903-917.

Gracia, R, and Perron, P. (1996): "An Analysis of the Real Interest Rate under Regime Shifts", *Review of Econometrics and Statistics*, 78: 111-125.

Han, Kim E. and Singal, Vijay (2000): "Stock Market Openings: Experience of Emerging Economics", *Journal of Business*, 73: 25-65.

Kaminsky, Graciela Laura and Schmickler, Sergio L. (2001): "On Boom and Crashes: Financial Liberalisation and Stock Market Cycles", *World Bank Research Paper*.

Kaminsky, Graciela Laura and Schmickler, Sergio L. (2003): "Short-Run Pain, Long-Rain Gain: The Effects of Financial Liberalisation", *NBER Working Paper 9787*.

Kwan, B.F. and Reyes, M.G. (1997): "Price Effects of Stock Market Liberalisation in Taiwan", *The Quarterly Review of Economics and Finance*, 37.

Lamoureux, Christopher G. and Lastrapes, William D. (1990): "Persistence in Variance Structural Change and the GARCH Model", *Journal of Business and Economic Studies*, 8: 54-75.

Levine, Ross and Zervos, Sara (1998): "Capital Control Liberalisation and Stock Market Development", *World Development*, 26: 1169-1183.

Mandelbrot, B. (1963): "The Variation of Certain Speculative Prices", *Journal of Business*, 36: 394-419.

Nelson, B. Daniel (1991): "Conditional Hetroscedasticity in Asset Returns: A New Approach", *Econometrica*, 59: 347-370.

Nilsson, B. (2002): "Financial Liberalisation and the Changing Characteristics of Nordic Stock Returns", *Working Paper*, Department of Economic Lund University.

Pal, Parthapratim (1998): "Foreign Portfolio Investment in India Equity Markets: Has the Economy Benefited?", *Economic and political weekly*, 3: 589-598.

Porterba, J. and Summers, L. (1986): "The Persistence of Volatility and Stock Market Fluctuations", *American Economic Review*, 76: 1142-41.

Richards, A.J. (1996): "Volatility and Predictability in National Stock Markets: How do Emerging and Mature Markets Differ?" *IMF Staff Paper*, 43: 461-501.

Samal, Kishore C. (1997): "Emerging Equity Market in India: Role of Foreign Institutional Investors", *Economic and political weekly*, 32: 2729-2723.

Schill, M.J. (2003): "Sailing in Rough Water: Market Volatility and Corporate Finance", University of Virginia.

Singh, Ajit (1993): "The Stock Market and Economic Development: Should Developing Countries Encourage Stock-Markets?", *UNCTAD Review*, No 4.

Tauchen, George E. and Pitta, Mark (1983): "The Price Variability: Volume Relationship on Speculative Markets," *Econometrica*, 51: 124-45.

Security and Trust in Electronic Payments

9

Ashutosh Saxena

The growth of the Internet as a medium of transaction has made possible an economic transformation in which commerce is becoming electronic. The critical factors of success for every commercial entity to implement and operate an electronic business mechanism are money flow; material flow and authentication information flow. The majority of trust theories are built upon the basis that there is a history of exchanges between partners, i.e. past experiences, but the fluid nature of e-commerce market makes the issue of trust hard because of the weakness to scale the reliability of participants. Strong and long-lasting business relationships have always depended on trust. The transition to digital economy, forces enterprises not only to develop customer intimateness but also to ensure that security requirements are part of the customer relationship strategy.

Transactions in electronic commerce can occur without any prior human contact or established interpersonal relationships. This lack of interpersonal trust creates a circumstance for a security threat. Generally, security is a set of procedures, mechanisms and computer programs to authenticate the source of information and guarantee the integrity and privacy of the information (data).

The focus of every processing e-commerce transaction is to minimize the transaction risk. In parallel, a trust framework in e-commerce must address scalability and cost. It is characteristic that there are no face-to-face operations and all transactions are performed electronically with the use of communication networks. This demands establishment of the concepts of trust and security.

1. Electronic Payments

Requirements

The security requirements can be considered as follows (Spinellis et al., 1999).

- *Authentication*: persons participating in a transaction are the one they claim to be.
- *Identification*: unique identification of a person or entity.
- *Confidentiality*: prevention of unauthorized parties to capture, interpret or understand data.
- *Integrity*: certainness that data have not been altered or manipulated by unauthorized parties, i.e. sureness that information has not been altered since the data were signed
- *Non-repudiation*: prevention of denying the action of participating into a transaction by a person or entity.
- *Fraud prevention and tolerance*: prevention of parties from fraud and financial losses in case the system crashes or the network fails.
- *Access control*: control on the actions of a person or entity, based upon its identity.
- *Availability*: uninterrupted provision of banking and other related services.

This list by no means can be considered as comprehensive and can be extended to include other security requirements more specific to environment. But broadly the security with regard to electronic payment can be categorised into three areas.

1. *Systems security*: technical infrastructure and implementation.
2. *Transaction security*: secure payment according to specific and well-defined rules.
3. *Legal security*: a legal framework for electronic payment.

Properties

- *Divisibility*: possibility of multiple denominations.
- *Transferability*: spending via electronic payments without the need to contact the issuer.
- *Double-spending prevention*: prevention of copied coins to spend repeatedly.
- *Payment confidentiality*: payment details including payer, payee, account numbers, amounts, date and time must not become known to electronic observers, who are able to monitor network traffic.
- *Payment anonymity*: the payee will know only pseudonym of the payer.
- *Payer untraceability*: payment system cannot trace payer payments.

We must mention that all these properties are of an ideal electronic payment system. No currently working electronic payment system meets all of these properties.

2. Identification of Trust

The phase of electronic payment (e-payment) is confidential when all phases of the process are capable to satisfy the needs of participants and their security expectations. A fundamental prerequisite must be that all participants have absolute trust in the system that they participate in. Trust has been defined as "the willingness of a party to be vulnerable to the actions of another party based on the expectation that the other will perform a particular action important to the trustor, irrespective of the ability to monitor or control that other party" (Mayer et al., 1995).

Trust requires a party to make a rational decision based on the knowledge of possible rewards for trusting and not trusting. Trust enables higher gains while distrust avoids potential loss (Jean Camp, 2003). "Generally, an entity can be said to 'trust' a second entity when it (the first entity) makes the assumption that the second entity will behave exactly as the first entity expects" (X.509 ITU, 2000).

The purpose of modeling trust is to establish a secure way to describe the decision of commerce process. A trusted environment is characterised by:

- the fact that all entities are uniquely identifiable;
- that there is a minimum number of a priori trusted entities; and
- that these entities have unquestionable trust to other participating entities.

To design for trust, it is necessary to determine if, and under what conditions trust mechanisms are brittle. Security architecture presumes that a trust model defines the trusted relationships between all involved components.

Trust and trustworthiness are fundamental for every security solution. The needs for these trust aspects and the means that are used to implement it, affect the security mechanism of any commercial system. But there is distinction between trust and trustworthiness. Trust is an act of a trustor, in which an entity places trust in some object. In contrast, trustworthiness is a characteristic of someone or something that is the object of trust. Trust is the enabling of confidence that something will or will not occur in a predictable or promised manner. The enabling of confidence is supported by identification, authentication, accountability, authorisation, and availability (Andert et al., 2002).

3. Cryptography and PKI

A logical question arises concerning which is the mechanism that could establish and efficiently implement both security and trust on Internet environment, knowing that Internet is referred as "the network of networks"; a set of interconnected networks, which is open, independent, heterogeneous and universal. It is an environment that is driven by demand, not supply.

Cryptography provides the only feasible way in which business can work as compared to traditional paper based mechanisms. Cryptographic methods should be trustworthy in order to generate confidence in the use of information and communication systems. Cryptographic methods are mainly developed in response to the needs and demands of businesses. The development of cryptographic methods is determined by the market in the competitive environment. The premise approach enables that solutions are in accordance to technology, the demands of market and needs of information and communications systems. The development of standards and protocols related to cryptographic methods must also take into the consideration the prevailing demand of the industry. Cryptography is represented in two forms. The first is called symmetric or secret key cryptography, uses one common key for both encryption and decryption and a second named public key cryptography or asymmetric, uses two different keys (a private and public) to transform plaintext into ciphertext. In symmetric schemes, the sender and recipient of data, share a single encryption key, and the shared keys must not be revealed or exposed to unauthorized parties. In asymmetric schemes, two keys are used; a "public" and a "private" key. Public keys can be freely distributed but recipients still require a way to know that a key can be trusted. To certify each public key, a central Certification Authority (CA) is required. Symmetric cryptography schemes are based on the concept that only the users of the encrypted information should have the keys needed to decrypt it into something understandable. Public Key Cryptography (Sanderson and Forcht, 1996) is based on the principle that the two keys should be different, but related to each other. In a sense, they need to be inverses of one another. This form of cryptography relies heavily upon the assumption that it is computationally infeasible to determine the decryption key if the encryption key and algorithm, are known. This means that the problem cannot be solved in deterministic polynomial time and since the parameters are large, the time that is required for problem to solve will also be very large. All commonly used public key encryption techniques are based on mathematical functions which are easy to compute, and hard to invert.

The PKI (Public Key Infrastructure) comprises a complex infrastructure of hardware, software, networks, security procedures public key encryption techniques, policies and procedures for distribution and management of certificates, a group solution for key distribution problems (Benantar, 2001) in a business environment and how it addresses the trust issues inherent in business models. The PKI is a business enabling initiative, one may refer (Saxena, 2004) for details in the area of PKI. It provides a means for both trusted digital identity verification and data encryption in transit. In e-business, we want to establish relationships and identify the parties (Adams and Lloyd, 2002). Certificates address the problem to verify the identity of the parties exchanging encrypted information over the Internet.

In the public key technology, an essential process for establishing a trust relationship is for the first entity to import a public key from the second one and protect its integrity for storage or communication to other entities. The entity that imports the public key is known as the relying party (intends to rely upon the public key) for protecting the succession exchange with the key-holder, the entity from whom the key is imported.

With this background, we now discuss the initiatives and the actions taken by the Reserve Bank of India (RBI) to support electronic payments in the country.

4. RBI Initiatives

The RBI, the apex body for providing the guidelines for banking and financial industry, has said that it would set up an institution at the national level to own and operate all retail payment systems of the country. In its payment systems in India—Vision 2005-08, RBI said it will also establish a national settlement system through which the clearing houses/clearing organizations can settle the net position of the participating banks at the national level. To start with, all clearing settlements from four centres (Mumbai, New Delhi, Kolkata and Chennai) would be settled through National Settlement System by December 2005. Coverage of all major clearing centres—the 40 MICR clearing centres—would be completed by December 2006. Towards this, RBI will take steps to build a sound legal base for payments systems. These include enactment of payment and settlement systems act, framing of regulations for authorized payment and settlement systems, finalization of electronic funds transfer regulations and drafting regulations for electronic clearing system (debit clearing). To mitigate risks in payment systems, RBI plans to migrate inter-bank transactions at all places to Real Time Gross Settlement (RTGS) system and make high value clearing systems secured netting systems by introduction of guarantee funds. The Central Bank will also implement national settlement system for posting the net position of the clearing participants in all clearing houses in the country. And to address operational and legal risks, it will introduce digital signatures using PKI for enhanced security of messages, encourage credit transfers in electronic mode and provide for high availability of all systems. The RBI will strive to have every cheque with MICR standards and make all payment and settlement services to be available on a national level—National ECS and National EFT. It will rationalize clearing operations by setting up new clearing houses, expansion of geographical jurisdiction of the clearing houses and merger and amalgamation of clearing houses.

The Reserve Bank had earlier in December 2001 published its "Payment Systems—Vision Document" detailing its vision, goals, objectives and proposed measures relating to the payment systems in India for a three-year period. An evaluation of the results of the steps taken as per the broad directions contained in the Vision statement for the period 2001-04 reveal that most of the goal sets outlined have been met with while a few are at various stages of implementation.

Under the approach to computerisation and networking, with the definitive role of technology in facilitating large-scale developments in payment and settlement systems, the main requirements of INdian FInancial NETwork (INFINET) in becoming the secure, dedicated communication backbone for the banking and financial sector, namely a generic architecture model for connectivity, standardisation of hardware, operating systems, systems software, application software and messaging middleware, prescribing a Common Minimum Requirement Level for hardware and networking requirements for payment gateways, secured connectivity between INTERNET and INFINET, link between SWIFT and INFINET have all been achieved; applications for ATM transactions, intra-bank transactions like remittances and foreign exchange transactions do use INFINET. The setting up of Credit Information Bureau of India Ltd. (CIBIL) facilitates the banking industry to carry out a credit check on credit card holders and thus, reduces the incidence of frauds and default by individuals.

With the operationalisation of Real Time Gross Settlement (RTGS) System, this service is available at more than 4800 branches at 398 centres as at the end of April 2005. The implementation of Structured Financial Messaging Solution (SFMS) and Centralised Funds Management System (CFMS) showing the results, facilitating the banks with several value added services and options. Using CFMS, banks maintaining accounts with RBI at its various offices are in a position to know their balances at each location from their treasury branch. Enhancement in scope and coverage of Electronic Funds Transfer (EFT) system has been achieved through the Special EFT and the proposed National EFT; many banks have also integrated EFT with their own product offerings. With regard to upgradation of processing environment, banks are undertaking BPR as a part of implementing core banking, security standards have been prescribed, PKI based Digital Signatures are used for security and legal protection.

On the legal front, the Negotiable Instruments Act, 1881, has already been amended to enable cheque truncation and to define e-cheque. A Payment and Settlement Systems Bill has been drafted. Consequent upon Government of India Gazette Notification dated February 18, 2005 of the Reserve Bank of India (Board for Regulation and Supervision of Payment and Settlement Systems) Regulation, 2005, a Board for Payment and Settlement Systems has been constituted with effect from March 7, 2005.

All these have benefited directly or indirectly to the customers. The Internet based banking which was one of the goals to be achieved has been implemented in 26 banks. The need for core banking solutions at banks, which is at the base of many centralised initiatives such as Internet and mobile banking is also being implemented by banks and as many as 39 banks have implemented core banking solutions while 29 are at various stages of implementation. The delivery channels for customers have also improved with ATMs taking over a large number of cash related functions. Recognising the potential of this delivery channel, the Reserve Bank not only set the direction for banks to share ATMs but also helped the settlement process in the form of an ATM switch which has been set up and is being operated by the IDRBT, Hyderabad. Thus, card holders of any bank among the group can use their cards at the ATMs of any bank in the group.

4.1. What is INFINET?

The INFINET is the communication backbone for the Indian banking and financial sector. All banks, public sector, private sector, foreign, cooperative, etc., and premier financial institutions in the country are members of the INFINET. The INFINET is a Closed User Group (CUG) Network and uses a blend of communication technologies such as VSATs and Terrestrial Leased Lines. The network consists of over 2,051 VSATs located in approximately 400 to 500 cities of the country and utilizes one full transponder on INSAT 3A. The Hub of the VSAT network is situated at the Institute for Development and Research in Banking Technology, Hyderabad, and consists of an 11-meter antenna and other satellite earth station equipments.

The INFINET is primarily a TCP/IP based network. A detailed IP addressing scheme has been devised by IDRBT for all CUG members, which has to be strictly followed by all CUG members while interacting via the INFINET communication backbone. The INFINET had been expanded using leased line technology wherein 21 cities were connected by a judicious mix of bandwidth and enough redundancy and back-up leased line links. CUG members are being allowed to access the gateways to this leased line based network at each of these 21 cities. The leased line segment of the INFINET has been seamlessly integrated with the VSAT portion of the INFINET. Various inter-bank and intra-bank applications ranging from Simple Messaging to Inter-branch Reconciliation are being implemented using the INFINET.

4.1.1. The Technology—Best of Both Worlds

VSAT Network

VSATs were the natural choice when the INFINET was conceived as they were economical, affordable and reliable for a sprawling network of this nature, spanning the entire country (leased line costs were prohibitive at that time and, of course, there was the major problem of the last mile connectivity). The INFINET's VSAT Network uses TDM/TDMA for light data traffic and SCPC for enterprise application traffic. The present configuration consists of 48 × 128 Kbps inroutes and 3 × 512 Kbps and 1 × 2Mbps outroutes. It also provides for 100 simultaneous DAMA connections at any point of time. In the TDM/TDMA network various access mechanisms such as *Aloha, Transaction reservation* and *Stream* are used to allocate different bandwidth and offer different response times for different application on the network.

Leased Line Network

Now that communication lines have improved and the leased line costs have become reasonable; a seamless integration of the VSAT Network with a high bandwidth Leased Line Network (LLN) connecting 21 major cities across the country has been done with more than 600 circuits. Each Bank can develop its own intra-city or nearby cities network and come through a single gateway to get linked to the INFINET through the LLN Gateway. A dedicated port is allocated to each participating bank at the LLN gateway and dedicated bandwidth is also made available depending upon the requirements of each bank.

With the integration of the LLN with the VSAT Network, the users of INFINET have the option of dynamic routing between VSATs and the Leased Lines depending upon traffic volumes, specific application requirements and other factors like time criticality, etc.

4.1.2. Security

The INFINET is the most secure platform that technology can provide for this purpose. The salient features of security implementation on the INFINET are as follows:

- INFINET being a Closed User Group (CUG), it provides a high level of security against intruders. Outsiders cannot enter or penetrate the network.
- In the case of VSAT Network:
  (a) The IP Addresses for IDUs at the remote VSAT locations are allotted and maintained by the Hub and cannot be changed by the end-users.
  (b) In the space segment, the data transmission, even in broadcast mode, is encrypted using proprietary standards and the packets cannot be opened at any VSAT location except the one specified as the destination VSAT.
- In the case of Leased Line Network (LLN), IPSEC 56 provides state-of-the-art encryption and security.
- Apart from the above layers of network security, there are a host of in-built security mechanisms in each application that is deployed on the INFINET—like password, access control, encryption, digital signatures and certification and in some applications there are smart cards and/or bio-metric authentication as well.

4.2. Banking Applications on the INFINET

Various inter-bank and intra-bank applications ranging from Simple Messaging, MIS, EFT, ECS, Electronic Debit, Online Processing and Trading in Government Securities, Centralized Funds querying for Banks and Financial Institutions, Anywhere/Anytime Banking and Inter-bank reconciliation are being implemented using the INFINET.

INFINET can be used for both intra and inter-bank applications. Banks can develop and port intra-bank applications on their own. Inter-bank applications are being developed together by the Reserve Bank of India, IDRBT and member banks. Applications such as Real Time Gross Settlement, Central

Funds Management System, Security Settlement System, Electronic Clearing System and Electronic Funds Transfer, being developed by the RBI are ported on the INFINET and in a true sense, the INFINET has become the backbone for the National Payment Systems.

Some of the applications, which the CUG members are using on the network are Any Branch Banking (Multi-Branch Banking), Fast Collection of Cheques, Cash Management Products, ATM Network, Inter-bank Reconciliation, Corporate E-mails, etc.

Now we present the applications which are hosted by IDRBT on INFINET.

4.3. INFI-CERT

This single point contact for INFINET Closed User Group is a part of CERT-In. It keeps track of security issues, provides appropriate solutions/advises to its members and in turn updates itself by being in contact with other CERTs.

Functions

The following Table presents the broad functionality of INFINET:

Reporting and Response	- 24 X 7 contact center reacts to the incident reports from members and assigns a unique number. - The solution/ recommendations are sent to the members. - Feedback on the status is maintained for future references. - Provides telephonic support to System Administrators/IT Managers.
Reactive Measures	- Provides single point of contact for reporting security issues of banks and FIS. - Evaluates the Impact of the Incidents. - Provides recommendations to overcome the issues. - Documents the incidents for future reference.
Proactive Measures	- Monitors security related developments in global scenario. - Sends advisory information to INFICERT members. - Conducts training / workshop regularly. - Vulnerabilities & Risk Analysis on the security issues is carried out at the INFICERT center and outcome is shared with INFICERT members. - Security product evaluation is carried out and results are published. - Interacts with various product developers/ manufacturers for better understanding on their products

INFICERT receives incident reports through email, fax, telephone and web. It responds to the incidents with the objective of helping the reporting organizations to take immediate steps to restore the systems to operation.

4.4. SFMS

The primary need to have a secure and common messaging solution that would serve as the basic platform for intra-bank and inter-bank applications was recognised and emphasised by the INFINET Users Group (IUG). The IUG appointed a Subgroup to study this issue. This Subgroup recommended a SWIFT-like Messaging System to fulfill the needs of domestic financial messaging. Based on the recommendations of the Subgroup, a Working Group was appointed for the design of message formats for various transactions. The Working Group has grouped the requirements of Message Formats into the following four categories/volumes, which are available from the RBI.

Volume I: All Customer Transactions like Fund Transfers, Bills and Cheques, etc.

Volume II: All Government Transactions and Currency Chest Transactions.

Volume III: All Securities Transactions—Government Securities and Investments, PPF, Precious Metals, Travellers' Cheques, etc.

Volume IV: System Messages—Technical information on data types and file systems, message templates, trouble shooting, etc.

The major advantage of SFMS is that it can be used practically for all purposes of secure communication within the bank and between banks. Individual banks can integrate their existing applications with SFMS and could take full advantage of the secure messaging facility it provides. Integration of existing bank applications would require interaction among the concerned parties. Application Program Interfaces (APIs) are being provided for this purpose. As regards inter-bank applications, RBI has already taken initiative in implementing critical applications like Real Time Gross Settlement System (RTGS), Deliver Versus Payments (DVP), Centralized Funds Management System (CFMS), etc., which will piggyback on SFMS.

Banks can link all their important, high volume branches, irrespective of their category, to the SFMS through appropriate connectivity like PSTN/ISDN or Leased Lines to INFINET. Use of SFMS is not restricted to computerised or partially computerised branches or offices, and all that is required is a Windows based PC and link to the INFINET.

4.5. Mail Messaging System

IDRBT has set up a Mail Messaging System (MMS) on the INFINET for enabling basic communication between the users. MMS consists of high availability e-mail servers, which perform Clustering, Load Balancing, Certification, Domain Name Services, etc. A unique set up has also been created so that users of these e-mails can also send and receive mails from the Internet. Using this messaging backbone, banks can implement highly effective and productive workflow applications on the INFINET.

MMS is being used to provide a unique Corporate e-mail facility to the banks. Banks can now have a simple short e-mail address for their executives and officers across the country, like designation@bankname.co.in or username@bankname.co.in. The advantage of this facility is that this enables users to have a single, permanent e-mail address which can be used on their Corporate Intranet as well as on the Internet. The designation based official email addresses provide instant access to the new incumbent or ever-changing incumbents and the username based demi-official e-mail address provides instant access to the particular person, wherever official goes, on multiple transfers and so on, without the need for changing the e-mail address.

4.6. IDRBTCA

IDRBTCA fulfills the need for Trusted Third Party (TTP) services in Electronic Commerce by issuing Digital Certificates that attest to some fact about the subject of the certificate, thereby providing independent confirmation of an attribute claimed by a person offering a Digital Signature. For securing the transactions through INFINET, IDRBT provides high-end Public Key Infrastructure (PKI) based services and solutions that enable trust and security to individuals, organizations, and the government.

Banks can also implement security for their messaging and e-mail applications, using digital signatures and certification to take care of authentication, authorization, confidentiality, non-repudiation, etc.

4.7. NFS

In a major step towards ushering in convenience-banking for the citizens of the country, the Institute has set up the National Financial Switch (NFS). Dr. Y.V. Reddy, Shri. G.N. Bajpai, and Shri. C.S. Rao, dedicated this National Financial Switch to the Nation on August 27, 2004.

The customer-centric National Switch for ATMs enables access to a large number of ATMs of different banks for the citizens of the country. The NFS comprises a switch to facilitate inter-connectivity between the Banks' Switches, and Inter-bank Payment Gateway for authentication and routing the payment details of various e-commerce transactions, e-government activities, etc.

The NFS Network now connects more than 5,500 ATMs, which is the largest number of ATMs under a single network in the country. The National Financial Switch allows connecting directly to the individual bank's switch or through their shared ATM Network Switches. It is a win-win situation for all the banks and more importantly, for the customers.

The Clearing Corporation of India Limited (CCIL) is the clearing and settlement agency for the switch, which also facilitates the NFS Disaster Recovery Site from its premises at Mumbai. An NFS User Group has been set up to deliberate various issues related with the procedures, fee, etc., and a Steering Committee consisting of the banks' top management resolves various issues related to the National Financial Switch and policies from time to time.

Future Ahead

As the world is moving ahead, IDRBT is also planning to migrate from IPv4 protocol to IPv6 protocol for INFINET.

But for migration to IPv6 in the INFINET environment, it is essential that both IPv4 and IPv6 co-exist, therefore an initial test set-up is being planned at the Institute. Further, a hierarchical model is also required to be created, to appropriately decide the IP schema for INFINET members.

On the anvil are also plans to expand the reach of INFINET to rural and semi-urban places of the country.

To conclude, electronic commerce and finance are growing rapidly in the country. New payments mechanisms designed to aid electronic commerce have become routine. Predictions flourish about the capabilities of the information and communication technology to bring forth important tools for conducting electronic commerce and payments.

REFERENCES

Andert, Donna, Wakefield, Robin, and Weise, Joel. (2002): Professional services security practice. Sun BluePrints_ OnLined December.

Benantar, M. (2001): "The Internet Public Key Infrastructure", *IBM Systems Journal,* 40(3).

Carlisle, Adams, Steve, Lloyd. (2002): *Understanding PKI: Concepts, Standards, and Deployment Considerations*, 2nd ed., Addison-Wesley.

Jean Camp L. (2003): "Designing for Trust", *LNAI* 2631: 15-29.

Mayer R., Davis, J., Schooman, F. (1995): "An Integrative Model of Organizational Trust", *Academy of Management Review*, 20(3): 709-734.

Reserve Bank of India: *Payment System in India–Vision 2005-08 Online.*

Sanderson, Ethan and Forcht, A. Karen (1996): "Information Security in Business Environments", *Information Management and Computer Security*, 32-37.

Saxena Ashutosh. *PKI: Concepts, Design and Deployment*, Tata McGraw Hill, New Delhi, 2004.

Spinellis, D., Kokolakis, S., Gritzalis, S. (1999): "Security Requirements, Risks and Recommendations for Small Enterprise and Home-office Environments", *Information Management and Computer Security,* 121-128.

X.509 ITU-T Recommendation X.509. Information Technology, Open Systems Interconnection the Directory: Public-key and Attribute Certificate Frameworks; 2000.

10

Rural Credit Reforms in India: Critical Issues, Challenges and Perspectives

Debesh Roy

1. INTRODUCTION

The Indian economy is characterised by a great rural-urban divide in terms of various parameters. Such parameters include income and wealth, employment opportunities, and access to basic amenities of life, including banking and financial services. In order to achieve the status of a developed nation by the year 2020, India's annual GDP growth needs to accelerate from the present 8 per cent to 10-12 per cent. Needless to say, this Great Indian Vision cannot be achieved by being oblivious to the needs and requirements of the rural economy. In this connection, the banking sector has a key role to play in the development of the rural economy. Nationalisation of commercial banks in India was indeed a pioneering step towards accessibility of banking services to the vast rural population of the country. However, in spite of the enhanced outreach of banks in rural areas and the implementation of directed credit, farmers and rural artisans still did not receive adequate credit from banks during the post-nationalisation period. According to the Expert Committee on Rural Credit (NABARD, 2001), two distinct features characterise Indian rural credit policy: (a) it attempts to bring increasing number of rural households within the ambit of formal institutions, and (b) it aims at making credit an effective instrument of poverty alleviation in conjunction with other measures. It would indeed be a remarkable journey for banks in India from the post-nationalisation era, where they grudgingly financed the 'credit unworthy' rural poor through 'directed credit', to the era of Rural Banking Reforms, when they appreciate that a world of business opportunities lies at the 'bottom of the pyramid'.

The Indian rural credit system is operationalised by multiple agencies, viz. cooperatives, Regional Rural Banks (RRBs), commercial banks and a large network of informal credit outlets. The earliest rural credit institutions evolved during the early twentieth century in the form of cooperative credit institutions. However, the impact of these institutions on the rural economy was insignificant. The Rural Credit Survey Committee (1954) found that the share of institutional credit constituted only 3 per cent of total borrowings in the rural areas. The Committee summed up its findings in the oft-quoted dictum, "Co-operation has failed but co-operation must succeed" and observed that the cooperative institutions were the most suitable agencies for rural credit dispensation, and deemed their faster growth critical to rural development. The Committee's recommendations paved the way for State Bank of India to provide commercial banking facilities to rural and semi-urban areas and associate with the development of co-operative credit. With these measures, the share of cooperatives in the total borrowings of cultivators increased to 38 per cent by 1966-67. This was, however, still far short of expectations. There was a growing realisation that commercial banks should increasingly meet the credit requirements of the rural population, as the cooperative credit institutions alone were not in a position to meet the needs of Indian agriculture. The D.R. Gadgil Study Group (1968) set up by the National Credit Council recommended the involvement of commercial banks in rural credit through branch expansion and directed lending, and also to lend to primary agriculture credit societies (PACS), where District Central Cooperative Banks (DCCBs) were not financially strong. Accordingly, fourteen commercial banks were nationalised in 1969 and six more in 1980. This facilitated the large expansion of bank branches in rural and semi-urban areas. In 1975 the Narasimham Working Group reviewed the flow of institutional credit to the weaker sections, and concluded that reorganizing and restructuring cooperative or commercial banking systems could not meet major regional and functional gaps in rural credit within a reasonable time frame. The Group proposed the establishment of low-cost, state-sponsored, region-based and rural-oriented banks called Regional Rural Banks (RRBs), which were expected to possess the local feel and familiarity of problems of cooperatives, and business acumen, ability to mobilize deposits, access to money markets and modern outlook of commercial banks.

Along with restructuring of rural financial institutions (RFIs), several measures like the establishment of Lead Bank Scheme, directed lending to the Priority Sectors, banking sector's linkage with Government sponsored programmes for poverty alleviation, Differential Rate of Interest Scheme, and the Service Area Approach, were taken. Further, the National Bank for Agriculture and Rural Development (NABARD) was established in 1982 as an apex development financial institution for facilitating credit flow for promotion and development of agriculture and rural non-farm sector, and for promoting integrated and sustainable rural development. It was also vested with policy formulation and regulatory powers *vis-à-vis* cooperative banks and RRBs.

Subsequently, during the post-reforms era, several policy initiatives were undertaken to transform RRBs and cooperative credit institutions into organisationally strong, financially viable and operationally efficient units, viz. reduction in budgetary support and concessionality of resources, preparation of Development Action Plans and signing of Memoranda of Understanding (MoU) with controlling institutions, and introduction of prudential norms relating to income recognition, asset classification and provisioning. The lending rates for these institutions were also deregulated. Further, while RRBs were allowed to finance non-target groups and conduct non-fund business, State Cooperative Banks (SCBs) and District Central Cooperative Banks (DCCBs) were allowed direct financing. There has also been liberalisation in investment policies respect of RRBs and cooperative banks. These measures have contributed many RRBs to turnaround.

The SHG-Bank Linkage Programme, introduction of Kisan Credit Card, and Government of India's thrust on doubling of agriculture credit over a period of three years (2004-05 to 2006-07) promised to change the face of rural credit in India. There is a huge credit potential that needs to be tapped by rapid capital formation in agriculture, spread of hi-tech agriculture, horticulture and organic farming, development of allied activities (dairy, poultry, etc.), creation of rural infrastructure, development of rural non-farm sector (RNFS), capacity building of farmers, artisans and women, institutional development of RRBs and cooperative credit institutions, and an increasing role of the corporate sector in agriculture, allied activities, agro-based industries, and the service sector. These measures could raise the credit absorption capacity of the rural population and lead to a rapid increase in income and employment in rural areas, which in turn could accelerate demand for products of industrial and service sectors. Consequently, the Indian economy can be expected to grow at around 10-12 per cent per annum. Banks, therefore, need to realise that in addition to playing the role of a catalyst in the development process of the country, it makes real business sense to penetrate into the world of rural banking. Against this backdrop, this paper attempts to examine the problems, policy issues, and challenges of rural credit reforms in India.

2. SECTORAL DEPLOYMENT OF BANK CREDIT IN INDIA

An analysis of sectoral deployment of gross bank credit in the country reveals that the share of agriculture has increased by a mere 1 percentage point from 12 per cent to 13 per cent during the period end-March 2000 to end-March 2005 (Figures 1 and 2). While the share of small-scale industries (SSI) suffered a decline from 14 per cent to 8 per cent, the share of other priority sector (OPS) increased from 9 per cent to 16 per cent, during the same period. The share of Priority Sector as a whole increased from 35 per cent to 37 per cent. The share of industry, however, declined from 40 per cent to 31 per cent during the period under review.

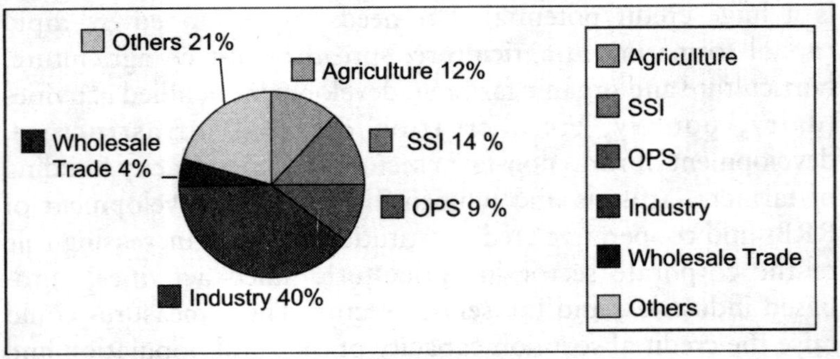

Figure 1: Sectoral Share of Gross Bank Credit (end-March 2000).

Source: *Report on Trend and Progress of Banking in India*, RBI (various issues)

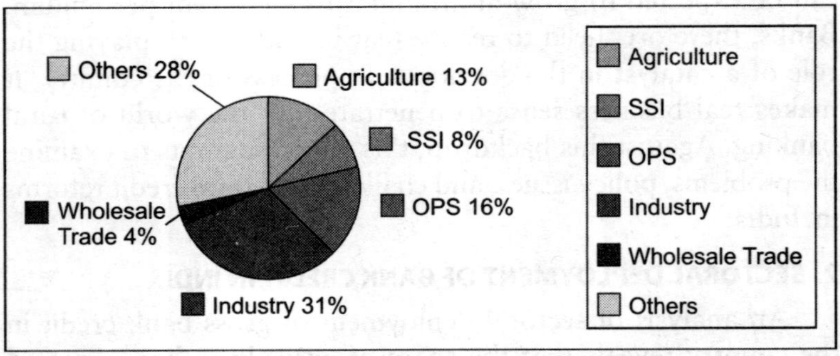

Figure 2: Sectoral Share of Gross Bank Credit (end-March 2005).

Source: *Report on Trend and Progress of Banking in India*, RBI (various issues).

It may, however, be observed that while the growth rate of deployment of agriculture credit increased steadily from 16.99 per cent during 2000-01 to 23.15 per cent during 2003-04, there was a sudden increase to 35.15 per cent during 2004-05 (Table 1). This was primarily due to the thrust on 'Doubling of Agriculture Credit', beginning with the year 2004-05. Similarly, the growth rate of credit to the Priority Sector as a whole increased from 17.13 per cent during 2000-01 to 31 per cent during 2004-05, mainly boosted by the substantial growth in agriculture credit during 2004-05. Although the share of SSI sector in gross bank credit suffered a decline from 14 per cent (end-March 2000) to 8 per cent (end-March 2005), mainly due to an increase in the share of OPS (comprising business and service sectors, housing and educational loans, etc.), there was a steady increase in the growth rate of deployment of bank credit to the SSI sector from 6.04 per cent (2000-01) to 15.58 per cent (2004-05). The OPS experienced a consistently high growth rate in credit deployment from 34.24 per cent (2000-01) to 36.96 per cent (2004-05). Credit to the industrial sector showed a sharp increase from 10.53 per cent (2000-01) to 36.47 per cent (2002-03), followed by a slump to 5.12 per cent (2003-04), and a recovery to 17.38 per cent (2004-05).

Table 1: Sectoral Deployment of Gross Bank Credit

(Amount in Rs. crore)

	March 24, 2000	March 23, 2001	March 22, 2002	March 21, 2003	March 19, 2004	March 18, 2005
Priority sector (i+ii+iii)	1,31,827	1,54,414 (17.13)	1,75,259 (13.50)	2,11,609 (20.74)	2,63,834 (24.68)	3,45,627 (31.00)
(i) Agriculture	44,381	51,922 (16.99)	60,761 (17.02)	73,518 (21.00)	90,541 (23.15)	1,22,370 (35.15)
(ii) SSI	52,814	56,002 (6.04)	57,199 (2.14)	60,394 (5.59)	65,855 (9.04)	76,114 (15.58)
(iii) OPS	34,632	46,490 (34.24)	57,299 (23.25)	77,697 (35.60)	1,07,438 (38.28)	1,47,143 (36.96)
Industry (Medium and large)	1,47,319	1,62,837 (10.53)	1,72,324 (5.83)	2,35,168 (36.47)	2,47,210 (5.12)	2,90,186 (17.38)
Wholesale Trade	16,818	17,845 (6.11)	20,459 (14.65)	22,578 (10.36)	24,867 (10.14)	33,814 (35.98)
Other sectors	79,163	94,066 (18.83)	1,14,707 (21.94)	1,50,700 (31.38)	1,92,511 (27.74)	2,61,839 (36.01)
Gross Bank Credit	4,00,818	4,69,153 (17.05)	5,36,727 (14.40)	6,69,534 (24.74)	7,64,383 (14.17)	9,72,587 (27.24)

Note: Figures in brackets indicate percentage growth over previous year.
Source: *Report on Trend and Progress of Banking in India*, RBI (various issues).

SSIs with a share of 6.5 per cent of the GDP, 95 per cent of all industrial units, 34 per cent of total exports, 20 million jobs and more than 7,500 products, have emerged as a key growth driver. In the post-WTO world, issues, such as, most favoured nation treatment, national treatment, freer trading system and predictable trading system need to be addressed to urgently to provide an enabling environment for a level playing field, providing SMEs with a reasonable period of time and pace for adjustment and adequate safeguards against unfair trade and investment. The steady growth of the SSIs is also constrained by entrenched debilities, e.g., delayed payment of bills, technological obsolescence, inadequate working capital availability, marketing bottlenecks, weak infrastructure, lack of technological synergy between technology seekers (SSIs) and technology developers (R&D), high cost of patents and ineffective coordination between institutions involved in promoting accelerated development. SSIs should be calibrated to emerge from the environment of protection to face the emerging challenges of competition by leveraging their dynamism, flexibility and innovativeness. Accent on various inter-related issues, e.g., speed, customer preference, quality certification, technology upgradation, cost reduction, professional learning, innovation promotion, marketing development and infrastructural support is imperative in the present day context. There are also issues relating to streamlining of SFCs, innovative financing of SSIs, microfinance, total quality management (TQM), venture capital, cluster development, coordination among institutions, credit rating, etc., for the SSIs to realize a high and sustainable growth trajectory (Sharma, 2005 a).

3. PROBLEMS OF RURAL CREDIT IN INDIA

3.1 Inadequacy of Rural Credit

The nationalisation of commercial banks and the setting up of RRBs facilitated the expansion of bank branches in the remotest corners of the country. However, while the rural branches of scheduled commercial banks outnumbered urban branches by more than one and a half times, the share of rural credit in total credit outstanding was a meagre 9.2 per cent as on 31 March 2005, having declined steadily from 10.58 per cent as on 31 March 1999 (Table 2). Similarly, the share of semi-urban credit declined from 12.38 per cent to 11.28 per cent during the period under review. But, the share of urban credit increased from 77.04 per cent (31 March 1999) to 79.52 per cent (31 March 2005).

Table 2: Population Group-wise Credit Outstanding of Scheduled Commercial Banks

(Amount in Rs. crore)

As on	Rural	Per cent share	Semi-urban	Per cent share	Urban/Metro	Per cent share	Total
31/03/99	41,192.86	10.58	48,229.53	12.38	3,00,037.63	77.04	3,89,460.02
31/03/00	47,396.02 (15.06)	10.10	55,021.85 (14.08)	11.73	3,66,613.84 (22.19)	78.16	4,69,031.71
31/03/01	56,016.65 (18.19)	10.07	63,857.47 (16.06)	11.48	4,36,561.83 (19.08)	78.46	5,56,435.95
31/03/02	65,700.28 (17.29)	9.61	73,354.81 (14.87)	10.73	5,44,535.61 (24.73)	79.66	6,83,590.70
31/03/03	74,775.52 (13.81)	9.85	84,683.65 (15.44)	11.15	5,99,751.12 (17.43)	79.00	7,59,210.29
31/03/04	83,244.00 (11.32)	9.36	1,01,334.00 (19.66)	11.40	7,04,268.00 (17.43)	79.23	8,88,846.00
31/03/05	1,06,497.00 (27.93)	9.20	1,30,596.00 (28.88)	11.28	9,20,714.00 (30.73)	79.52	11,57,807.00

Source: *Quarterly Statistics on Deposit and Credit of Scheduled Commercial Banks* (various issues), RBI.

Further, the per branch credit outstanding of rural branches increased from Rs. 1.25 crore as on 31 March 1999 to Rs. 3.33 crore as on 31 March 2005 (Table 3). On the other hand, per branch credit outstanding of urban branches increased from Rs. 16.56 crore to Rs. 44.3 crore during the period under review. The annual rate of growth per branch credit outstanding was, however, higher in rural branches (28.57 per cent) than in urban branches (24.92 per cent) as on 31 March 2005 (Table 3). This could be due to Government of India's thrust on 'Doubling of Agriculture Credit' since June 2004. Incidentally, agriculture credit disbursement during 2004-05 increased by 32.5 per cent (which was significantly higher than that of preceding years), as a result of this policy.

As per extant RBI guidelines agricultural advances should constitute at least 18 per cent of net bank credit. However, banks as a whole have never been able to achieve this benchmark. During the period 2000-01 to 2004-05, the share of agricultural advances to net bank credit in case of public sector banks increased marginally from 15.65 per cent to 15.68

Table 3: Population Group-wise Credit Outstanding Per Bank Office of Scheduled Commercial Banks

(Amount in Rs. crore)

As on	Rural	Semi-urban	Urban/Metro
31/03/99	1.25	3.41	16.56
31/03/00	1.45 (16.00)	3.85 (12.90)	19.82 (19.69)
31/03/01	1.72 (18.62)	4.40 (14.29)	23.14 (16.75)
31/03/02	2.03 (18.02)	4.99 (13.41)	28.41 (22.77)
31/03/03	2.32 (14.29)	5.72 (14.63)	30.95 (8.94)
31/03/04	2.59 (11.64)	7.23 (26.40)	35.44 (14.51)
31/03/05	3.33 (28.57)	8.49 (17.43)	44.30 (24.92)

Note: Figures in brackets indicate percentage growth over previous year.
Source: *Quarterly Statistics on Deposit and Credit of Scheduled Commercial Banks* (various issues), RBI.

per cent (Table 4). The same in respect of private sector banks increased from 9.55 per cent to 12.09 per cent during the period under review (Table 5). The inadequacy of rural credit can also be gauged from the fact that the share of credit to the weaker sections of the society ranged between 7.28 per cent and 8.85 per cent of net bank credit in case of public sector banks (Table 4), and declined from 1.7 per cent and 1.2 per cent in case of private sector banks (Table 5), as against the RBI stipulation of 10 per cent, during the same period. Although the RBI stipulation of 40 per cent of net bank credit towards priority sector advances has been achieved by both public sector and private sector banks, it was mainly due to the fact that the shortfall in priority sector lending targets are required to be deposited by scheduled commercial banks with the Rural Infrastructure Development Fund (RIDF).

Table 4: Advances of Public Sector Banks to Agriculture and Weaker Sections
(As on the last reporting Friday of March)

(Amount in Rs. crore)

Year	Total Agricultural Advances		Weaker Sections		Priority Sector Advances	
	Amount	Per cent to Net Bank Credit (Target 18per cent)	Amount	Per cent to Net Bank Credit (Target 10per cent)	Amount	Per cent to Net Bank Credit (Target 40per cent)
2000-01	53,685.36	15.65	24,805.33	7.28	1,46,545.96	42.99
2001-02	63,082.99 (17.51)	15.81	28,974.90 (16.81)	7.30	1,71,185.26 (16.81)	43.12
2002-03	73,507.06 (16.52)	15.34	32,303.75 (11.49)	6.76	2,03,094.92 (18.64)	42.50
2003-04	86,186.77 (17.25)	15.41	41,588.64 (28.74)	7.44	2,45,671.75 (20.96)	43.94
2004-05	1,12,474.95 (30.50)	15.68	63,492.11 (52.67)	8.85	3,10,093.30 (26.22)	42.23

Note: Figures in brackets indicate percentage growth over previous year.
Source: *Report on Trend and Progress of Banking in India*, RBI (various issues).

Table 5: Advances of Private Sector Banks to Agriculture and Weaker Sections
(As on the last reporting Friday of March)

(Amount in Rs. crore)

Year	Total Agricultural Advances		Weaker Sections		Priority Sector Advances	
	Amount	Per cent to Net Bank Credit (Target 18 per cent)	Amount	Per cent to Net Bank Credit (Target 10 per cent)	Amount	Per cent to Net Bank Credit (Target 40 per cent)
2000-01	5,394.38	9.55	958.94	1.70	21,540.80	38.15
2001-02	8,022.28 (48.72)	8.53	1,142.06 (19.10)	1.82	25,709.14 (19.35)	40.93
2002-03	11,872.60 (48.00)	10.78	1,223.40 (7.12)	1.48	36,704.93 (42.77)	44.35
2003-04	17,651.77 (48.68)	15.81	1,495.49 (22.24)	1.34	52,860.86 (49.40)	47.35
2004-05	21,472.63 (21.65)	12.09	1,913.86 (27.98)	1.20	69,383.68 (31.26)	43.33

Note: Figures in brackets indicate percentage growth over previous year.
Source: *Report on Trend and Progress of Banking in India*, RBI (various issues).

3.2 Low Credit-Deposit Ratio

Lower Credit-Deposit Ratio (CD Ratio) compared to urban centres reflects the inadequate deployment of credit in rural and semi-urban centres. During the period 1998-99 to 2004-05, the CD Ratio of scheduled commercial banks in rural centres increased from 40.15 per cent to 49.87 per cent (Table 6). While the annual growth in CD Ratio in rural centres increased from –1.99 per cent in 1999-00 to 3.26 per cent in 2002-03, it declined to 1.63 per cent in 2003-04, before achieving an impressive growth of 15.68 per cent during 2004-05. This was mainly due to an increase of 27.93 per cent in rural credit outstanding, reflecting the effect of the policy of 'Doubling of Agriculture Credit'. Nevertheless, CD Ratios in rural and semi-urban centers (Tables 6 and 7) fell far short of the RBI stipulation of a minimum CD Ratio of 60 per cent. The urban centres, on the other hand, achieved a healthy CD Ratio of 74.05 per cent as on 31 March 2005 (Table 8).

Table 6: Deposit and Credit of Scheduled Commercial Banks According to Population Group (as on 31 March)—Rural Centres

(Amount in Rs. crore)

Year	Offices	Deposit	Credit	CD Ratio
1998-99	32,856	1,02,601.85	41,192.86	40.15
1999-00	32,719	1,20,446.75 (17.39)	47,396.02 (15.06)	39.35 (-1.99)
2000-01	32,533	1,39,426.68 (15.76)	56,016.65 (18.19)	40.18 (2.11)
2001-02	32,423	1,59,925.31 (14.70)	65,700.28 (17.29)	41.08 (2.24)
2002-03	32,244	1,76,268.52 (10.22)	74,775.52 (13.81)	42.42 (3.26)
2003-04	32,080	1,93,111.00 (9.56)	83,244.00 (11.32)	43.11 (1.63)
2004-05	31,958	2,13,536.00 (10.58)	1,06,497.00 (27.93)	49.87 (15.68)

Note: Figures in brackets indicate percentage growth over previous year.
Source: *Quarterly Statistics on Deposit and Credit of Scheduled Commercial Banks* (various issues), RBI.

Table 7: Deposit and Credit of Scheduled Commercial Banks According to Population Group (as on 31 March)—Semi-urban Centres

(Amount in Rs. crore)

Year	Offices	Deposit	Credit	CD Ratio
1998-99	14,140	1,36,681.41	48,229.53	35.29
1999-00	14,301	1,60,060.15 (17.10)	55,021.85 (14.08)	34.38 (-2.58)
2000-01	14,508	1,86,733.26 (16.66)	63,857.47 (16.06)	34.20 (-0.52)
2001-02	14,688	2,15,473.55 (15.39)	73,354.81 (14.87)	34.04 (-0.47)
2002-03	14,813	2,40,523.25 (11.63)	84,683.65 (15.44)	35.21 (1.17)
2003-04	15,018	2,67,378.00 (11.16)	1,01,334.00 (19.66)	37.90 (7.64)
2004-05	15,375	2,96,303.00 (10.82)	1,30,596.00 (28.88)	44.07 (16.28)

Note: Figures in brackets indicate percentage growth over previous year.
Source: *Quarterly Statistics on Deposit and Credit of Scheduled Commercial Banks* (various issues), RBI.

Table 8: Deposit and Credit of Scheduled Commercial Banks According to Population Group (as on 31 March)—Urban/ Metropolitan Centres

(Amount in Rs. crore)

Year	Offices	Deposit	Credit	CD Ratio
1998-99	18,122	4,62,578.92	3,00,037.63	64.86
1999-00	18,501	5,41,625.86 (17.09)	3,66,613.84 (22.19)	67.69 (4.36)
2000-01	18,867	6,24,545.41 (15.31)	4,36,561.83 (19.08)	69.90 (3.26)
2001-02	19,165	7,21,649.94 (15.55)	5,44,535.61 (24.73)	75.46 (7.95)
2002-03	19,379	8,61,875.37 (19.43)	5,99,751.12 (17.43)	69.59 (-7.78)
2003-04	19,872	10,54,711.00 (22.37)	7,04,268.00 (17.43)	66.77 (-4.05)
2004-05	20,783	12,43,334.00 (17.88)	9,20,714.00 (30.73)	74.05 (10.9)

Note: Figures in brackets indicate percentage growth over previous year.
Source: *Quarterly Statistics on Deposit and Credit of Scheduled Commercial Banks* (various issues), RBI.

An Expert Group constituted by Government of India (2005a) to go into the problems of low CD Ratio has made the following major recommendations:

- While the existing indicator of credit as per sanction should continue to be used to monitor the CD Ratio of banks in a district, it should give way to credit as per utilisation for the purpose of monitoring at the State and bank level.

- The CD Ratio at the State and bank levels should also factor in the contribution made by banks towards RIDF.
- District is to be the unit of implementation, overseeing and monitoring. The districts are to be organised into groups having CD Ratio below 20 per cent, between 20-40 per cent, 40-60 per cent and more than 60 per cent.
- Special Sub-Committees (SSC) of the District Level Consultative Committee (DLCC) are to be set up in districts where the CD Ratio is less than 40 per cent. The SSCs are required to draw up Monitorable Action Plans (MAPs) for improving CD Ratio in their districts on a self-set graduated basis, and set a definite time frame for the CD Ratio beyond 60 per cent in annual increments. The recommended framework for implementation in districts with CD Ratio less than 20 per cent is to be the same as that below 40 per cent, except that the district is to be jointly 'adopted' by the district administration and the Lead Bank.
- The State Government may give an upfront commitment regarding its responsibilities for the creation of identified infrastructure together with support towards creating an enabling environment for banks to lend and recover their dues.

Earnest implementation of the recommendations of the Expert Group (GoI, 2005a) would definitely make a positive impact on the CD Ratio of banks in rural and semi-urban centres. In this connection, the State Governments, through budgetary support, RIDF loans, grant assistance under Rashtriya Sam Vikas Yojana (RSVY), or private- public partnership model (PPP), etc., may develop the infrastructure requirements as identified in the Potential Linked Credit Plans (PLPs) prepared by NABARD at the district level. Further, banks may increase the share of investment credit in their rural credit portfolio, which would not only help increase CD Ratio substantially, but also lead to increase in capital formation in agriculture.

3.3 Non-Performing Assets (NPAs)

There has been an overall improvement in gross and net NPAs in respect of scheduled commercial banks in the country during 2004-05. The sharp rise in credit growth was underpinned by a steady improvement in asset quality (RBI, 2005a). However, it has been observed that the share of NPAs in the priority sector increased from 45.43 per cent at end-March 2001 to 49.05 per cent at end-March 2005, and that of non-priority sector declined from 51.35 per cent to 50 per cent, during the same period, in case of public sector banks (Table 9). Further, while the share of NPAs in agriculture increased from 13.87 per cent to 15.21 per cent, NPAs of SSI sector declined from 19.44 per cent to 16.43 per cent, during the period under review. In case of private sector banks, the share of NPAs in the priority sector decreased from 28.62 per cent at end-March 2001 to 24.87 per cent at end-March 2004-05, and NPAs of non-priority sector increased from 69.45 per cent to 74.65 per cent, during the same period, in case of private sector banks (Table 10). Further, while the share of

Table 9: Non-performing Assets of Public Sector Banks – Sector-wise (As at end-March)

(Amount in Rs. crore)

Year	Agriculture (per cent to Total NPA)	SSI (per cent to Total NPA)	OPS (per cent to Total NPA)	Priority Sector (per cent to Total NPA)	Public Sector (per cent to Total NPA)	Non-Priority Sector (per cent to Total NPA)	Total NPA
2000-01	7,376.65 (13.87)	10,339.41 (19.44)	6,440.18 (12.11)	24,156.24 (45.43)	1,710.87 (3.22)	27,307.01 (51.35)	53,174.12
2001-02	7,821.54 (13.84)	10,583.95 (18.73)	6,733.85 (11.92)	25,139.34 (44.49)	1,115.85 (1.97)	30,251.15 (53.54)	56,506.34
2002-03	7,707.35 (14.60)	10,161.53 (19.24)	7,069.48 (13.39)	24,938.36 (47.23)	1,087.15 (2.06)	26,781.41 (50.72)	52,806.92
2003-04	7,240.30 (14.44)	8,837.92 (17.62)	7,762.11 (15.48)	23,840.33 (47.54)	610.23 (1.22)	25,697.75 (51.24)	50,148.31
2004-05	7,254.05 (15.21)	7,834.96 (16.43)	8,308.37 (17.42)	23,397.38 (49.05)	450.49 (0.94)	23,848.61 (50.00)	47,696.48

Source: *Report on Trend and Progress of Banking in India*, RBI (various issues).

NPAs in agriculture increased marginally from 5.03 to 5.29 per cent, NPAs of SSI sector declined from 15.61 per cent to 10.96 per cent, during the period under review. As bulk of priority sector lending is done by public sector banks the increasing trend in the share of NPAs under priority sector in general and agriculture sub-sector in particular in case of public sector banks is a cause for concern and necessitates immediate steps to arrest the rising trend of NPAs.

Table 10: Non-performing Assets of Private Sector Banks – Sector-wise (As at end-March)

(Amount in Rs. crore)

Year	Agriculture (per cent to Total NPA)	SSI (per cent to Total NPA)	OPS (per cent to Total NPA)	Priority Sector (per cent to Total NPA)	Public Sector (per cent to Total NPA)	Non-Priority Sector (per cent to Total NPA)	Total NPA
2000-01	322.47 (5.03)	1,000.73 (15.61)	511.51 (7.98)	1,834.71 (28.62)	123.37 (1.92)	4,452.26 (69.45)	6,410.34
2001-02	439.16 (3.76)	1,485.26 (12.73)	621.93 (5.33)	2,546.35 (21.82)	31.18 (0.27)	9,089.77 (77.91)	11,667.30
2002-03	536.78 (4.52)	1,261.86 (10.63)	646.76 (5.45)	2,445.40 (20.61)	94.51 (0.80)	9,326.52 (78.60)	11,866.43
2003-04	459.12 (4.43)	1,262.41 (12.19)	760.39 (7.35)	2,481.93 (23.97)	74.58 (0.72)	7,795.81 (75.30)	10,352.32
2004-05	465.40 (5.29)	964.31 (10.96)	758.76 (8.62)	2,188.46 (24.87)	42.34 (0.48)	6,569.03 (74.65)	8,799.83

Source: *Report on Trend and Progress of Banking in India*, RBI (various issues).

It is also a matter of serious concern that cooperative banks have been suffering from high level of NPAs. In case of State Cooperative Banks (SCBs), the NPA ratio varied from less than 3 per cent (as on 31 March 2004) in case of Haryana, Punjab and Rajasthan, to more than 50 per cent in States like Arunachal Pradesh, Assam, Bihar, Manipur and Nagaland. The NPA ratio also varied significantly across the States from 5 per cent to 68 per cent (as on 31 March 2004), in case of DCCBs. Further, while NPAs in case of State Cooperative Agriculture and Rural Development Banks (SCARDBs) varied between zero per cent (Haryana and Punjab) and 100 per cent (Manipur) as on 31 March 2004, the same in respect of Primary Cooperative Agriculture and Rural Development Banks (PCARDBs) ranged between 15.5 per cent in Chhattisgarh and 83.8 per cent in Maharashtra (RBI, 2005a).

The cooperative banks have been advised to make a proper assessment of their NPA position and draw up strategies to bring them down to reasonable levels. The measures suggested included the implementation of the one time settlement scheme (OTS), *Lok Adalats* and referring high value advances to the Debt Recovery Tribunals (DRTs). Further, the refinance policy of NABARD was revised and linked to NPAs so as to restrict the flow of refinance to banks with high level of NPAs (RBI, 2005a).

3.4 Problems of Rural Credit Delivery System

The cooperative credit institutions and RRBs together constitute the backbone of the rural credit delivery system, in terms of outreach. However, these institutions have been plagued with serious problems like high level of NPAs, massive accumulated losses, poor quality of human resources, lack of professionalism in management, and poor corporate governance (Sharma, 2004a). The advent of financial sector reforms led to a paradigm shift in policy issues in respect of the rural credit institutions. Various steps taken by Government of India/ RBI/ NABARD led to an improvement in the financial viability of these institutions, especially the RRBs. However, the cooperative credit institutions and some RRBs continue to suffer from financial and structural weaknesses.

The cooperative credit institutions suffer from low resource base, high dependence on refinancing agencies, high level of imbalances, poor business diversification, low recoveries and huge accumulated losses. The apex level State Cooperative Banks (SCBs) are financially stronger than the District Central Cooperative Banks (DCCBs), while the grassroots level institutions, viz. Primary Agriculture Cooperative Credit Societies (PACS) are the weakest entities in the three-tier Short Term Cooperative Credit Structure (STCCS). Most of the PACS are too small in size to be economical and viable. Out of 1.12 lakh PACS in the country, 62 per cent were viable, 29.7 per cent were potentially viable, 3.5 per cent were dormant and 1.7 per cent were defunct, as on 31 March 2003 (RBI, 2005a). The PACS are heavily dependent on borrowed funds and are not self-reliant, as a result of which their level of business is stagnant.

Out of 31 SCBs, 26 were in profit as on 31 March 2004 with a total profit of Rs. 393 crore (Table 11). The number of loss-making SCBs declined from 6 as on 31 March 2002 to 4 as on 31 March 2004. The amount of losses also declined from Rs. 87 crore to Rs. 20 crore, during the period under review. During the same period the number of profit-making DCCBs increased from 262 to 263, and the amount of profit increased from Rs. 702 crore to Rs. 859 crore. On the other hand while the loss making DCCBs reduced from 105 to 102, the amount of loss increased from Rs. 737 crore to Rs. 758 crore (Table 11). Further, while the accumulated losses of SCBs decreased substantially from Rs. 569 crore (31 March 2002) to Rs. 262 crore (31 March 2004), the same in respect of DCCBs increased from Rs. 3685 crore to Rs. 4981 crore (Table 12).

Table 11: Working Results of Cooperative Banks

Agency/ Year	Total (No.)	In Profit (No.)	Amount (Rs. crore)	In Loss (No.)	Amount (Rs. crore)
SCBs					
2001-02	30	24	258	6	87
2002-03	30	25	500	5	30
2003-04	31	26	393	4	20
DCCBs					
2001-02	368	262	702	105	737
2002-03	367	243	742	122	954
2003-04	365	263	859	102	758
SCARDBs					
2001-02	20	9	85	11	182
2002-03	20	8	62	11	164
2003-04	20	10	97	9	210
PCARDBs					
2001-02	768	196	47	572	323
2002-03	768	211	51	557	357
2003-04	768	276	74	439	411

Source: *Annual Report 2004-05*, NABARD.

The SCARDBs experienced an increase in the number of profit making institutions from 9 (31 March 2002) to 10 (31 March 2004), and the amount of profit increased from Rs. 85 crore to Rs. 97 crore. Further, while the number of loss-making SCARDBs declined from 11 to 9, the amount of loss incurred increased from Rs. 182 crore to Rs. 210 crore (Table 11). The accumulated losses, however, increased substantially from Rs. 494 crore to Rs. 854 crore, during the period under review (Table 12). In case of PCARDBs, while the number of profit-making institutions increased from 196 to 276, the profit increased from Rs. 47 crore to Rs. 74 crore. The number of loss-making PCARDBs decreased from Rs. 572 crore to Rs. 439, but the amount of losses increased from Rs. 323 crore to Rs. 411 crore. PCARDBs also have experienced an increase in accumulated loss of Rs. 2054 to Rs. 2649 crore (Table 12).

Table 12: Accumulated Losses (as on 31 March)

(Amount in Rs. crore)

Year	SCBs	DCCBs	SCARDBs	PCARDBs
2002	569	3685	494	2054
2003	343	4475	657	2381
2004	262	4981	854	2649

Source: Annual Report 2004-05, NABARD.

Compared to cooperative banks the financial position of RRBs has been improving steadily during the period of banking sector reforms. The total profit of RRBs increased from Rs. 699.93 crore as on 31 March 2002 to Rs. 952.33 crore as on 31 March 2004 (Table 13). However, the number of RRBs incurring losses increased from 29 (31 March 2002) to 40 (31 March 2003), before declining to 33 (31 March 2004). The total accumulated losses increased from Rs. 2694.06 crore (31 March 2002) to Rs. 2725.35 crore (31 March 2004). The performance of RRBs, however, varied across States. On the recovery front, there was a general improvement in the performance of RRBs as on 30 June 2004, compared to the previous year. There was also a declining trend in NPAs of RRBs (NABARD, 2005a). Nevertheless, in order to face growing competition with commercial banks, and the need to increase profitability and to improve viability, through expansion in their loan portfolio, it has been maintained by RBI/NABARD that there is a strong case for amalgamation of RRBs.

Table 13: Working Results of RRBs (Rs. crore)

Particulars/ Year	2002	2003	2004
No. of RRBs	196	196	196
RRBs earning Profit (No)	167	156	163
Amount of Profit	699.93	733.97	952.33
RRBs incurring Losses (No.)	29	40	33
Amount of Losses	92.05	214.68	183.65
Accumulated Losses	2694.06	2752.25	2725.35

Source: Annual Report 2004-05, NABARD.

3.5 Inadequacy of Investment Credit, Capital Formation and Infrastructure

A robust increase in capital formation is a pre-requisite to the sustainable development of agriculture. This is mainly due to the daunting task of increasing agricultural production in tandem with the increase in population. Judicious use of natural resources for sustainable production of agriculture, adoption of advanced technology and development of infrastructure for facilitating all agricultural activities, ensuring food security in the broader sense of making adequate nutritious food available and accessible to all and making agriculture a profitable commercial activity at par with other industries in the arena of global economy require a strong and robust capital base (Government of India, 2003). Agricultural development cannot be ensured by confining attention to the activities within the boundaries of agricultural fields. It should encompass activities fully or partially meant for agriculture such as production of fertilizers and pesticides, development of agricultural markets, rural roads and communication; augmentation of facilities for agricultural credit for small and marginal farmers, agricultural education, research and development of agricultural technology which are the main sources of increasing production under the limited availability of natural resources (*ibid.*). While on the input front capital formation and infrastructure development help to ensure timely and adequate delivery to farmers, on the output fronts they help to integrate local markets with national and international markets.

One of the most alarming features of the development of agricultural sector in India during the last couple of decades has been the decline in capital formation. The share of agriculture sector's Gross Capital Formation (GCF) in GDP declined from 1.92 per cent in 1990-91 to 1.7 per cent in 2004-05. This declining share was mainly due to stagnation or even a decline in public investment in irrigation particularly since the 1990s (Table 14). While the public sector investment in agriculture reached the highest level since the early nineties at Rs. 12,809 crore in 2003-04, quick estimates for 2004-05 indicate a decline to Rs. 12,591 crore. The GCF in agriculture also declined from Rs. 47,833 crore in 2003-04 to Rs. 43,123 crore in 2004-05. The share of the agriculture sector's capital formation in GDP, too, declined from 2.2 per cent in 2001-02 to 1.7 percent in 2004-05. During the period 1992-93 and 1998-99 the growth rate of public investment in agriculture was lower than private investment only during the year 1994-95 (Table 14). During the period 2000-01 to 2004-05, however, the growth rate of public investment in agriculture experienced a substantial increase during the year 2003-04, but fell sharply during 2004-05, although it was marginally higher than that of private investment. Capital formation in agriculture is dominated by the private sector, with its share in the total having increased from 70.4 per cent in 1990-91 to 82.9 per cent in 2002-03. However, subsequently, there has been a sharp decline to 70.8 per cent in 2004-05. The basic components of private investment in agriculture are farm equipments, farm machinery, irrigation, land development and land reclamation. These investments help increase agricultural productivity and also facilitate farmers to take up cultivation of non-conventional and high-value crops. Availability of enabling infrastructure, investible resources and expected rate of return on investment are the principal factors, which determine private investment in agriculture. While infrastructure development falls under the purview of public investment, the expected rate of return to an investor is largely determined by the prices of agricultural inputs and outputs. It is in the context of availability of investible resources that institutional credit becomes critically important (RBI, 2005b). Private investment in agriculture can be boosted with improved availability of credit for agriculture and liberalised trade for agricultural products.

Table 14: Gross Capital Formation in Agriculture

(Amount in Rs. crore)

Year	Public	Per cent growth	Private	Per cent growth	Total	Per cent growth	Investment in agriculture as per cent of GDP
Old series (at 1993-94 prices)							
1990-91	4395 (29.6)		10441 (70.4)		14836		1.92
1991-92	3871 (29.9)	-11.92	9518 (70.1)	-8.84	13389	-9.75	1.7
1992-93	4076 (28.1)	5.30	10432 (71.9)	9.60	14508	8.36	1.8
1993-94	4467 (33.0)	9.59	9056 (67.0)	-13.19	13523	-6.79	1.6
1994-95	4947 (33.0)	10.74	10022 (67.0)	10.67	14969	10.69	1.6
1995-96	4849 (33.9)	-1.98	10841 (69.1)	8.17	15690	4.82	1.57
1996-97	4668 (28.9)	-3.73	11508 (71.1)	6.15	16176	3.10	1.51
1997-98	3979 (25.0)	-14.76	11963 (75.0)	3.95	15942	-1.45	1.43
1998-99	3870 (26.0)	-2.74	11025 (74.0)	-7.61	14895	-6.57	1.26
1999-00	4221 (24.4)	9.07	13083 (75.6)	18.67	17304	16.17	1.37
New Series (at 1999-00 prices)							
1999-00	7754 (17.8)		35719 (82.2)		43473		2.2
2000-01	7018 (18.4)	-9.49	31158 (81.6)	-12.77	38176	-12.18	1.9
2001-02	8529 (18.2)	21.53	38215 (81.8)	22.65	46744	22.44	2.2
2002-03	7849 (17.1)	-7.97	38018 (82.9)	-0.52	45867	-1.88	2.1
2003-04	12809 (26.8)	63.19	35024 (73.2)	-7.87	47833	4.29	2.0
2004-05	12591 (29.2)	-1.70	30532 (70.8)	-12.82	43123	-9.85	1.7

Note: Figures in brackets indicate percentage share in agricultural gross investment.
Source: *Economic Survey*, Government of India, 2003-04, 2004-05 and 2005-06.

An essential prerequisite for rapid capital formation in agriculture is an increase in investment credit. It is, however, a matter of serious concern that, while the share of production credit in total agriculture credit increased from 62.6 per cent (1999-00) to 63.2 per cent (2003-04), the share of investment credit declined from 37.4 per cent to 36.8 per cent, during the same period (Table 15).

Table 15: Ground Level Credit Flow in Production and Investment Credit in Agriculture

(Amount in Rs. crore)

Sl. No.	Sector/ Sub-sector	1999-00	2000-01	2001-02	2002-03	2003-04	Growth Rate*
1.	Production Credit	28,965 (62.6)	33,314 (63.1)	40,509 (65.3)	45,586 (65.5)	54,977 (63.2)	17.3
2.	Investment Credit	17,303 (37.4)	19,513 (36.9)	21,536 (34.7)	23,974 (34.5)	32,004 (36.8)	15.4
	Total (I&II)	46,268	52,827	62,045	69,560	86,981	16.6

* Annual Compound Growth Rate.
Note: Figures in brackets indicate percentage share in total agriculture credit.
Source: *Annual Report 2004-05*, NABARD.

The Expert Group (RBI, 2005b) observed that the gap between the credit flow on the basis of current trends and the 10th Five-Year Plan estimates is wider than the estimated gap of doubling of credit dispensation. In fact if the sub-sector wise credit flow grows at the current level, reaching the expected level of credit by the end of 2006-07 appears possible. The Expert Group identified the constraints on investment credit as follows:

- Meagre growth in minor irrigation and farm mechanization which are the major sub-sectors in primary agriculture;
- Declining public sector investment;
- Limited credit absorptive capacity;
- Lack of effective mechanism for technology transfer and poor extension services;
- Inadequate extension services;
- Limited infrastructure for agro-processing, storage, warehousing, value addition and marketing;
- Restrictions on purchases outside the *mandis*;

- Weather aberrations and output fluctuations;
- Inadequate risk mitigation mechanism; and
- Non-availability of land records.

The Expert Group (RBI, 2005b) also identified the following factors that affect the banking institutions in the deployment of investment credit:

- High transaction costs;
- Structural deficiencies in rural credit delivery system resulting in limited outreach;
- Issues relating to credit worthiness, viz. collateral for low asset base farmers;
- Low volume of loans associated with high risk; and
- High manpower requirement in bank branches.

4. RURAL CREDIT IN INDIA: REFORMS, CHALLENGES AND POLICY ISSUES

4.1 An Overview of Rural Credit Reform Initiatives in India

Financial sector reforms were initiated in India during the early nineties, following the publication of the Report of the Committee on the Financial System (RBI, 2001). During the period of reforms financial viability and operational efficiency of rural financial institutions were accorded top priority by the Reserve Bank of India and NABARD. Directed credit and loan waiver schemes announced by the government had weakened rural financial institutions. Loan waiver schemes in particular vitiated the recovery climate in the rural areas. Moreover, the quality of loan assets worsened due to the implementation of target oriented subsidy based government sponsored programmes like the Integrated Rural Development Programme (IRDP), which suffered from poor implementation right from the stage of identification of beneficiaries to the grounding of projects. Further, most of the rural branches were unremunerative and lacked viability in their operations. Internal control over rural branches became weak and ineffective. Information retrieval had been hampered by delays and inaccuracies and quality of assets was severely affected by, amongst other things, absence of post-credit supervision (*ibid.*).

Notwithstanding their geographical and functional expansion in the country, the RFIs suffered from huge overdues and NPAs. A large number of cooperative banks and RRBs had turned into non-viable institutions. The financial sector reforms were aimed at transforming these institutions into organisationally strong, financially viable and operationally efficient units. Several measures were taken in this regard, viz. reduction in budgetary support and concessionality of resources, preparation of Development Action Plans and signing of Memoranda of Understanding (MoU) with controlling institutions, and introduction of prudential norms relating to income recognition, asset classification and provisioning for RRBs and cooperative banks. The lending rates for these institutions were also deregulated. Further, while RRBs were allowed to finance non-target groups and conduct non-fund business, State Cooperative Banks (SCBs) and District Central Cooperative Banks (DCCBs) were allowed direct financing. There has also been liberalisation in investment policies in respect of RRBs and cooperative banks. These measures have contributed many RRBs to turnaround. However, while a greater awareness about profitability and sustainable viability has been created, a large number of cooperative banks continue to remain non-viable entities.

In order to strengthen the capital base of RRBs, the Government of India has since 1994-95 infused capital through budgetary allocations. Recapitalisation has resulted in substantial improvement in the profitability of RRBs. The Report of the Committee on Banking Sector Reforms (RBI, 1998) recommended that Capital Adequacy prescription may be extended to RRBs and cooperative banks, in order to develop a sound and healthy rural financial system. Accordingly, 8 per cent capital to risk weighted assets was prescribed by the Committee (*ibid.*) for RRBs and cooperative banks, to be achieved within a period of five years. The Committee suggested that a review of the capital structure of RRBs be undertaken with a view to enlarging public subscription in line with the recommendations of the Working Group (1975) on establishing RRBs, and also that sponsor banks should be given greater ownership and responsibility in the operation of RRBs. As regards the cooperative banking system, the Committee urged that consideration be given to de-layering of the system with a view to reducing the intermediation costs and providing the benefit of cheaper NABARD credit to the ultimate borrowers. Further, the cooperative credit institutions need to enhance their capital through their members and not by Government. The Committee also recommended that the duality of control of the cooperative credit institutions by State Government and RBI/ NABARD should be eliminated and all cooperative banking institutions should come under the discipline of the Banking Regulation Act, 1949 under the aegis of RBI/ NABARD/ BFS.

Recent reforms in rural credit have involved various policy initiatives including:

- Institutional reforms in the form of consolidation of RRBs through amalgamations and the restructuring/ recapitalisation process of cooperative banks.
- Repositioning RRBs as an effective instrument of credit delivery in the Indian financial system by: (a) enhancing their resource base through line of credit from sponsor banks at reasonable rates, and access to inter-RRB term money/ borrowings, access to repo/ CBLO market; (b) issue of credit/ debit cards and setting up ATMs; (c) opening of currency chests; (d) conduct of various types of foreign exchange transactions by RRBs; and (e) handling pension and other government business as sub-agents.
- The coverage of rural credit has been extended to include storage facilities as also credit through NBFCs.
- Procedural and transactional bottlenecks are being removed, including elimination of Service Area Approach (except in case of government sponsored programmes), reducing margins, and redefining overdues to coincide with crop cycles.
- The scope of Kisan Credit Cards has been widened to

include investment credit component, and issue of General Credit Cards.

- Public and private sector banks are being encouraged to enhance credit delivery while strengthening disincentives for shortfall in priority sector lending.

The reform initiatives taken so far have the potential to accelerate rural credit and expand its outreach through innovations in loan product and delivery, and strengthening of the credit delivery system.

4.2 Doubling of Agriculture Credit

In order to ensure adequate credit availability to farmers so as to achieve 4 per cent growth in agriculture sector during the Tenth Five-Year Plan period, Government of India announced a credit package for doubling of agriculture credit during the three-year period 2004-05 to 2006-07, over and above the disbursement during the year 2003-04. The following strategy has been adopted by RFIs to achieve doubling of agriculture credit:

- Increase annual agriculture credit disbursement of commercial banks, RRBs and cooperative credit institutions by 30 per cent.
- The Special Agriculture Credit Plan envisaged financing by commercial banks to: (a) at least 100 new farmers by each rural and semi-urban branch, resulting in financing about 50 lakh new borrowers; (b) 2 to 3 new investment projects in plantation and horticulture, fisheries, organic farming, etc.; and (c) at least 10 agri-clinics in each district during 2004-05.
- Public sector banks may lend more to small and marginal farmers with emphasis on provision of credit to tenant farmers and oral lessees.
- Debt restructuring by RFIs envisaged: (a) reschedulement/ restructuring of loans in respect of farmers in distress/ farmers in arrears; (b) One-Time Settlement (OTS) scheme for small and marginal

farmers; (c) to finance redemption of past debts from non-institutional lenders.

- Revising scales of finance and realigning them to meet the realistic needs of farmers, especially of capital-intensive agricultural operations.
- Implementation of special package to promote technological upgradation in agriculture, agro-processing and agri-biotech.

The policy of 'Doubling of Credit' has given a proper direction to the acceleration of agriculture credit. This can be corroborated by the data for the year 2004-05, viz. (a) there was a 32 per cent growth in the flow of agriculture credit by all RFIs from Rs. 86,981 crore to Rs. 1,15,243 crore; (b) 7.88 million new farmers were financed by all RFIs taken together; (c) one-third of the total disbursement at Rs. 21,875 crore by public sector banks had gone to new farmers, out of which around Rs. 360 crore (or 1.65 per cent) was disbursed to tenant farmers, who in the past were almost ignored by the institutional credit mechanism.

During the period 1999-00 to 2004-05, the growth rate of agriculture credit as a whole increased from 14.18 per cent to 32.50 per cent (Table 16). It may also be observed that the share of cooperative banks in the ground level credit in agriculture and allied activities, has declined steadily from 39.47 per cent (1999-00) to 26.59 per cent (2004-05). While the share of RRBs increased from 6.86 per cent to 10.17 per cent, the same in respect of commercial banks increased from 53.46 per cent to 63.24 per cent, during the period under review. Further, the rate of growth of agriculture credit disbursed by RRBs increased from 33.04 per cent (2000-01) to a massive 54.57 per cent (2004-05), propelled by the policy on 'Doubling of Agriculture credit'. Commercial banks also showed a robust increase in agriculture credit from 12.43 per cent (2000-01) to 38.99 per cent (2004-05).

Table 16: Agency-wise Ground Level Credit Flow for Agriculture and Allied Activities

(Amount in Rs. crore)

Agency	1999-00	2000-01	Per cent growth	2001-02	Per cent growth	2002-03	Per cent growth	2003-04	Per cent growth	2004-05	Per cent growth
Cooperative banks	18,260 (39.47)	20,718 (39.22)	13.46	23,524 (37.91)	13.54	23,636 (33.98)	0.48	26,875 (30.90)	13.70	30,639 (26.59)	14.01
RRBs	3,172 (6.86)	4,220 (7.99)	33.04	4,854 (7.82)	15.02	6,070 (8.73)	25.05	7,581 (8.72)	24.89	11,718 (10.17)	54.57
Commercial banks	24,733 (53.46)	27,807 (52.64)	12.43	33,587 (54.13)	20.79	39,774 (57.18)	18.42	52,441 (60.29)	31.85	72,886 (63.24)	38.99
Others	103 (0.22)	82 (0.16)	-20.39	80 (0.13)	-2.44	80 (0.11)	0.00	84 (0.10)	5.00	-	-
Total	46,268	52,827	14.18	62,045	17.45	69,560	12.11	86,981	25.04	1,15,246	32.50

Note: Figures in brackets indicate percentage share to total credit disbursement.
Sources: (1) *Annual Report 2004-05*, NABARD, (2) *Economic Survey*, 2005-06, Government of India

4.3 Streamlining RFIs

The Planning Commission estimated demand for food grains during 2011-12 at 298.38 million tonnes. The increase of about 50 per cent in food production in a decade requires augmenting the credit flow substantially. In view thereof as also considerations of equity and distributive justice, the Central Government has been pushing for increased lending to the agricultural and other priority sectors. Doubling of credit growth within a period of 3 years effectively means a growth of 30 per cent over three years. To provide a sense of balance and proportion, it needs to be pointed out that some banks were already achieving this growth rate. Without in any way belittling the significance of such improvement in terms of quantitative parameters, given the decrepit state of rural banking in India, a much more important issue is that of streamlining the quality of the credit delivery system.

RFIs, particularly cooperatives, continue to suffer from systemic weaknesses, such as, high transaction cost, high risk costs, low margins, high NPAs and low capitalisation. Hence, there is a discernible need to make these banks sound and vibrant not only to enhance the functioning of these banks but also to provide a stable macro-economic environment. In view of the severity of the crisis the RFIs are afflicted with, attempts to improve credit delivery systems, need to be well supported by multi-dimensional strategies comprising general strategies, thrust on recovery performance and institution and area specific measures. What is fundamentally needed today is a paradigm shift and a frontal attack on the basic problems afflicting RFIs because the viability of RFIs is inexorably linked to business-related factors, viz. low level of deposits with a large proportion of high cost deposits, low level of advances with an unprofitable mix and injudicious funds management. An efficient and vibrant rural credit delivery mechanism requires maintaining a higher capital adequacy ratio, facilitating restructuring of the system through an exit and privatisation policy, implementing stricter and more transparent accounting and disclosure norms, enhancing rule-based supervision and reduced reliance upon public sector funding because of its unsustainability, highly volatile and socially/economically undesirable nature. Any strategy to streamline the banking system must necessarily address these basic concerns with the support of all players in the system to bring about a marked improvement for sustained development. While financial recapitalisation is expected to cleanse the balance sheets of cooperative banks, its success is contingent on organisational, structural, operational and systemic reforms (Sharma, 2004 b).

4.4 Accelerating Investment Credit

In order to achieve the goals set for the agricultural sector under the Tenth Five-Year Plan, major reform initiatives need to be carried out in this sector. In the context of viable and sustainable development of the sector, the efficient management of land and water resources assumes critical importance. The conservation of land and water resources through watershed development in ecologically fragile areas is intrinsic to sustainable development in agriculture. Out of the country's irrigation potential of 139.89 million hectares only about 68 per cent has been achieved till 2004-05. Development of irrigation projects through Accelerated Irrigation Benefits Programme (AIBP) and Rural Infrastructure Development Fund (RIDF) have been facilitating the development of available potential. An area endowed with a good network of irrigation, roads and power will yield high returns to agricultural investment. Animal husbandry has become an important sub-sector contributing nearly one-fourth of GDP of the agriculture sector. Research and Development efforts should focus on bringing about further improvement in the production potential. Further food and agro-processing sector involving value addition should be a thrust area.

Trade liberalisation in the agricultural sector in the wake of the 'Agreement on Agriculture' under the WTO, is expected to improve the scope for increasing the exports of non-traditional agricultural commodities. The Ministry of Commerce, Government of India, is promoting the establishment of Agri-Export Zones in collaboration with State Governments to boost agricultural exports.

Total institutional credit disbursed to the agriculture sector during the period 1999-2000 to 2003-04 has grown at an annual compound growth rate of 16.6 per cent, with crop loan and investment credit growing at the rate of 17.3 per cent and 15.4 per cent, respectively (Table 17).

Table 17: Sub-sector-wise Ground Level Credit Flow in Agriculture and Allied Activities

(Amount in Rs. crore)

Sl. No.	Sector/ Sub-sector	1999-00	2000-01	2001-02	2002-03	2003-04	Growth Rate* (per cent)
1	Crop Loan	28,965 (62.6)	33,314 (63.1)	40,509 (65.3)	45,586 (65.5)	54,977 (63.2)	17.3
2	Investment Credit	17,303 (37.4)	19,513 (36.9)	21,536 (34.7)	23,974 (34.5)	32,004 (36.8)	15.4
a.	Minor Irrigation	2,345	1,820	1,845	1,976	2,730	3.9
b.	Land Development	318	290	307	393	579	16.2
c.	Farm Mechanisation	3,889	4,125	3,847	3,600	3,986	-
d.	Plantation and Horticulture	777	755	765	1,195	1,436	18.4
e.	Animal Husbandry	2,118	2,188	2,221	2,637	2,928	8.7
f.	Fisheries	404	318	508	539	1,142	29.8
g.	Hi-tech agriculture	1,360	2,088	2,257	2,268	4,017	25.2
h.	Others	6,092	7,929	9,786	11,366	15,186	24.4
	Total (1&2)	46,268	52,827	62,045	69,560	86,981	16.6

* Annual Compound Growth Rate.

Note: Figures in brackets indicate percentage share in total credit to agriculture and allied activities.

Source: *Annual Report 2004-05*, NABARD.

Further, the share of term credit to total agriculture credit has shown a decline from 37.4 per cent during 1999-2000 to 36.8 per cent during 2003-04. During the same period the share of crop loan increased from 62.6 per cent to 63.2 per cent. Under investment credit, sectors like plantation and horticulture, land development, fisheries and hi-tech agriculture experienced substantial gains, while minor irrigation, and farm mechanisation, which together accounted for a substantial share in investment credit (36 per cent during 1999-2000), have lost momentum as well as their relative share in recent years (20 per cent during 2003-04).

The continued higher proportion of short-term credit could probably be due to the relatively higher comfort level of those who demand and those who supply credit. Since expenditure on inputs is inevitable to sustain their agricultural operations, irrespective of weather conditions obtaining in the field, farmers prefer to borrow short-term credit as it provides them necessary control over resources through continued liquidity. The suppliers, on the other hand, favour providing short-term credit due to relatively lower lending and risk costs, lower supervision and monitoring costs and a better asset liability management (RBI, 2005b).

Given the importance of agriculture in India, in terms of its contribution to GDP, employment and income, a low growth rate in agriculture will have an adverse impact on the growth of the economy. Investment, the prime mover, therefore needs to be accelerated to achieve the desired level of growth. However, the investment needs to be appropriately structured, timed and well implemented to have the maximum effectiveness. The National Agriculture Policy adopted in July 2000 and various committees appointed earlier had envisaged an annual growth in agriculture of over 4 per cent per annum and highlighted adequate and timely supply of institutional credit to farmers. Total credit flow to agriculture and allied sectors during the Tenth Plan period was projected at Rs. 7,36,570 crore, including Rs. 3,59,701 crore short-term credit and Rs. 3,76,859 crore medium and long-term credit. The Ground Level Credit (GLC) flow to agriculture has been growing over the years and has reached a level of over Rs. 2,60,540 crore during the three year period (2002-03 to 2004-05) of Tenth Five-Year Plan (i.e. 36 per cent), it is clear that there is a wide gap in supply of credit requiring a large increase in credit, particularly investment credit, to facilitate capital formation in agriculture and to achieve the stipulated growth rate. There is, therefore, a need for evolving a strategy to increase investment in agriculture.

Over the past few years, several discerning changes have been observed in rural India, which will go a long way in redefining agriculture and would also have a significant impact on the investment credit requirements for primary production, areas of diversified activities, trends in value addition and supply chains (RBI, 2005b). While the face of traditional on-farm activities has altered significantly since the onset of the Green

Revolution, some of the basic features of this remarkable change relate to: (a) an increasing number of small and marginal farmers with progressive decline in average size of holding; (b) increased usage of high yielding varieties of seeds, quality inputs and modern equipment necessitating higher investment credit; (c) deceleration in rate of growth in production of food crops particularly in agriculturally advanced states like Punjab; and (d) limited progress in technology adoption especially in rainfed areas. The diversified and new farm activities observed are: (a) an increased trend towards commercial and horticulture crops but with almost imperfect markets for these crops; (b) greater importance for food cash crops like sugarcane, oilseeds, spices and condiments, fruits and vegetables, etc.; (c) emergence of high-tech agriculture and organic farming; (d) a shift towards market-led demand-led agricultural production; and (e) a significant increase in the share of output of allied sectors, viz. dairy, poultry and fisheries and horticulture crops in the agricultural GDP.

Concomitantly, there has been an emergence of new off-farm activities, viz. (a) food processing; (b) storages, godowns, market yards and activities related to grading and certification which are supporting agriculture; and (c) increasing importance of services sector in rural areas. The share of non-agricultural households in rural areas has also increased from 29 per cent in 1983 to over 35 per cent in 2001-02.

In view of the foregoing developments, the Expert Group (RBI, 2005b) identified the following broad thrust areas for increasing investment credit in agriculture:

- Emphasis needs to be laid on traditional investment such as land development, irrigation, and farm mechanisation and integration of small and marginal farmers in the mainstream in the case of marketing and exports;
- Focus of investment must be on the entire value chain of agricultural products;

- In particular reform of agricultural markets and investments in enabling competitive market deserves priority; and
- Public investment in agricultural infrastructure should get a greater priority especially in poorer states, viz. Eastern and North Eastern regions for facilitating greater private investment.

As recommended by the Expert Group (RBI, 2005b), the following policy issues need to be addressed to enable greater deployment of investment credit in agriculture:

- **Legal provision for computerization of land records:** Updating land records regularly and making appropriate amendment in the laws pertaining to ownership rights and land alienation, to enable farmers to offer land as a security for obtaining loans above Rs. 50,000. There is also a need to explore the possibility of simple charge on the land/ crops in place of mortgage, which involves elaborate procedure and payment of heavy stamp duty.
- **Legal support for recovery:** Poor recovery of loans and increasing NPAs not only affect financial health of the credit institutions, but also arrest the flow of funds to various sectors. State Governments should make suitable amendments in the Public Demand/ Revenue Recovery Act and extend all possible help to banks in their recovery efforts. Banks may also take recourse to the services of Lok Adalats, for speedy recovery of their dues and even consider outsourcing recovery to government departments like Revenue Department on commission basis.
- **Reforms in agricultural marketing:** Weak marketing links often deny farmers their due in share price, thereby adversely affecting their cash flows. In some States Agriculture Produce Marketing Committee (APMC) Act restricts the sale of produce outside market yards. Such restrictive provisions may be removed.

In the changing agricultural environment, Research and Development (R&D) in agriculture needs to be demand driven, with involvement of farmers in technology development. While the public sector could play a catalytic role, the entire R&D process could be made more pluralistic by involving public, private farmers' organisations, and the voluntary sector. In this connection, the corporate sector can play a major role in funding R&D and transfer technology from lab to land, as part of an integrated contract farming model. There is a need to refocus R&D agenda from crop centric research in irrigated areas to location specific cropping systems in dry lands and hills and tribal areas. Greater attention may have to be paid to horticulture crops which are land and water saving. Efforts may also be made in harnessing remote sensing technologies to optimise application of inputs and exploring areas in emerging capital-intensive biotechnology. Major, medium and minor irrigation projects sanctioned should have a component of R&D. There is a need for NABARD and banks to collaborate with agriculture universities, *Krishi Vigyan Kendras*, etc., to help farmers improve and diversify farm produce. NABARD has also been advocating the need for banks to focus on financing Area Development Projects in agriculture and allied activities for intensified area development, leading to rapid capital formation, and acceleration of investment credit.

Noted agricultural scientist Professor M.S. Swaminathan has mooted the idea of an 'Evergreen Revolution'. This implies not just increase in crop yield but also productivity without social or ecological damage. Professor Swaminathan has demonstrated that there is a need for agricultural renewal which would address the aspects of soil health, irrigation and water supply, technology from lab to land in post harvest phases, and market advice to farmers, which calls for a more responsible coordination from extension workers. In this connection, there is a need for doubling food production in the country, with a special focus on increasing the output of fruits and vegetables.

In view of the structural weaknesses of cooperative banks and the limited area of operation of RRBs, commercial banks will have to increasingly shoulder the responsibility of supporting private investment in agriculture. At the same time there is a need for consolidation of RRBs and strengthening of cooperative banks. In order to meet the investment credit needs of farmers, banks have been integrating term credit as well as an element of consumption needs with the crop loan requirements under KCC. The Expert Group (RBI, 2005b) suggested that banks could consider determining the normal credit requirements in a given geographic area, for various sizes of holdings and for investments that farmers generally make on their farms such as crop practices, animal husbandry activities, purchase of small implements, etc. Further, tenant farmers and oral lessees may be financed for production, consumption and investment purposes under KCC through Joint Liability Groups (JLG). Banks may also consider developing general-purpose credit cards with features such as fixed repayment schedules, etc. In order to make KCC a more effective instrument for meeting the credit needs of the farmers throughout the year, banks may devise IT enabled cards and also install low-cost cash dispensation machines at their rural branches. Banks could also consider charging differential rates of interest within a narrow band to borrowers depending on their credit utilisation and repayment performance, thereby reducing transaction costs and improving repayments.

4.5 Risk Mitigation and the Role of Commodity Exchanges

With commercialisation of agriculture and an increasing emphasis on financing of the value chain, keeping in mind the need to infuse global competitiveness into Indian agribusiness, there is a need for stepping up of pledge financing, credit for marketing and introduction of Negotiable Warehousing Receipt System. The RBI constituted a Working Group on Warehouse Receipts and Commodity Futures (RBI, 2005c) with a view to examining the role of banks in providing loans against Warehouse Receipts and evolving a framework for participation of banks in the commodity futures market. Price discovery and hedging are the major economic uses of futures contracts. Producers and users of a commodity can use futures contracts to reduce the risk they run due to volatility in the price of the commodity (RBI, 2005c). In this connection, some of the major recommendations of the Working Group are as follows:

- The Central Government may issue a notification under Section 6(1)(o) of Banking Regulation Act, 1949 permitting banks to deal in the business of agricultural commodities including derivatives.
- The creation of Closed User Group (CUG) for everyone engaged in the agricultural commodity business, and it is envisaged as an electronic platform that would offer straight through processing.
- Proprietary positions in agricultural commodity derivatives could be used by banks to mitigate their risk in lending to farmers. To achieve this they have to buy options and options on futures.
- Farmers often incur losses due to volatility in the prices of their produce. With consequent non-performing loans, their access to bank finance is further reduced. Hedging with the use of commodity derivatives is not very easy. Availability of options would give a simpler alternative to the farmers.
- Paper Warehouse Receipts suffer from shortcomings such as difficulty in splitting, risk of forgery and theft/ mutilation, etc., and hence may be replaced by electronic Warehouse Receipts.
- Popularising Warehouse Receipt based lending would help farmers to realise better price for their produce, will lower access barriers, overcome the problem of lack of track record and enable banks to screen borrowers with minimum delay.
- It is desirable that a Warehouse Receipt Act be passed putting the negotiability of Warehouse Receipts on firm legal footing.
- Banks may be permitted to have independent proprietary position in commodity futures linked in a macro way to their credit portfolio. This is the best way in which banks can cover their risks.

- As the farmers are likely to find it difficult to assume positions in future market of their own, banks may offer non-standard contracts to farmers to suit their needs. Further, banks may be permitted to offer commodity derivative based products to farmers to enable them to hedge their commodity price risk.

Commodity Exchanges in India, viz. National Commodities and Derivative Exchange (NCDEX) and Multi-Commodity Exchange of India (MCX) have an important role to play in trading in commodities, both in the spot and futures market, by farmers as well as banks and traders. Generally, farmers in the country (who are mainly small and marginal farmers) lack market information and holding capacity and, therefore, have to resort to distress selling of their produce soon after harvest when there is a glut in the market. Normally, the farmers sell their produce to middlemen/ *artiyas* in rural markets (*mandis*), at prices below the market-determined prices. In an increasingly liberalised environment, commodity exchanges offer market-based instruments to the farmers for managing risk and uncertainty. For the commodity exchanges to make inroads into trading in farm produce there is a need to organise and educate farmers. In this connection, NCDEX has been organising awareness camps for farmers, and making arrangements for soil testing and supply of quality seeds and fertilizers through accredited agencies, in order to ensure good quality of farm produce. Farmers are required to carry their produce to the accredited warehouses of NCDEX, where quality check of the produce is conducted. Once the produce is accepted at the warehouse, the farmers are issued Warehouse Receipts. The farmers have the option of selling the commodities at the spot or futures markets, as per their needs, based on the spot or future prices, respectively, displayed online at centres affiliated to NCDEX members at the village level. The credit needs of the farmers could be met by bank loans against Warehouse Receipts, or through KCC (the scope of which could be enlarged by meeting post harvest and marketing needs).

While the initiative taken by NCDEX promises to benefit the farmers through price discovery, spot and futures trading, and improvement in the quality of farm produce, there are issues relating to logistics like the transportation of the produce of farmers to the nearest warehouse accredited to NCDEX, which could be as far as 100 km from a particular village. There is a need for banks to finance rural godowns under the Centrally sponsored Capital Investment Subsidy Scheme for Rural Godowns, to individuals, entrepreneurs/agri-preneurs, cooperative societies, groups of farmers, etc., in every block headquarters of a district. These godowns could then be accredited to a commodity exchange. In this connection, it is important for farmers to organise into Farmers Clubs (attached to every rural bank branch) under NABARD's Farmers Club Programme, which can play an important role in transfer of technology to the farms for improving productivity and quality of produce, educating farmers about online trading in commodities and about the availability of bank credit, helping bank branches in recovery of loans, and also for facilitating the transportation of farm produce to the warehouses or to the *mandis*.

4.6 Rural Infrastructure

While infrastructure has always been considered a key element of the overall development process, the significance of rural infrastructure has been increasingly realised in attaining the avowed goals of growth and structural transformation (Sharma, 2005b). Increase in credit flow in a given area depends on credit absorption capacity, which in turn depends on supporting infrastructure in the form of connectivity, power and allied linkages including market related linkages like grading and standardizing. Such infrastructure gaps need to be identified and projects prepared by district level functionaries. These projects could be financed under different financial arrangements including Rural Infrastructure Development Fund (RIDF) (RBI, 2005b).

The corpus under RIDF has been increased over the years from Rs. 2000 crore under RIDF – I (1995-96) to Rs. 8000 crore under RIDF – X (2004-05). While the number of projects sanctioned has increased from 4,168 to 60,015, the amount sanctioned has increased from Rs.1,910.54 crore (RIDF – I) to Rs. 8,282.75 crore (RIDF – X) (NABARD, 2005a). The aggregate disbursements under RIDF I-X stood at Rs. 25,384.02 crore. The assistance provided under various tranches of RIDF for rural infrastructure projects has been observed to facilitate the expansion of the production base in rural areas and creation of additional employment opportunities (*ibid.*). The corpus under RIDF – XI was retained at Rs. 8,000 crore. The sanctions under RIDF – XI stood at Rs. 7,301 crore as on 31 January 2006. A special feature during 2005-06 has been a sanction of Rs. 346 crore to the North Eastern States, and is likely to reach Rs. 600 crore by the end of the financial year. Keeping in view the expanding requirements for creating rural infrastructure, the corpus of RIDF – XII has been enhanced to Rs. 10,000 crore (Chidambaram, 2006).

Ineffective implementation of rural infrastructure projects has brought to fore the need for proper appraisal and close monitoring for efficient project management, cost saving and better impact. Given the importance of rural infrastructure and limited quantum of funds under RIDF, there is a case for NABARD to design appropriate products for financing rural infrastructure projects outside RIDF by mobilising resources from the market or banks at competitive interest rates, especially for such projects that are to be implemented through community participation and close involvement of civil society organizations (RBI, 2005a). There also is a need for additional funding of rural infrastructure, possibly through the issue of Rural Infrastructure Bonds with appropriate tax benefits to investors, and also by utilising a part of the country's burgeoning foreign exchange reserves. Development of infrastructure is expected to enhance the credit absorption capacity in rural areas, which in turn would have a multiplier effect on rural income and employment generation.

There is a need to enhance public investment in agriculture in order to give a boost to agricultural production. In this connection, the Central Government has stepped up investment in rural roads and rural employment programmes. Major initiatives taken by the government for agricultural development through enhanced capital formation are as follows: (a) a roadmap for agricultural diversification has been prepared with focus on floriculture, horticulture, animal husbandry and fisheries; (b) strengthening of agricultural marketing infrastructure; (c) national scheme for repair, renovation and restoration of water bodies; (d) focus on micro-irrigation, microfinance, micro-insurance and rural credit; (e) setting up a Knowledge Centre in every village; (f) setting up a National Fund for Strategic Agricultural Research; and (g) provision of urban amenities in rural areas (PURA).

Further, enabling policies to attract private investment in irrigation projects and setting up of power transmission and distribution lines in rural areas, setting up of private R&D units and herbal parks may have to be put in place. Public investment in medium and major irrigation needs to be stepped up, particularly in Eastern and North-Eastern States (RBI, 2005b). Also, commercial banks may review their portfolios and focus on supporting cost-effective sprinkler, drip, and other such systems, not only in water scarce but also in water surplus areas.

The Central Government has announced that assured irrigation, credit, diversification and creation of market for agricultural products are thrust areas (Chidambaram, 2006). The outlay under Accelerated Irrigation Benefits Programme (AIBP) has been increased from Rs.4,500 crore during 2005-06, to Rs. 7,121 crore for the year 2006-07. The programme for repair, renovation and restoration of water bodies is being implemented in 23 districts in 13 States. The first phase is expected to cover 20,000 water bodies with a command area of 1.47 million hectares.

The experience of NABARD in participatory investments with community based watershed development projects in dry land areas under the Watershed Development Fund has shown that watershed projects, when designed, implemented and maintained through community participation and voluntary community labour, are better executed in terms of technical parameters and lead to substantial downstream benefits for all participants. Similarly, Watershed Development Projects implemented by NABARD under Indo-German Watershed

Development Programme in water scarce districts of Maharashtra can be replicated in other States having similar environment.

4.7 Institutional Reforms

4.7.1 *Consolidation of RRBs*

The process of recapitalisation of RRBs started in 1994-95 and continued till 1999-2000 and covered 187 RRBs with an aggregate financial support of Rs. 2,188 crore from the shareholders (Central Government, sponsor banks and State Governments). Further, under the guidance of NABARD preparation of annual development action plans for attaining financial viability within a definite time frame was introduced in 1994-95. These initiatives led to an impressive turnaround of loss-making RRBs. However, there was a general perception that the RRBs did not fully meet the expectations of their role as a critical channel for rural credit delivery. According to the Advisory Committee on Flow of Credit to Agriculture and Related Activities from the Banking System (RBI, 2004), the turnaround of most of the RRBs emanated largely from their treasury operations rather than from their commercial banking operations. The Committee highlighted the following external and internal factors, responsible for hampering the working of RRBs: (a) Limited area of operations and narrow client base of RRBs; (b) High transaction cost caused in part due to a large number of small accounts; (c) Lack of professionalism in management; (d) Inappropriate and inadequate training of their staff; (e) Ineffective board of directors, since government/ sponsor bank still retained most decision-making powers.

The Advisory Committee (*ibid.*) was of the view that RRBs had an important role to play, particularly because of their strong rural branch infrastructure and rural orientation of their staff. There is, thus, a need to restructure RRBs into viable financial institutions, while retaining their regional character and rural focus. Different committees and working groups have over the years suggested various measures to restructure RRBs into viable entities. The options suggested by these committees are: (a) merger of RRBs with sponsor banks; (b) all RRBs sponsored by a single sponsor bank to be amalgamated into a single, wholly owned subsidiary of the sponsor bank; (c) each RRB to be a wholly owned subsidiary of the sponsor bank; (d) consolidation of RRBs into a National Rural Bank; (e) continuation of the existing structure; (f) privatisation of RRBs; (g) amalgamation of RRBs into zonal banks; (h) amalgamation of RRBs into state level banks; and (i) state level amalgamation of a sponsor bank.

The Advisory Committee (RBI, 2004) was of the opinion that there was a need to adopt a hybrid model combining different options, with a view to making RRBs viable, stronger and vibrant institutions. It also recommended the merger of all RRBs in North-Eastern States into a zonal bank, with its equity being held by NABARD (26 per cent), State Bank of India (37 per cent) and United Bank of India (37 per cent). The Committee also recommended a two-step reorganisation of RRBs for the rest of the country. As a first step, the Committee recommended that all RRBs of a sponsor bank in a state would be amalgamated into a single unit in that state, and in the process reducing the number of RRBs in the country from 196 to 74. As a second step the Committee recommended state-wise consolidation and formation of state level RRBs within a period of three to five years, reducing the total number of RRBs to 20.

An Internal Group on RRBs has suggested that in order to improve the operational viability of RRBs, the route of merger/ amalgamation of RRBs may be considered on two lines: (a) merger between RRBs of the same sponsor bank in the same State; and (b) merger of RRBs sponsored by different banks in the same State (RBI, 2005d). It was argued that a change in sponsor banks may, in some cases, help improve competitiveness, work culture and efficiency of the concerned RRBs, and that the new sponsor bank could even be a private bank. The following major recommendations of the Internal Group promise to turn RRBs into viable and professionally managed institutions:

- The merged entities and existing RRBs that have accumulated losses can be capitalized to wipe out the losses and satisfy minimum capital requirements. The CRAR could initially be kept at 5 per cent;

- An exit route subject to extant legal provisions may be considered for RRBs which cannot turnaround within 3 to 5 years;
- Professionalising and strengthening the Boards of RRBs;
- An appropriate recruitment policy, providing for greater flexibility and freedom to the RRBs;
- Appropriate incentive structure, career planning, and relevant training for the employees of RRBs;
- RRBs may actively consider distribution of products of mutual funds/ insurance companies, rationalisation of branch network, participate in consortium lending within their areas of operations; and
- RRBs may be considered for currency chest facility and empowered to collect taxes by the State Government.

During the year 2005-06, the options for amalgamation of statewise sponsor-bankwise RRBs (e.g., Bank of Baroda sponsored Baroda Gujarat Gramin Bank) and region-wise sponsor-bank-wise within a State (e.g., Bank of Baroda sponsored Baroda Eastern Uttar Pradesh Gramin Bank, and SBI sponsored Purvanchal Gramin Bank), were exercised. It is interesting to observe that the newly formed Bank of Baroda sponsored RRBs have adopted uniform operational practices including Information Technology at par with those prevalent in Bank of Baroda. Even the logo of the sponsor bank forms part of the logo of these banks. It is not improbable that in the long run these RRBs could either become fully owned subsidiary of the sponsor bank or could even be merged with the latter.

It is expected that the formation of strong RRBs would enable them to upscale their operations by increasing and diversifying their loan portfolio, conducting non-fund business more efficiently, conducting foreign exchange transactions, and setting up ATMs or sharing them with commercial banks. It is also expected that the emergence of stronger and more professionally managed RRBs would help meeting the ever-increasing credit needs of the rural areas in a more cost-effective and efficient manner.

4.7.2 *Restructuring, Revitalizing and Strengthening of Cooperative Credit Institutions*

The cooperative credit institutions are the oldest rural credit delivery agencies in India. They also have the widest network of credit outlets, covering every state and union territory. One of their major strengths is their proximity to their members, both physical and conceptual (NABARD, 2001). These institutions are also an important constituent of the institutional structure necessary for the development of the rural areas. However, the health of the rural cooperative credit institutions (both short-and long-term structures) has been a major cause of concern. Government of India, RBI and NABARD have over the years set up several committees/ expert groups to study the problems of the cooperative credit system and recommend measures to revive, revitalise, restructure and reform the rural cooperative credit institutions so as to enable them to transform into strong and viable entities.

The Capoor Task Force (RBI, 1999) suggested a four dimensional strategy of strengthening the rural cooperative credit system that included the financial, operational, organisational and systemic aspects. The Task Force focused on raising of the resource base and business of the cooperative credit institutions by facilitating them to become member-driven enterprises. The need to adopt the essential features of the Model Cooperative Societies Act (GoI, 2001) by all State Governments or to bring in necessary amendments in the State Cooperative Societies Act so as to reflect the spirit of democratisation and self-reliance, was also highlighted. Various committees (viz. Capoor Task Force and ECRC) broadly agreed about the need to infuse professionalism and accountability in cooperative credit institutions. Another vital issue highlighted by these committees has been the duality of control over the cooperative credit institutions between the State Government on one hand and

RBI/ NABARD on the other. It has, therefore, been suggested that the provisions of the Banking Regulation Act, 1949 should override the provisions of the State Acts/ By-laws/ Rules, which run counter to it. It has also been broadly agreed that the cooperative credit institutions should devise attractive banking products and diversify their credit portfolio in order to compete effectively with commercial banks and RRBs.

An important issue deliberated upon by various committees, viz. ACRC (1989), Narasimham Committee II (1998), Capoor Task Force (1999), ECRC (2001), Vikhe Patil Committee (2003), is the de-layering of the three-tier short-term cooperative credit structure. While it was broadly agreed that de-layering *per se* might not bring about the desired efficiency or economy in the operations of the institutions, the Narasimham Committee II urged that consideration be given to de-layering of the system with a view to reducing the intermediation costs and providing the benefit of cheaper NABARD credit to the ultimate borrowers (RBI, 1998). The Capoor Task Force argued that the existing three-tier structure should continue in the bigger states, and was of the opinion that for the structure as a whole to work as a cohesive system, the organisational tiers have to be made stronger, and the responsibility in this regard should rest on the higher tiers. The Task Force also suggested that wherever necessary measures should be taken for strengthening the cooperatives, if necessary, by voluntary amalgamation/ merger based on economies of scale, particularly in areas, where DCCBs are unviable and are not in a position to ensure uninterrupted credit flow to agriculture.

Being a major player in the rural credit structure, cooperative credit institutions need to be financially strong and viable. While these institutions have been following prudential norms, viz. asset classification, income recognition and provisioning, they have so far been exempt from meeting capital adequacy norms. Therefore, the need to recapitalise the weak cooperative credit institutions has been broadly agreed to by various committees, so that over the years they could conform to these norms.

A Task Force on Revival of Rural Cooperative Credit Institutions (Vaidyanathan Committee) was constituted by

Government of India to propose an action plan to revive the rural cooperative banking institutions and suggest appropriate regulatory framework for these institutions. The Task Force (GoI, 2005b) made the following major recommendations to strengthen the Short-Term Cooperative Credit Structure:

- The Cooperative Credit Structure is impaired in governance, managerial and financial fronts and hence needs to be revived and restructured.
- Financial assistance to be made available for wiping out accumulated losses; covering invoked but unpaid guarantees by the State Governments; increasing the capital to a minimum specified level; retiring government share capital; and technical assistance.
- Availability of financial assistance from Government of India shall be strictly subject to legal and institutional reforms in the cooperative sector by the State Governments, to ensure that the cooperatives become truly democratic and member-driven. These reforms shall include: (a) ensuring full voting membership rights on all users of financial services including depositors; (b) removing state intervention in administrative and financial matters in cooperatives; (c) removing provision for Government equity and participation in the Boards of cooperatives; (d) withdrawing restrictive orders on financial matters; (e) permitting cooperatives the freedom to take loans from any financial institution and similarly place their deposits with any financial institution of their choice; (f) permitting cooperatives under the parallel Acts to be members of upper tiers under the existing cooperative societies Acts and *vice versa*; (g) limiting powers of the State Government to supersede Boards; (h) ensuring timely elections before expiry of the terms of the existing Boards; (i) facilitating full regulatory powers for RBI in case of cooperative banks; and (j) introducing prudential norms including CRAR for all financial cooperatives including PACS.

- Certain major amendments to the Banking Regulation Act, 1949 has been suggested by the Task Force to enable the removal of dual control and bringing the cooperatives under the regulatory control of the RBI, viz. all cooperative banks would be on par with commercial banks as far as regulatory norms are concerned; the RBI will prescribe 'fit and proper' criteria for elections to the Boards of the cooperatives; the RBI will prescribe certain criteria for professionals to be in the Boards of cooperative banks; the CEOs of the cooperative banks would be appointed by the respective banks themselves.
- Total financial assistance has been tentatively fixed at Rs. 14,839 crore.
- NABARD to be designated as the Nodal Implementing and Pass Through Agency to coordinate and monitor the progress of the programme representing the Government of India.

Consequent upon submission of the aforementioned Report, Government of India had entrusted the work of suggesting an implementable action plan for the revival of the Long-Term Cooperative Credit Structure (LTCCS) to the Vaidyanathan Committee. The Draft Report of the Task Force reiterated that like the Short-Term Cooperative Credit Structure, the revival and revitalisation of the LTCCS would also require amendments in the existing laws (GoI, 2005c). It has also been suggested that the primary units in the structure be at liberty to join the higher tier of their choice. The reform measures, including financial assistace, suggested by the Task Force (LT) are similar to those suggested for the Short-Term Cooperative Credit Structure. In addition, the measures specific to the LTCCS, suggested are as follows:

- Enabling LTCCS to undertake credit business other than long-term loans and also loans for non-agricultural purposes.
- Enabling accepting of deposit by Primary Cooperative Agriculture and Rural Development Banks (PCARDBs)

from members and State Cooperative Agriculture and Rural Development Banks (SCARDBs) from the public, subject to regulatory norms on the lines of those specified for loan companies.

- Converting unitary structures to federal ones.
- Providing full autonomy to the primary and apex units in the appointment of CEO and all other operating personnels.

Various committees, including the Vaidyanathan Committees (STCCS and LTCCS), have considered the need to integrate the STCCS and LTCCS in the long run. In this connection, the experience of the integration of the two structures in Andhra Pradesh has not been satisfactory. However, the Vaidyanathan Committees have recommended the need to revive the system, in terms of vision, conditionalities, and operational methodologies, and to create an environment in which both the structures are enabled to come together, meet on a common platform, so that in the long run they move towards integration. In order to achieve the long-term vision of an integrated cooperative system, it is also necessary to bring the LTCCS under the purview of the Banking Regulation Act, 1949. But the Vaidyanathan Committees have not been able to agree with this view, on the grounds that the LTCCS does not have the experience of banking in the wider sense of the term. Nevertheless, keeping the long-term vision in mind and the need to develop and sustain financially strong and viable credit institutions to enable them to meet the growing rural credit requirements, it would be advisable for the SCARDBs to transform themselves into full-fledged banks, within a specified time frame.

It is now widely agreed that the growing needs of rural credit can only be met by financially strong and viable entities, viz. commercial banks, RRBs and the cooperatives. Hence, the time has arrived for the State Governments concerned to carry out the reforms suggested by Vaidyanathan Committees (STCCS and LTCCS), so that the cooperative credit institutions are able to compete with commercial banks and RRBs on an equal footing, and serve the rural population more effectively.

4.8 Role of Information Technology (IT)

An infrastructure of village level kiosks is being promoted across the country by internet service providers, public-private partnerships and agri-business corporates. ITC's *e-choupal* is by far the most successful model that has unlocked value for all the stakeholders. Another application of IT is in terms of providing timely information to farmers. A case in point is the Information Village Research Project implemented by the M.S. Swaminathan Research Foundation for Pondicherry fishermen. As a part of the project, computers were placed in the village centre and connected to the Internet, through which regular weather reports of the Indian Meteorology office could be accessed. The 2005-06 Union Budget had announced an allocation of Rs. 100 crore from RIDF for setting up of Rural Knowledge Centres. Village level internet kiosks can be an effective channel to deliver financial services to the unorganized sector right at their doorstep, at a lower cost.

Computerisation in rural branches is expected to lead to substantial improvement in their profitability and productivity. However, infrastructural bottlenecks, high cost of software, high investment in hardware and cost of servicing and maintenance of computers are certain problems, which could discourage computerisation. But these problems can be overcome by developing suitable low-cost software and compatible hardware for the rural/ semi-urban centres. While the initial investment would be high the benefits likely to accrue from computerisation are immense. This would provide the banks more time to devote to business planning and development, deposit mobilisation efforts, recovery of loans and devising innovative credit delivery systems to serve the customers better (Roy, 2003).

The Committee on Banking Sector Reforms (RBI, 1998) had recommended the networking of bank branches for the achievement of branch automation. It had also suggested the introduction of "cluster" automation approach for providing the facilities of 'anywhere banking'. Further, service providers who enable outsourcing of branch/ bank automation should be encouraged. Banks need not, therefore, invest in expensive technological investments in small, isolated branches and can yet automate such branches by hooking up to the service provider. ICICI Bank is reportedly planning to install low cost ATMs in rural areas. In this connection, banks should convert Kisan Credit Cards to electronic credit cards, which would enable farmers to withdraw cash from ATMs anywhere in the country. In order to demonstrate the concept of branch automation with specific reference to the use of memory/ processor cards for SHGs and other clients, a pilot project has been launched in five branches of Sri Visakha Gramin Bank in Andhra Pradesh which would test the acceptability and adaptability of IT in rural areas as also to address MIS needs in rural banks. The project envisages the issue of processor cards to KCC holders and SHGs and also automation of book-keeping in SHGs, with a view to reducing paper work, saving time and improving efficiency (NABARD, 2005b).

4.9 Credit Planning

Capital formation is crucial for economic development, and when it occurs rapidly, it helps to create a sound base for further development. In this context, banks play a crucial role in the process of economic development as purveyors of credit to individuals and institutions. The nationalisation of commercial banks focused on expansion of bank branches in the hitherto unbanked and underbanked rural and semi-urban areas of the country. It was realised that a major bottleneck in the process of economic development was rural indebtedness. The rural poor were heavily dependent on non-institutional sources of credit and were trapped in the vicious cycle of poverty. It was recognised that the development planning process could be effective only when it was aligned with credit planning. A systematic approach to rural credit planning was conceived by the RBI under the Lead Bank Scheme in December 1969. Lead Banks were required to formulate comprehensive District Credit Plans (DCPs) in consultation with bankers and Government functionaries which were to be implemented by banks operating in the respective districts. However, the experience was that the DCPs were largely divorced from ground level potentials and absorptive capacity of the area and they essentially remained bankers' budgetary plans.

The Service Area Approach to rural lending was introduced by RBI in 1989. Under this approach every rural and semi-urban branch of commercial banks and RRBs which are allocated a number of villages, prepare a credit plan for each of the allocated villages. Such village-wise credit plans are consolidated into Branch Credit Plans. The Branch Credit Plans are aggregated into Block Credit Plans, which in turn, are added up to form the District Credit Plan. NABARD in 1998-99 took the initiative of preparing Potential Linked Credit Plans (PLPs), which were to reflect the ground level potential, credit and non-credit linkages as well as the macro-level policies and interventions and micro-level demands/ needs. The objective was to arrive at a comprehensive document of potentials for various rural economic activities, both in physical and financial terms. It was felt that this would facilitate a meaningful direction to the flow of ground level credit and enable the GoI/ RBI/ NABARD to assess the gap in credit supply and take corrective policy measures. Co-terminous with each Five-Year Plan, a Base PLP is prepared. Its formulation envisages estimation of long term potential for the entire plan period in each sector of agriculture and rural development. The annual phasing for the second and remaining years of the Five-Year Plans is updated every year to keep the projections in tune with the changes in priorities of the Government, availability of infrastructure, attitude of clients and avenues for deployment of bank credit.

With the relaxation of Service Area norms by the RBI in the recent past, PLPs have been made the basis for preparation of DCPs. Thus, the entire PLP process has been made consultative. Accordingly, there is a provision for pre-PLP and post-PLP meetings where views of all stakeholders in the development process are sought. The PLPs also provide a proper and comprehensive estimation of infrastructure requirements in the district to facilitate State Governments to identify projects under RIDF. The idea behind this paradigm shift in the credit planning process is to make the DCP realistic and implementable with a view to realising the full potential of the district.

5. CONCLUSION

The Indian economy is one of the fastest growing economies in the world. But to sustain this momentum there is a need to accelerate rural development. Majority of the rural population lives in poverty and rural areas lack basic socio-economic and physical infrastructure. In this context banks have a critical role to play by meeting the credit needs of the rural population. Problems of rural credit, viz. inadequacy of credit, sectoral imbalances, institutional weaknesses, high level of NPAs, lack of capital formation in agriculture and low CD Ratio, need to be addressed through comprehensive reforms in rural credit.

Various reform initiatives have been undertaken in recent years, which have the potential to accelerate rural credit. An essential prerequisite for meeting the growing rural credit needs is the existence of strong and viable rural credit institutions. Institutional development of RRBs and cooperative banks, through consolidation, recapitalisation and restructuring has received focused attention from GoI, RBI and NABARD. The emergence of stronger and more professionally managed RRBs and cooperative credit institutions would help meet the ever-increasing credit needs of the rural areas in a more cost-effective and efficient manner.

In order to ensure adequate credit availability to farmers so as to achieve 4 per cent growth in agriculture sector during the Tenth Five-Year Plan period, Government of India announced a credit package for Doubling of Agriculture Credit during the three-year period (2004-05 to 2006-07), over and above the disbursement during the year 2003-04. The target for disbursement of agriculture credit during 2004-05 has been achieved, and it is expected that the same for the year 2005-06 would also be achieved. However, such high growth rate can be sustainable only when there is a comprehensive plan of action to accelerate investment credit, leading to capital formation in agriculture, and also to identify and develop rural infrastructure. Increase in credit flow in a given area depends on credit absorption capacity, which in turn depends on supporting infrastructure in the form of connectivity, power and allied linkages including market related linkages like grading and standardizing. In this context, reforms in the rural credit planning process initiated recently in the form of refinement in preparation of PLPs which form the basis for preparation of DCP are expected to lead to a more balanced sectoral credit flow.

The commodity exchanges, viz. NCDEX and MCX have an important role in facilitating farmers in price discovery and spot and futures trading in commodities, as well as improvement in productivity and the quality of farm produce. In this connection, the role of Farmers Clubs in transfer of technology to the farms for improving productivity and quality of produce, educating farmers about online trading in commodities and about the availability of bank credit, helping bank branches in recovery of loans, and also for facilitating the transportation of farm produce to the warehouses or to the *mandis*, would be critical.

Information Technology would be a critical component in the rural credit delivery system. Computerisation in rural branches and installation of ATMs (preferably low cost cash dispensation machines) and conversion of Kisan Credit Cards to electronic credit cards, are expected to lead to substantial improvement in their profitability and productivity. The role of ITC's *e-choupals,* and Information Village Research Project implemented by the M.S. Swaminathan Research Foundation and Rural Knowledge Centres, in providing information relating to price of farm produce, and weather conditions, etc., would pave the way for sustainable rural development. Village level internet kiosks can be a cost-effective channel to deliver financial services to the unorganized sector right at their doorstep.

A fast growing rural economy will have a multiplier effect on the growth of the rest of the economy. In this context, the role of rural credit institutions in the creation of capital and investment opportunities in the rural areas, assumes great significance. Contrary to popular perception, the issue of streamlining of rural credit institutions has both quantitative and qualitative dimensions. While underscoring the significance of increasing rural credit in quantitative terms, it is important not to be impervious to the qualitative aspects of the rural credit system, particularly the century old cooperative system. Clearly the realisation of the Great Indian Vision of achievement of the status of a developed nation by 2020 depends on balanced and equitable development—a process of economic growth that is inclusive, equitable and all encompassing. In this overarching scenario, it is manifestly clear that the rural economy has to be vibrant and resilient to achieve the avowed goals of development.

REFERENCES

Chidambaram, P. (2006): *Budget Speech 2006-07*, Government of India.

Government of India (1991): *Report of the Committee on Model Cooperatives Act,* Planning Commission (Chairman: Chowdhary Brahm Perkash).

—— (2003): *Report on the Committee on Capital Formation in Agriculture*, Directorate of Economics and Statistics, Dept. of Agriculture and Cooperation, Ministry of Agriculture.

—— (2005a): *Report of the Expert Group on Credit-Deposit Ratio* (Chairman: Y.S.P. Thorat).

—— (2005b): *Report of the Task Force on Revival of Rural Cooperative Credit Institutions (Short-Term)* (Chairman: A.Vaidyanathan).

—— (2005c): *Draft Report of the Task Force on Revival of Rural Cooperative Credit Institutions (Long-Term)* (Chairman: A.Vaidyanathan) www.finmin.nic.in, www.rbi.org.in, www.nabard.org

——. (2006): *Economic Survey, 2005-06*, Ministry of Finance, Economic Division.

NABARD (2001): *Report of the Expert Committee on Rural Credit* (Chairman: V.S. Vyas).

—— (2005a): *ABARD Annual Report 2004-05.*

—— (2005b): *Progress of SHG-Bank Linkage in India, 2004-05.*

Reserve Bank of India (1991): *Report of the Committee on the Financial System* (Narasimham Committee I).

—— (1998): *Report of the Committee on Banking Sector Reforms* (Narasimham Committee II).

—— (1999): *Report of the Task Force to Study the Cooperative Credit System and Suggest Measures for its Strengthening* (Chairman: Jagdish Capoor).

—— (2004): *Report of the Advisory Committee on Flow of Credit to Agriculture and Related Activities from the Banking System* (Chairman: V.S. Vyas).

—— (2005a): *Report on Trend and Progress of Banking in India, 2004-05.*

—— (2005b): *Report of the Expert Group on Investment Credit,* June 2005 (Chairman: Y.S.P. Thorat).

—— (2005c): *Report of the Working Group on Warehouse Receipts and Commodity Futures* (Chairman: Prashant Saran).

—— (2005d): *Report of the Internal Group on Regional Rural Banks.*

Roy, Debesh (2003): *Dynamics of Bank Deposits: The Developing States in India*, Social Science Press, New Delhi.

Sharma, Manoranjan (2004a): "Resuscitating Rural Financial Institutions in India: Catalytic Role of Micro Finance", *Sixth Conference on Money and Finance*, IGIDR, Mumbai, March 28.

—— (2004b): "Financing of SMEs in a Globalised World – Expedient Issues and Paradigm Shifts", *FICCI Conference on Global Banking: Paradigm Shift,* September.

—— (2005a): "Rural Non-Farm Sector in India: Issues and Evidence", *Leading Issues in Indian Economy*, (ed.) Manoranjan Sharma, Atlantic Publishers and Distributors, New Delhi.

—— (2005b): "Bracing for Tomorrow: Renewed Thrust on Rural Infrastructure Imperative", *Bankers' Conference*, November.

Day of the Week Effect and Market Efficiency—Evidence from Indian Equity Market Using High Frequency Data of National Stock Exchange*

11

Golaka C. Nath and *Manoj Dalvi*

Introduction

In recent years the testing for market anomalies in stock returns has become an active field of research in empirical finance and has been receiving attention from not only in academic journals but also in the financial press. Among the more well-known anomalies are the size effect, the January effect and the day-of-the-week effect. The day-of-the-week effect is a phenomenon that constitutes a form of anomaly of the efficient capital market theory. According to this phenomenon, the average daily return of the market is not the same for all days of the week, as we would expect on the basis of the efficient market theory.

---

* The authors thank Dr. A.K. Nag of RBI and Prof. Bidisha Chakrabarty of John Cook School of Business, St. Louis University for their comments on the preliminary draft of this paper. The authors are thankful to Dr. Abhiman Das of MIT for help in SAS codes. The authors thank NSE for providing the high frequency data at a very nominal cost for the research work undertaken in this paper. The authors also would like to thank Prof. Bhagwan Chowdhry of CUNY and now at ISB, Susan Thomas of IGIDR and now at ISB and participants in the Financial Analytics Conference (2004) at ISB, Hyderabad. Thanks due to the participants at the International Conference of SEBI-ICFAI on Emerging Securities Market: Challenges and Prospects (2005). Usual disclaimer applies.

Earlier studies have found the existence of the day of the week effect not only in the USA and other developed markets but also in the emerging markets like Malaysia, Hong Kong, Turkey. For most of the Western economies, (USA, UK, Canada) empirical results have shown that on Mondays the market has statistically significant negative returns while on Fridays statistically significant positive returns. In other markets such as Japan, Australia, Singapore, Turkey and France the highest negative returns appear on Tuesdays.

The most satisfactory explanation that has been given for the negative returns on Mondays is that usually the most unfavorable news appears during the weekends. These unfavorable news influence the majority of the investors negatively, causing them to sell on the following Monday. The most satisfactory explanation that has been given for Tuesdays' negative returns are that the bad news of the weekend affecting the USA's market, influence negatively some markets lagged by one day.

In most developed markets such as the USA's, the United Kingdom's and Canada's, most studies, Cross (1973), Gibbons & Hess (1981), Keim & Stambaugh (1984), Theobald and Price (1984), Jaffe & Westerfield (1985), Harris (1986), Simrlock & Starts (1986), Board and Sutcliffe (1988), and Kohers and Kohers (1995), Tang and Kwok (1997) for six indices [Dow Jones Industrial Average Index (US), Financial Times Index (UK), Nikkei Average Index (Japan), Hang Seng Index (Hong Kong), FAZ General Index (Germany) and All Ordinary Index (Australia)] and many others, have come to the conclusion that Mondays' average returns are negative and Fridays' are positive. In other words, the stock exchange market starts downwards and ends upwards. However, in some other studies such as Condoyanni, O'Hanlon & Ward (1987), Solnik & Bousqet (1990) in the French stock market; Athanassakos & Robinson (1994) in the Canadian market; Jaffe & Westerfield (1985) in the stock markets of Australia and Japan; Kim (1988) in the stock markets of Japan and Korea; Aggarwal & Rivoli (1989) in the stock markets of Hong Kong, Singapore, Malaysia and Philippines; Ho (1990) in the stock markets of Australia, Hong

Kong, Japan, Korea, Malaysia, New Zealand, Philippines, Singapore, Taiwan and Thailand; Wong, Hui and Chan (1992) in the markets of Singapore, Malaysia, Hong Kong and Thailand; Dubois & Louvet (1996) in the stock markets of Japan and Australia; Agrawal and Tandon (1994) for eighteen countries and many others, the negative average returns are observed on Tuesdays. Also, for the Istanbul stock exchange there were negative average returns on Tuesdays [Aydoðan (1994), Balaban (1995), Bildik (1997) and Özmen (1997)].

On the other hand, studies on the Spanish stock market have revealed that there is no day of the week effect [Santemases (1986), Pena (1995) and Gardeazabal and Regulez (2002)]. Solnik and Bousquet (1990) focused on the period 1978-1987 and examined the CAC Index of Paris Bourse. Their results showed strong and persistent negative mean returns on Tuesdays. Solnik (1990) wondered whether the settlement procedure could explain the pattern of daily returns observed in previous studies of the Paris Bourse.

Dubois and Louvet (1996) re-examined the day of the week effect for the French stock market along with other markets such as the US, UK, German, Japanese, Australian and Swiss markets, during the period 1969-1992 using standard statistical approaches and moving averages. They observed that Wednesdays presented the highest return while the day with the lowest (negative) return was Monday for all the above markets except the Japanese and the Australian. The null hypothesis of the equality among the mean returns of all days of the week was rejected at the 1% confidence level. The authors concluded that probably, the different settlement systems could account for difficulties in comparing the results internationally, but could not explain the possible reasons for this anomaly in the US and the European markets they examined.

If an anomaly exists in the market, the investors can take advantage of the same and adjust their buying and selling strategies accordingly to increase their returns with timing the market.

The day of the week effect in Indian market was examined by many researchers—Chaudhury (1991), Poshakwala (1996), Goswami and Anshuman (2000), Choudhry (2000), Bhattacharya, Sarkar and Mukhopadhyay (2003). All studies except Choudhry (2000) and Bhattacharya et al. (2003) have been based on data of mid-1980s and mid-1990s and all these studies have used conventional methods like serial autocorrelation tests and or fitting an OLS. Choudhry (2000) examined seasonality of returns and volatility under a unified framework but the study has a misspecification issue with regard to conditional mean. Bhattacharya et al. (2003) used GARCH framework by incorporating the lagged returns (BSE 100[1]) as explanatory variables in the conditional mean. They have used reporting and non-reporting weeks[2] to study the day of the week effect. All these studies have used end of day data.

The availability of high frequency data from NSE has opened up many avenues of research that helps us to look closer into the market activities. The present study aims to find the day of the week effect on India equity market using high frequency data. This study is different in two aspects: (1) it uses the high frequency data to study the day of the week effect and for the same we have to calculate the 1-minute returns and then aggregate the same for the day to get the daily returns. This is primarily done to understand the market dynamic observed during the whole day and to conduct a micro-analysis. The closing value that is generally available is the average of last 30 minutes of trade and may not suitably bring out the dynamics of the market and most of the information that happens during the day is not absorbed in the last 30 minutes of trades; (2) the study also does a comparative analysis using

---

1. BSE (The Stock Exchange, Mumbai) calculates BSE 100 that covers 100 most liquid stocks on the basis of the closing prices of these stocks using a market capitalisation method.
2. Reporting week means the week in which Banks send their Friday report to the Reserve Bank of India and on reporting Fridays, banks are expected to conform to the CRR and SLR requirements specified by RBI.

the closing values to understand if any additional valuable information can be obtained from high frequency data.

The rest of the paper has been presented as below: Section II talks of data and data characteristics, Section III talks of methodological issues, Section IV talks of results and Section V gives the concluding remarks.

Data and Data Characteristics

We have used the high frequency data for the index S&P CNX NIFTY from January 1999 to December 2003. S&P CNX Nifty is a benchmark stock index based on the selected stocks traded at National Stock Exchange (NSE). It is owned and managed by India Index Services and Products Ltd. (IISL), which is a joint venture between NSE, India's most advanced and leading Stock Exchange and CRISIL, India's leading Credit Rating Company. IISL is the first specialised company in the country focused upon developing the stock indices as a core product. It has a consulting and licensing agreement with Standard & Poor's (S&P), who are world leaders in index services. The average total traded value of all Nifty stocks is approximately 77% of the traded value of all stocks available for trading on the NSE. The S&P CNX Nifty stocks represent about 61% of the total market capitalisation as on August 31, 2004. The impact cost of S&P CNX Nifty for a portfolio size of Rs. 5 million is 0.10%. Liquid derivative products on S&P CNX NIFTY are available for trading in NSE. S&P CNX Nifty is computed using market capitalisation weighted method, wherein the level of the index reflects the total market value of all the stocks in the index relative to a particular base period. The method also takes into account constituent changes in the index and importantly corporate actions such as stock splits, rights, etc. without affecting the index value. The base period selected for S&P CNX Nifty index is the close of prices on November 3, 1995, which marked the completion of one year of operations of NSE's equity market segment. The base value of the index has been set at 1000 and a base capital of INR 2.06 trillion. Companies eligible for inclusion in Nifty must have a six monthly average market capitalisation of

Rs. 5000 millions or more during the last six months. Companies eligible for inclusion in S&P CNX Nifty should have at least 12% floating stock. For this purpose, floating stock shall mean stocks which are not held by the promoters and associated entities (where identifiable) of such companies. A new company with a fresh IPO is eligible for inclusion in the index, if it fulfills the normal eligibility criteria for the index like impact cost, market capitalisation and floating stock, for a 3 month period instead of the usual requirement of 6 months.

In order to control the effect of market, wide factors from international markets as well as in the domestic market, we have to introduce additional independent variables in the equation. Fortunately for the Indian stock market we have another index, the CNX Nifty Junior that comprises stocks for second rung liquid stocks. The 50 stocks in the CNX Nifty Junior are filtered for liquidity, so they are the most liquid of the stocks excluded from the S&P CNX Nifty are included in this index. The maintenance of the S&P CNX Nifty and the CNX Nifty Junior are synchronized so that the two indexes will always be disjoint sets, i.e. a stock will never appear in both indexes at the same time. Hence it is always meaningful to pool the S&P CNX Nifty and the CNX Nifty Junior into a composite 100 stock portfolio. CNX Nifty Junior represents about 10% of the total market capitalisation as on August 31, 2004 and the average traded value for the last six months of all Junior Nifty stocks is approximately 8% of the traded value of all stocks on the NSE and the impact cost for CNX Nifty Junior for a portfolio size of Rs. 2.50 million is 0.30%. The lagged S&P500 index return is used as an independent variable to remove the effects of worldwide price movements on the volatility of the Nifty Index return. For example, if the Indian market is influenced by US markets, this will be reflected through the lagged S&P500 return.

During the period of our study, the stock market in India has seen many changes in terms of trading and settlement rules. The trading has moved to a one-day rolling settlement and the settlement cycle moved to T+2 from T+5. Corporate governance has become more effective.

We have 1,228 days of data running into millions of tick level index values. Normally we have 335 minutes of trade between 9.55 AM to 3.30 PM but there are few missing values due to unavailability of data or due to some reason the trade halted in the stock exchange. We have more than 410,652 data points of 1 minute index values from where we compute the logarithmic returns. The same has been taken out from millions of S&P CNX NIFTY values that we handle from daily data provided by NSE. We also notice that for 30 days the data is missing from high frequency records supplied to us by NSE. For comparison purpose, we have also made suitable adjustments in the close-to-close data set. However, we have calculated the returns for all days and then removed the days but kept the return series generated for the remaining successive day which depended on the closing values of the days which were not considered. For the 1-minute value we take the last index value recorded before the relevant time stamp and if there are more than 1 index value at the relevant time (the index values are provided by NSE in time format as HH:MM:SS), we take the average of the values and calculate the 1-minute returns as the difference between successive log values of the index and express these in percentages as given in equation 1:

$$R_{t,d} = 100 * LN(P_{t,d} / P_{t-1,d}) \qquad ...(1)$$

where $P_{t,d}$ is the value at time *t* during the day and $P_{t-1,d}$ is the value of the index at time t-1.

And we have also calculated the close-to-close return using the equation 2.

$$R_t = 100 \; LN(P_t / P_{t-1}) \qquad ...(2)$$

The 1-minute logarithmic return series of 410,652 data points as well as the squared logarithmic return series are plotted in Chart 1 and Chart 2 below. We can see the returns are heavily concentrated on zero or its close vicinity in the Chart 1. There are certain extreme cases which are the characteristics of any financial time series data.

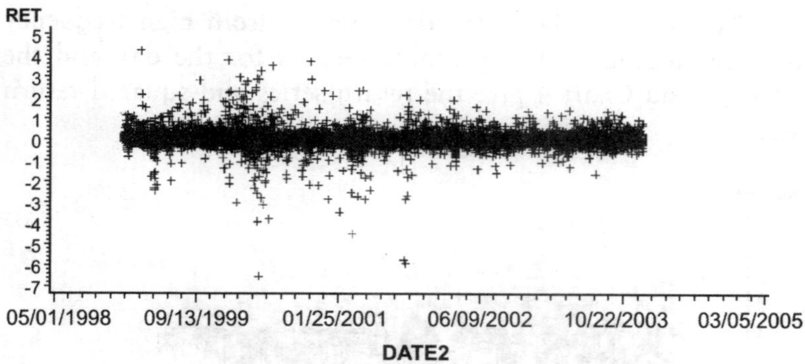

Chart 1: Scatter Plot of 1-minute Return Using High Frequency Data.

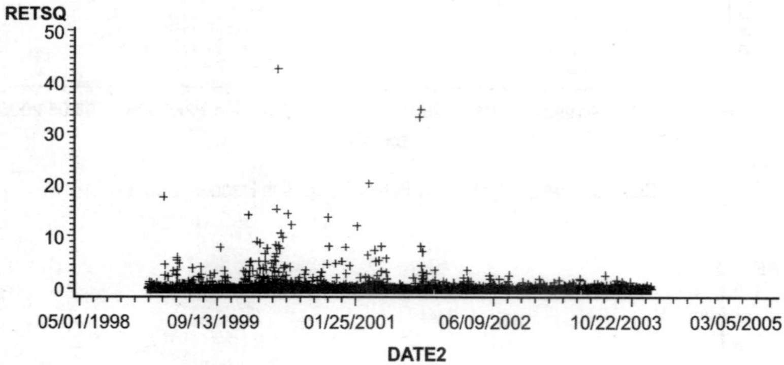

Chart 2: Scatter Plot of 1-minute Squared Return Using High Frequency Data.

The descriptive statistics of the high frequency 1-minute return is given in Table 1.

Table 1: Descriptive Statistics of 1-minute Returns Using High Frequency Data

N	Mean	Std Deviation	Skewness	Kurtosis	Std Error Mean	t-statistic	Min	Max
406670	0.0001 (0.1560)	0.0777	-2.71104	582.36789	0.00012	1.4185	-6.5239	4.2006

The mean has been found to be statistically zero as expected from a high frequency return series (as expected from a normally distributed data series). We have considered this measure on the basis of normally distributed mean as we have large number of small lag difference values and most of the values are expected to be close to zero.

We have calculated the daily return from high frequency data by adding all the 1-minute returns for the day and the Chart 3 and Chart 4 give the return series and squared return series.

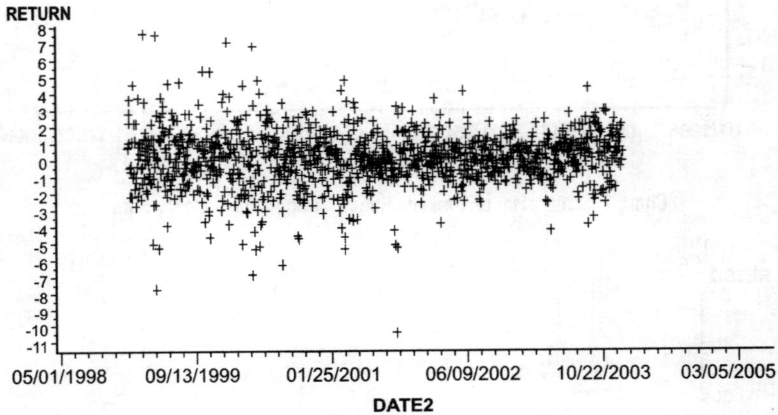

Chart 3: Scatter Plot of Daily Return Using High Frequency Data.

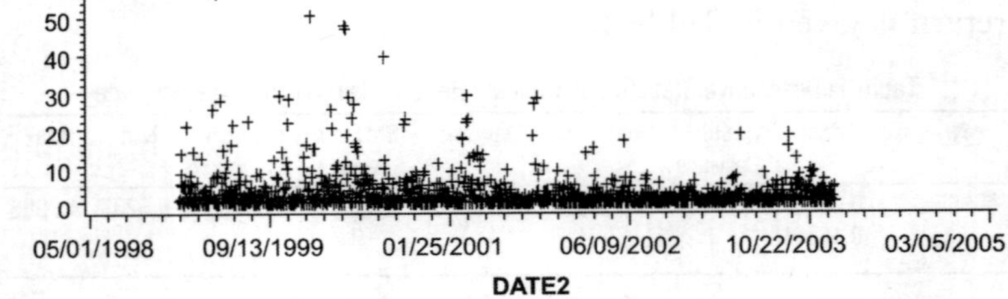

Chart 4: Scatter Plot of Daily Squared Return Using High Frequency Data.

The descriptive statistics of the daily return series is given in Table 2.

Table 2: Descriptive Statistics of the Daily Return Using High Frequency Data (1999 to 2003)

N	Mean	Std Deviation	Skewness	Kurtosis	Std Error Mean	t-statistic	Min	Max
1228	0.0573 (0.223)	1.6463	-0.2915	3.5061	0.04698	1.2193	-10.4256	7.6262
Descriptive statistics of the daily squared return using high frequency data (1999 to 2003)								
1228	2.7113 (.0001)	6.3252	7.4808	86.7648	0.18050	15.0210	0.00002	108.6941
Descriptive statistics of the daily return using high frequency data (1999 to 2001)								
731	0.01671 (0.8116)	1.8942	-0.2629	2.8243	0.0700621	0.238448	-10.4256	7.6262
Descriptive statistics of the daily return using high frequency data (2002 to 2003)								
497	0.11697 (0.0290)**	1.19055	-0.11861	0.81946	0.0534	2.190105	-4.2917	4.2642

** indicates significant at 5% level.

For the period from 1999 to 2003 as well as the sub-period of 1999 to 2001, it is found that mean is statistically zero for the daily returns arrived after summing 1-minute high frequency returns for the day whereas in the sub-period of 2002 to 2003, the mean is statistically non-zero and significant at 5% level. Chart-5 plots the histogram of the daily return series for the entire period and it can be seen that the return series is non-normal and has a negative skewness and excess kurtosis.

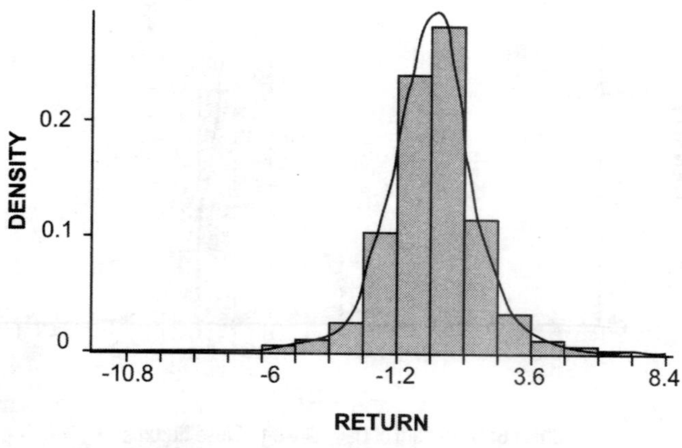

Chart 5: Histogram of Daily Returns from High Frequency Data.

In comparison to the above, for the sub-period 1999 to 2001, we find the mean return is having a negative sign for the mean return calculated using close-to-close daily end of day data (though not significant at conventional level). However, for the period 2002 to 2003, the mean is statistically significant at 10% level and positive. We also see that the mean of the daily return using close-to-close data for the entire period 1999 to 2003 is statistically zero. The descriptive statistics for the same is given in Table 3:

Table 3: Descriptive Statistics of the Return Series Using Close-to-Close Index Values (1999 to 2003)

N	Mean	Std Deviation	Skewness	Kurtosis	Std Error Mean	t-statistic	Min	Max
1228	0.01552 (0.7274)	1.5596	-0.2466	3.3154	0.04451	0.3487	-9.7053	7.2971
Descriptive statistics of the daily close return using end of day data (1999 to 2001)								
731	-0.03674 (0.5772)	1.78095	-0.2040	2.7725	0.06587094	-0.5578	-9.7052	7.2970
Descriptive statistics of the daily close return using end of day data (2002 to 2003)								
497	0.09239 (0.0757)	1.157136	-0.12710	0.77341	0.0519	1.7799	-4.2325	3.8306

* indicates significant at 10% level.

Chart 6 depicts the histogram of daily close-to-close returns. Charts 7 and 8 give us the plot of daily returns and squared returns using close-to-close values.

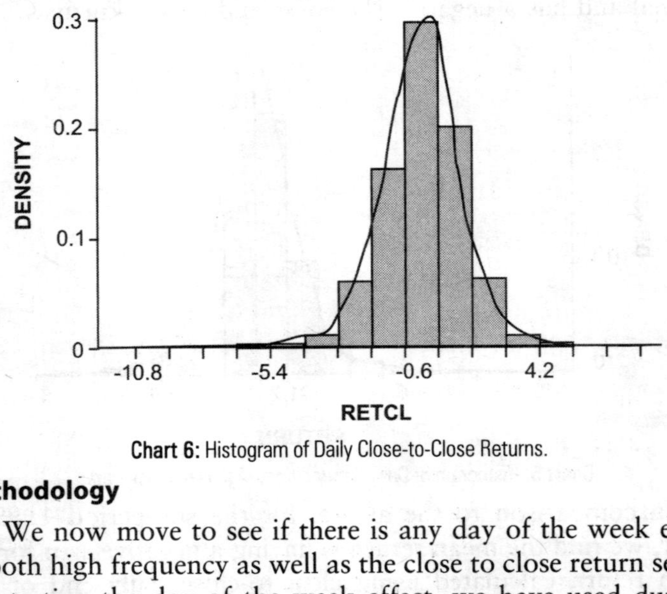

Chart 6: Histogram of Daily Close-to-Close Returns.

Methodology

We now move to see if there is any day of the week effect in both high frequency as well as the close to close return series. For testing the day of the week effect, we have used dummy

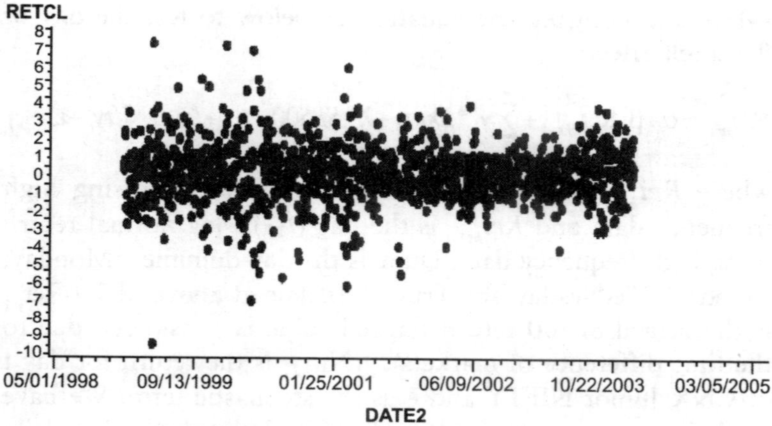

Chart 7: Scatter Plot of Close-to-Close Return.

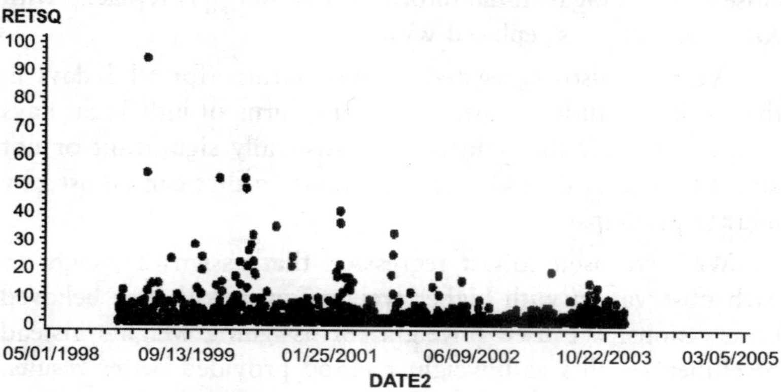

Chart 8: Scatter Plot of Close-to-Close Squared Return.

variables. We assigned values of 1, 2, 3 and 5 for Monday, Tuesday, Wednesday and Friday respectively (leaving out 1 day for robustness of the regression results)[3] as dummy variable

3. We have shortlisted Thursday for elimination from the regression as Monday and Friday cannot be ignored as these days are first and last day of the week which can bring some psychological pressure on the market. The competing stock exchange, BSE, earlier followed a trading cycle from Monday to Friday and this used to have effect on the trading at NSE because market participants would move their exposures from NSE to BSE and BSE to NSE depending on closing dates of trading cycle. Tuesday and Wednesday can not be ignored because Wednesday was the first day of trading cycle at NSE and Tuesday being the last day of trading cycle.

values and designed the equation as below to test the day of the week effect:

$$Ret_{hf\,t} = \alpha + \beta^{*} Ret_{hf\,t-1} + \sum_{1}^{4} \gamma_i * Dum_i + \lambda * SP500_{Ret,t-1} + \zeta * JrNifty_t + \varepsilon_t \quad (3)$$

where $Ret_{hf,t1}$ is the day *t*'s logarithmic return using high frequency data and $Ret_{hf,t-1}$ is the day (*t-1*)'s log normal return using high frequency data, Dum_i is the day dummies (Monday, Tuesday, Wednesday and Friday) explained above $SP500Ret_{t-1}$ is the lagged SP500 return (lagged value is considered due to the time difference of markets), $JrNifty_t$ is the return for day t of CNX Junior NIFTY and ε_t is the stochastic term. We have used the same equation to study the relationship using daily close to close logarithmic returns where $Ret_{hf,t1}$ is replaced with Ret_{t1} and $Ret_{hf,t-1}$ is replaced with Ret_{t-1}.

We have also segregated daywise return (for all 5 days in the week) to study the behaviour of returns of individual days to understand if the returns are statistically significant or not and if they provide additional information that can be used by market participants.

We have used robust regression that assigns a weight to each observation with higher weights given to better behaved observations. We used biweight for assigning weights instead of Huber weights as biweight method provided better results. The biweight[4] (bisquare) transformation is used in robust analysis.

---

4. For many applications, it combines the properties of resistance with relatively high efficiency. Resistance means that changes in a small part of the data do not cause large changes in the estimate. The mean is an example of a non-resistant estimate while the median is an example of a resistant estimate. Efficiency is a measure of how well the estimate performs for data from a given distribution. For example, the mean is a 100% efficient estimator for normally distributed data. However, it has poor efficiency for heavy tailed distributions. A desirable property for robust estimators is that they maintain high efficiency under a variety of distributions. The biweight transformation of a variable has this property for many applications.

Bisquare:

$$w(u) = \begin{cases} \left(1-\left(\frac{u}{4.684}\right)^2\right)^2 & |u| \leq 4.685 \\ 0 & |u| \leq 4.685 \end{cases} \qquad ...(4)$$

In fact, extremely deviant cases, those with Cook's D greater than 1, can have their weights set to missing so that they are not included in the analysis at all. The observations that have the lowest weights would be those with the largest residuals and the observations with the highest weights would be with low residuals. Robust regression with biweights is more robust than an OLS.

Results

The regression results using dummy variables for the high frequency return series is given in Table 4. The results show that the index movement is explained by market wide movement in India as well as movement in international markets as measured by lagged values of S&P500.

Table 4: Results of Dummy Variable Tests Using High Frequency Data from January 1999 to December 2003 (Robust Regression with Biweights)

Variable	Parameter Estimate	Std Error	t- Value	p-value
Intercept	0.08991	0.05157	1.74	0.0815*
Lag1 return	-0.05479	0.01473	-3.72	0.0002***
S&P500 return	0.08678	0.01766	4.91	<.0001***
Jr. Nifty return	0.64077	0.01237	51.81	<.0001***
Monday	-0.25092	0.07360	-3.41	0.0007***
Tuesday	0.01511	0.03653	0.41	0.6792
Wednesday	-0.04349	0.02451	-1.77	0.0762*
Friday	0.01232	0.01472	0.84	0.4028

Model DF 7 Sum of Squares 1653.53920 Mean Square 236.21989F Value 402.95 Pr > F (<.0001)** *
Error DF 1214 Sum of Squares 711.67484 Mean Square 0.58622.
Root MSE 0.76565 R-Square 0.6991.
Corrected Total DF 1221 Sum of Squares 1735.71106.
Dependent Mean 0.06874 Adj R-Sq 0.6974.
Coeff Var 1113.91355
***, **, * indicates significant at 1%, 5% and 10% level.

For the period from 1999 to 2003, the coefficient of the mean return arrived from the high frequency data for Monday and Wednesday are negative and significant while for other days the same is insignificant. However the significance is mild at 10% level for Wednesday. The adjusted R-squares have been significantly high at about 0.70 indicating robustness of the results obtained. The robust regression also shows the previous day's coefficient is significant.

We have carried the similar regression using close to close returns. The closing index value is guided by the market activity during last 30 minutes of trade and hence may not capture the essence of market activity during the entire day. The weighted average prices are used to calculate the close index. The results for the close to close returns are given in Table 5.

Table 5: Results of Dummy Variable Tests Using Close-to-Close Data from January 1999 to December 2003 (Robust Regression)

Variable	Parameter Estimate	Std Error	t- Value	p-value
Intercept	0.04563	0.04878	0.94	0.3497
Lag1 return	-0.01847	0.01487	-1.24	0.2144
S&P500 return	0.07578	0.01675	4.52	<.0001***
Jr. Nifty return	0.60938	0.01178	51.73	<.0001***
Monday	-0.14908	0.06956	-2.14	0.0323**
Tuesday	0.00188	0.03445	0.05	0.9564
Wednesday	-0.05616	0.02331	-2.41	0.0161**
Friday	-0.00212	0.01394	-0.15	0.8792

Model DF 7 Sum of Squares 1473.42148 Mean Square 210.48878 F Value 400.64 Pr > F (<.0001).
Error DF 1214 Sum of Squares 637.81334 Mean Square 0.52538.
Corrected Total DF 1221 Sum of Squares 2111.23482.
Root MSE .72483 R-Square 0.6979.
Dependent Mean 0.02370 Adj R-Sq 0.6962.
Coeff Var 3058.39675.
***, ** indicate significant at 1% and 5% level.

For the period from 1999 to 2003, the coefficient of the mean return arrived from the end of day data for Monday and Wednesday are negative and significant while for other days the same is insignificant. The robust regression also shows the previous day's coefficient is significant.

Wednesday may be significant as NSE used to follow the trading cycle of Wednesday to Tuesday where Wednesday used to be the first day of the trading cycle at NSE and due to carry forward system many traders used to carry over their positions to the next trading cycle. Further, auctions used to be conducted for shortages in deliveries on Wednesdays.

For checking the robustness of the results we have at hand, we did a sub-sample analysis by dividing the period into two parts using the major regime change as the logic. The compulsory rolling settlement was introduced in Indian equity market from the first trading day of January 2002. Accordingly we have divided the entire data set into two parts, January 1999 to December 2001 having about 731 observations and the other period was from January 2002 to December 2003 having 497 observations. The results of the first period for both high frequency data and close-to-close data for the period from January 1999 to December 2001 are given in Tables 6 and 7 respectively.

For the high frequency as well as the end of day data, the results for the sub-sample period 1999-2001 shows that the coefficient of mean return is significant for Monday and Wednesday. The sign is negative for both days.

Table 6: Results of Dummy Variable Tests Using High Frequency Data Using Sub-sample January 1999 to December 2001 (Robust Regression)

Variable	Parameter Estimate	Std Error	t- Value	p-value
Intercept	0.19507	0.07513	2.60	0.0096***
Lag1 return	-0.06412	0.01877	-3.42	0.0007***
S&P500 return	0.11681	0.02641	4.42	<.0001***
Jr. Nifty return	0.63018	0.01557	40.48	<.0001***
Monday	-0.38741	0.10842	-3.57	0.0004***
Tuesday	-0.00209	0.05378	-0.04	0.9690
Wednesday	-0.06251	0.03597	-1.74	0.0827*
Friday	-0.02612	0.02156	-1.21	0.2262

Model DF 7 Sum of Squares 1339.17522 Mean Square 191.31075 F Value 254.29 Pr > F (<.0001)***
Error DF 720 Sum of Squares 541.68030 Mean Square 0.75233.
Corrected Total DF 727 Sum of Squares 1880.85552.
Root MSE 0.86737 R-Square 0.7120.
Dependent Mean 0.03541 Adj R-Sq 0.7092.
Coeff Var 2449.39321.
*** (*) indicates significant at 1% (10%) level.

Table 7: Results of Dummy Variable Tests Using Close-to-Close Returns Using Sub-sample January 1999 to December 2001 (Robust Regression)

Variable	Parameter Estimate	Std Error	t- Value	p-value
Intercept	0.11380	0.07192	1.58	0.1140
Lag1 return	-0.04144	0.01940	-2.14	0.0330**
S&P500 return	0.09683	0.02544	3.81	0.0002***
Jr. Nifty return	0.58450	0.01503	38.90	<.0001***
Monday	-0.21864	0.10364	-2.11	0.0352**
Tuesday	0.00072	0.05120	0.01	0.9887
Wednesday	-0.08451	0.03469	-2.44	0.0151**
Friday	-0.03705	0.02070	-1.79	0.0739*

Model DF 7 Sum of Squares 1114.37053 Mean Square 159.19579 F Value 231.58 Pr > F (<.0001)***
Error DF 723 Sum of Squares 495.63665 Mean Square 0.68743.
Corrected Total DF 728 Sum of Squares 1610.00718.
Root MSE 0.82911 R-Square 0.6922.
Dependent Mean -0.02353 Adj R-Sq 0.6892.
Coeff Var -3523.12610.
***, **, * indicate significant at 1%, 5% and 10% level.

The results for the second period for both high frequency data and close-to-close data from January 2002 to December 2003 are given in Tables 8 and 9 respectively.

Table 8: Results of Dummy Variable Tests Using High Frequency Data Using Sub-sample January 2002 to December 2003 (Robust Regression)

Variable	Parameter Estimate	Std Error	t- Value	p-value
Intercept	-0.05962	0.06947	-0.86	0.3912
Lag1 return	-0.04516	0.02657	-1.70	0.0898*
S&P500 return	0.05218	0.02293	2.28	0.0233**
Jr. Nifty return	0.66262	0.02340	28.32	<.0001***
Monday	-0.07489	0.09814	-0.76	0.4458
Tuesday	0.04206	0.04843	0.87	0.3856
Wednesday	-0.00366	0.03251	-0.11	0.9103
Friday	0.06022	0.01970	3.06	0.0024**

Model DF 7 Sum of Squares 358.23161 Mean Square 51.17594 F Value 120.23 Pr > F (<.0001)***
Error DF 489 Sum of Squares 208.14210 Mean Square 0.42565.
Corrected Total DF 496 Sum of Squares 566.37371.
Root MSE 0.65242 R-Square 0.6325.
Dependent Mean 0.11999 Adj R-Sq 0.6272.
Coeff Var 543.71563.
***, **, * indicates significant at 1%, 5% and 10% level.

Obtain starting weights for all cases

= Obtain residuals e_i from and ordinary least squares fit

= Obtain the scaled residual u_i:

$$u_i = \frac{e_i}{MAD}$$

were

$$MAD = \frac{1}{6.75}\, median\{\| e_i - median\{e_j\}\|\}$$

which is called the median absolute deviation.

Table 9: Results of Dummy Variable Tests Using Close-to-Close Returns Using Sub-sample January 2002 to December 2003 (Robust Regression)

Variable	Parameter Estimate	Std Error	t- Value	p-value
Intercept	-0.07791	0.06331	-1.23	0.2190
Lag1 return	0.02543	0.02465	1.03	0.3028
S&P500 return	0.05583	0.02091	2.67	0.0078***
Jr. Nifty return	0.67152	0.02134	31.47	<.0001***
Monday	-0.04395	0.08924	-0.49	0.6226
Tuesday	0.01658	0.04411	0.38	0.7071
Wednesday	-0.00280	0.02970	-0.09	0.9248
Friday	0.04416	0.01790	2.47	0.0140***

Model DF 7 Sum of Squares 368.02024 Mean Square 52.57432 F Value 148.94Pr > F (<.0001)***
Error DF 488 Sum of Squares 172.26026 Mean Square 0.35299.
Corrected Total DF 496 Sum of Squares 540.28050.
Root MSE 0.59413 R-Square 0.6812.
Dependent Mean 0.08857 Adj R-Sq 0.6766.
Coeff Var 670.80405.
***, ** and * indicates significant at 1%, 5% and 10% level.

The results show that the coefficients for none of the days except Friday are significant. The sign has been found to be positive indicating the effect of Wednesday has vanished after introduction of rolling settlement. This clearly indicates the Friday being the last day of the week; traders would like to close their positions before the weekends. This clearly indicates that markets have become more efficient after introduction of rolling settlement. The coefficients for Monday and Wednesday have the negative sign but not significant. The adjusted R-square is at 0.68 indicating the robustness of the results.

We further went to study the daywise behaviour of returns to see if any day is giving better returns or any particular day has some negative bias. The results are given in Table 10 below.

Table 10: Daywise Behaviour of Returns

N	Mean (*p*-value)	Median	Std Deviation	Minimum	Maximum	t-Stat (mean)
Monday						
High Frequency Data						
244	-0.1179 (0.3387)	0.0033	1.9209	-10.4256	7.6262	-0.9587
Close-to-Close						
244	-0.0388 (0.7155)	0.0383	1.6612	-5.8437	7.1623	-0.3649
Tuesday						
High Frequency Return						
247	0.0351 (0.7184)	0.1113	1.5280	-6.9043	5.2966	0.3611
Close-to-Close Return						
247	-0.0228 (0.8086)	0.0140	1.4772	-7.1566	4.8366	-0.2425
Wednesday						
High Frequency Return						
247	0.3374 (0.0004)***	0.3014	1.4752	-4.2522	4.7969	3.5950
Close-to-Close Return						
247	0.3000 (0.0160)**	0.2271	1.49047	-4.0944	5.9560	2.4246
Thursday						
High Frequency Return						
251	0.04238 (0.6569)	0.0687	1.5096	-4.3017	5.3695	0.4448
Close-to-Close Return						
251	0.0052 (0.9545)	0.1024	1.4291	-4.4622	5.2664	0.0571
Friday						
High Frequency Return						
239	-0.01485 (0.8952)	0.0398	1.7121	-7.7099	7.5368	-0.13187
Close-to-Close Return						
239	-0.1006 (0.3669)	0.0000	1.7197	-9.7053	7.2971	-0.9039

We find that the daywise returns on Wednesdays are not statistically zero for both high frequency as well as close to close return series indicating the existence of arbitrage opportunities for investors. The results have also pointed out that Mondays have the highest standard deviation for high frequency data while for close to close data Fridays have the highest standard deviation. For Wednesdays, the returns are not only positive and significantly different from zero but also the risk (standard deviation) is less compared to other days. This indicates existence of arbitrage opportunity for investors who could have benefited from the above syndrome. Both Monday and Friday returns have shown negative signs for both intraday and close to close returns though the returns are statistically zero.

In order to check the robustness of our analysis, we divided the data into two parts as already explained and carried out the above exercise. The results are given in Table 11 for the first part of the data (January 1999 to December 2001) and in Table 12 for the second part of the data (January 2002 to December 2003).

For the data period from January 1999 to December 2001, the results find clearly that the coefficients for Wednesday and Friday are significant indicating the presence of day of the week effect. The sign for both Monday and Friday are negative indicating pressure on first and last day of the week. Wednesday returns are positive and significant but are associated with less risk compared to other days giving an indication of risk being not efficiently priced.

The period from January 2002 to December 2003 has witnessed lesser volatility (as measured by standard deviation) compared to the earlier period. The results from the second part of the data show some very interesting results. It shows that the effect for Wednesday has gone off after the introduction of rolling settlement and the returns for all days except Friday are not statistically significant from zero. The Friday returns are positive. This indicates existence of arbitrage opportunity for an investor.

Concluding Remarks

The present study examined the day of the week effect anomaly in Indian stock market for the period from 1999 to 2003 using both high frequency and close to close returns calculated using the main market index S&P CNX NIFTY.

Table 11: Daywise Behaviour of Return Series (January 1999 to December 2001)

N	Mean	Median	Std Deviation	Minimum	Maximum	t-Stat (mean)
Monday						
High Frequency Data						
143	-0.2053 (0.2768)	-0.0430	2.2485	-10.4256	7.6262	-1.0917
Close-to-Close						
143	-0.0986 (0.5364)	-0.1435	1.9017	-5.8437	7.1623	-0.6197
Tuesday						
High Frequency Return						
146	0.0270 (0.8526)	0.2344	1.7549	-6.9043	5.2966	0.1862
Close-to-Close Return						
146	-0.0236 (0.8664)	0.0687	1.6935	-7.1566	4.8366	-0.1685
Wednesday						
High Frequency Return						
149	0.4972 (0.0005)***	0.4251	1.7163	-4.2522	4.7969	3.5361
Close-to-Close Return						
149	0.3286 (0.0226)**	0.3431	1.7411	-4.0944	5.9560	2.3040
Thursday						
High Frequency Return						
152	0.01732 (0.8987)	-0.1378	1.6743	-4.3017	5.3695	0.1276
Close-to-Close Return						
152	-0.0397 (0.7546)	-0.0569	1.5637	-4.4622	5.2664	-0.3132
Friday						
High Frequency Return						
141	-0.27730 (0.0965)	-0.1538	1.96760	-7.7099	7.5368	-1.67347
Close-to-Close Return						
141	-0.37055 (0.0255)	-0.2349	1.94931	-9.7053	7.2971	-2.25726

Table 12: Daywise Behaviour of Return Series (January 2002 to December 2003)

N	Mean	Median	Std Deviation	Minimum	Maximum	t-Stat (mean)
Monday						
High Frequency Data						
101	0.0058 (0.9650)	0.1422	1.3269	-3.8984	2.9045	0.0440
Close-to-Close						
101	0.04677 (0.7078)	0.15457	1.2505	-3.1632	2.8594	0.3758
Tuesday						
High Frequency Return						
101	0.0468 (0.6785)	0.0197	1.1303	-2.5077	4.2643	0.4158
Close-to-Close Return						
101	-0.0216 (0.8438)	-0.0572	1.0994	-2.6011	3.7093	-0.1975
Wednesday						
High Frequency Return						
98	0.09454 (0.3331)	0.0963	0.96203	-2.0306	3.6308	0.9728
Close-to-Close Return						
98	0.07989 (0.4241)	0.1634	0.9852	-2.1555	3.5387	0.8027
Thursday						
High Frequency Return						
99	0.0809 (0.5116)	0.1997	1.2212	-4.2917	2.4214	0.6587
Close-to-Close Return						
99	0.07405 (0.5399)	0.2245	1.1978	-4.2326	2.2132	0.6151
Friday						
High Frequency Return						
98	0.3628 (0.0055)	0.3738	1.2659	-2.6088	4.0847	2.8367
Close-to-Close Return						
98	0.2879 (0.0226)	0.3964	1.2303	-2.7907	3.8306	2.3168

The data consisted of 1,228 days of trading. We have left out some few days due to missing data. The robust regression with biweights was used in place of ordinary least square methods for arriving at the results. When we looked at the entire sample for analysis and used the dummies for finding out the day of the week effect in Indian equity market, we found that the coefficient for logarithmic returns series for Wednesday and Monday were significant for both high frequency and close to close data, though for the high frequency data it showed mild significance at 10% level for Wednesday. In order to understand the robustness of the findings, we divided the data into two parts on the basis of a significant regime change – introduction of compulsory rolling settlement. The compulsory rolling settlement was introduced in India from January 2002 and hence the data was divided accordingly. For the period from January 1999 to December 2001, we found that the coefficients for Monday and Wednesday was significant for both high frequency and close-to-close data. But when we analysed the second part of the data from January 2002 to December 2003, we found that the coefficient for Friday had become significant while other days had lost their significance. All the regression results had shown the previous days' returns as well as market wide movement in domestic and international markets as significant. In Indian market, some days of the week have been found to be significant though earlier it was Monday and Wednesday but after introduction of compulsory rolling settlement, it is Friday which is significant.

We analysed the data in order to find if day-wise returns were significant or not and could provide an arbitrage opportunity to investors. When we took the entire period for analysis, we found that only for Wednesdays the mean returns were significantly different from zero and positive, indicating existence of clear arbitrage opportunity for investors who could buy on other days and sell on Wednesdays where the chance of making profit is higher. Mondays and Fridays returns were negative though not significant for both high frequency and close-to-close data. However, in terms of risk, we found that both Mondays and Fridays have higher standard deviation for high frequency as well as close-to-close data in comparison to Wednesdays. Wednesdays provided for lowest standard deviation (less risky) with significantly positive returns indicating market inefficiency.

However, when we did the robustness check dividing the data into two separate buckets as already explained, we found that, for the period from January 1999 to December 2001, the coefficients for Wednesdays and Mondays were found to be significant and negative for both the datasets. The period from January 2001 to December 2003 showed the coefficient of Fridays being significant and positive.

While looking at the return and risk aspect of the data, for the entire period, we find that returns on Wednesdays are significantly different from zero and positive while both Mondays and Fridays showed negative returns (but not significant) for both high frequency and close-to-close data. The risk measured by standard deviation was found to be higher on Mondays and Fridays for both high frequency and close-to-close data. We also noticed that generally most of the extreme observations (maximum and minimum) are on Mondays and Fridays. Wednesdays have lower risk compared to Mondays and Fridays but with significant positive returns. This shows clear existence of market imperfection and mis-pricing of risk before the introduction of rolling settlement.

When we divided the period into two different blocks on the basis of an important event like introduction of rolling settlement and analysed the data, we found that for the first period (January 1999 to December 2001) the returns for Wednesdays and Fridays were significant and positive while returns for other days were not significantly different from zero. In terms of risk, we also found that Mondays and Fridays have very high standard deviation of the returns compared to any other day. Wednesday had a clear arbitrage opportunity for investors who could take lesser risk but can expect high return.

For the second period (January 2002 to December 2003), we found that mean returns on Fridays are positive and significantly different from zero for both high frequency and close-to-close data at 1% and 5% level respectively. We have also noticed that the risk as measured by standard deviation has come down significantly after rolling settlement for all weekdays. However, in terms of risk, Mondays and Fridays were found to have higher standard deviations though returns were not significantly different from zero for Mondays. This also indicates that Fridays, being the last days of the weeks have become significant after rolling settlement. The existence of market inefficiency is clear for the second part of the data as we see Friday's returns have lower standard deviations but significantly positive returns compared to Mondays which have returns not significantly from zero but higher standard deviations.

We feel that Wednesday had been a significant day historically as NSE used to follow a trading cycle from Wednesday to Tuesday. Wednesday being the first day of the trading cycle must have reflected the action of market participants who used to roll over their positions from Tuesdays (the closing day of the trading cycle). But in recent times, Fridays, being the last day of the week, have become significant. The market inefficiency still exists and market is yet to price the risk appropriately. However, the risk as measured by standard deviation, has come down significantly after the introduction of rolling settlement.

REFERENCES

Aggarwal, R. and Rivoli, P. (1989): "On the Relationship between the United States' and Four Asian Equity Markets", ASEAN *Economic Bulletin*, 6: 110- 117.

Agrawal, Anup and Tandon, Kishore (1994): "Anomalies or Illusions?: Evidence from Stock Markets in Eighteen Countries", *Journal of International Money and Finance,* 83-106.

Alexakis, P. and Xanthakis M. (1995): "Day-of-the-Week Effect on the Greek Stock Market", *Applied Financial Economics*, 5: 43- 50.

Athanassakos, G. and Robinson, M.J. (1994): "The Day of the Week Anomaly: The Toronto Stock Exchange Experience", *Journal of Business Finance & Accounting*, 21: 833-56.

Balaban, E. (1995): "Day-of-the-Week Effects: New Evidence from an Emerging Stock Market", *Applied Economics Letters*, 2: 139- 143.

Ball, Clifford, Torous, Walter, and Tschoegl Adrian (June 1982): "Gold and the Weekend Effect", *Journal of Futures Markets*, 175- 182.

Barone, E. (1990): "The Italian Stock Market", *Journal of Banking and Finance*, Vol. 14, No. 3, 431-439.

Bekaert, G., Erb, C.B., C.R. Harvey, and T.E. Viskanta (Winter 1998): "Distributional Characteristics of Emerging Markets Returns and Asset Allocation", *Journal of Portfolio Returns*, 102-116.

Bhattacharya, K., Sarkar, N. and Mukhopadhyay (2003): "Stability of the Day of the Week Effect in Return and in Volatility at the Indian Capital Market: A GARCH Approach with Proper Mean Specification", *Applied Financial Economics*, 13: 553-563.

Board, J.L. and Sutcliffe, C.M. (1988): "The Weekend Effect in UK Stock Market Returns", *Journal of Business, Finance & Accounting*, 15: 199- 213.

Bollerslev, T., Engle, R. and D. Nelson (1994): "ARCH Models" in Chapter 49 of *Handbook of Econometrics*, Volume 4, North-Holland.

Bollerslev, T. and J. Wooldridge (1992): "Quasi-Maximum Likelihood Estimation and Inference in Dynamic Models with Time Varying Covariances", *Econometric Reviews*, 11: 143–172.

Chang E., Pinegar M. and Ravichandran R. (1993): "International Evidence on the Robustness of the Day-of-the-Week Effects", *Journal of Financial and Quantitative Analysis*, 28: 497-513.

Chaudhury, S.K. (1991): Seasonality in Share Returns: Preliminary Evidence on Day of the Week Effect, *Chartered Accountant (India)*, 40, November: 107-9.

Choudhury, T. (2000): "Day of the Week Effect in Emerging Asian Stock Markets: Evidence from GARCH Model", *Applied Financial Economics*, 20: 235-42

Condoyanni, I., O' Hanlon, J. and Ward, C.W.R.: "Day of the Week Effects on Stock Returns: International Evidence", *Journal of Business Finance and Accounting*, 14 (2): 159-174.

Cross, F. (November/December 1973): "The Behavior of Stock Prices on Fridays and Mondays", *Financial Analysts Journal*, 67-69.

Dubois, M. and Louvet, P. (1996): "The Day-of-the-Week Effect: International Evidence", *Journal of Banking and Finance*, 20: 1463- 1484.

Dyl, E. and Maberly, E. (1986): "The Weekly Pattern in Stock Index Futures: A Further Note", *Journal of Finance*, 41(5): 1149- 1152.

Eisemann, P.C. and Timme, S.G. (Spring 1984): "Intraweek Seasonality in the Federal Funds Market", *Journal of Financial Research*, 47- 56.

Flannery, M. and Protopapadakis, A. (June 1988) "From T-Bills to Common Stock: Investigating the Generality of Intra-Week Return Seasonality", *Journal of Finance*, 431- 450.

Gardeazabal, J. and Regulez, M. (June 2002): "The Weekend-Dividend Effect in the Spanish Market", Presentation at the 2002 European Finance Management Association, Annual Conference, London, UK.

Gay, G. and Kim, T. (1987): "An Investigation into Seasonality in the Futures Market", *Journal of Futures Markets*, 7: 169- 181.

Gibbons, M. and Hess, P. (October 1981): "Day of the Week Effects and Asset Returns", *Journal of Business*, 579-596.

Goswami, R and Anshuman, R (2000): "Day of the Week Effect on Bombay Stock Exchange", *ICFAI Journal of Applied Finance*, 6: 31-46.

Haroutounian, M. and Price, S. (2001): "Volatility in Transition Market of Central Europe", *Applied Financial Economics*, 11: 93-105.

Harris, L. (1986): "A Transaction Data Study of Weekly and Intradaily Patterns in Stock Returns", *The Journal of Financial Economics*, 16: 99-117.

Ho, Y.K. (1990): "Stock Return Seasonalities in Asia Pacific Markets, *Journal of International Financial Management and Accounting*, 2: 44-77.

Jaffe, J. and Westerfield, R. (June 1985): "Patterns in Japanese Common Stock Returns: Day of the Week and Turn of the Year Effects", *Journal of Financial and Quantitative Analysis*, 261- 272.

Jaffe, J., Westerfield, R. and Christopher M.A. (1989): "A Twist on the Monday Effect in Stock Prices", *Journal of Banking and Finance*, 13: 641- 650.

Johnston, R., Karacaw, W. and McConnel (1991): "Day-of-the-Week Effects in Financial Futures", *Journal of Financial and Quantitative Analysis*, 26: 23- 44.

Jordan, Susan D. and Jordan, Bradford D. (June 1991): "Seasonality in Daily Bond Returns", *Journal of Financial and Quantitative Analysis*, 269- 285.

Keim, D. and Stambaugh, R. (July 1984): "A Further Investigation of the Weekend Effect in Stock Returns", *Journal of Finance*, 819- 837.

Kim, S.W., (1988): "Capitalizing on the Weekend Effect", *Journal of Portfolio Management*, 15: 61-64.

Kohers, T. and Kohers, G. (1995): "The Impact of Firm Size Differences on the Day of the Week Effect: A Comparison of Major Stock Exchanges", *Applied Financial Economics*, 5: 151-60.

Lee, I., Pettit, R. and Swankoski, M. (Spring 1990): "Daily Return Relationships among Asian Stock Markets", *Journal of Business, Finance & Accounting*, 17(2): 265- 284.

Lyroudi, K., Subeniotis, D. and Komisopoulos, G. (June 2002): "Market Anomalies in the A.S.E.: The Day of the Week Effect", Presentation at the 2002 European Finance Management Association, Annual Conference, London, UK.

Murinde, V. and Pashakwale, S. (February 2002): "Volatility in the Emerging Stock Markets in Central and Eastern Europe: Evidence on Croatia, Czech Republic, Hungary, Poland, Russia and Slovakia", *European Research Studies Journal.*

Pena, I. (1995): "Daily Seasonalities and Stock Market Reforms in Spain", *Applied Financial Economics*, 419-423.

Santemases, M. (1986): "An Investigation of the Spanish Stock Market Seasonalities", *Journal of Business, Finance & Accounting*, 13(2): 267- 276.

Smirlock, M. and Starks, L. (September 1986): "Day-of-the-Week and Intraday Effects in Stock Returns", *Journal of Financial Economics*, 197- 210.

Solnik B. (1990): "The Distribution of Daily Stock Returns and Settlement Procedures: The Paris Bourse", *Journal of Finance*, 45(2): 1601-9.

Solnik, B. and Bousquet, L. (1990): "Day- of-the-Week Effect on the Paris Bourse", *Journal of Banking and Finance*, 14: 461-468.

Tang, G.Y.N. and Kwok, K. (1997): "Day of the Week Effect in International Portfolio Diversification: January vs. Non-January", *Japan World Economics*, 9: 335-352.

Theobald, M. and Price, V. (1984): "Seasonality Estimation in Thin Markets, *Journal of Finance*, 39: 377- 392.

Wong, K.A., Hui, T.K. and Chan, C.Y. (1992): "Day- of- the- Week Effects: Evidence From Developing Stock Markets", *Applied Financial Economics*, 2: 49-56.

Managing Risk: Insurance for the Poor?

12

Amir Ullah Khan and *Saleema Razvi*

1. Introduction

Vulnerability is both a cause and a symptom of poverty. It resides in the many shocks that pervade the lives of the poor. The frequent occurrence of these shocks can easily erode hard won gains and force households quickly back into poverty.[1] Over the past few years, a growing body of evidence[2] shows that microfinance has had a positive impact on the poor. Growth of enterprise revenues and, in turn, increased household incomes have brought important benefits to many households. However, focusing only on static measures of household earnings and income tends to mask the more dynamic side of poverty, the vulnerability of the poor to risk.

Risk comes in many forms, for example, illness, death, fire or theft. These risks could occur frequently and create financial pressures that exacerbate the ever-present stress of meeting regular needs such as food, rent and school fees. To cope with risk the poor use a diversity of strategies. These include borrowing, saving, selling productive and non-productive assets, and other forms of 'self-insurance', informal group-based risk sharing systems, and, occasionally, formal insurance. Yet, the effectiveness of these strategies is limited. Factors such as lack of timeliness, limited coverage and high costs suggest an insurance landscape that is far from perfect. In addition, poverty

1. World Bank, *Investing in Health.* World Development Report 1993. New York: Oxford University Press for the World Bank.
2. Miller, M. Northrip, Z., *Bamako 2000: Innovations in Microfinance,* 2001.

impedes many from taking risks and gaining access to what is on offer.

In the absence of insurance, the poor often avoid risky but potentially profitable economic activities and enter into informal insurance arrangements or rely on precautionary savings. It has been found that the largest gap between demand and access for the rural people is for insurance. This paper examines the vulnerability of the poor farmer with regard to risks faced especially of health and illness. It also examines the health insurance schemes available for the poor in India. With a population of over 1 billion growing at the rate of approximately 2 per cent every year, India presents immense opportunities for investment in the health care sector. The sheer size of the existing health care infrastructure in India gives an idea of the growth potential that this sector offers to domestic and foreign investors. With more than 15,000 hospitals, 500,000 doctors, 737,000 nurses, 170 medical colleges and 350,000 retail chemist outlets, Indian health care sector is by far one of the largest in the world.

The Indian health care delivery market is nearly US$ 18.7 billion, growing annually at the rate of 13 to 15 per cent. There have been estimates that by the end of 2012, the health-care sector shall be equivalent to more than 8% of the GDP, and the share of private sector shall increase to 75% from the present share of 63%. The strong Indian middle-class acts as a prime driver of growth of health-care facilities in the country. Changing demographic and socio-economic profile of the population in favour of the youth, and changing lifestyle patterns are opening unprecedented demands for preventive and curative health care facilities.

Health Infrastructure	
Hospitals (public & private)	15000
Doctors	500,000
Nurses	737,000
Medical Colleges (public and private)	170
Retail Chemist Outlets	350,000

Source: ICRA.

Less than 10% of the Indian population is covered by some form of health insurance. It is expected that the major international players will establish networks of affiliated hospitals and seek direct involvement in the development of new facilities. The voluntary health insurance market is expected to grow fast with estimates of Rs. 130 billion by 2005. Privatisation of insurance will extrapolate into a new health care delivery system in India. Currently, only 2 million people—which is 0.2 per cent of the total population—are covered under Mediclaim with estimates that there are 315 million potentially insurable lives in the country. Insurance companies estimate that with health insurance coming in, 6 per cent of household income will be spent on health care up from the current 2 per cent.

The Industry is now expected to undergo a drastic change with the advent of Managed Care Systems in the form of Preferred Provider Organisations—which will metamorphose in to Health Maintenance Organisations in the long run....

India has made significant progress in the past several decades in improving the health and well-being of its people. Over the past 40 years, life expectancy has risen by 17 years to 61 years, and infant mortality has fallen by more than two-thirds to 74 deaths per 1,000 live births. Despite these significant strides, the country continues to bear a heavy burden of both communicable and non-communicable diseases. Furthermore, India is experiencing a slow epidemiological evolution from infectious and parasitic diseases to non-communicable diseases. Also, the emergence of AIDS has begun to affect national and regional epidemiological profiles and priorities.

The government has sought to help states to improve their health policy environment and access to quality of services, with particular attention to building institutional capacity, the first-referral level, and services for the poor. This will help in establishing sustainable health systems that focus on cost-effective programs, and also make sufficient use of the private sector. The priority will be to develop effective and sustainable health systems that can meet the dual demands posed by the growth in non-communicable diseases and peoples' needs for better quality and higher levels of health care. Government sector that provides publicly financed and managed curative and preventive health services from primary to tertiary level, throughout the country and free of cost to the consumer (these account for about 18% of the overall health spending and 0.9% of the GDP).

The private sector plays a dominant role in the provision of individual curative care through ambulatory services and accounts for about 82% of the overall health expenditure and 4.2% of the GDP. Nationwide health care utilisation rates show that private health services are directed mainly at providing primary health care and financed from private resources, which could place a disproportionate burden on the poor. Most of these costs are out of pocket costs, State Governments contribute 15.2%, Central Government 5.2%, and third-party insurance and employers put in 3.3% of the total.[3] Private sector has 70% specialists and 85% of technology in their facilities. It accounts for 49% beds and occupancy ratio of 44%, whereas occupancy rate in public sector is 62%. More than 75% of service delivery for dental health, mental health, orthopedics, vascular and cancer diseases and about 40% of communicable diseases and deliveries are provided by the private sector.

The provision of health care by the public sector is a responsibility shared by State, Central and local Governments, although it is effectively a state responsibility in terms of service delivery. State and local Governments incur about three-quarters and the Center about one-quarter of public spendings on health. The responsibility for health is at three levels. First, health is primarily a State responsibility. Second, the Center is responsible for health services in Union Territories without a legislature and is also responsible for developing and monitoring national standards and regulations, linking the States with funding agencies, and sponsoring numerous schemes for implementation by State Governments. Third, both the Center and the States

3. Bhat, Ramesh and Jain, Nishant, "Analysis of Public and Private Health-care Expenditures", *Economic and Political Weekly*, Vol. XLI, No.1, 2006, pp. 57-68.

have a joint responsibility for programmes listed under the concurrent list. Goals and strategies for the public sector in health care are established through a consultative process involving all levels of government through the Central Council for Health and Family Welfare.

2. Risk Assessment

It was once assumed that poor people had no need for financial services, and perhaps needed only credit. Yet the conditions under which the poor live suggest otherwise. For poor people, risk is familiar and high. Strategies for managing and coping with risk are part of everyday life. Research[4] and experience have shown that the poverty and uncertainty poor people face require diverse financial services. Borrowing helps households achieve food security and alleviate poverty. In times of stress, the poor need to borrow to pay for essential consumption. But borrowing alone is not enough to pull households out of poverty. Poor people also require savings services to help them better manage their resources over time and to enable them plan and finance their investments. And most importantly, the poor need access to insurance to lessen the blow when, for instance, a breadwinner falls ill, crops fail, or prices for their products plummet.

Types of Risks

• Life Cycle Needs

Low-income households are most commonly exposed to expenditure requirements for life cycle needs, such as paying for a child's education, re-stocking household supplies, paying a sufficient dowry, or saving for retirement. These needs arise when flows of income do not coincide with required expenditures. While households are generally aware whether and when these events will occur, the high likelihood and frequency of their occurrence create an ongoing uncertainty as to whether the household will have sufficient income or assets to cover the cost associated with these events. While individually

4. Freiberg, J., *Social Security for the Poor—Options and Experiences*, 1999.

these events have the least severe impact, their frequency makes managing them a pressing need for many low-income households.

- **Death Risks**

Death risks include the costs that result from the death of a family member. The degree of uncertainty regarding death is greater than that caused by life cycle events, but less than that caused by most other risks faced by low-income households. This is because family members are sure that they will at some point die. However they experience uncertainty regarding when this may happen. The loss a household experiences when a death occurs (apart from the emotional loss) includes both a one-time component (e.g., cost of proper burial, cost of settling the deceased's accounts, etc.) and, potentially, an ongoing component to replace income that the deceased formerly provided to the family.

- **Property Risks**

Property risks include events leading to theft, damage, loss, or destruction of a household asset. Crop losses, livestock illness or death, and fire, are all examples of the types of asset losses that low-income households may need to protect against. Given the range in value of these assets and the situation specific nature of property risks (i.e. the likelihood of theft varies substantially by community), the impact of property risks will vary by family and locality. In general, property risks are likely to cause households greater uncertainty than death risks or life cycle needs because they cannot be sure whether, when, or how often a fire or theft might occur. The relative value of a household's loss due to a property risk will depend on the asset at risk.

- **Health Risks**

Besides life cycle needs, health risks—accidents, illnesses, and injuries that require households to pay for medical treatment—are among the most common concerns of low-income households. The cost to a household of each accident, illness or injury is generally one-time and, like property risks, can vary from relatively small, such as purchasing aspirin, to relatively large, such as major surgeries. The frequency with which health risks can occur, and the household's limited ability to predict whether or when they will be affected, suggest that health risks generate a greater degree of uncertainty than other risks.

- **Disability Risks**

The causes of disability risks are essentially the same as those for health risks (accidents, illnesses, and injuries), however there is a greater relative cost to a household of having a family member disabled than injured or sick. A disabled family member may require ongoing treatment expenses besides the cost of the initial medical attention. Households may also incur additional costs in replacing lost income if the family member is no longer able to work. This is especially problematic if the disabled family member is young. Instead of becoming a future source of income for the family, his/her disability requires an ongoing expense. Consequently, when these risks occur, low-income households have greater difficulty in overcoming disability risks than health risks.

- **Mass, Covariant Risks**

Mass, covariant risks are the threat that an event, such as an epidemic, a natural disaster, and war, could cause substantial losses for a large portion of a population at the same time. These risks could fit into the categories described above based on the impact they have on households. Death, property damage, illness, and disability are all associated with mass, covariant risks.

Mass, covariant risks are considered separately[5] because:

(1) They tend to be difficult or impossible to predict;

(2) They affect many people at the same time, thus hampering the ability of risk-pooling mechanisms to protect against these risks; and

(3) The cost associated with mass, covariant risks tends to be significantly greater than that resulting from other risks. This is because households are forced to deal with multiple losses at the same time (e.g., severe

5. Miller, M. and Northrip, Z., *Bamako 2000: Innovations in Microfinance*, 2001.

flooding leading to death of a family member, destruction of the family's home and several injuries to remaining family members); and a households' traditional risk coping strategies, such as intra-family gift giving, reciprocal exchange and non-financial savings tend to be weakened or destroyed because neighbors and local family members are suffering the similar losses at the same time.

3. Why Health Insurance?

Insurance protects against unexpected losses by pooling the resources of the many to compensate for the losses of the few. The greater the uncertainty of the event more the insurance becomes the economical form of protection. Insurance replaces the uncertain prospect of large losses with the certainty of making small, regular, affordable premium payments. The primary function of insurance is to act as a risk transfer mechanism, to provide peace of mind and protect against losses.

Insurance is not the only way of dealing with risks, and not all risks are insurable.[6] However, health risks such as those relating to illness, injury, disability, maternity and the like are considered to be eminently insurable as these risks are mostly independent or idiosyncratic, that is, not correlated among community members.[7] Moreover, among several risks facing poor households, health risk is considered to be crucial as it has a destabilising effect on household finances: directly, by thrusting health expenditure in the event of illness and indirectly, by affecting the income earning capacity of households.[8]

---

6. Brown, W; Churchill, C; *Providing Insurance to Low-Income Households*, USAID, 1999.
7. Alderman and Paxson. (1994). "*Do the Poor Insure?*" A Synthesis of Literature on Risk and Consumption in Developing Countries. In Bacha (ed.) Economics in a Changing World: Vol. 4: Development, Trade and the Environment. Macmillan Press, London, England.
8. Asfaw, A., von Braun, J., Assefa, Admassie A., and Jütting, J., *The Economic Costs of Illness in Low Income Countries: The Case of Rural Ethiopia*. Mimeo.

Health insurance enables access to better medical services and a longer and better quality of life. Thus, access to adequate insurance protection can assist the poor to achieve sustainable growth and provide them with the capability to attain a better standard of living. It can mitigate the impact of personal and environmental calamities on the build-up of assets and provide escape from the vicious circle of poverty. Insurance can also protect those that have risen above the poverty level against unforeseen events that may cause them to fall back into poverty.

For most people living in developing countries, "health insurance" is however an unknown word. It is generally assumed that, with the exception of the upper classes, people cannot afford such type of social protection. This is unfortunate, as poor people need protection against the financial consequences of illnesses. Illness still represents a permanent threat to their income earning capacity. Beside the direct costs for treatment and drugs, indirect costs for the missing labour force of the ill person have to be shouldered by the household.

Health insurance schemes are an increasingly recognized factor as a tool to finance health care provision in low-income countries. Given the high latent demand from people for health-care services of a good quality and the extreme under-utilisation of health services in several countries, it has been argued that social health insurance may improve the access to health care of acceptable quality. Whereas alternative forms of health care financing and cost recovery strategies like user fees have been heavily criticised, the option of insurance seems to be a promising alternative as it is a possibility to pool risk transferring, unforeseeable health care costs to fixed premiums. Recently, mainly in Sub-Saharan Africa and also in a variety of other countries, non-profit, mutual, community-based health insurance schemes have emerged. These schemes are characterised by an ethic of mutual aid, solidarity and the collective pooling of health risks. In several countries these schemes operate in conjunction with health care providers, mainly hospitals in the area.

This study focuses on rural areas because here the need for insurance is especially high, but private insurance markets do not exist and public measures often fail to reach their target population. It looks at community-based health insurance as a means of financing health care for the rural poor.

4. Community Based Health Insurance (CBHI)

Community based health insurance is seen as an effective way in financing health care costs. Health insurance by pooling of risks across members who participate in health insurance lessens the financial burden of members affected by illness. Indeed, several types of community based health insurance schemes have emerged in Sub-Saharan Africa,[9] Asia and in other regions.[10]

Community health care financing schemes are usually based on the following characteristics: voluntary membership, non-profit objective, link to a health care provider (often hospital in the area), risk pooling and relying on an ethic of mutual aid/solidarity.

Benefits

The real benefit of CBHI lies in keeping the transaction costs low, in the design of schemes suited to the community needs, in influencing health behavior through health education, and in influencing the supply of health care. Its advantage lies in being able to reach low-income people in rural areas and working in the informal sector who are otherwise difficult to reach, to exploit social capital in bringing about greater awareness, correct adverse selection and moral hazard problems, encourage preventive measures and increase access to health care. Popularizing insurance among low-income people requires conveying the idea, canvassing for it, collecting premium, and verifying claims and then reimbursing these claims, thus incurring high costs. In case of formal providers, all these

---

9. Wiesmann, D., and Jütting, J. (2000), "The Emerging Movement of Community Based Health Insurance in Sub-Saharan Africa: Experiences and Lessons Learned", *Afrika Spectrum*, 2/2000, pp. 193-210.

10. Bennett, S., Creese, A., and Monash, R. (1998), *Health Insurance Schemes for People Outside Formal Sector Employment*. ARA Paper No. 16, WHO, Geneva.

functions typically take up a significant part (at least 20 per cent) of the premium amount. In CBHI schemes such costs can be kept low, say to 5-6 per cent. This is because many of these tasks can be performed by the community members themselves.

Besides, in poor communities, the financial barrier is only one of the barriers to accessing health care. Often, there are many non-financial barriers that must also be overcome through the design of schemes, which ought to take into account characteristics of the community. All these aspects can best be handled if the scheme is community based. Additionally, the problems of adverse selection and moral hazard that arise due to informational asymmetries too can be reduced by making use of local knowledge that is readily available among people living in close communities.

Limitations

But community based schemes also have certain weaknesses such as low capital base, low level of revenue mobilisation, frequent exclusion of the poorest of the poor, small size of risk pool, limited management capacity, and isolation from more comprehensive benefits. Some forms of CBHI also have important limitations.[11] For example, where an NGO itself provides insurance (acts like an insurer), the ability of the NGO to have a pool of well diversified risk is limited. This in turn restricts the ability of the NGO to cover or insure variety of risks facing the target population. Moreover, where CBHI schemes are critically dependent on external funding, extending the reach of these schemes then depends on the amount of such funding available. Furthermore, the insurance schemes launched either by national or State-level Governments when elections are in sight tend to be populist or vote-catching ploy. Since such schemes have to be renewed every year, these tend to be dropped once the elections are over. It is to be seen if the universal health insurance scheme belongs to this category.

A few micro-level studies that have tried to estimate demand for health insurance based on the willingness-and-ability-to-

11. Gumber, A., *Hedging the Health of the Poor—The Case for Community Financing in India*, 2001.

pay for health insurance have come out with positive findings. A survey-based study[12] on the willingness to pay even in case of Ethiopia—one of the poorest countries in the Sub-Sahara Africa—shows that the poor are willing to pay up to 5 % of their monthly income for a scheme that can take care of their costs of illness.

5. Health Insurance for the Poor In India

Health insurance for the poor in India is still very much in the nascent stage. It takes different forms, being either community-based (CBHI) or non-community-based (like Jan Arogya policy of the government). The Community Based Health Insurance (CBHI) can itself take several forms.[13]

Community and self-generated financing programmes are those usually run by non-governmental organizations (NGOs) or non-profit-making organisations.[14] These organisations rely on finances from various sources, including government, donor agencies, and community and self-generated sources. Also many innovative methods of financing health care services have been used, like progressive premium scales, community-based pre-payment/insurance schemes, and income-generating schemes. The target population for provision of health care services by such organisations is primarily workers and families outside the formal sector. The sources of revenue for the programmes can be categorised as:

(a) User fees defined as the payment made by the beneficiaries directly to the health care provider, such as fees for services or prices paid for drugs/immunisation. This mode of financing is not common.

(b) Prepayment/insurance schemes, including payment by members for drugs either at subsidised rate or at cost price.

---

12. Asfaw, A., von Braun, J., Assefa Admassie, A., and Jütting, J., *The Economic Costs of Illness in Low Income Countries: The Case of Rural Ethiopia*. Mimeo.

13. Gumber, A., *Hedging the Health of the Poor—The Case for Community Financing in India*, 2001.

14. Dave, Priti., *Community and Self-Financing in Voluntary Health Programs in India*, Health Policy and Planning, Vol. 6 (1).

(c) Commercial schemes for profit actively run by organisations to finance health care.

(d) Fund raising activities by organisations for financing health care services. In some cases the revenue raised in this manner constitutes more than 5 per cent of the total funds of the organisations.

(e) System of making contributions in kind (such as rice, sorghum, community labour, etc.). This method is not very popular due to difficulty in management.

(f) Other sources of community-based and self-financing include instances like Tribhovandas Foundation providing health care through village milk cooperatives and Amul Union (the milk cooperative organisation) contributing significantly towards health services through putting a cess on milk collection.

All these forms currently exist in the country but only in small pockets, depending on the local conditions that vary considerably across regions. The most pertinent point about these schemes is their rural orientation and ability to mobilise resources in a village community. However, most of these schemes have catered to a small section of population with limited health coverage restricted to elementary, preventive, and maternal and child health (MCH) care.

CBHI schemes are designed in a number of ways, depending on the socio-economic characteristics of the target population, health profile of the population, and the health risks prevalent in the region. The decentralisation process initiated in the country with the 73rd and 74th Constitutional Amendment aimed at promoting local bodies, like Panchayati Raj Institutions (PRIs) in the rural areas and Nagar Palikas in the urban areas, has raised hopes of being able to reach the poor through community based initiatives with some subsidy to those who cannot afford the costs.[15]

15. Gumber, A. and V. Kulkarni, Paper presented in the National Consultation on Health Security in India organised by Institute for Human Development and UNDP with support from Ministry of Health and Family Welfare, Government of India, July 26-27, 2001.

Community Based Universal Health Insurance Scheme

Prior to the announcement of the proposed community based universal health insurance scheme by the finance minister of India, various States Governments were contemplating launching a health insurance scheme for their poor population. State Governments intensified their efforts when a similar announcement by the Central Government in the budget 2002-03, did not take off. Without sufficient knowledge base, the State Governments were trying to enter into an arrangement with the providers of medical services, public insurance companies and the target community whereby insurance companies would reimburse treatment costs of the target community and the governments would subsidise the premium to the insurance company for the insurance sold to the target community. Some State Governments had thought of paying the premium through their general revenues while others had planned to cross-subsidise premium by bringing State Government employees also under Mediclaim policy (Punjab and West Bengal Governments were thinking along these lines).[16]

Features

The scheme comes in three different categories:

(i) Re. 1 per day per year for an individual;

(ii) Rs. 1.5 per day per year for a family of up to five members; and

(iii) Rs. 2 per day per year for a family of upto seven members.

Benefits include providing medical expenses upto Rs. 30,000 per family in case of hospitalisation. If an earning member falls sick, the scheme also provides for the loss of livelihood at the rate of Rs. 50 per day upto maximum of 15 days, and in case of death of the earning head of the family due to personal accident Rs. 25,000 is to be given to the nominee.

In all these categories, the government provides a subsidy of Rs. 100 which remains fixed whether it is an individual who buys insurance or a family of five or of seven. While the

16. Ahuja, R., *Health Insurance for the Poor in India*, ICRIER, 2004.

scheme is open to anybody who wants to participate in it, the subsidy is given only to families below the poverty line. Moreover, the scheme is designed to cover not a poor individual/ family on Indian streets but those who are members of some group or the other such as cooperative societies, bidi workers, handloom weavers, etc. In other words, the proposed scheme is a group insurance scheme with membership of at least 100 families.

The scheme is not designed to cover the entire population below the poverty line (BPL), at least not in the initial phase. If the scheme survives and does not get extended to include other BPL families, State Governments would then need to think of reaching those poor who are not a part of any occupation-based or any self-help group for which the scheme is currently intended.

Some other salient features of the scheme are: (i) individuals between the age of 3 months and 65 years can join the scheme; (ii) total hospital expense that can be reimbursed under the scheme for any one illness can be up to Rs. 15, 000, with a cap on the amount payable for different types of hospital expenses; (iii) a number of illnesses/ situations are excluded, for example maternity insurance is not included; and (iv) claims will be settled either by an intermediary called third party administrators (TPAs) or by the insurance companies themselves.

In principle, both public and private insurance companies can participate in the scheme. In reality, participation of private insurance companies seems unlikely, especially when there are other more lucrative areas still to be tapped.

Health insurance schemes for the poor should take care of not just the inpatient or hospital care, but also of the outpatient care. It is often suggested that insurance be provided only for inpatient care and that outpatient care be left outside the ambit of insurance. The reasons given are that people can, by and large, afford out-patient care because it is relatively inexpensive; it is the in-patient care that pushes them into poverty trap; that administratively it is difficult to include out-patient care; and, that out-patient care would lead to cost escalation. Ideally, both in-patient care and out-patient care should be covered, and the decision of whether or not a patient needs hospitalisation should be professionally made and should not be a function of whether or not the patient has health insurance cover.

Conclusion

In the current debate on health security for the poor, health insurance is made out to be panacea for all the ills facing the poor. Health insurance, no doubt, has emerged as an important financing tool as it promises to mobilise some resources from the people themselves, i.e. those who buy insurance. But health insurance, which strengthens demand side, makes sense only when the supply of health care is reasonably well developed. Where this is not so, health insurance is meaningless. The supply of health care in the rural and remote areas of country is far from satisfactory. Although public health care centers are pervasive, these centers have degraded overtime in most states due to lack of funds, accountability and so forth. Any attempt at introducing health insurance for the poor must also be accompanied by revival of health care facilities at these centers. Finally, both the provision and access to health care services should be a part of a bigger health strategy which includes other public health programs such as safe drinking water, sanitation, family planning, etc., as each of these are important determinants of health outcomes.

REFERENCES

Berman, P.A. (1997): "Rethinking Health Care Systems: Private Health Care Provision in India", Harvard School of Public Health, July.

Berman, P. (1996): "Health Care Expenditure in India" Monica Dasgupta et al. (Eds.), *Health, Poverty and Development in India,* Oxford University Press, Delhi.

Berman, P. and Khan, M.E (Eds.) (1993): *Paying for India's Health Care*, Sage Publications, New Delhi.

Bhat, R. (1996): "Regulation of the Private Health Sector in India", *International Journal of Health Planning and Management*, 11: 253-74.

Burgess, R. and Stern, N. (1991): "Social Security in Developing Countries: What, Why, Who, and How?" Ahmad, Drèze and Hills, Sen (Eds.): *Social Security in Developing Countries: Wider Studies in Development Economics*. Oxford: Clarendon Press, 41-80.

Business World, Cover Story, October 1999.

Central Statistical Organization (2003): "Selected Socio-Economic Statistics, India 2001", Ministry of Statistics and Programme Implementation, Government of India.

Garg, Charu (1998): "Equity of Health Sector Financing and Delivery in India", *Takemi Working Papers*, Harvard School of Public Health.

Chollet, D.J. and Lewis, M. (1997): "Private Insurance: Principles and Practice", *Innovations in Health Care Financing*. Washington, DC: World Bank.

Duggal R. (1993): "Employee Medical Benefit in Corporate Sector", *The Foundation for Research in Community Health*, Bombay.

Duggal, R. and Amin, S. (1989): "Cost of Health Care: A Household Survey in an Indian District", *The Foundation for Research in Community Health*, Bombay.

Economic Survey, 2002-2003, Government of India, Ministry of Finance & Company Affairs, Economic Division.

Giridhar, G. (1993): "Concepts and Practices in Health Care Insurance Schemes and Recent Examples in India", *Paying for India's Health Care*. Eds: Berman & Khan. Sage Publications.

Griffin, C. and Shaw, P.R. (1995): "Health Insurance in Sub-Saharan Africa: Aims, Findings, Policy Implications", P. Shaw and M. Ainsworth (Eds.): *Financing Health Services through User Fees and Insurance*. Washington, DC: World Bank.

Jesani, A. and Anantharam, S. (1989): "Private Sector and Privatization in the Health Care Service", *Foundation for Research in Community Health*, Bombay.

Jutting, J. (1999): "Strengthening Social Security Systems in Rural Areas of Developing Countries", *ZEF Discussion Paper on Development Policy*, Center for Development Research, Bonn.

Outreville, J.F. (1998): "The Health Insurance Sector: Market Segmentation and International Trade in Health Services", S. Zarrilli and C. Kinnon (Eds.): *International Trade in Health Services*. Geneva: UN, WHO. Review, 53 (5): 941-973.

Ron, A., Abel-Smith, B. and Tamburi, G. (1990): *Health Insurance in Developing Countries*. Geneva, ILO.

Sanyal, S.K. (1996): "Household Financing of Health Care", *Economic and Political Weekly*, Vol. XXXI, May.

Shariff, A. (1995): "Health Transition in India", *Working Paper No. 57*, National Council of Applied Economic Research, New Delhi.

Uplekar, M. (1989): "Private Doctors and Public Health", *Takemi Program in International Health*, Report No. 40, Harvard School of Public Health.

Viswanathan, H. and Rohde, J.E. "Diarrhoea in Rural India: A Nationwide Study of Mothers and Practitioners", New Delhi.

WHO (1978): "Primary Health Care", Report of the International Conference on Primary Health Care, Alma-Ata, 6-12 September Geneva.

Williams, A. (1997): "Priority Setting in Public and Private Health Care", A.J. Cuyler and A. Maynard (Eds.): *Being Reasonable about the Economics of Health*.

World Bank (1993): "World Development Report: 1993, Investing in Health", New York: Oxford University Press.

World Bank (1995): "India: Policy and Finance Strategies for Strengthening Primary Health Services", *Report No. 13042*, Population and Human Resources Division, Washington DC.

Microfinance in India: Impressive Achievements but Miles to Go

13

Manoranjan Sharma

Introduction

Micro-credit and Microfinance (MF) are often used synonymously. But MF is a much more broader concept than micro-credit. MF encompasses micro-credit, micro-savings, micro-insurance and payment services. MF emerged as an innovative savings and loan mechanism in developing countries because of market distortion and financial repression (Shaw, 1973; McKinnon, 1973), lack of an adequate social safety net for the poor and absence of conveniently accessible and flexible products and services, simplified documentation and the insistence on collateral (Fisher and Sriram, 2002).

Development pushed from above by the State distorted accelerated industrialization (Korten, 1981: Stohr and Taylor, 1981; Schumaker, 1973). This necessitated an accent on MF, which has been characterized by bottom-up approach, targeted credit supply, entrepreneurial drive, sustainability and replicability. Some positive results are already palpable in recent years across countries as the product of inclusive development, micro-credit and other socio-economic innovations.

Microfinance in Global and National Setting

The utter neglect of the poor (now globally estimated at 2 billion people) emanates not only from relations of power but also complete inadequacy of economic theory in resolving the peculiar but interrelated problems of widespread poverty, deprivation, unemployment and highly skewed pattern of distribution of income and wealth. In this setting of widespread poverty and deprivation, the determinants of production and productivity need to be carefully examined to effectively address the challenge of the new millennium. There is a fair measure of consensus that labour-intensive and equitable robust economic growth together with larger outlays of social expenditures focused on the poor is a must for launching a direct assault on poverty. In the pursuit of growth with distributive equity, there has been a heightened consciousness of the necessity of empowering all people by increasing their access to all factors of production, including credit and the role of non-governmental organizations (NGOs).

Micro-credit encourages the latent capacity of the poor for entrepreneurship with small-scale loans. About 3,000 microfinance institutions in developing countries make the poor more self-reliant, create employment opportunities and promote gender empowerment. Micro-credit also helps to create deeper and more widespread financial markets. This is why Nobel Laureate Dr. Muhammad Yunus has repeatedly urged that credit should be accepted as human right because of the emergence of money economy and the need for credit reform like other reforms. Speaking at the Reserve Bank of India (RBI) on the topic 'Credit as Human Right' on February 2, 2007, he made a strong case for the creditworthiness of the poor, who have been left unbanked by traditional banks. Dr. Yunus stressed that the poor are the victims of the poverty created by policies, institutions, concepts and systems built by ourselves. Grameen Bank, founded by Dr. Yunus is based on a banking model without collateral. Taking a leaf out of Professor Yunus' speech, RBI Governor, Dr. Y.V. Reddy said that the central bank would frame a charter to make credit a human right. Pointing to the disparity created by conventional banking he said, "Only one-third of the world's population has access to credit while the rest is not considered creditworthy by the system. The remaining two-third doesn't have the money to start with".

According to the *2005 State of the Microcredit Summit Campaign Report*, in 1997 only about 7.6 million families were served by micro-credit worldwide. As of Dec. 31, 2004, about 3,200 micro-credit institutions reported reaching more than 92 million clients. Almost 73% of such clients were living in dire poverty at the time of their first loan. Cross-country studies explain and reflect that microfinance slashed poverty through increasing income levels. There is also incontrovertible evidence that microfinance discernibly improved health care, children's education and nutrition, and women's empowerment. In particular, the ability to borrow, save, and earn income reduces economic vulnerability for women and their households. Thus, development of MF must be central to any development strategy.

Micro-credit dispensation is characterised by loans of usually small amounts, frequent, for short durations and mainly for unconventional purposes, high repayment rate, loaning mainly on the basis of mutual need and trust with minimum documentation and without any tangible security, variable rate of interest and creation of confidence building in the target group. These characteristics are succinctly summed by the title of Bouman's book *Small, Short and Unsecured* (1989). To be sure, microfinance is not without its defects. For example, microfinance has been criticised on the grounds of its relatively greater impact on the moderately poor more than the truly destitute because of higher skill levels, better market contacts and higher initial resource base, variable impact per income group, etc.

The widely acclaimed Grameen Bank model has sometimes been criticised because of low repayment rate with 19% of their loans one year overdue; 10% loans over 2 years overdue; use of coercive methods for repayment, such as, removing the tin roof from people's homes; the bank's attempt to conceal problem loans by relabelling and hiding account information; lack of formal supervision in its operation and an overemphasis on microfinance to combat poverty leading to a reduction of other assistance to the poor, such as government welfare (Pearl et al. 2001). But given its enormous reach and impact, MF has rapidly emerged as a catalytic instrument of socio-economic transformation. Of the range of diverse microfinance in vogue, mention may here be made of the following mechanisms:

- OPP-OCT, Karachi, Pakistan
- ACCION International

- ACDI/VOCA
- Aga Khan Agency for Microfinance.
- A Self-help Assistance Program (ASAP Africa).
- The Consultative Group to Assist the Poor.
- DOEN Foundation attempts to improve access to the financial sector in both transition and developing countries.
- Cooperative
- Grameen Bank
- Grameen Foundation
- FINCA
- Freedom from Hunger
- Village Enterprise Fund
- Negroes Women for Tomorrow Foundation
- NICA Fund (Nicaraguan Credit Alternatives Fund)
- Opportunity International provides opportunities for people in chronic poverty to transform their lives.
- Microloan Foundation focusses on Malawi and sub Saharan Africa.
- The ProCredit Group
- Unitus is an innovative group using a hybrid venture capital model to increase local access to microfinance.
- www.kiva.org
- Microfinance Opportunities
- M2i Consulting-Microfinance Management and Investnment Advisory.
- Mifex Solutions for creating easier access to financial services and business training.
- Ujjivan, an urban microfinance organization, based in Bangalore, India.
- Andromeda, is a fund supporting the empowerment of entrepreneurs in developing countries.

Indian Scenario—Strategy for Development

MF provided by formal institutions (banks and cooperatives), semiformal institutions (non-government organisations) and informal sources (money-lenders and shop keepers) is contemporarily significant. Of the one billion poor people globally, about 200 million persons live in India. Despite typically providing thrift, credit and other financial services and products of small amounts to the poor, self-help, savings and credit groups streamlined existing credit delivery mechanism by increased credit outreach and enhanced viability of rural financial institutions (RFIs) in India.

Absence of conveniently accessible and flexible products and services, simplified documentation and the insistence on collateral marked the Indian rural credit scenario. High transactions costs of rural lending in India arise because of small loan size, frequent transactions, large geographical spread, heterogeneous borrowers, widespread illiteracy and inappropriate "financial climate". The concept of the "joint liability" is the basic feature distinguishing microfinance from the conventional mechanism of credit disbursement.

Cross-country analysis clearly brings out that in a welfare state, equitable distribution of costs and benefits is a basic desideratum of any development project. MF is not entirely new or novel to India because of the implementation of Integrated Rural Development Programme (IRDP) for twenty years leading to cumulative financial assistance of around Rs. 250 billion to roughly 55 million families and an elaborate network of cooperatives, 196 RRBs and 27 public sector banks (PSBs). World Bank-NCAER Survey's on rural access to finance shows that despite the large size and depth of the Indian financial system, 70 per cent of the rural poor lack a bank account and 87 per cent are without any access to credit from a formal source. Access to other financial services, such as, savings accounts, life, health and crop insurance also remains extremely constricted for the rural poor with 80 per cent of the Rs. 450 billion market for micro-financial services being met by informal sources.

Gaps in macro approaches induced retooling of RFIs in designing financial services for the rural poor. There are also several spin-off effects of micro credit for banks, e.g. increase in outreach measured by the number of new clients, volume of savings mobilized and credit deployed, empowerment of the poor, particularly women, creation of clusters, federations and social clusters, etc. While the poor are under-banked, they are certainly not unbankable and micro-enterprises are viable and sustainable in extricating the poor from the vicious circle of poverty.

Complete deregulation of interest rates on loans by banks to MFIs and by these organisations to their members and beneficiaries, except for government sponsored programmes, mainstreamed micro-credit and accelerated flow of bank credit to MFIs without damaging their decentralised, voluntary and non-bureaucratic character. MF provides a fairly good risk-adjusted return with very low non-performing assets from clients considered as vulnerable as strikingly revealed by the experience of diverse countries like Indonesia, Thailand, Bangladesh, Bolivia, El Salvador and India. This methodology of banks/ Microfinance Institutions (MFIs) adopting a profit-centre approach with customer-friendly savings and loan products has important policy prescriptive lessons in dealing with poverty and economic related issues for the developing and poverty-ridden nations.

MFIs are an extremely heterogeneous group comprising NBFCs, societies, trusts and cooperatives. The number of private MFIs in India is estimated to be around 1000. Of this, not more than a dozen MFIs have an outreach of 1,00,000 clients and the large majority of MFIs operate with clients ranging from 500-1500. Loans up to Rs. 25,000 in India are covered under microfinance. Thirt-six per cent of the credit needs in the rural areas is still met informally, viz. moneylenders, landlords, friends and relatives and chit fund. Given the high risk factors, viz. poor quality of security, inadequate documentation, crop failure, moneylenders continue to perform an important function in the Indian socio-economic setting. MF is a rational, relevant instrument of strengthening poor.

This instrument is entirely in conformity with the interests of the banking system because of the efficacy of MF in credit dispensation, improved loan recovery and removal of poverty. This is why the 2005 Union Budget provided an impetus to microfinance with the Finance Minister Mr P. Chidambram announcing, "Government intends to promote MFIs in a big way. The way forward, I believe, is to identify MFIs, classify and rate such institutions, and empower them to intermediate between the lending banks and the beneficiaries".

Conceptual and Methodological Frame

The Task Force on Supportive Policy and Regulatory Framework for Microfinance (1998) defined "Microfinance" as "provision of thrift, credit and other financial services and products of very small amounts to the poor in rural, semi-urban and urban areas for enabling them to raise their income levels and improve living standards". MFIs, however, provide other non-credit services and capacity building, training, marketing of the products of the SHGs, micro-insurance, etc. MFIs have developed effective poverty targeting strategies, viz. contextual factors, outreach and impact measurement methodologies. Aggressive MF expansion to qualitatively improve the lives of the vulnerable sections requires focused attention on exploration of new products, delivery methodologies and strategic partnerships to overcome high transaction costs, limited sources of funds, determination of suitable rate of interest. These are necessary to ensure long-term viable operations, networking with locally feasible integrated development projects and business competence.

RBI prohibits commercial banks from using agents in collection of savings services. Use of agents in collection of savings services could, however, reduce transaction costs for providers and customers, rightly align incentives for the collector and customers, while checking transaction costs, reducing cost of branch opening and providing greater flexibility. However, the 2005 Budget broke fresh ground. This approach was carried forward by the RBI in its subsequent Annual Policy Statement: "As a follow-up to the Budget proposals, modalities for allowing banks to adopt the agency model by using the infrastructure of civil society organisations, rural kiosks and village knowledge centres for providing credit support to rural and farm sectors and appointment of microfinance institutions (MFIs) as banking correspondents are being worked out". But what is prognostically alarming is that even this refreshingly different approach revealed the customary pre-occupation with "credit".

Strategies for Inclusive Growth—Learning from Global Experiences

Improved access to credit for small rural or urban producers, landless farmers and other people with low or no income, with special attention to the needs of women and disadvantaged and vulnerable groups has customarily been stressed. But despite the challenge and the desperate need for strategic action, not much happened on the ground. Hence, the World Summit for Social Development (Copenhagen, March 1995) advised Governments to review national legal, regulatory and institutional frameworks restricting the access of people living in poverty, especially women, to credit on reasonable terms; to promote realistic targets for access to affordable credit, providing incentives for improving access to and strengthening the capacity of organized credit systems to deliver credit and related services to people living in poverty and vulnerable groups; and to expand financial networks, building on existing networks, promoting attractive opportunities for savings and ensuring equitable access to credit at the local level (United Nations, 1995).

There is a growing recognition that MF provides a practical way of making the developing countries' financial systems more accessible to poor people. Ms. Mercedes Benavides, Manager, Global Network for Banking Innovation in Microfinance, Women's World Banking cited international experiences in financial inclusion in her Special Address to the BANCON 2006 held at Hyderabad in November 2006. She cogently argued that microfinance provides faster and better services with low-income people loans being better than group loans. Top performing microfinance institutions have demonstrated high growth and huge return on investments. The Colombian experience in financial inclusion demonstrated that GNBI was able to achieve financial penetration of 26 per cent. Consequently, there is an imperative need for specialized training for the underprivileged sections, high product integration and low costs.

Success Stories in India

Institutions like the National Bank for Agriculture and Rural Development (NABARD), Sidbi Foundation for Micro-Credit (SFMC), Sa-Dhan (an association of Community Development Finance Institutions), Rashtriya Mahila Kosh (RMK), Mysore Resettlement and Development Agency (MYRADA) in Karnataka, Cashpor Financial and Technical Services Ltd. (CFTS) in eastern Uttar Pradesh, Development of Humane Action (DHAN) Foundation in Tamil Nadu, Andhra Pradesh and Karnataka, Friends of Women's World Banking (FWWB), SHARE Microfin Ltd., etc., have played a pioneering role in selection and training of staff and adopting deposit products, credit services and collateral requirements to the target group to build a sustainable microfinance programme. No wonder, then, microfinance programmes have steadily burgeoned in recent years as strikingly reflected, for example, in the membership of Sa-Dhan and loans outstanding of its member MFIs, remarkable increase in the outreach of the CARE CASHE Programme and the impressive increase in the outreach of SHARE Microfin Limited. The 'Velugu' Project in Andhra Pradesh, the Bidar innovation in Karnataka—these and other developments have brought about a silent revolution in rural areas—a paradigm shift from debt-driven development to self-driven development. Such examples of changes with far-reaching implications can easily be increased. What is urgently needed is replication of these examples on a much larger canvas.

Criticality of SHGs

Given their historical experience and the socio-economic setting, banks were initially hesitant to reach the multitude of poor necessitating grass root level initiatives by voluntary organizations (VOs)/ NGOs. With around 90 per cent of groups linked with banks being exclusive women-SHGs', SHGs enhanced gender empowerment. With a modest beginning of 255 SHGs 'credit-linked' to the banks as at end-March 1993, the number of such SHGs rose to16.18 lakh linked with 35,294 bank branches of 560 banks in 563 districts across 30 States as at end-March 2005, cumulative bank loans disbursed rose from about Rs. 0.3 crore to around Rs. 6,898 core, reduced vulnerability of the target group and infusion of professionalism into services to rural poor, viz. landless and marginal farmers and women, reflecting the process of widening, deepening and strengthening of credit access among SHGs. Mushrooming SHGs has, however, adversely affected quality of SHGs. Some SHGs fail because of entry of non-poor from middle classes into the system or natural calamities. Limiting involvement of government departments in promoting groups, providing long-term incentives to NGOs for sustained nurturing, enhancing management of SHG groups with greater financial investment and technical support could arrest deteriorating quality of SHGs.

There are three extant SHG-Bank Linkage Models-Model I-Bank as SHPIs, Model II-Bank-Facilitator Agency-SHGs-Members and Model III-Bank-NGO-MFI-SHG-Members. But Model II is the most widely acceptable. As the Tenth Plan allocated Rs. 7,36,570 crore for agriculture, banks had to substantially enhance ground level credit disbursement. The slew of measures announced in the Union Budget, 2005-06 would considerably bolster credit dispensation by MFIs in conjunction with SHGs and NGOs. RBI's April 2005 Annual Policy Statement indicated access to External Commercial Borrowings for NGOs engaged in microfinance activities and working out of modalities for allowing banks to adopt the agency model by using the infrastructure of civil society organisations, rural kiosks and village knowledge centres for providing credit support to rural and farm sectors and appointment of microfinance institutions (MFIs) as banking correspondents. Banking correspondents, who are from the local areas, can identify and disburse small loans to the rural populace. This innovative mechanism could address uncertainties about the quality of borrowers and assets and thus contribute to risk mitigation. Banks benefit through two ways: reduced transaction cost and the distinct possibility of charging higher interest rates and earning higher returns.

Apart from direct bank lending to SHGs, NGOs themselves have transformed into financial intermediaries. Important non-SHG bank-linkage approaches include Cooperatives and Grameen replicators *a la* Bangladesh. Inadequate attention on such approaches led to the present situation, where we still have neither a suitable legal entity for non-SHG-Linkage micro-finance for the poor, nor a supportive policy and regulatory framework. But both models—direct credit linking by the banks and credit linking through NGOs and MFIs—have been extremely successful. RBI instructed banks to consider lending to SHGs as a normal lending activity and such lending with flexible margins, security norms, repayment schedules, etc., forms part of priority sector lending. SHGs eminently meet the test of physical and financial sustainability, defined as the ability of the group to continue to function and grow without financial, managerial and other organisational support from Self-Help Promoting Institutions (SHPI) and others on subsidised terms.

SHG-Bank Linkage

MFIs typically have a strong developmental impact. Banks' commercial microfinance techniques provide better access to finance for micro-enterprises, accelerate their growth, boost overall confidence in the financial sector and create new jobs. Flexible SHGs help in aggregation of small individual saving and borrowing requirements of members obviating the need for the bank to maintain multiple accounts for all group members. While some groups attempt credit management out of their own savings, most others rely on linkages with banks. Such linkages necessitate proper credentials, track record, and system of maintaining accounts and records, regular audits in place and manpower for closer supervision and follow-up. The synergy built in the programme between the informal sector comprising the poor and their SHGs, the semi-formal sector comprising NGOs, and the formal sector comprising banks, government and the development agencies like the 'twice-blessed' Shakespearean quality of mercy needs to be fully exploited.

Demand-side Perspective—Yawning Chasm in Credit

Despite credit linkage of over one million SHGs and mobilization of Rs. 3000 crore as credit from formal financial institutions, MF still forms a miniscule proportion of the total bank credit in India. Notwithstanding the truly remarkable growth of SHG-Bank Linkage, particularly since the 1990s, there continues to be a serious demand-supply imbalance. On the basis of modest \$200 on average for each micro-enterprise and \$100 for each landless household, it has been estimated that 90 million farm holdings, 30 million non-agricultural enterprises and 50 million landless households in India collectively need approximately US\$30 billion credit annually, constituting about 5 per cent of India's GDP.

Table 1 attempts to construct two scenarios of credit requirement under microfinance in India, i.e. (a) credit available at prevailing trend, i.e. @ Rs. 5,000 per member and (b) credit required for sustainable livelihood, i.e. @ Rs. 35,000 per member.

Table 1: Regionwise Credit Flow and Potential Under Microfinance in India (Position as on 31.03.2005)

(Amount- Rupees Crore)

Sl. No.		Average Credit (in Rs.)	Central	East	North	South	West	All India
A. Coverage so far (Adjusted Total) @								
1.	SHG formed		810308	846955	164819	1734915	50634	4060631
2.	Members already in SHG fold	14/SHG	11344313	11857373	2307467	24288813	7050870	56848837
3.	SHG Credit Linked	65697	2268	2909	585	6268	1610	13640
4.	Members Credit Linked	4542	2243	2885	602	6500	1631	13862
B. Potential Credit Requirement for Sustainable Livelihood								
5.	Additional Credit for Members already credit linked (4 above) for sustainable livelihood	0 30458	0 15045	0 19345	0 4039	0 43591	0 10935	0 92956

(Contd...)

6.	Members from unlinked SHGs (2-4) for	5000	3202	2753	491	4988	1730	13165
	sustainable livelihood	35000	22417	19271	3434	34919	12112	92154
7.	Members left out of BPL families	5000	8550	3399	0	0	2105	14055
	for sustainable livelihood	35000	59851	23796	0	0	14736	98383
8.	Additional 10% of APL population	5000	2448	1352	840	2036	1831	8506
	for sustainable livelihood	35000	17137	9461	5879	14253	12815	59545
9.	Total Potential of Credit (5+6+7+8)for	5000	14201	7504	1330	7025	5666	35726
	sustainable livelihood	35000	114450	71874	13353	92764	50599	343038
C. The Gap in Credit for Indian Microfinance (9-2)								
Existing Gap for	subsistence	5000	11957	4619	728	524	4035	21864
	for sustainable livelihood	35000	112206	68989	12750	86263	48968	329176

Source: *A Resource Book for Livelihood Promotion*, BASIX, Hyderabad.

Real and Worrisome Concerns

The inexorability of the MFI movement gathering steam is incontrovertible. But an analysis of the overall scene needs to be tempered by gaps in adequacies and competencies, viz. small size, limited collective outreach of MFIs and region-specificity in the spread of SHGs and the MFIs with States in South India, accounting for over three-fifth of this credit linkage. Even among the Southern States, a skewed pattern is discernible with Andhra Pradesh (AP) way ahead. Apart from well-developed banking infrastructure and outreach, AP's remarkable success is attributable to routing of all State Government schemes through SHGs, uniform treatment of SHGs above and below the poverty line, exemption of stamp duty on loan documents, operationalisation of NABARD's 'critical rating index', training of government officials, local cultures and practices, etc.

There are also the problems of inadequacy of addressal by MFIs and NGOs alone as 80 per cent of the financial sector is still controlled by public sector institutions, modest involvement of commercial banks, miniscule involvement of the MFIs in terms of the proportion of poor households served, covering less than 5 per cent of India's rural poor (as compared to 65 per cent in Bangladesh) and lack of capital, technology and human resources.

Medium-term and long-term capacity building of MFIs requires both enhanced financial and non-financial capacity through value-added information, including education, training and on-the-job learning to create cost-effective and self-sustaining MFIs. Financial capacity building helps an MFI to absorb and manage increased funds for loan disbursement, increased number of loans, clientele base, and savings, etc. Non-financial capacity building primarily focuses on institutional and human resources of an MFI through networking and partnership for training, skill development, information management systems, etc. Capacity building through training and education, documentation of best practices and ideas, strategies, tools and ideas and microfinance business support services also broadly involves advocacy and networking. A virtuous cycle of regenerative, broad-based growth in an age of seamless symbiosis and of shrinking horizons now needs to be fostered by both cost efficiency and earnings efficiency for systemic long-run viability and sustainability.

It is generally agreed that micro-credit transcends money and access to credit. Despite the criticality of MFIs in providing composite services, given the wide array of financial transactions (both borrowing and lending, often simultaneously, and at all levels of income) characterizing the financial life of the poor (Ruthven, 2001; Patole and Ruthven, 2001), the scope of Indian MFIs continues to be extremely narrow. This severely constrains the potential of microfinance as a development tool. With only India's three top MFIs offering composite services, RFAS-2003 also reinforced this reality check. With an average of 15 persons per SHG, a crore and fifty lakh people, mostly women are now organised as SHGs but the average size of the loan is still grossly inadequate at Rs. 2500. Consequently, there is a strong demand for non-SHG-linkage types of microfinance. MFIs are constrained by the need to become a non-bank finance company to accept deposits, with high capital requirements, regulatory limits on raising debt from foreign sources and foreign equity limitations.

These compelling issues need to be addressed through appropriately structured policies, participative strategies and continuing consultative process to sustain the pace of expansion, fostering growth of NGOs in non-Southern regions, reducing cost of promotion of NGOs and enhancing per capita credit outlays. The recalcitrance of banks and financial institutions to lend to micro and small businesses, given their high failure rate, economic uncertainties and lack of collateral, makes it necessary to stress a holistic approach for development of micro-enterprises among SHGs with innovations in financial services, product development and business development services. Towards this end, skill and technology development and upgradation and effective marketing strategies with active participation of the rural poor are called for to enable access to financial services to the poor. While Canara Bank has worked in extending capacity building assistance to community-based institutions through 33 training institutes set up by it, Women's World Banking emphasizes an understanding of the environment, market and institutional capabilities in planning microfinance interventions.

Development Outcomes—Quantiative and Qualitative Impact Assessments

Development is a multi-dimensional, systemic process springing from the culture, values and social and political structures of each society; it also conditions the way society manages the challenges, constraints and opportunities of an often alien modernisation process. The process of economic development reveals that the analysis of transformation cannot be fully conducted merely on a macro-economic level. Successful progress on sound, scientific and sustainable line necessitates a paradigm shift and micro-economic analysis. Microfinance impact relates to economic impact; socio-political or cultural impacts and personal or psychological impact. With MF going far beyond conventional "credit for enterprise" to encompass "financial services to reduce the vulnerability of the poor", transformed MFIs have started delivering a wide spectrum of financial products. The International Year of Micro-credit 2005's Fact Sheet *Microfinance and the Millennium Development Goals* (MDGs) shows that microfinance provides a frame of action directly attacking the vulnerabilities debilitating the rural populace leading to discernible improvement in the household income of beneficiaries. MF thus leads to eradication of extreme poverty and hunger through improved living standards—both at the individual and household level *vis-à-vis* those without access to financial services, e.g. the clients of BRAC (Bangladesh) increased household expenditures by 28 per cent and assets by 112 per cent; the weekly income of FINCA clients increased on an average by 145 per cent in El Salvador. The programme promoted achievement of universal primary education in poor households with access to financial services, both by sending children to school in larger numbers and by prolonging the duration of stay in school. In Bangladesh, almost all girls in Grameen client households had some schooling, compared to 60 per cent of non-client households.

Access to financial services and the resultant transfer of financial resources to poor women enhanced gender equality and women's empowerment, e.g. female clients of Bank Rakyat Indonesia (BRI) were more likely than non-clients to make joint decisions with their husbands regarding allocation of household money, children's education, use of contraceptives and family size, and participation in community events. The programme also resulted in a range of other benefits. Such benefits included reduced child mortality, improved maternal health and control of HIV/AIDS, malaria, and other diseases through better nutrition, housing and health, reduced credit dependency on informal money lenders and other non-institutional sources. Malaria, which can be controlled for $3 billion a year, costs Africa millions of lives a year with over $12 billion in lost productivity. A simple mosquito net costing $2-$5 is effective in preventing malaria for a household. But even this capital cost is often considered prohibitive by a farmer with earnings of ~$250 per year. In cases where preventative measures exist, microfinancing can help make these solutions more universally affordable and facilitate the achievement of almost all MDGs.

A study by National Bank for Agriculture and Rural Development (NABARD), which covered 560 SHG member households from 223 self-help groups, spread over 11 States showed that average value of assets increased by 72 per cent, from Rs. 6,843 to Rs. 11,793, average annual savings per household registered over threefold increase from Rs. 460 to Rs. 1444, the average borrowing per year per household increased from Rs. 4,282 to Rs. 8,341 and average net income increased per household increased by about 33 per cent. Impressive quantitative outreach achievements are inextricably linked to systematic and sustainable solutions of socio-economic issues. Such commendable efforts lead to a silent revolution in improving the quality of life of the vast multitude mired in abject poverty. Empirical evidences clearly reveal the successful impact of the programme on reduced incidence of poverty and vulnerability of poor households, improved asset position, increased savings, shifted borrowing patterns and activities financed, increased employment and consumption expenditure and a beneficial social impact, including reduced credit dependency on informal money lenders and other non-institutional sources, building "capacity" at the SHG level and space for different stakeholders to innovate, learn and replicate and reduced feminisation of poverty. RFAS, 2003 for AP and UP shows that despite significant regional differences, nearly 54 per cent of SHG members are from the poorest groups and hence the payoff in terms of cohesive maturity and understanding is significant.... But usurious lending and exploitation by moneylenders is checked only partially because the SHGs are customarily given credit at comparatively higher interest rate of 12-36 per cent per annum. Asset creation at higher rates dissipates the extra income in debt servicing and undermines the socio-economic impact on poor clients.

Impact assessment has evoked trenchant criticisms. But Susy Cheston, et al. (1999) support the use of impact measurement tools incorporating financial measures and indicating transformation among clients. The issue of impact assessment is beset with problems of non-serious nature of most impact studies, high financial cost and rather disappointing tangible results, reasonable proxies for impact data provided by the marketplace, justification of development expenditures for institutions unable to meet marketplace standards of profitability and high portfolio quality.

The model is riddled with serious theoretical, methodological and operational problems. This makes it difficult to quantify qualitative aspects, such as, life, health, leadership, women's roles, empowerment, etc. But impact needs to be measured because of the general tendencies and movements of a wider geographical impact on a permanent basis through quality financial products delivered by competitive, effective microfinance institutions (outreach approach) and/or in reaching the poorest of the poor (in-depth targeting) by long-term planning and setting up of proper appraisal mechanisms.

Need to Bridge Dichotomy between Sustainability and Outreach Approaches

"Sustainability related to outreach" has important implications for product design and delivery system. "Outreach refers to the central purpose of microfinance: to provide large numbers of poor people, including the very poor and women, access to quality financial services. Financial sustainability entails the institutional capacity to become independent of donor or government subsidies" (CGAP, Focus Note No. 2). While the two schools of thought, viz. "sustainability" or "institutionist" approach and the "poverty" or "welfarist" approach share a common concern for the poor, their prisms of looking at the whole issue of MF differ markedly. The "institutionist approach" spearheaded by the Ohio State University Rural Finance Program, the World Bank, the CGAP, USAID, Maria Otero and Elisabeth Rhyne focuses on creating financial institutions to serve clients who either are not served or are under-served by the formal financial system. "The emphasis is on achieving financial self-sufficiency; breadth of outreach (meaning numbers of clients) takes precedence over depth of outreach (meaning the levels of poverty reached); and positive client impacts are assumed. The centre of attention is the institution, and institutional success is generally gauged by the institution's progress toward achieving financial self-sufficiency" (Woller).

Besieged by mounting instances of unduly heavy reliance on external support and folding up of MFIs, the "Institutionists" stress long-term viability, economies of scale and more effective mobilization of savings and financial resources from private investors in the form of loans, equity or participations demand for microfinance services by financially sound MFIs. "Best practices" in respect of the identification, standardisation, and widespread adoption are a prerequisite to industry-wide financial self-sufficiency, capital market access, and maximum outreach to poor clients. "Best practices refer to those practices that improve institutional efficiency and effectiveness in areas such as management and management systems, finance and accounting, marketing, service delivery, or product design and development" (Woller).

Important protagonists and institutions of the welfare school include (a) Jonathan Morduch, Gary Woller, and Christopher Dunford and (b) the Grameen Bank in Bangladesh and its replicates elsewhere, and FINCA-style village banking programs in Latin America and, more recently, in Africa, Asia and in Eastern Europe. "The 'welfarist approach'... is quite explicit in its focus on immediately improving the well-being of participants. They are less interested in banking per se than in using financial services as a means to alleviate directly the worst effects of deep poverty among participants and communities, even if some of these services require subsidies"(Rice). They emphasise "depth of outreach" with a commitment to serve the destitute. Their objective tends to be self-employment of the poorer among the economically active poor, especially women, whose control of modest increases of income and savings is assumed to empower them to improve the conditions of life for themselves and their children. The centre of attention is the "family".

Cost of Credit for Clients and MFIs

There is a lack of conclusive evidence views on cost of credit for clients and MFIs. The debate rages on with the welfarist approach making a strong case for provision of loans at subsidised interest rates for enhanced credit access to the destitute. The institutional approach, however, suggests, the pursuit of institutional self-sufficiency through sustainable interest rates (covering all costs of running a MFI, including cost of capital and transaction costs) to clients with excellent repayment history for project sustainability and long-term viability of MFIs. Apart from the interest rate charged on loans, the amount outstanding also influences the income.

"Cost covering interest rates only cover costs if they are actually paid by a sufficient number of borrowers (amount outstanding). To ensure this, the lending rate and other lending conditions, need compare attractively with other financial products accessible to low-income households. This brings to the fore the need to consider the environment within which the MFI operates when determining interest rates" (Moll)."Experience with successful MFIs operating at a substantial scale and with a reasonable efficiency shows that these institutions are able to provide small, short-term loans at lending rates of 3 to 5 per cent per month"(Moll). There are many institutions resisting such high interest rates with an interest rate of 2.5 per cent a month being generally accepted.

The "Institutionist" approach is grounded on belief of the apparent willingness and ability of poor borrowers to pay exorbitantly high interest rates from moneylenders and the continued demand for loans and high repayment rates. MFIs should offer financial services with increased availability and flexible repayments. The combination of credit with insurance and trade enables their clients to make use of several spin-off benefits.

It is also important not to be impervious to the issues of the ability of all micro-entrepreneurs in capable of paying sustainable rates as brought to the fore by the welfarists. This requires keeping interest rates within manageable proportions to increase access to financial services to the very poor by subsidising some services. "While petty traders and a few others with high-margin, quick turnaround businesses can pay high real interest rates, most poor households cannot...Others may borrow from moneylenders at rates above 100 per cent a year, but they are generally doing so to meet short-term consumption needs, not to make long-term productive investments" (Rice).

The apparent dichotomy between the "welfarist" approach and the "Institutionist" approach has often led to both conflicting theoretical formulations and policy prescriptions. This is why the much-needed synthesis of the "welfarist" approach and the "Institutionist" approach highlights the necessity of viewing the interrelation of development and viability in a broader framework of 'political economy'. There is, therefore, a felt need to reorient the policy framework and institutional context for evolving feasible alternative development strategy by using a judicious mix of both these sets of instruments. This new approach challenges the traditional paradigms and calls for a partnership based on a close analysis of the constraints to rapid development, review of the past policies and a careful assessment of basic objectives of the future development strategy. There is, therefore, a manifest need for a middle (not muddle) path with MFIs charging sustainable interest rates at reasonable levels by reducing operating costs (particularly by reducing salaries and introducing (non)-financial incentives for staff), improving efficiency, by attaining economies of scale, and reducing default (effective loan monitoring system and recovery programme).

Financially sustainable institutions can reach the poor because there is no trade-off between reaching the poor with credit and financial sustainability. Irrespective of the approach adopted, competitive and sustainable financial system is the key to delivering quality and permanent services to the poor. Technology needs to be increasingly used to enhance institutional efficiency and access to the markets as clearly borne out by the innovations of ICICI bank to improve efficiencies in microfinancial transactions. Technology could be leveraged as an enabler for the efficient provision of microfinance services and the possibilities of using Simple Inexpensive Multilingual People's Computer (SIMPUTER) devices in microfinance on the lines of ABN AMRO bank's pilot with these devices growingly explored.

Institutionalization of social performance management for translation of the mission into effective practice requires addressing the basic problems of outreach to excluded segments, broadening scope of MF services and minimizing transaction costs, e.g. micro-insurance services, delivery mechanisms and technologies. Cross-section studies reveal that the success of SHGs is attributable to the sense of solidarity, group size, self-consciousness, self-reliance and transparency, leadership and practical regulations together with peer pressure and group dynamics. Given the degree of success achieved, SHGs now need to shift from a minimalist approach of only financial intermediation to an integrated approach, including provision of enterprise development services to take on the livelihood interventions, e.g. marketing infrastructure with direct linkage between the borrowers and potential buyers, repayment incentive structures, streamlined administration, market-based pricing, introduction of technology and design development. MF attempts in a modest way to unleash forces transforming lives from debt-driven to self-driven development. It thus facilitates a structural transformation in meeting the needs of the poor, the deprived and the women. But taking MF to the next level requires addressing the issues of financial standards, governance, ethical norms, transparency and accountability of MFIs.

Financial Sustainability of MFIs

Depth of outreach is based on value-based commitment to serve the destitute, fear of commercialisation of microfinance, diverting the industry away from its original mission of serving the very poor and withdrawal of donor support resulting in resource allocation on the basis of good institutional performance alone, regardless the impact of the actual programme. There is also the issue of definition and codification of "best practices" stifling innovation and experimentation in the design of new products and delivery systems for the destitute.

In the ultimate analysis, development of microfinance requires effective, stable, transparent and efficient microfinance institutions. Since long-term survival and sustainability is the prerequisite to an MFI reaching its target clientele and covering administrative and other costs, this paradigm stresses financial intermediation with self-sustainability of institutions and qualitative/quantitative outreach to the poor in scaling up services to reach the estimated three billion people, who still lack access to formal financial services, in developing countries. This is essential to influence the livelihoods of the poor. Strengthened financial institutions, cost recovery for continued business and intermediation benefits to clients and a financial system approach to functional specialization and market coverage are essential (Otero et al., 1994).

Sustainability of MFIs requires greater use of market incentives and directed initiatives to promote the virtuous cycle. Sustainability has internal and external implications—internal in terms of deposit and savings mobilization, financial performance, staff motivation, loan and administrative costs, etc.; external in terms of availability of funds for loan disbursement, grants for community organizing and training etc. Sustainable MFIs also attract external financial investment, satisfy central bank reporting requirements, build trust among its clients and supporting institutions and satisfy and attract commercial bank partners. The process of sustainability can be enhanced by greater role of NGOs, training and research institutions, evaluators and rating agencies, sharing of experiences and materials, etc. But there are issues of innovative mechanisms for delivering financial services to low-income households, rating of MFIs and other performance standards, funds availability and its cost implications, grants for 'non-financial' activities and programme initiation. Hence current trends, best practices, emerging issues and persisting concerns need to be carefully examined to make an objective assessment of the technologies and strategic business issues in expanding the world of the possible.

There are three levels of cost recovery for MFIs with ultimately all institutions moving from subsidy dependence to operational self-sufficiency and finally to financial self-sufficiency (Christen, 1997). As most MFIs continue to be heavily subsidy dependent and only some are able to cover more than 80 per cent of their costs, it becomes necessary for MFIs to develop strategies for sustainable microfinance by increasing the range and volume of their financial services. This requires overcoming the problems of limited institutional and managerial capacity at the level of retail microfinance institutions starkly reflected in inadequate management information systems, poor strategic planning, and high operating costs; paucity of organizations providing safe savings facilities, which can be sustainably mobilized for on-lending to the poor.

While there is a manifest need to create an inclusive, competitive and vibrant financial system with high quality, client-responsive products and services to all on a commercial basis, sustainability and commercialisation of MFIs is fraught with the danger of compromising on the inclusion of the poorest of the poor. Sustainability hence needs an introspection based on a realistic assessment. Sustainability can also be examined by demand and supply characteristics, mission of MFIs, organizational and financial sustainability (Mahajan, 2001). But self-sustainability alone cannot improve the 'process' of delivery of MF necessitating other attendant measures to mainstream MF in India. MFIs can contribute to sustainable poverty alleviation by credit and combination of savings, credit and insurance services. Union Budget, 2005-06 proposed appointment of MFIs as agents for micro-insurance products.

Increasing outreach while maintaining and improving sustainability requires focused attention on quality SHGs, particularly financial sustainability, governance and management structures and adequate internal controls and financial discipline; an enabling policy, legal and regulatory environment, clear targeting of clients, appropriate products and services and good staffing policies, inclusiveness and competition and removal of extremely skewed distribution. While the problem of borrowings of MFIs from banks has considerably eased, most MFIs still lack adequate access to financial capital and have high debt equity ratio. Consequently, the reoriented Microfinance

Development Equity Fund (MFDEF), set up with NABARD, could partially alleviate the problem of equity needs of MFIs.

Huge and Still Growing Global Market

Traditional banking services are largely unavailable to the 2.5 billion people from low-income countries and many of the 2.7 billion from middle-income countries. But there have been events and developments, such as, the pioneering work of Professor Muhammad Yunus with Bangladesh's Grameen Bank, important academic works (e.g., books by Professors Prahalad, Harper et al.) and empirical cross-country evidence. Such evidence relates to the context of the poor and nature of poverty, employment, income generation and cash flows of poor households, indigenous savings and credit systems and practices and need for providing financial services to the poor. Consequently, there is a heightened consciousness of the viability and practicality of microfinance in subserving the needs of the poor and the downtrodden across diverge regions. On the basis of 18 incisive case studies drawn from 15 countries, Harper et al. demonstrate that commercial banks have successfully provided financial services to poorer people.

To be sure, the microfinance sector in India is still evolving. But "poverty and a predominantly rural population is no bar to commercial banks' entry to microfinance". Clearly, then, small customers do not only constitute a large market but are also profitable and financially sustainable. Harper et al. cogently argue that "Bank Rakyat Indonesia (BRI) has proven that institutional viability, sustainability and outreach to low-income people are compatible". Similarly, the Equity Building Society in Kenya (formed 1984) developed a viable business serving small customers. Equity now serves 252,000 depositors and 66,000 borrowers with an average loan of $360 from five branches and 24 other outlets. With growing profits since 1994, it achieved a return on equity of 30 per cent and return on assets of 3.6 per cent in 2003. AgBank, Mongolia, "has disbursed 878,000 loans (the average loan is $382) between late 2000 and February 2004, while maintaining an arrears rate consistently below 2 per cent and becoming the most profitable bank in Mongolia, with return on equity of 44 per cent in 2003".

Prahalad persuasively argues that India's millions of have-nots, often neglected by corporations as having no purchasing power, brought into the fold of the fastest-growing market through innovations that tailor products affordably to their needs. Simply selling the same product at the lowest price point may not be best strategy. Innovative business solutions are needed for rural India to reach the inflection point. This market-led and synergy-driven thesis of reaching the under-banked and unbanked markets is not as far-fetched as it may apparently seem and can easily be substantiated by the hugely successful experience of Bank Rakyat (Indonesia), Bank Pichincha's subsidiary CREDIFEC (Ecuador), ICICI (India), etc. in "building people's organisations to build people". Banque du Caire estimates that only 7 per cent of the 2.4 million small entrepreneurs in Egypt have access to microfinance.

Sweeping Change

While bankers have customarily been recalcitrant to unsecured lending, they are now increasingly looking at micro-finance as a growth opportunity given its excellent repayment record with NPLs of about 2 per cent. In sharp contrast to the Grameen Bank's peer-group monitoring, the Bank Rakyat of Indonesia, which serves 2.5 million clients and 12 million small savers, relies on character references and locally recruited lending agents in place of physical collateral. Thailand's Bank of Agriculture and Agricultural Cooperatives serves approximately 1 million micro-borrowers and 3.6 million micro-savers. Impressive progress has also been made by the Association for Social Advancement of Bangladesh, the People's Credit Funds of Vietnam, the Association of Cambodia Local Economic Development Agencies, Buro-Tangail of Bangladesh, the Self-Employed Women's Association Bank of India, Amanah Ikhtiar Malaysia, Accion Internacional through a network of 19 affiliates in Latin America and North America, Banco Solidario of Bolivia, the Association for the Development of Micro-Entreprises of the Dominican Republic and Accion Comunitaria del Peru.

No wonder, then, some of the world's biggest banks like the Citigroup attempt to strengthen and expand microfinance programmes by reaching deeper and providing services for a new group of profitable customers with an excellent repayment record. Other banking majors, such as the Netherlands' ABN AMRO, are strengthening their involvement in microfinance through a combination of equity, guarantees and debt as well as technical assistance to local microfinance partners. Shorebank, the leading US community development and environmental banking corporation, has worked in the microfinance area in 30 countries for more than 15 years and in 2003 established a London-based subsidiary ShoreCap International to make equity investments in MFIs in Africa, Asia and eastern Europe. ShoreBank and the CGAP have helped microfinance gather steam. What is needed is scale and finding the right structures to give a wider range of people financial access and choice. Against this backdrop, MF is growingly being looked at as an effective instrument of poverty reduction and sub-serving the goals of equity and distributive justice while providing an opportunity to expand profitable ventures (high risk adjusted returns) (Harper and Arora, 2005). What is sparking all these changes? As demonstrated by C.K. Prahalad in his classic book *The Fortune at the Bottom of the Pyramid* (2004), there are teeming millions with little money. They nevertheless constitute a potentially profitable market estimated by the World Bank at US $ 225 billion a year—a market that by no stretch of imagination can be trifled with and is growing strongly.

Micro-credit is profitable and indeed sustainable. While the MFIs face daunting challenges, the impressive repayment track record of MFIs demonstrates that microfinance, despite providing financial services to the poor, can be a profitable business. High-performing microfinance institutions have developed innovative and out of box mechanisms to extend credit, savings and other services to poor clients through reduced cost and risk by greater use of IT. While several variants of partnership models between banks and MFIs have been tested, ICICI Bank has been a pioneer in lending wholesale loan funds, microfinance debt (securitisation), testing and rolling out specific retail products such as the *Kisan* (Farmer) Credit Card, engaging microfinance institutions as agents, which are paid for loan origination and recovery, with loans being held on the books of banks, equity investments into newly emerging MFIs and banks and NGOs jointly promoting MFIs.

Financial services for poor people covering their full costs, through adequate interest spreads, accent on efficiency and proper repayment ethics is no longer a distant dream but a viable reality. There are immense possibilities of reaching poorer people profitably. For example, microfinance services are increasingly being provided by profitable institutions, even after adjusting for subsidies received. Infact it has sometimes been justifiably argued (Table 2) that the profitability of MFIs far exceeds the profitability of even the banking sector in India.

Table 2: Profitability of MFIs vis-à-vis Banking Sector in India

Microfinance Institutions	Return on Assets (%)	Return on Equity (%)	Profit Margin (%)	Loan Assets (Rs. Crore)	No. of borrowers
Spandana	8.35	-6.50	48.07	238.75	385,996
Share Microfin	3.15	24.63	16.69	175.79	368,996
Sanghamitra	2.02	6.07	13.34	15.22	112,029
Basix	0.04	0.10	3.05	56.86	89,953
Bandhan	N.A	N.A	26.25	18.75	82,260
Swayam Krishi Sangam	-6.50	-6.50	-0.21	33.25	73,635
Grama Vidyal	0.60	10.99	2.62	16.32	55,566
Global benchmark*	1.6-2.8	5.1-11.5	8-11.6	-	-
Banks					
SBI and its associate Banks	0.95	18.76	10.60		
Nationalized Banks	0.92	16.53	10.84		
HDFC Bank	1.47	18.45	17.80		
ICICI Bank	1.59	18.86	15.60		

All figures are for 2004-05. For banks, data on loan assets and number of borrowers has not been included. Only MFIs with more than 50,000 borrowers have been included.

*Global benchmark data is for companies that have been in business for more than five years.

Source: www.mixmarket.org for MFIs and Reserve Bank of India for banks.

This peculiar situation has given rise to increasing concerns about the terms and conditions of lending of MFIs and what is generally perceived as exorbitant and usurious rates of interest charged by MFIs. But the interest rates decrease over time as competition in micro-credit grows and economies of scale and greater efficiency contribute to profitability leading to a win-

win situation all around. Consequently, there are several cases in India of corporates funding SHGs, directly or by partnerships, and supporting NGOs, e.g. Citibank, ABN Amro, Hindustan Lever Ltd. (Stree-Shakti project), ITC (e-chaupal), Mahindra & Mahindra (Subha Labh), Tata Group (Kisan Sansar), HDFC, Max New Life Insurance, etc. Cashphor Financial & Technical Services (CFTS) is based on the model of Grameen Bank, where a group of 5-6 members is made and loans are given to individual members but the liability to repay is still collective. With financial help from NABARD, ICICI, UCO bank, UTI Bank, Deutsche Bank, Mumbai, Grameen Foundation USA, etc., at 6 to 12 per cent interest, CFTS lends to villagers at 20 per cent interest.

Small-scale lending programmes rely on lending to small enterprises in agriculture, distribution, crafts, trading and similar activities. The participatory nature of these projects, together with the emphasis on women entrepreneurs and employment creation, attempts to slash poverty. Cross-country experiences clearly reveal that the innovative MF mechanism helps to expand and diversify local markets, boosts production of consumer goods, increases production through subcontracting and ancillary goods, e.g. toy-making, embroidery, candle-making, rearing cattle, making *papad,* pickles, automobiles, electronics, leather, textiles, furniture, electronic assemblies, handicrafts, etc. With some institutional support mechanisms in the form of credit, marketing, technology, infrastructure and training, such production can easily be upscaled to cross the barriers of 3 Ps (papad, pickle and petticoat) while recovering almost the full cost. Large producers can use this success as a platform to penetrate new markets or consolidate the present position in the existing markets.

Complementarity relationship based on the indivisibility of demand exists between small scale (SSIs) and large-scale industries (LSIs). In case of forward linkages, the LSIs find the demand of their intermediate products, emanating from downstream SSIs, which produce final consumer goods. Similarly, the backward linkage effect takes place when the LSIs outsource their components and other intermediate raw materials from SSIs because LSIs find it cost effective to subcontract the supply of certain components to SSIs, so that LSIs can concentrate on their core competency. Hence, this process of ancilliarization through strengthening of forward and backward linkages leads to complementarity and supplementarity between LSIs and SSIs. LSIs attempt to forge strategic alliances with the SSIs, wherein SSIs takeover quality production of certain key components leaving LSIs to concentrate on "core competencies" like scale of production, technology development and markets leading to enhanced competitive advantage of both SSIs and LSIs, e.g. Maruti, Hero Honda, Bajaj, etc., in India. Development of enterprise opportunity, growth of existing enterprises and jobs and strengthened sustainability of local communities requires restructuring and innovative approaches to streamline organizational, managerial and techno-financial capacities. The present stage of microfinance development requires significant upscaling and broad basing with much greater commercial funding. Commercial funding of this order necessitates transparent financial reporting. The Microfinance Information Exchange (MIX) is an information exchange website where more than 600 MFIs and 75 funds post information on their organisations and their performance.

Box 1: The Nobel Peace Prize for 2006

The Norwegian Nobel Committee has decided to award the Nobel Peace Prize for 2006, divided into two equal parts, to **Muhammad Yunus** and **Grameen Bank** for their efforts to create from below. Lasting peace cannot be achieved unless large population groups find ways in which to break out of poverty. Micro-credit is one such means. Development from below also serves to advance democracy and human rights.

Muhammad Yunus has shown himself to be a leader who has managed to translate visions into practical action for the benefit of millions of people, not only in Bangladesh, but also in many other countries. Loans to poor people without any financial security had appeared to be an impossible idea. From modest beginnings three decades ago, Yunus has, first and foremost through Grameen Bank, developed micro-credit into an ever more important instrument in the struggle against poverty. Grameen Bank has been a source of ideas and models for the many institutions in the field of micro-credit that have sprung up around the world.

Every single individual on earth has both the potential and the right to live a decent life. Across cultures and civilizations, Yunus and Grameen Bank have shown that even the poorest of the poor can work to bring about their own development.

> Micro-credit has proved to be an important liberating force in societies where women in particular have to struggle against repressive social and economic conditions. Economic growth and political democracy cannot achieve their full potential unless the female half of humanity participates on an equal footing with the male. Yunus's long-term vision is to eliminate poverty in the world. That vision cannot be realised by means of micro-credit alone. But Muhammad Yunus and Grameen Bank have shown that, in the continuing efforts to achieve it, micro-credit must play a major part.-Oslo, 13 October 2006

Agricultural Microfinance

The Consultative Group to Assist the Poor (CGAP), supported by the International Fund for Agricultural Development (IFAD), examined over 80 providers of microfinance to identify "agricultural microfinance". CGAP stresses that successful agricultural microfinance rests on a judicious mix of 10 principal features, but it is not necessary for an effective model to incorporate all features. The features indicate that repayments are not linked to loan use, character-based lending techniques are combined with technical criteria in selecting borrowers, setting term loans, and enforcing repayment and provision of saving mechanisms. There is also highly diversified portfolio risk, loan terms and conditions adjusted to accommodate cyclical cash flows and bulky investments. Contractual agreements reduce price risks, enhance production quality and help guarantee repayments, financial service delivery piggybacks on existing institutional infrastructure, or is extended using technology, membership-based organisations can facilitate rural access to financial services and be viable in remote areas. Area-based index insurance can protect against the risks of agricultural lending, insulation of agricultural microfinance from political interference.

Regulatory and Supervisory Concerns

The government's socio-economic policies and the level of development of the financial sector influences the ability of MFIs to deliver financial services to the poor. The macro-environmental setting, viz. the government's monetary policy with regard to the stability of the domestic currency and the exchange rate, the institutional structure of the financial system, the legal framework for the operations of the formal financial institutions, interventions in the determination of interest rates, the allocation of credit to priority sectors, regions or groups, and the interference in loan recovery procedures, have an important bearing on MF. "These interventions affect the operations of formal financial institutions and their competitive position *vis-à-vis* informal financial operators in rural financial markets" (Moll, 1999). The government should also create a regulatory environment (including appropriate legislation) fostering the growth of MFIs. However the government's attempt to cap interest rates renders MFIs less capable to achieve their financial sustainability and financial viability.

Cross-country evidence unmistakably brings out that governments should refrain from the process of the design or delivery of microfinance services because of inherent structural deficiencies (UNCDF, 1999). Historically, government-sponsored rural credit programmes failed to bring out desired results. Such deficiencies included reliance on subsidised interest rates, inappropriate terms and conditions, lack of repayment enforcement, and corruption. "Direct government intervention in financial institutions has met with little, if any, success; thus intervention is an inappropriate way to stimulate agriculture and the rural sector. Instead, financial institutions should be allowed to perform their tasks of mediation guided by business criteria. If agriculture requires promotion through subsidies, the government should not use financial institutions for this purpose, but should explore more direct ways of subsidising this sector" (Moll, 1999).

An understanding of the functions and working of MF led to more efficient and sustainable microfinance programmes. But as the number of MFIs and their clients and portfolios steadily burgeon, the stakes rise higher in creating an enabling policy environment at the local and national levels. It might, therefore, be advisable for such 'formal' policies to be directed at the overall financial system as a whole and those for commercial banks together with new policies for MFIs to recognise the beneficial role of MFIs in serving the needs of low-income households and micro-enterprises and focus on financial and non-financial support services required by MFIs. Policies also need to factor the 'social' face of MFIs in terms of their role in poverty alleviation, and therefore use evaluation and monitoring criteria sensitive to this orientation. As the basic origin of MFIs lies in the failures of formal banking systems, systems of reporting and other requirements different from those for commercial banks are needed. This requires an accent on 3As. These 3As relate to **Awareness** (creating opportunities to learn about values, principles, and practice of microfinance), **Assessment** (developing resources and tools for communities and microfinance organizations to monitor progress and track good practices in their region) and **Action** (promoting wider participation in making microfinance available to all low-income households and micro-enterprises).

Given MF's essential informality and flexibility, the developmental aspects have justifiably occupied center-stage. With MFIs coming of age, MFIs are increasingly exploring the possibility of deposit mobilisation from the general public. The case for deposit mobilisation rests on investible decision of the funds with the MFIs, cheaper source of funds than bank loans, partial overlapping of borrowing and depositing channels and a primary source of funds for meeting steadily rising loan requirements. But it is difficult to distinguish, for regulatory requirements, micro-credit institutions from microfinance institutions. This difficulty arises because of the need of microfinance institutions for more varied skills and multiple regulators. As the SHGs lack any formal organisational structure, there is skepticism about covering them under proposed formal framework for the MFIs. The issue of accepting public deposits, against the backdrop of unhappy experience of repeated collapse of non-banking financial companies (NBFCs) in India, poses major legislative and moral hazard challenges of systematic stability and safeguarding of small depositors interest, particularly because they function as depositories for the most vulnerable groups at the bottom of the income pyramid.

MFIs have diverse organisational forms, viz. Trusts, Societies, Cooperative Societies, Not-for-Profit Companies and NBFCs. Further large corporates provide micro-credit as a part of their Corporate Social Responsibility (CSR) endeavours. Consequently, there is no consensus on recognition of one or more or all the organisational forms under a formalised regulatory framework for the MFIs. The difficulty arises because central bank rules on supervision, reporting, etc., rules and regulations on savings and deposit mobilization, rules and regulations on loan disbursement and collection, registration and incorporation systems for MFIs, alternative performance standards, gender dimensions of microfinance, etc., differ across countries. This is why intelligent regulation and an enabling policy and programme frame are needed from local to national and international levels for proper development of both the microfinance sector and the MFIs themselves. But generally a regulatory framework is most effective when microfinance activities have reached a critical mass and several MFIs have become licensed institutions.

Non-prudential regulations (NPR) imply enabling the formation and operation of micro-lending, protecting consumer, preventing fraud and enhancing the per capita credit outlays, setting up credit information services, supporting secured transactions, interest rate management, etc. Prudential regulations, which imply disclosure of effective interest rates, disclosure of controlling interest and ownership of a company and fit and proper screening norms, are far more stringent.

Regulatory issues manifest themselves differently in various institutional frameworks. The Latin American experience suggests the need for regulation to enable the MFIs to significantly upscale their operations. The viability and solvency of MFIs requires resolution of important issues of high level reserve requirements discouraging deposits, frequent and detailed reporting requirements on the number, volume, and loan recovery status of outstanding portfolios and inappropriate criteria for loan portfolio classification and provisioning. This necessitates taking a call on the three policy options of examining the scope and effectiveness of a self regulatory organisation for the MFIs and bringing these MFIs under strict market discipline, regulating only large MFIs with a systemic impact on the entire financial system or the microfinance market or covering all MFIs under regulation. But in view of the myriad complexities involved in the issue, the jury in India, as indeed in most other countries, is still out on the need and modalities of regulating MFIs, self-regulation and market discipline, prudential regulation and supervision structures, development of prudential norms and reporting standards.

Rapid upscaling of MFIs must be consistent with prudential practices. Hence, regulators, apex development banks, the government and MFIs themselves have to carefully consider globally recommended principles on regulation and supervision. Such principles include the CGAP's Guiding Principles on Regulation and Supervision on Microfinance, in devising appropriate safeguards in conformity with the distinctive macro-economic needs (including the challenge of financial inclusion), differences in organisation, structure and methods of working of MFIs and growth objectives. The regulation of MFIs could conceivably be restricted at the State-level without any involvement of the RBI as a banking regulator or for extending deposit-insurance. RBI's recent Technical Paper on Policy relating to Development, Regulation and Supervision of Microfinance Services together with the draft report of the internal group of RBI on Rural Credit and Microfinance (Khan Committee) is expected to lead to suitable policy formulation. The Khan Committee report considers (a) policy options and strategies for deepening and widening of financial services; (b) promotion, development and rating of microfinance institutions and other outreach entities; and (c) regulatory issues and concerns.

At the Bankers' Conference (BANCON 2006) held at Hyderabad on 3-4 November 2006, Sri P. Chidambaram, the Hon'ble Finance Minister in his inaugural address, stressed that the Microfinance Bill being drawn up by the Government will have minimal regulations on microfinance activity. The RBI has requested states to exercise caution while interfering with the activities of Microfinance Institutions (MFI). "We have a mindset of microfinance in India that any interest rate not less than 20 per cent-25 per cent is exploitation. A rate of 25 per cent charged by moneylenders may be usurious. But for funds generated from banks, that passes through intermediaries and reaches the end customer, there is a cost in the process. We have to recognise that microfinance activity carries a price and educate people accordingly," Sri Chidambaram asserted. The Government is in the final stages of preparing the Microfinance Bill.

Credit Rating for MFIs-unfinished Agenda

Given the conspicuous absence of a plausible framework to ensure the accountability of MFIs, accountability and transparency are key issues in governance. Credit ratings are current opinions in respect of creditworthiness. Such ratings are usually assigned for specific instruments issued or for a defined purpose, often on a continuing basis. But such ratings are limited by their respective definitions and do not constitute investment or financial advice. Rating is *inter alia*, a function of marketing strategies, competitive edge, level of technological development, operational efficiency, competence and effectiveness of management, risk factors involved, cash-flow trends and potential, financial flexibility.

Micro-Credit Ratings International Ltd. (M-CRIL), established in 1998, promotes development of a rigorous system of appraising credit risk by an independent third party. Cluster-wise identification of MFIs could economise cost and time. MFI credit rating methodology must combine credit and performance factors by several parameters measuring operational, financial, business and management related issues to enhance the utility and quality of rating exercises and to add value to the localised operations of the MFIs. CRISIL's rating methodology relies on MICROS (Management, Institutional analysis, Creditworthiness, Resources and cost of funds, Operational effectiveness and Scalability and sustainability).

Credit rating of MFIs provides the depositors, investors and creditors a transparent, credible, independent and objective assessment of the institutions' capacity to meet their short-term and long-term obligations, gauge future outlook, and enables them to make informed decisions about investment and deposit, etc., in the institutions to gain credibility in the market, with the public, issuers, investors and regulators and potential donors, it is necessary to develop norms of governance, promote an accreditation system and promote capacity-building initiatives for MFIs. Hence ratings definitions, criteria and methodologies need to be periodically reviewed to bring them in line with rapidly unfolding realities.

Both quantitative and qualitative factors go into the making of a comprehensive assessment of MFIs. Quantitative aspects considered include provisions and loan loss reserves, credit and savings performance data, portfolio quality, etc. Simultaneously, a descriptive rating report looks at the qualitative dimensions, viz. salient aspects of the MFI programme, creditworthiness and relative strengths and weaknesses of the organisation. All these aspects together with the feedback of the rated MFI are factored in a holistic view of overall assessment grade for the rated MFI with recommendations on the absorptive capacity and the lendable amount to the MFI.

Rapid expansion and the complexities involved in examining the gamut of issues involved in ascertaining the financial, managerial and organizational strengths of MFIs suggest that credit rating will pick up steadily. Some of the main strands of this debate relate to credit ratings for a defined purpose and often, on a continuing basis, utility and quality of rating exercises, addition of value to the localised operations by ratings, transparency, integrity and independence of the rating and surveillance processes compromised by conflicts of interest, abuse of confidential information or other undue influences, etc. These complex issues need to be addressed to urgently because of the varied forms and the level of development of the MFIs and to make the growth of the MFIs sustainable. Organizations like M-CRIL and CRISIL in India have established policies and procedures designed to promote and protect the independence, objectivity and rigor of their credit rating process for all market-place participants. These frameworks need to be increasingly used to discernibly improve the ground realities.

Emerging Role of Information Technology (IT)

Some of the major dimensions of cataclysmic change relate to the growing importance of knowledge and growth in information and communication technologies (IT & C). Accelerated pace of creation of new knowledge received an impetus through vast expansion of computing power, plummeting cost of transmitting information and convergence of computing and telecommunications. In the overarching context of rapid technological developments, effective use of IT by MFIs can slash transaction costs and bridge the digital divide. It could thus make MF commercially viable and even profitable.

The issue of technology in the MF sector in addressing credit, livelihood and credit plus services has evoked wide-ranging and at times even acrimonious debates on the digital divide, appropriate technology versus esoteric, indigenous versus exotic, expensive or economical, high end versus low end, generic or customized and finally specific or customized technology products. Despite the immense latent potential of IT & C, it has not yet been sufficiently harnessed. The realization of this potential rests on simultaneous action on two fronts: technology downscaling in terms of price and products, and the MF sector upscaling in adopting technology into its operations in conformity with the needs of the rapidly evolving situation.

The unfolding role of IC&T in the MF sector is a function of the interaction of several factors. Some of the important factors could be isolated and identified as the emergent technology needs of the MFIs, technological advancement in IC&T sector, the infrastructure and the wider economy. With MFIs scaling up and technology developing, such interaction is poised to increase in the future. There is no doubt that the role of IT & C in microfinance will increase significantly as strikingly illustrated by the examples of SEWA (Self Employed Women's Association) Bank, BASIX and Swayam Krishi Sangham (SKS), The Activists for Social Alternatives (ASA) and Development for Humane Action (DHAN) Foundation. Eventually, new age tools like digital marketing, product promotion and web analytics would bridge the digital divide. But given the suitability of manual operations and cost-effectiveness, manual operations would certainly persist for some more time.

It needs no clairvoyance to perceive that at the nascent stage of development, optimization of benefits requires co-existence and integration of both the manual and technology systems. Hence IT needs to be increasingly leveraged to bring banking services to the rural populace with flexible timing of banking transaction to be cost-effective. The implementation of efficient information systems and the computerization of the networks could conceivably be done through upgradation of information on insurance, savings, credit, pilot testing of handheld devices like palmtops, Personal Digital Assistants (PDAs), smart card, etc., for automatic transaction and data entry integration, customized software integrating financial functions with HRM, CRM and MIS, fuzzy-neuro techniques. CGAP has identified over 200 domestic retail banks or consumer credit companies getting involved in microfinance. These institutions attempt to reduce transaction costs and reach larger poorer clients through e-banking, smart cards and telephone technology, etc.

Considered in a proper historical and comparative perspective, the catalytic role of the government in the development of IT and MF is a tribute both to the efficacy of IT and MF and to the enabling policy frame. But clearly much more needs to be done to ensure optimal returns from the huge investments made in IT. Towards this end, provision of soft loans for development of software, tracking the usage of the software by the organization, rating the available software and developing rating standards and benchmarks for spatial and sectoral spread of MF is urgently needed.

Going to Scale Across Geographical Regions and Functional Areas

The system has many components and their individual problems could be analysed in detail. But the totality of the system and a SWOT analysis of MFIs are imperative to meet the challenges of the present and the expectations of the future. This requires an understanding of general problems in micro-credit, multiple ramifications, causes and consequences and systematic interrelatedness. In this overarching scenario, the higher transactions and operational costs, cost of serving the rural poor is justified because of the extraordinarily high repayment rates and attendant socio-economic benefit of extending financial services in both rural and urban areas for ensuring financial inclusion of all persons.

NABARD's success model of SHG-bank linkage together with intensifying competition in urban areas through multinational banks has induced most banks and even major financial institutions like Housing Development and Financial Corporation (HDFC), ICICI to increasingly consider microfinance as a growth option. Even though ICICI Bank entered the market in 2001, by offering wholesale finance to other institutions and direct service delivery, its microfinance portfolio grew from $16 million to $63 million with an average loan of $223 in 2001 and the bank envisages a potential portfolio of $4 billion from this market. Similarly, State Bank of India (SBI) allows informal SHGs of 10-20 women to open bank accounts and borrow from the bank. SBI lent to 174,666 such SHGs in March 2004 (with an average loan of $53) as against only 12,200 SHGs four years earlier. SBI envisages to reach one million SHGs, with approximately 15 million mainly women members, by 2008. Canara Bank has taken equally impressive strides in this area. Despite growth of this magnitude, there is a manifest need to significantly upscale this movement by simultaneous development of investment potential and improvement of skill levels of the borrowers with synchronized attempts by NGOs, MFIs, RBI, banks and financial institutions, the Government and apex institutions like NABARD and SIDBI together with delivery of non-credit financial services, such as, insurance and mutual funds by microfinance institutions. All these are areas, where immediate, easy answers may not be available. This is because working towards sustainability is a dynamic process that must essentially be viewed in the context of long-term issues.

Microfinance is not the panacea for all ills of development of the poor, as for example, demonstrated by a study (OECD, 1997). The study showed that credit needed to be supplemented with access to land and appropriate technology for the programme to be successful. The poor have manifold needs viz. health, education, insurance and the like. Convergence of MF and livelihood requires effective use of a range of competing delivery channels, enhanced urban and rural coverage and provision of financial services—not just loans but also greater application of information technology and credit ratings. The spectre of marginalisation of the poor in India requires a renewed thrust on MF. This needs to be done on the basis of available knowledge, capital and technology. There has to be a comprehensive vision encompassing the numerous delivery models and methodologies, organisational innovation and market segmentation, clear operational freedom and incentives and surge in economic growth to create in the lives of rural poor.

The literature on MF has proliferated in recent years across Asia, Africa and Latin America. This proliferation has brought to the fore the need for far-reaching changes in conceptual constructions to overcome the problems of theoretical inadequacies and transformation of the interpretative context of development. What is needed is an investigation into the entire gamut of issues afflicting MFIs including the MFI's organizational and operational structure (supply studies) and on its clients (demand studies). Specific evaluation of operational aspects could include replication, scaling up, innovations and best practices, capacity building for microfinance, micro-credit, community credit mobilization, informal credit markets, community participation, credit access for women, micro-enterprises, etc. Major organizational issues relate to NGOs, community groups, people's organizations, self-help groups, credit unions, cooperatives, commercial banks, international NGOs/agencies, etc. The evidence suggests that the impact of such initiatives has remained limited and regional-specific in terms of the situation in low-income countries, Asia, Africa, Latin America, Central and Eastern Europe. These early lessons on monitoring and evaluation, documentation and analysis of 'best' and 'worst' practices in microfinance, sharing ideas goes beyond making MFIs more efficient and self-sufficient may help improve the implementation, equitable impact and sustainability of future development programmes.

The promotion of wholesome development is not easy. But with cutting edge policy advice, advocacy and networking services, together we can and must make a difference to the management of the dynamics of the developmental process. The success of this strategy requires turning the campaign for strengthening microfinance into a mass movement. The focus on emerging trends must cover a judicious mix of local experiences and global case studies to drive home the considerable contemporary significance of change management in the microfinance industry in sub-serving the needs of the poor across diverse regions. Important issues of scale (reaching a larger number), sustainability (restricting subsidies to innovations, capacity building and sectoral infrastructure), impact (measurement and enhancement), capital markets (attracting more mainstream debt and equity), regulation and transparency (building a more supportive regulatory environment) must constitute some of the key elements of the development strategy. Hence, such aspects need to be comprehensively addressed not just as a random or disconnected set of activities but as a 'system', where different constituents form parts of an organic whole. The Government must be proactive in building the infrastructure necessary to facilitate both microfinance and livelihood interventions for the poor. While MFIs have significant potential, they need to make an increasing contribution to "scale" consistent with cost, sustainability and efficiency of operations. Progress in this area needs to tracked in terms of objectively verifiable indicators. The crux of these measures boils down to upscaling direct credit linking by the banks and credit linking through NGOs and MFIs, distinctly identified goals and effective execution strategy, institutional commitment, operating autonomy and a responsive management culture. Solutions to the future may not come easily, but we must make all-out efforts to broaden the availability of credit to such enterprises with a sense of urgency.

REFERENCES

Alba, J.D. and Park, D. (2003): "The Role of Group-based Lending and Microcredit in Economic Development", *Savings and Development*, 27 (4).

Adams, D.W. and Von Pischke J.D. (1992): "Microenterprise Credit Programs: Déjà vu" , *World Development*, Vol 20, No. 10.

Adams, D.W., Douglas H. Graham and Von Pischke, J.D. (Eds.) (1984): *Undermining Rural Development with Cheap Credit*, Boulder: Westview Press.

Aghion, Beatriz Armendáriz de and Jonathan Morduch (2005): *The Economics of Microfinance,* Cambridge, Mass.: MIT Press.

Anderson, L.C., Locker, L. and Nugent, R. (2002): "Microcredit, Social Capital, and Common Pool Resources", *World Development,* 30: (1)

Bédard, G. (1993): *Development Banking for the Benefit of the Poor: A New Model for Banking*, Working Paper No. 7, Eschborn: GTZ Section Banking and Financial Systems Development.

Bouman, F.A.J. (1989): *Small, Short and Unsecured: Informal Rural Finance in India*, Oxford University Press, Delhi, Oxford, New York.

Chaves, Rodrigo A. and Claudio Gonzalez-Vega. (1996), "The Design of Successful Rural Financial Intermediaries: Evidence from Indonesia", *World Development*, Vol. 24, No. 1.

Charitonenko, Stephanie, Anita Campion and Nimal A. Fernando (2004): *Commercialization of Microfinance: Perspectives from South and Southeast Asia*. Manila: ADB.

Charitonenko, Stephanie and Dulan de Silva (2002): *Commercialization of Microfinance: Sri Lanka*. Manila: ADB.

Chastri, Pradip (2002): *Synthesis Report for Microfinance Development and Microenterprise Development,* Hull: Canadian International Development Agency.

Cheston, Susy et al. (1999): "Measuring Transformation: Assessing and Improving the Impact of Microcredit", Microcredit Summit website at *www.microcreditsummit.org*.

Cohen M. and Gaile G., *CGAP Working Group* (1997): Paper Impact Assessment Methodologies, *Discussion Paper*, CGAP, 1997.

Consultative Group to Assist the Poorest (2004): *Building Inclusive Financial Systems: Donors Guidelines on Good Practice in Microfinance.* Washington, DC: CGAP, World Bank.

Christen R., Rhyne E. and Vogel R. (1995): "Maximising the Outreach of Microenterprise Finance: The Emerging Lessons of Successful Programs", *USAID Program and Operations Assessment Report No. 10*. Washington, D.C.: U.S. Agency for International Development.

Christen, R.P. (1997): *Banking Services for the Poor: Managing for Financial Services*, ACCION, USA.

Christen R. and Rosenberg R. (2000): The Rush to Regulate: Legal Frameworks for Microfinance, *Microenterprise Best Practices.*

Copestake, J. (2003): "Inequality and the Polarizing Impact of Microcredit: Evidence from Zambia's Copperbelt", *Journal of International Development*, 14(6).

Daphnis, Franck and Bruce Ferguson (2004): *Housing Microfinance: A Guide to Practice,* Bloomfield, CT: Kumarian Press.

De Silva, Donauts and Vailla Deuby (1992): *Banking the Unbankable: Bringing Credit to Poor,* Horizon India Books, New Delhi.

Development Centre of the Organisation for Economic Cooperation and Development (1997): *Microfinance for the Poor*, Hartmut Schneider (ed.).

Dohn, A.L., Chavez, A., Dohn, M.N., Saturria, L., and Pimentel, C. (2004): "Changes in Health Indicators related to Health Promotion and Microcredit Programs in the Dominican Republic", Revista Panamericana de Salud Publica. *Pan American Journal of Public Health*, 15(3).

Dowla, A. and Alamgir, D. (2003): "From Microcredit to Microfinance: Evolution of Savings Products by MFIs in Bangladesh", *Journal of International Development*, 15(8).

Drake, Deborah and Elisabeth Rhyne (ed.) (2002): *The Commercialization of Microfinance: Balancing Business and Development,* Bloomfield, Conn: Kumarian Press.

Duflos, Eric et al. (2005): *Aid Effectiveness Initiative: Microfinance Donor Peer Reviews,* Washington, DC: Consultative Group to Assist the Poorest, 2004.

Evers J., Jack S., Loeff A and Siewertsen H. (2000): Reducing Cost and Managing Risk in Lending to Micro-Enterprises, *Handbook for Micro-lending in Europe*, FACET/IFF.

FACET (2000): *New Paradigms, Productive Roles and Actions.*

Fisher, Thomas and M.S. Sriram (ed.) (2002): *Beyond Micro-credit: Putting Development Back into Microfinance*, New Delhi: Vistaar Publications; Oxford.

Foundation for Development Cooperation (1991): *Best Practice of Banking with the Poor,* Brisbane, U.K.

Gonzalez-Vega, Claudio (1994): "Stages in Evolution of Thought on Rural Finance: A Vision from the Ohio State University", *Occasional Paper No. 2134*, Rural Finance Program, Ohio State University.

Gonzalez-Vega, Claudio (1997): "The Challenge of Growth for Microfinance Organisations: The Case of Banco Solidario", Hartmut Schneider (ed.), *Microfinance for the Poor?* Paris: OECD.

Gonzalez-Vega, Claudio (1998): "Microfinance: Broader Achievements and New Challenges", *Occasional Paper No. 2518*, Rural Finance Program, Ohio State University.

Harper, M. (1998): *Profit for the Poor: Cases in Microfinance*, IT publications.

Hulme D. and Mosley P. (1996): *Finance against Poverty*, Volumes 1 and 2. Routledge, London.

Harper, Malcolm. (2002): "Promotion of Self Help Groups under the SHG Bank Linkage Program in India", Seminar on *SHG-bank Linkage Programme*, New Delhi, November 25-26.

Harper, Malcolm (ed.) (2003): *Microfinance: Evolution, Achievements and Challenges*, London: ITDG; New Delhi: Samskriti.

Harper, Malcolm and Sukhwinder Singh Arora (eds.) (2005): *Small Customers, Big Market: Commercial Banks in Microfinance*, Warwickshire, UK: ITDG Pub.; New Delhi TERI.

Harris, Sam Daley (ed.) (2002): *Pathways Out of Poverty: Innovations in Microfinance for the Poorest Families*. Bloomfield, CT: Kumarian Press.

Horan, J.C. (2002): "Indigenous Wealth and Development: Micro-credit Schemes in Tonga", *Asia Pacific Viewpoint*, 43 (2).

Hulme, D. (1995): "Finance for the Poor, Poorer or Poorest? Financial Innovation, Poverty and Vulnerability", University of Manchester. *Paper for Finance Against Poverty Conference*, University of Reading, 27-28 March.

Hulme D. (1997): "Impact Assessment Methodologies for Microfinance: A Review". *Assessing the Impact of Microenterprise Services*. Washington, D.C.: Management Systems International.

Izugbara, C.O. (2004): "Gendered micro-lending schemes and sustainable women's empowerment in Nigeria". *Community Development Journal*. 39 (1)

Jain, Pankaj and Mick Moore (2003): *What Makes Microcredit Programmes Effective?: Fashionable Fallacies and Workable Realities*. Brighton: Institute of Development Studies.

Johnson S. and Rogaly B. (1997): *Microfinance and Poverty Reduction, Actionaid and Oxfam.*

Johnson, S. (2004): "The Impact of Microfinance Institutions in Local Financial Markets: A Case Study from Kenya", *Journal of International Development*. 16(3).

Johnson, Susan (2004): "Milking the Elephant: Financial Markets as Real Markets in Kenya", *Development and Change*, 35, No. 2 April.

Klobuchar, Jim and Susan Cornell Wilkes (2003): *The Miracles of Barefoot Capitalism: A Compelling Case for Microcredit*. Minneapolis, Minn.: Kirk House Publishers.

Korten, D. (1981): "Putting People First", *Bureaucracy and the Poor*, D. Korten and F.B. Alfonso (eds.), Asian Institute of Management.

Krahnen J.P. and Schmidt R.H. (1994): *Development Finance as Institution Building: A New Approach to Poverty-Oriented Banking*, Westview Press, Boulder.

Kumar, Anjali et al. (2005): *Access to Financial Services in Brazil*, Washington, DC: World Bank.

Ledgerwood J. (1999): "Sustainable Banking with the Poor", *Microfinance Handbook: An Institutional and Financial Perspective*, The World Bank, Washington.

Levitsky, Jacob and Lene Hojmark (eds.) (2001): *Micro-and-Small Enterprises in Latin America: Experience of Business Development Services*, Mikkelsen. London: ITDG Publishing.

Lont, Hotze and Otto Hospes (2004): *Livelihood and Microfinance: Anthropological and Sociological Perspectives on Savings and Debt*, Delft: Eburon.

Lopez, Euqemian Piza and March, Canadida (1991): "Gender Considerations in Economic Enterprises", *Report of the workshop held in Philippines,* Oxfam Gender and Development Unit, Women Resources and Research Centre, Oxford.

Malhotra, M. (1997): "Micro-finance: The New Emerging Market?" *CGAP Newsletter No. 3*. Washington, D.C.: The World Bank.

Mahajan, V., B.G. Ramola, and M. Titus (1998): "Starting Microfinance in India", *Workshop on Kick-Starting Microfinance: A Challenge for the Indian Banks*, BIRD, Lucknow, October.

Mahmud, S. (2003): "Actually How Empowering is Microcredit?" *Development and Change*, 34 (4).

Masanjala, W.H. (2002): "Can the Grameen Bank be Replicated in Africa? Evidence from Malawi", *Canadian Journal of Development Studies*. 23 (1).

Matin, I., Hulme, D., Rutherford, S. (2002): "Finance for the Poor: From Microcredit to Microfinancial Services", *Journal of International Development,* 14 (2).

McKinnon, Ronald (1973). *Money and Capital in Economic Development,* Oxford University Press, New York.

Moll, H. (1999): *Microfinance and Development*, Selected articles, February.

Morduch, J. (1998): "The Microfinance Schism", *Development Discussion Paper No. 626*. Cambridge: Department of Economics and HIID, Harvard University.

Mosley, Paul, and David Hulme (1998): "Microenterprise Finance: Is There a Conflict between Growth and Poverty Alleviation?" *World Development*, Vol. 26, No. 5.

Mosley, P. and Rock, J. (2004): "Microfinance, Labour Markets and Poverty in Africa: A Study of Six Institutions", *Journal of International Development*, 16 (3).

Mosley, Paul and Steel, Lucy. (2004): "Microfinance, the Labour Market and Social Inclusion: A Tale of Three Cities", *Social Policy and Administration*, 38, No. 7 D.

NABARD (1999) *Task Force on Supportive and Regulatory Framework for Micro-finance.* Revised draft, Mumbai, 24 June.

Navajas, Sergio, Mark Schreiner, Richard L. Meyer, Cluadio Gonzalez-Vega, and Jorge Rodriguez-Meza (1998): *Microcredit and the Poorest of the Poor: Theory and Evidence from Bolivia*, October 22-24, Buenos Aires, Argentina.

Navajas, S., Schreiner, M., Meyer, R.L., Gonzalez, Vega C., Rodriguez, Meza J. (2000): "Microcredit and the Poorest of the Poor: Theory and Evidence from Bolivia", *World Development*, 28 (2).

Nelson, C., MkNelly, B., Stack, K. and Yanovitch, L. (1995): *Village Banking: The State of the Practice*, SEEP.

Otero, Maria and Elisabeth Rhyne (eds.) (1998): *The New World of Microenterprise Finance-Building: Healthy Financial Institutions for the Poor,* West Hartford, CN: Kumarian Press.

Pallen, Dean (2001): *Reinventing the City: The Role of Small Scale Enterprise,* Hull: Canadian International Development Agency.

Pearl, Daniel and Michael M. Phillips (2001): "Small Change: Bank that Pioneered Loans for the Poor Hits Repayment Snag—'Microcredit' Icon Grameen Faces Questions as Rate of Delinquencies Rises—Mrs. Begum's Missing Cow", *The Wall Street Journal* (Eastern edition), November 27.

Prahalad, C.K. (2004): *The Fortune at the Bottom of the Pyramid: Eradicating Poverty Through Profits*, Watson School Publishing.

Remenyi, Joe and Benjamin Quiñones, Jr. (2000): *Microfinance and Poverty Alleviation: Case Studies from Asia and the Pacific,* London: Pinter Publishing.

Reserve Bank of India (1954). *All-India Credit Survey*. Bombay: RBI.

Reserve Bank of India (1996). Linking of Self Help Groups with Banks—Working Group on NGOs and SHGs—Recommendations—Follow up. Circular. Rural Planning and Credit Department, 2 April.

Rhyne, Elisabeth. (1998): "The Yin and Yan of Microfinance: Reaching the Poor and Sustainability", *Micro-Banking Bulletin*, Vol. 2, No. 1.

Rhyne, Elisabeth (2001): *Mainstreaming Microfinance: How Lending to the Poor Began, Grew and Came of Age in Bolivia,* Bloomfield, Conn.: Kumarian Press.

Robinson, Marguerite S. (2001): *The Microfinance Revolution: Sustainable Finance for the Poor,* Washington, D.C.: World Bank; New York: Open Society Institute.

Robinson, Marguerite S. (2002): *The Microfinance Revolution Lessons from Indonesia.* Washington, D.C.: World Bank; New York: Open Society Institute.

Rutherford, S. (1997): "A Critical Typology of Financial Services for the Poor", *Actionaid Working Paper No.1*.

Rutherford, S. (2000): *The poor and their money*, (PFID), Oxford University Press.

Ruthven, Orlanda (2001): *Money Mosaics: Financial Choice and Strategy in a West Delhi Squatter Settlement*, University of Manchester Institute for Development Policy and Management, Finance and Development Research Programme, Paper 32.

Ruthven, Orlanda and Sushil Kumar (2002): *Fine-grain Finance: Financial Choice and Strategy among the Poor in Rural North India,* University of Manchester Institute for Development Policy and Management, Finance and Development Research Programme Paper 57.

Schumaker, E.F. (1973): *Small is Beautiful: A Study of Economics as if People Mattered*, London: Blond and Toniggs.

Sebstad, J. and G. Chenn (1996): *Overview of Studies on the Impact of Microenterprise Credit*, AIMS, USAID, Washington.

Sharma M., Zeller M., Henry C., Lapenu, C and Helms, B. (2003): *Assessing the Relative Poverty Level of MFI Clients*, IFPRI/CGAP.

Shaw, Edward S. (1973): *Financial Deepening in Economic Development*, Oxford University Press, New York. Smidt R.H. and Zeitinger C.P. (1998): *Critical Issues in Small and Micro Business Finance*, IPC.

Shylendra, H.S. (2006): "Mainstreaming Microfinance for Poverty Alleviation: Need for a Proactive and Regulatory Framework," *Towards Sustainable Microfinance Outreach in India: Experiences and Perspectives*, NABARD, Mumbai.

Stohr, W.B. and Taylor, D.R.F. (1981): *Development from Above or Below?* Boston, MA: John Wiley and Sons.

Tawney, Claire (2005): "International Year of Microcredit Theme Issue: The Financing of Microfinance", *Special Issue of Small Enterprise Development,* 16 (1).

Thillairajah, Sabapathy (1994): "Development of Rural Markets in Sub-saharan Africa", *World Bank Discussion Papers 219*, World Bank, Washington.

Trape, P. and Benhamou, J.F. (1996): "French Assistance for the Development of Microfinance Institutions", *CGAP Newsletter No. 2.* Washington, D.C.: The World Bank.

UNCDF (1999): *Working Paper on Microfinance*, UNDP.

UNDP, Commission on the Private Sector and Development (2004): *Unleashing Entrepreneurship: Making Business Work for the Poor,* Report to the Secretary-General of the United Nations, New York.

Webster, L. (1995): "The Informal Sector and Microfinance Institutions in West Africa", *CGAP Newsletter No. 1,* Washington, D.C.: The World Bank.

Whiley, C., Kempson, E. and Evers, J. (2000): *Banks and Micro-lending: Support, Co-operation and Learning*, PFRC/IFF.

World Bank (2003): *Microfinance in India: Issues, Challenges and Policy Options*, Washington DC: World Bank.

World Bank (2003a): *Improving Access to Finance in Brazil.* Washington DC: World Bank.

World Bank (2003b): *India: Development Policy Review: Sustaining Reform, Reducing Poverty.* Washington DC.

Wright, G., Kasente, D., Ssemogerere, G. and Mulsesasira, L. (1999): "Vulnerability, Risks, Assets, and Empowerment: The Impact of Microfinance on Poverty Alleviation", *Microsave Africa,* Uganda Women's Finance Trust, UNDP/DFID.

Wright, G.A.N. (1999): "A Critical Review of Savings Services in Africa and Elsewhere", *Microsave Africa,* UNDP/DFID, 1999.

Yaron J., P. Mcdonald, Benjamin and Piprek, G. (1997): *Rural Finance: Issues, Design and Best Practices*, World Bank, 1997.

Yunus, M. (1994): "Building Solidarity between the North and the Bottom Fifty Per Cent of the South", *Grameen Dialogue*, Issue 18, Grameen Trust, April.

Yunus, Muhammad with Alan Jolis (2005): *Banker to the Poor: Micro-lending and the Battle against World Poverty*, New York: Public Affairs.

Ypeij, Annelou (2000): *Producing against Poverty: Female and Male Micro-entrepreneurs in Lima, Peru.* Amsterdam: Amsterdam University Press.

Zeller, Manfred and Meyer, Richard L. (Eds.) (2002): *The Triangle of Microfinance: Financial Sustainability, Outreach, and Impact,* Baltimore, London: Johns Hopkins University Press.

Articles and Other Information

- Commercialization: Overcoming the Obstacles to Accessing Commercial Funds while Maintaining a Commitment to Reaching the Poorest, June 15, 2006.
- Alleviating Global Poverty through Microfinance, October 10, 2005: Factors and Measures of Financial, Economic, and Social Performance.

- *The New Yorker,* Millions For Millions, October 30, 2006.
- *The Economist.* The Hidden Wealth of the Poor: A Survey of Microfinance, November 2005.
- *The MicroBanking Bulletin* published by The MIX.
- Measuring the Impact of Microfinance: Taking Stock of What We Know; Nathanael Goldberg, December 2005.
- Hype and Hope: The Worrisome State of the Microcredit Movement, Thomas Dichter.

Online Resources

- MicroLINKS
- Rural Finance Learning Centre: Rural and Microfinance Training Materials
- ACCION Publications
- CGAP Publications
- The MIX Market
- Symbiotics Microfinance Directory
- Rural Finance Program—The Ohio State University
- kiva.org
- Freedom from Hunger Technical Resource Center
- Gender and Micro Credit: Useful Resources
- The Microfinance Gateway
- MicroVest
- The Virtual Library on Microcredit
- Microfinance.
- devdir-microfinance.org.

Websites

CGAP, Maximising the outreach of microenterprise finance: Emerging lessons of successful programs, CGAP, Focus Note No. 2, October 1995. http://www.cgap.org/html/p focus-notes02.html

Fruman, C. and Paxton, J., Outreach and sustainability of savings-first vs. Credit first financial institutions. http://www.worldbank.org/html/esd/agr/sbp/may/compeng.htm

Rice, E., Sustainability and its effects on the poor. What is said, and does it hold? http://www.evans.washington.edu/faculty/cla/599 00/RicePaper.htm

Woller, G.M., Dunford, C. and Woodworth, W., Where to microfinance? (available in part two: selected readings). http://www.gdrc.org/icm/where-to-mf.html

Financial Inclusion, Microfinance and SMEs—Business Opportunities

14

Manoranjan Sharma

PERSPECTIVE

The global economy recorded its fourth consecutive year of over 4 per cent expansion in 2006. This growth was led by developing world, with growth in real gross domestic product (GDP) of 6.9 per cent as against 3 per cent of the developed world. China, India and Russia have spearheaded the global success story. No wonder, then, that the cover story on the Indian economy in *Time* magazine stressed that over the last three years India has achieved "the second fastest (growth) rate in the world".

The deregulation of the Indian economy, which started in the 1980s, received an impetus in 1991. Against virtual stagnation in the period 1900-50, India's GDP grew by a modest 3.5 per cent in the period 1951-79. The Indian economy is now on a higher growth trajectory of sustained 8 per cent growth. The acceleration in macroeconomic growth to a robust 8.4 per cent in 2005-06 is manifested in economic indicators across the development spectrum, e.g. 7 per cent GDP growth for four consecutive years, 20 per cent rise in exports for three years in a row, a record 30 per cent increase in corporate loans, 40 per cent increase in investment, 14 per cent rise in salaries in 2005, spending spree spearheaded by 50 per cent growth in home loans, 40 per cent rise in consumer credit, wealth creation in stock markets, 50 per cent growth in mobile phones, booming airlines and auto industries, etc. Moderate inflation and buoyant foreign exchange reserves of over US$ 180 billion also augur well.

Key growth drivers of contemporary India are diverse industrial base, 250 million resourceful middle-class, the emergence of new entrepreneurial class and the world's youngest workforce, strong agriculture sector, robust services sector and mature capital market. India's economy is thus in a growth mode at once high and broad-based transcending IT and other service sectors to encompass traditional industries like textiles, steel, ready-made garments, etc. Remarkably, institutions, including Goldman Sachs, Boston Consulting Group and McKinsey Global Institute share a consensus about India's high growth prospects.

The economy is on a roll. India's economy could expand by 10 per cent a year in the next few years. This would help to smash the 'vicious circle of poverty'. The economy is likely to grow at 8 per cent with growth impulses emanating from various segments. As the Hon'ble Prime Minister, Dr. Manmohan Singh has repeatedly stressed, 10 per cent growth, over the medium term, is "eminently feasible" with increased savings rate, growth in agricultural output, infrastructural expansion and expansion of services because of a rapidly urbanising India and rising per capita income.

EXTENT OF FINANCIAL EXCLUSION—REAL AND WORRISOME

These are clear indications of an India that has come of age. But such exhilaration needs to be tempered by the sobering thought that several developing countries—and not just China—are way ahead of India in terms of Human Development Index (HDI). India is placed at a lowly 126th among 177 countries in HDI. This unenviable position of India, which hampers the process of economic growth and the mismatch between social and economic indicators is attributable to low employment (phenomenon of jobless growth), the disarray in agriculture, the poor position of women and the decay in public services. Clearly, then, there is the basic issue of widespread financial exclusion emanating from deeply entrenched poverty, employment, skewed pattern of distribution of income and wealth. Liberating agriculture, education and health could result in a "New Deal" discernibly improving the quality of life of the teeming millions of Indians and significantly bridging the educational, economic and social divide.

Financial exclusion can be described as the "inability of individuals, households or groups to access necessary financial services in an appropriate form. Exclusion can come about as a result of problems with access, prices, marketing, financial literacy or self-exclusion in response to negative experiences or perceptions" *(Centre for Research into Socially Inclusive Services, UK)*. Financial exclusion occurs because of fear of banks (environment and staff), fear of temptation (and getting into debt) and fear of failure (or lack of confidence that they will achieve a successful outcome).

GROWTH SANS DEVELOPMENT

A quick reality check would immediately bring to the fore several disconcerting aspects of the process and pattern of economic development. Some such multi-dimensional aspects include:

- Collapse of agricultural GDP to less than 2 per cent since 1996. Widespread rural distress is reflected in the spate of suicides by farmers. Such distress is caused by under-investment and over-regulation in agriculture.
- Inadequate provision of basic health services to millions of Indians or prevent diseases long since eradicated in other countries as clearly brought out by the recent National Family and Health Survey, the third in the series.
- Poor quality of education in most government schools and high drop-out rates.
- Lack of access for the physically challenged acts as a barrier to education and employment.
- Absence of a social security net for the elderly.
- Poor status of women reflected in abysmal sex and literacy ratios and low skills causing higher unemployment among women.
- According to the year 2005 Report "Children Under Threat" by UNICEF, although 108 million children

attend primary school, nearly 48 million children from the lower strata of society are out of school.

- Compelled by poverty and hunger, deprived children are either out on the streets begging or doing menial jobs for a plate of meal.
- Hunger and malnutrition contribute to the death of 5-6 million children world-wide—the equivalent of 10 children a minute.
- A 2006 Report Card on Nutrition by UNICEF reveals that 57 million children in India are malnourished—the highest number in the school.
- Hunger and malnutrition also impair children's cognitive and social development, making them less productive throughout their growing phase.
- Unless children's hunger needs are addressed, they will remain illiterate, wiping out the benefits of education, the potent tool for development.

It has been increasingly realised all over the world that inclusive growth has to be an integral element of the overarching framework for national policy formulation. What is now needed is a direct assault on the deeply ingrained problems of poverty, unemployment and inequalities in income and wealth, which perpetuated class divisions and gender discrimination. In this context, it is instructive to note that the World Bank describes the changes in the position of poor as continuous. On the one end of this continuum, the poor are beneficiaries as recipients of services, resources and development interventions. While community organizing, training and one-way flow of resources through grant mechanisms may be helpful, the provision of benefits extended might not enhance the ability of the people to act for themselves and thus may not be sustainable in the long-term. As the capacity of the poor people is strengthened and their voices begin to be heard, they become "clients", who are capable and demanding and paying for goods and services and private sector agencies. This necessitates a shift from welfare-oriented approaches and focus on building sustainable, market-based, decentralising authority and strengthening local resources. This leads us to the far end of the continuum, when these clients ultimately become owners and managers of their assets and activities. This stage ranks highest in the intensity of participation involved.

Against this overarching backdrop, financial inclusion is no longer just one of many objectives, it is an integral part of the growth process and indeed the structure of growth sought to be achieved most likely to achieve inclusiveness. To this end, other strategic objectives (i.e., economic growth, human development, regional imbalances and improving the status of women) need also be effectively pursued to promote financial inclusion. Apart from financing investments and policy reforms aimed at promoting growth, employment, human development, gender equity and environmental protection, there has to be an accent on projects that directly target the poor (e.g., for basic education, nutrition, health, and family planning services) or establish mechanisms to protect vulnerable groups. The key elements of the financial inclusion strategy relate to robust labour-intensive economic growth expanding economic opportunities and raising worker productivity and wages together with a comprehensive programme for socio-economic development to assuage concerns of lop-sided development. This requires adequate budgetary allocations for human capital, targeting of basic social services to the poor, removal of gender discrimination, an effective population policy and social protection. Hence India has to significantly reduce the extent of financial exclusion by augmenting employment and infrastructure and enhancing literacy rates and health facilities to become a developed nation in the true sense.

IMPERATIVE FOR A SHARPER FOCUS ON FINANCIAL INCLUSION IN INDIA

- Vast swathes of the rural hinterland are still underdeveloped, with very little safety nets for both employment generation and poverty alleviation. Agriculture is still sensitive to the vagaries of nature. Government directed approach may not always optimise returns. But empirical studies show that such approaches contribute to employment generation and poverty alleviation substantially, especially in those areas where sections of the populace have very poor skills or knowledge base. Hence issues relating to "inclusive" growth, distributive equity, "banking at the bottom of the pyramid", thrust on the development of agriculture and rural non-farm sector (RNFS) have increasingly come to the fore.

- Revolution of 'rising expectations'. Almost 60 per cent of enterprises and individuals lack access even to basic financial services, such as, savings and credit. Small, marginal and sub-marginal farmers constitute nearly 80 per cent of the total cultivators cultivating fragmented land holdings averaging around 1.41 hectares. Financial security is available to only 12-15 per cent of the 40 crore labourers, i.e., 5-6 crore labourers. The NSSO 2003 survey underscored that of the 89.35 million cultivator households, 43.42 million (48.6 per cent) are indebted. Households with 1 hectare or less land accounted for 66 per cent of all cultivator households. About 45 per cent of these marginal farmers were indebted to either formal sources or non-formal sources or to both. While institutional sources accounted for 57 per cent of loans, non-institutional sources accounted for the remaining 43 per cent. Nearly 55 per cent of cultivator households are not indebted at all making it necessary for the banking system to reach out to them to improve both volumes and outreach at the branch levels.
- The Rural Financial Access Survey conducted by the World Bank and NCAER in the states of Andhra Pradesh and Uttar Pradesh in 2003 also reached at the same conclusion. Only 21 per cent rural households had access to formal credit; only 11.8 per cent of marginal farmers in Andhra Pradesh and 13.5 per cent in Uttar Pradesh obtained loans from banks; the time taken for final clearance of a loan proposal ranged from 24 to 33 weeks and was generally collateralized

and only 42 per cent rural households had access to savings deposits.

- Fulfillment of financial needs in terms of accessibility, affordability and timeliness of loans to the vulnerable sections in the transforming socio-economic milieu has emerged as a key policy variable. Clearly this situation brooks no delay and necessitates a renewed thrust on increasing the ground level credit disbursement for agriculture and non-farm sector, percolating consumer banking to grass-roots, issue 'softer' credit cards to masses, bring 90 per cent of their branches to the 'anywhere banking' platform, launch no-frills accounts with miniscule balance and install a wider ATM network with low-cost machines.

GANDHIJI'S TALISMAN

"I will give you a talisman. Whenever you are in doubt or when the self becomes too much with you, apply the following test: Recall the face of the poorest and the weakest man whom you may have seen and ask yourself if the step you contemplate is going to be of any use to him. Will he gain anything by it? Will it restore him to control over his own life and destiny? In other words, will it lead to Swaraj for the hungry and spiritually starving millions? Then you will find your doubts and self melting away."

INADEQUACY OF REPLICATION OF THE WESTERN INSTITUTIONAL SYSTEM

The western institutional system cannot easily be replicated in vastly different Indian conditions because of different institutional environment (Willamson 1994) and the prerequisites of attendant institutional structures (Bardhan 1989). The case for intervention of the Government in the sphere of rural credit emanated from well documented market failures because of the difficulty in achieving allocative efficiency in a competitive and information system (Herath 1996; Stiglitz 1990). Accordingly the intervention took the forms of government ownership of banks, branch expansion, subsidisation, selective allocation of credit, etc. But the operation of these policies accentuated 'financial repression' characterised by regulation of interest rates both deposit and lending, large preemption of resources by government at rates lower than even the cost of raising them, cross-subsidisation of interest rates, high level of non-performing assets (NPAs), etc., resulting in gross overall inefficiency of the financial system (Besley, 1994).

A crucial objective of the present transitional phase of development is to develop sustained critical inquiries into the large and growing body of literature on the relationship between banks and inclusive growth and as a part of the process of developing critical inquiries, redefine the role of banks in fostering faster and more meaningful development. Further, as Patel (1994) demonstrates cross-subsidisation is a defining characteristic of a civilised society. This would also help us to realise development with the changing face India—a face designed to reflect vibrancy, resilience and efficiency despite structural bottlenecks and vicissitudes. This undoubtedly is a task of mammoth proportions and calls for evolution and strengthening of a collaborative forum, which would provide actionable solutions for critical areas for intervention impacting on the teeming millions of India. Such areas include augmenting availability of seeds/planting materials of high yielding varieties, developing and promoting use of hybrid, particularly for rainfed eco-systems, small farm mechanisation, transfer of technology through continuous assessment and refinement, developing infrastructure for post-harvest management, processing, marketing and agri-business and enhancement of export potential in selected areas with comparative advantage. What is basically needed is a broad-basing of the rural development process. This process looks at different programmes not in isolation but as part of an organic whole aimed at tackling the fundamental problems of widespread poverty, growing inequality, rapid population growth and high level of unemployment and underemployment. The key determinants of the rural development programme include selection of appropriate policy options, institutional development and orderly management of implementation of programmes.

The strategy of inclusiveness is all pervasive and now forms an integral part of the blueprint of the country's development planning. This was, therefore, the focal theme at the well-attended meeting of bankers–BANCON 2006-at Hyderabad on 3-4 November 2006. Sri P. Chidambaram, the Hon'ble Finance Minister in his Inaugural Address, drove home the point that while banks have made good strides in several areas, much remains to be done with only 50 per cent of GDP being financed by bank credit. Forty-eight per cent of households lack access to banking services and 58 per cent of farm households and 70 per cent of non-farm household in rural India lack access to banking. Consequently, there have been increasing concerns that banks have been unable to include vast segments of the population, particularly 300 million persons below the poverty line in India, into the fold of basic banking services. Given the wide extent of financial exclusion, there is no doubt that financial inclusion is the *sine qua non* for broad-based, equitable and inclusive growth.

India will remain a leader in the services sector and this sector would continue to be the largest contributor to the GDP. But India should also become a hub for manufacturing. While each bank is attempting to think 'out of the box' for greater inclusion, banks should reach out and lend more to productive sectors and vulnerable sections of population. The Microfinance Bill being drawn up will have minimal regulations on microfinance. RBI has requested states to exercise caution while interfering with the activities of Microfinance Institutions (MFI).

Growth touching bottom of the pyramid is imperative for developing countries. RBI Governor Dr. Y.V. Reddy asked commercial banks to lend more to farmers and urban entrepreneurs to ensure that more people reap the benefits of record economic growth. Dr. Reddy stressed "You have to move to the masses. Banks have to concentrate on loans to agriculture and small and medium enterprises because large companies can access global markets for funds". As he pointed out "Financial inclusion is not a matter of philosophy but can lead to a win-win situation for the banks and the customers...treat financial inclusion as an investment for business. It is the mass movies that make money". But he asked bankers to prudently expand loans to rural areas, which can be treated as a profit opportunity. Dr. Reddy cautioned, "Banks are not expected to be in the business of philanthropy. Banks are trusted custodians of depositors' money". This entails heavy responsibility on bankers. While significantly expanding financial inclusion, bankers have to constantly monitor such accounts, and effect course corrections, wherever needed in various districts and branches.

Banks have, therefore, initiated programmes to improve financial inclusion to ameliorate the financial conditions and improve the standard of living of the unprivileged segments in conformity with the Government's policy focus. But given the squeeze on spreads with over 60 per cent of banks' total outstanding advances above Rs. 2 lakh at rates below Prime Lending Rates (PLRs), pressure from corporates for finer rates, intensifying competition in the retail banking segment and the need for a "balanced scorecard", banks now increasingly need to look at financial inclusion as a business opportunity.

FINANCIAL INCLUSION: MEANING AND CONCEPT

Inclusive growth has been differently defined because of the semantic difficulty in conveying various meanings and different connotations implicit in the term. But as the Prime Minister Dr. Manmohan Singh recently stressed in his address at the University of Cambridge "prosperity is not divisible". An active inclusive policy will enhance economic benefits by raising the quality of work and the rate of employment thereby raising the standard of living of the masses. It thus becomes important to understand better the nature of this multi-layered problem, its multiple aspects, causes and consequences and their systemic interrelatedness.

Financial inclusion is broadly defined as the provision of affordable financial services, viz. access to payments and remittance facilities, savings, loans, and insurances services by the formal financial system to the vast sections of disadvantaged and low income groups. In other words, the term 'financial inclusion' implies the coexistence of a continuum of financial services outlets that work within their comparative advantage to serve the poor and low-income people. In India, many people, particularly those living on low incomes, cannot access mainstream financial products, such as, bank accounts and low cost loans. This obviously leads to great financial strain and unmanageable debt. Even in the UK, the Financial Inclusion Task Force in UK identified three priority areas as access to banking, access to affordable credit and access to free face-to-face money advice.

The socio-political ramifications of financial exclusion in developing countries are extremely complex. Not only do they vary from country to country and from sector to sector of a nation's economy, they are also different for the various segments of its population. Generalizations therefore have scant pertinence. Inclusive growth can have differing indices of the indebtedness of the households (47 per cent access to credit both from institutional and non-institutional sources), indebtedness of the households only from institutional sources (27 per cent), including MFIs and through SHG Model, etc. National Sample Survey Organisation (NSSO) 2005 Report shows that 46 million of farmers' households (51 per cent) are financially excluded, from institutional and non-institutional sources. The Report revealed that 27 per cent of the indebted farmers at the all-India level have availed loans from Commercial Banks (including Regional Rural Banks-RRBs) and that 26 per cent from Cooperatives. The Report also brought out that 29 per cent of the indebted farmers at the all-India level had taken loans from moneylenders, 12 per cent from traders and 18 per cent from friends and relatives. The number of bank accounts per 100 of population in India is 31 and the number of accounts per adult population is 59. Another study reckons the financial inclusion at 59 per cent taking into account the number of savings and current accounts as a proportion of adult population. The financial inclusion by way of Savings and loan accounts to the total number of adult population is 56 per cent and 12 per cent respectively, from banking industry.

While 2-3 billion people globally are still excluded from access to financial services, 900 million people, or 75 per cent of the world's poor people live in Asia. Nearly one in three Asians is poor. Although the proportion of people below the poverty line has declined, the trends in poverty reduction have recently worsened. Population growth also increases the absolute number of poor. South Asia, one of the poorest sub-regions in the world, has more than half a billion poor people, of whom 450 million are in India. The People's Republic of China has 225 million poor, and about 55 million more are in Southeast Asia. In other parts of the Asia-Pacific region, many people in the Central Asian republics have slipped into poverty with the economic disruptions of transition to a market economy. There could also be frequent crises because of social instability and unrest, particularly with rising inflation. Hence, the diverse experience in different national and international settings needs to be carefully considered to make the market economy more inclusive of marginalized people. This is a tall order but a beginning could be made by reviewing national legal, regulatory and institutional frameworks that restrict the access of people living in poverty to credit on reasonable terms; promote realistic targets for access to affordable credit, provide incentives for improving access to and strengthen the capacity of organized credit systems to deliver credit and related services to people living in poverty and vulnerable groups; and to expand financial networks, building on existing networks, promoting attractive opportunities for savings and ensuring equitable access to credit at the local level. These and other aspects bring to the fore the issues of dynamics of inclusion, institutional reforms, cooperation among public and private sectors, promotion of equitable growth, capacity building, making governments function in an efficient and evenhanded way, inclusive livelihood and coordination among different stakeholders to discernibly alter the ground realities.

GOOD GOVERNANCE

Participatory, pro-poor policies and sound macroeconomic management are a prerequisite to financial inclusion. Good governance ensures the transparent use of public funds, encourages growth of the private sector, promotes effective delivery of public services and helps to establish the rule of law. A sound macroeconomic framework encourages efficient and productive domestic investment and contains inflation to protect real incomes of the poor. It also helps prevent interest and exchange rate distortions artificially reducing the cost of capital and discouraging the use of labor. Good public expenditure management is necessary for fiscal discipline, economic growth, and equity.

GENDER AND POVERTY

Women continue to play a marginal and peripheral role in the overall national context despite constituting almost half the population and their critical role in the production and social processes of the economy. This is not only inequitable but also hampers the development of the nation with high efficiency cost. For, no country can sustain its development if it underutilises its women as a productive resource. It could also justifiably be maintained that men's emancipation is organically linked to that of women. Despite some basic changes in the status and role of women in the society, it can safely be maintained that viewed in an international setting, no society treats its women as well as its men. Consequently, women continue to suffer from diverse deprivations from the cradle to the grave across nations. All this leaves one with an uncomfortable feeling of frustration, of opportunities missed and challenges avoided.

While nearly two-thirds of the world's poor are in the Asian and Pacific region, two-thirds of the region's poor are women. Given such stark gender divides in education, health care, economic participation, and incomes, women are the most vulnerable category. The number of women living in poverty has increased disproportionately over the past decade, compared to the number of men. The plight of women in India today is reflected in the Gender Related Development Index (GDI), which takes into account life expectancy at birth, adult literacy rate, combined primary, secondary and tertiary gross enrollment ratios and share in earned income. In terms of GDI, Human Development Report (HDR) India ranked poorly. Similarly, in terms of gender empowerment measure (GEM) India was placed at the same lowly position. The widespread discrimination against women is structural and entrenched reflected in the persistent pattern of under representation of women in Parliament, Administration and Management, Professional and

Technical work and share in earned income. The gross under representation of women is strikingly reflected in several areas of employment like the police, the judiciary and the law, etc. The correction of this tradition of unhappy and unequal development of women necessitates, *inter alia*, focused intervention targeting education, training, child care, health, nutrition, credit, employment, welfare services support and legal safeguards. Investing in women's capabilities and empowering them is the surest way to contribute to economic growth and overall development.

Considered in a historical perspective, the role of women has increased manifold over the years. During India's struggle for Independence the contribution of women to the national cause was by no means insignificant and the potentially important role of women was repeatedly emphasised. For, as Gandhiji stressed 'subjugation and exploitation of women was a product of man's vested teachings and women's acceptance of them.' Similarly Pandit Jawaharlal Nehru maintained that 'in order to awaken the people, it is the woman who has to be awakened. Once she is on the move, the household moves, the nation moves and thus we build the India of tomorrow.' It was thus realised that political freedom must, in the ultimate analysis, lead to emancipation of women by eliminating shortcomings in terms of education, nutrition and health.

Conscious efforts in the form of constitutional and legal provisions, social reforms and directed economic upliftment programmes were initiated in the post-Independent India to provide *de jure* equality to women by measures, such as, The Hindu Women's Property Act (1937), Hindu Marriage and Divorce Act (1955), The Special Marriage Act (1954). Hindu Succession Act (1956), Hindu Adoptions and the Maintenance Act (1956), Widow Remarriage Act (1956), The Dowry Prohibition Act (1961, amended in 1986 to give it more teeth). The Indian political system has also been characterised by concern with women's status and rights. This is reflected in various constitutional provisions, e.g., Article 14 granted equality to men and women in political, economic and social spheres, Article 15(3) allowed affirmative action in favour of women and Article 16 provided legal opportunities of employment. A fundamental duty is also enjoined on every citizen to renounce practices derogatory to women. Not only were such legal measures largely inadequate but because of their inherent problems, e.g., laws relating to marriage, divorce, maintenance and inheritance, these laws have not been fully effective. Some secular laws like The Equal Remuneration Act and introduction of a new section on dowry death in The Indian Penal Code have also been framed but they do not go far enough. Social legislation has to go beyond social acceptance to take the form of a social movement for effective implementation. It can therefore justifiably be maintained that attempts to provide *de jure* equality to women have not been carried to their logical conclusion necessitating their reinforcement by tougher laws, stricter enforcement and exemplary punishment. There is also a compelling need to resolve certain basic issues about the socialisation processes inherent in a hierarchical society, resource and power distribution patterns and cultural values in India. Evidently, the E-components—education, employment, earnings, empowerment, entitlement to property and effects of violence—continue to be significant in India.

Reservation for women at the level of villages, districts and local bodies has been introduced to empower roughly about a million women at the village council level. But a situational analysis reveals that the majority of positions are cornered by men acting on behalf of women and women continue to suffer from a wide range of *de-facto* inequities because of pronounced gender bias in the complex socio-economic milieu (Agarwal, *2000)*. Further, the scuttling, despite both a functional and moral case, of the proposed 81st Constitutional Amendment Bill seeking to reserve 33 per cent seats for women in national and state legislatures would restrict the political participation of women in the decision-making process since women must have a critical 30 per cent representation in all decision-making processes—economic, political and social—nationally and locally to influence decisions that vitally affect them.

The patriarchal family system practiced in most parts of the country places a heavy premium on the boy while the girl is considered a liability from the moment of her conception in the womb. It is a commonplace to observe that gender-based inequalities occur within families/households. But it is not so commonly realised that women continue to be underprivileged in terms of almost all facets of gender equality, viz. nutrition, maternity, life expectancy, health care, education, training, participation in the polity and economy, etc. While rural women have been shouldering a heavy burden in the agricultural sector, their role has been largely confined to the lower socio-economic strata of the society. This is a cause for concern. Is it not time then for us to do some introspection, to ascertain how and why have we failed in brining about emergence of a healthy and vibrant economy? Is structure and quality of growth not as important as the quantity of growth? With greater concern for the emancipation of women, exploratory questions like what development, development for whom and when need to be raised. These questions are not merely academic but are central to the process and pattern of economic development in India. This necessitates an identification of the factors responsible for impeding the advancement of women, such as lack of access to housing and basic services, inadequate support services and technologies for reducing drudgery and occupational health hazards and for enhancing their productivity and devising a broad-based strategic action plan for the realisation of equal partnership of men and women in all spheres of economic activity. This can also be substantiated by the observation of Hillary Clinton, First Lady of the United States: "In country after country women have demonstrated that when given the tools of opportunity—education, health care, access to credit, political participation and legal rights—they can lift themselves out of poverty, and as women realise their potential, they lift their families, communities and nations as well."

An avowed objective underlying the plan programmes has been to increase the access to resources and ownership of productive assets to the weaker and resource-poor sections of society, of which women constitute a significant part. Women were traditionally subjected not only to denial of access to resources and ownership of productive assets but also to a host of social and other taboos. Initially the Five Year Plans focused on women as target of welfare policies. But the later Plans marked a changed viewpoint about women as 'critical inputs for national development rather than as targets for welfare policies' and stressed the necessity to train women in need of income and protection. Subsequently, there was a shift from 'welfare' to 'development' and the extension of women's areas of concern from the social services sector of education, health and welfare to the critical areas of economic development. There has also been a greater awareness of the need for inculcating confidence among women, generating awareness about their rights and privileges and training them for economic activity and employment. An attempt has also been made to extend the benefits of development to women both qualitatively and quantitatively. Women are expected to function as equal partners and participants in development and not merely as beneficiaries of various schemes by creation of an enabling environment, where women can freely exercise their rights both within and outside home as equal partners along with men. Improvement in women's economic status could be brought about by ensuring joint ownership of land, recognition of women-headed household, promoting women's self-help groups, encouraging women entrepreneurs/beneficiaries to avail of bank loans, increasing the number of women's cooperatives and changing rules and practices of women agriculture workers.

The Indian society has also been characterised by the symbiotic and mutually complementary relationship between the government, the women's movement and non-governmental organisations (NGOs). The women's movement in India continuously interacts with and influences public opinion and governmental action. The scheme of Support to Training and Employment Programmes (STEP) for women, Training-cum-Production Centres (TPCs), Rashtriya Mahila Kosh (RMK), Integrated Child Development Services (ICDS)—these and other schemes have, in their own distinctive ways, attempted to empower women and bring them into the mainstream of the development process. This has also been attempted by women-related policies like the National Health Policy (1983), National Policy on Education (1986), National Population Policy (1993) and National Nutrition Policy (1993). Several committees like the National Commission for Self-Employed Women and Women in the Informal Sector (1988), Shramshakti Committee on the Status of Women in India (1974), National Plan of Action for Women (1976), Working Group on Employment of Women (1978), which critically examined the role of women in both rural and urban areas to the growth of the formal economy. These Committees recommended recognition of women's work in both formal and informal sectors as socio-economic producers, establishment of exclusive credit institutions for women, provision and linking of training programmes to employment. While all these reports vary in details, they unmistakably bring out the importance of practical gender need as the basis on which to build a more secure system and a means through which more strategic interests of women may be realised. But it has not been easy so far with the impoverishment of society and sex-based discrimination despite significant regional variations all along the line. This is why while gender-specific policies with emphasis on activities and resources beneficial to women may help in providing equal opportunities and reaping the benefits of development, what is basically required is affirmative action in a situation of structural and entrenched discrimination. In other words, a gender transformative policy is alone incapable of eliminating systemic inequalities.

It is not always realised–much less felt–that the task of initiating such a transformative policy seeking to alter the existing distribution of resources, responsibilities and power cannot be accomplished solely by State intervention, few enlightened social groups or the advocates of the feminist movement working in isolation. Development of women in India continues to be constrained *inter alia* by inadequate market information, inability to scale up production because of scarce capital, inability to adopt technology transformation for quality standards, absence of adequate infrastructure, absence of brand equity and tendency to remain small. This necessitates coordinated and concerted action from all sections of society.

Gender-bred inequalities are historically determined. Hence, these can only be corrected by rethinking the frame of gender equity and bringing about attitudinal changes. While gender is never absent, it is inextricably linked with class and other social relations. Accordingly, the inclusion of gender-equity in the overall framework of distributive equity would also facilitate the attainment of the cherished objective of social justice. The challenge of development of women relates to traditional role prescriptions, behavioural biases, gender role ideology, socio-cultural/psychological biases, limit on outside monitoring, inadequate access to credit, technology, etc. A SWOT analysis of the position of women in India today reveals that while the strength lies in the commitment and dedication of women, the weaknesses relate to the inability of women to take calculated risks. There are emerging opportunities of the spread of education and liberalism but there is also the potent threat of competition from small and big units and the necessity of having to give up enterprise due to family reasons. Against this backdrop, Bina Agarwal cogently pursues the question of women's equality through the prism of economic equality as a central mediator (though not the sole determinant) in the achievement of gender equality in other spheres. Development of women entrepreneurs in a big way requires access to information on entrepreneurs to women; encouragement to association of women entrepreneurs; design, planning and implementation of women of programmes for women on a continuous basis; an active role of women entrepreneurs associations and NGOs in implementation of income-generating schemes; initiation of vocational courses; proactive role of apex institutions like SIDBI, NABARD, etc.; Centre and States to assist women entrepreneurs in participation of international fairs; networking of trade centres in all States linked up with trade centres in all foreign centres; simplification of rules, regulations, procedures, etc.; adequate insurance coverage and consideration of the scheme of providing 100 per cent loan without any collateral.

No strategy, which seeks to empower women can succeed unless women take the initiative themselves all along the line and are also duly supported by men. If women are denied their rightful place in political power-sharing and economic decision-making, the entire development process would be rendered ineffective in checking perpetuation of aggravated gender inequities. The spectre of marginalisation of women because of the triple exposure to discrimination by gender, class and caste requires a renewed thrust on all round development of women.

The national policy for empowerment of women stresses that policies, programmes and systems be established to ensure mainstreaming of women's perspectives in all developmental processes, both as agents and beneficiaries. This is essential because no strategy, which seeks to empower women can succeed unless women take the initiative themselves all along the line and are also duly supported by men. If women are denied their rightful place in political power-sharing and economic decision-making, the entire development process would be rendered ineffective in checking perpetuation of aggravated gender inequities. The spectre of marginalisation of women because of the triple exposure to discrimination by gender, class and caste requires a renewed thrust on all round development of women. Technology should be geared towards the most deprived, underprivileged and unexposed section of society, i.e., women. The solutions to problems associated with gender, science and technology are an integral part of a much larger agenda of promoting new, more ecologically sustainable and socially just approaches to development. This requires active participation of all stakeholders in the development process, including the society at large, government, educational institutions, premier technological institutions, voluntary agencies, policy matters and women themselves.

INSTITUTIONAL STREAMLINING

Institutions are defined as a set of constraints, which govern the behavioural relations among individuals and groups. Institutional development could be enhanced by strengthening of institutions, promotion of sustainable and equitable agriculture, effective credit support, improving the outreach of the banking system, modification of the regulatory framework and the promotion of competition and privatisation. In conformity with the winds of change sweeping the country, an efficient and performing credit delivery system must be an integral part of any design of rural development. This necessitates fundamental changes for successful working on a long-term basis.

MACROECONOMIC SETTING

Post-reforms, India has been a key driver of global economic growth. But high uneven growth has created new challenges as poignantly brought out by the recent World Bank publication (2006). This publication focuses on ensuring institutional reform to enhance the capability of public sector institutions and sustaining rapid growth and making the process of economic growth more inclusive—across sectors, across regions and bringing the benefits of higher incomes and living standards to more people.

Core public services, such as healthcare, education, power and water supply need to be improved through empowerment of people to demand better services through more effective systems of public sector accountability. Options include decentralizing to local governments, producing regular and reliable information for citizens, undertaking internal reforms of public sector agencies or creating public-private partnerships. But ultimately, implementation is most important.

Rapid and inclusive growth requires more, and more effective, investment in infrastructure to create more jobs for low and semi-skilled workers. Growth has to be equitably shared. Promoting inclusive growth includes revamping labor regulations, improving agricultural technology and infrastructure, reducing imbalances across states and regions and empowering the poor through proactive policies facilitating fair and equitable market participation. All these aspects necessitate empowerment and opportunity. Policies must move from protecting people from markets to empowering people to participate fairly in markets. Development must sustainably improve human well-being with emphasis on the less well-off. Dr. Amartya Sen and others have powerfully demonstrated that development transcends increasing material well-being to include expansions in capabilities and in both positive and negative freedoms. This requires a more consistent attention to assessing development progress not simply as a measure of an aggregate of economic activity but as an assessment of the inclusiveness of economic growth, with emphasis not only on the distribution of gains but also on the security, vulnerability, empowerment and sense of full participation enjoyed by people in social civic life. Disconcertingly in both economic progress and in service delivery, the chasm between the best and worst is growing.

SYSTEMIC REFORM, NOT MORE OF THE SAME

There is a growing consensus that improved implementation requires much more than policy tinkering or stronger internal management. What is required is a paradigm shift "moving from inputs to outputs and outcomes" or "from asset creation to asset operation". The message is clearly conveyed by the slogan "don't fix the pipes, fix the institutions that fix the pipes".

Financial inclusion, in the sense of extending banking products at an affordable cost to the vast sections of disadvantaged and low-income groups, is not new to India. Post-bank nationalization, Indian banking system underwent robust branch expansion. But there continued to be major gaps in terms of outreach. Hence, the need for a sharp focus on inclusive growth is greater than ever before to increase household incomes, reduce poverty and the vulnerability of the poor to shocks.

The year 2006 was characterized by major decisions taken by the Ministries of Finance, Rural Development, Urban Poverty Alleviation, Planning Commission, RBI, NABARD to address various policy and operational constraints to enhance financial inclusion. Of the several initiatives, mention may here be made of Kisan and Swarozgar Credit Cards, General Kisan Credit Cards (GCC), opening of no frills account, forming and supporting SHGs and Joint Liability Groups, capacity building of farmers through farmers' club, watershed associations, water users' association, use of microfinance institutions (MFIs), non-governmental organizations (NGOs), SHGs, etc., as business facilitators and correspondents to enable banks increase their outreach and ensure greater financial inclusion. Some other major initiatives related to extension of farm credit at 7 per cent, concessional refinance to commercial banks and RRBs, earmarking Rs. 1000 crore for Agro-Processing and Interest Incentive Scheme to boost farm credit. Other strategic interventions include subsidy-linked schemes for post harvest management, farm ponds, irrigation systems, etc., designed to encourage farm investment through bank credit, support for strengthening rural infrastructure through public-private partnerships to enhance farm productivity and rural connectivity. The whole process was also attempted to be given a big push through the constitution of Committee on Financial Inclusion headed by Dr. C. Rangarajan, working group on development of competitive micro-credit market in the Planning Commission, a task force on access to finance, raw materials and marketing under the National Commission of Enterprises for the unorganized Sector.

RBI's Annual Policy Statement for 2005-06 provided strongly the justification for the pursuit of financial inclusion as follows: "There has been expansion, greater competition and diversification of ownership of banks leading to both enhanced efficiency and systemic resilience in the banking sector. However, there are legitimate concerns in regard to the banking practices that tend to exclude rather than attract vast sections of population, in particular pensioners, self-employed and those employed in unorganised sector. While commercial considerations are no doubt important, the banks have been bestowed with several privileges, especially of seeking public deposits on a highly leveraged basis, and consequently they should be obliged to provide banking services to all segments of the population, on equitable basis."

RBI has attempted to promote financial inclusion through no frills account with either nil on minimum balances and charges, simplified KYC norms for opening account with maximum limit of deposits Rs. 50,000 and credits in the account Rs. 1,00,000 in a year, overdraft facility with 'no frill' account without collateral, One Time Settlement Scheme for borrowers with principal less than Rs. 25,000, Credit Cards facility in urban areas with cash withdrawal facility, General Purpose Credit Card in rural areas with a revolving credit facility upto Rs. 25,000 and reasonable bank charges. The action points with reference to the above include the following:

- RBI will implement policies to encourage banks, which provide extensive services while disincentivising those banks unresponsive to the banking needs of the community, including the underprivileged.
- The nature, scope and cost of services will be monitored to assess whether there is any denial, implicit or explicit, of basic banking services to the common person.
- Banks are urged to review their existing practices to align them with the objective of financial inclusion.
- Streamlining of rural financial institutions (RFIs). RFIs, particularly cooperatives, continue to suffer from systemic weaknesses, e.g., high transaction cost, high risk costs, low margins, high NPAs and low capitalisation. Improved credit delivery system requires multi-dimensional strategies comprising general strategy, thrust on recovery performance and institution and area specific measures. An efficient and vibrant rural credit delivery mechanism requires maintaining a higher capital adequacy ratio, facilitating restructuring of the system through an exit and privatisation policy, implementing stricter and more transparent accounting and disclosure norms, enhancing rule-based supervision and reduced reliance upon public sector funding. While financial recapitalisation is expected to cleanse the balance sheets of cooperative banks, its success is contingent on organisational, structural, operational and systemic reforms.

FURTHER SIMPLIFICATION OF NO-FRILLS BANK ACCOUNTS

With a view to achieving the objective of greater financial inclusion, all banks were advised to introduce 'no frills' account to bring a large section of population under the banking net. The basic characteristic of a no frills bank account is that it involves a nil or very low minimum balance as well as charges and offers limited transaction facilities. The 'no frills' account is a win-win opportunity for banks to cater to such segment and attract profitable customers. Banks will be able to create a database of these customers and can prudently use this information to target the customers in their databases to cross-sell various products. Banks are also required to report to the Reserve Bank on a quarterly basis and give wide publicity to the facility of such a 'no frills' account, including on their websites, indicating the facilities and charges in a transparent manner.

The Government has decided to relax the norms applicable under the Prevention of Money Laundering Act (PMLA) for no frill bank accounts, which were introduced to facilitate lending to the under-privileged and reduce credit rationing (a situation of excess demand of bank loans as compared to supply) for the poor and vulnerable sections of society. The RBI had written to the Finance Ministry expressing concern in this regard. Further, Know Your Customer (KYC) procedures for opening accounts of those who intend to keep balance less than Rs 50,000 in all their accounts taken together and the total credit in all the accounts taken together is not expected to exceed Rs 1,00,000 in a year have been simplified, to enable those belonging to low-income groups without documents of identity and proof of residence to open bank accounts. As a result, many of the guidelines for opening a no frills account became non-compliant with some of the rules under the PMLA. The PMLA, passed in 2003 and notified in 2005, is the Act governing the legal regime for anti-money laundering in the country.

CANARA BANK'S INITIATIVES

Historically, Canara Bank has played a pioneering role in the upliftment of the poor and the downtrodden. Some such initiatives include the following:

CanSaral, a "No Frills Savings Account": Unique features

- Account opening with an amount as low as Rs. 25/- and even maintains the same with zero balance.
- Simplified account opening procedures.
- Eligibility of individuals to withdraw up to 6 occasions per month without any charge.
- Interest earned is at Savings Bank rate.
- Free ATM-cum-Debit Card.
- Facility to accumulate balance up to Rs. 50,000/- in all the accounts taking together, with total credit in a year not to exceed Rs. 1.00 lakh.
- Facility of Internet & Mobile Banking Services.
- Issue of one cheque book free of cost

CanNE Savings Account: Features

- Offered to individuals in the North-Eastern States of the country.
- Accounts can be opened as zero balance account with maximum overdraft of up to Rs. 500/-.
- Maximum six transactions (including ATM withdrawal) allowed per month free of charges.
- Free ATM-cum-Debit Card facility.

Identification of Villages

- 1400 villages, across the country, have been earmarked by Canara Bank for implementation of total financial inclusion.

BUSINESS OPPORTUNITY—CONVERGENCE OF INTERESTS

The synergy built in the programme between the informal sector and the formal sector comprising banks, Government and development agencies, like the 'twice-blessed' Shakespearean quality of mercy, needs to be fully exploited by concerted marketing. Banks need to adopt a holistic household approach and look at the larger picture in creating awareness about financial products, education, and advice on money management, debt counseling, savings and affordable credit.

There is no doubt that financial inclusion can emerge as a commercial profitable business provided banks think out of the box!

FOSTERING INNOVATION—CONCERN BEYOND CONCERN

While banks have been talking extensively about technology-based approach towards financial inclusion, they are yet to build a suitable technology infrastructure to empower the rural population through knowledge. While technology is only an enabler and not a plug-and-play solution in banking, there is a need to map business architecture to technology. There should be no second thought in adopting technology when banks go in for financial inclusion. However, it would have to be a low-value high-volume proposition.

Financial inclusion can-and must-be used as a business opportunity by leveraging technology to reduce overall cost and incremental cost of transactions. This could be done through intelligent use of innovative mechanisms, such as, change from Maker-Checker concept to Maker cum Checker, installation of cash dispensers/low cost ATMs in select rural branches, connection of boutique/kiosk to the central server in villages, automatic kiosks for bill payment/cheque deposit, automated loan processing for small loans, etc. The adoption-and possible adaptation-of technologies and exploration of innovative mechanisms could provide alternative solutions in beneficial enduring outcomes for the poor and the disadvantaged in India.

KEY DELIVERABLES FOR BANKS

Indian public sector banks (PSBs) were not only conceived and functioned as instruments of social change and emancipation but also played a pivotal role in developing agriculture and rural development. Banks in India have been shouldering the onerous responsibilities of rural lending for a host of poverty alleviation/ self-employment programmes and directed lending to enhance the standards of living of the downtrodden/ neglected sections of society. The commercial banks (CBs) have been consistently directed by the RBI to earmark 40 per cent of their lending towards the priority sector, which constitutes agriculture, small scale industries, tiny sector, village and cottage industries, small traders, professionals and self-employed, etc.

Despite the impressive growth of the Indian financial system in terms of the elaborate network of CBs, RRBs and commercial banks financial institutions, non-banking financial companies (NBFCs) and the evolution of a wide range of financial instruments, there is immense latent potential for the formal credit delivery system (Annexure). Towards this end, rural India must occupy the center-stage of the development policy. Given that 27 per cent of the population still lives below the poverty line, financial inclusion process must be pursued with a holistic approach. There are three aspects of tackling financial inclusion, viz. (i) accessibility of credit, (ii) affordability of credit and (iii) actual facilities made available to the rural poor. Financial inclusion should be an integrated development plan.

Joseph Schumpeter (1942) propounded the thesis that the essence of capitalism is the process of "creative destruction"—the perpetual cycle of destroying the old and less efficient product or service and replacing it with new, more efficient ones. Andy Grove former CEO of Intel stressed that dramatic, industry-transforming innovations are today taking place faster and faster. There is a fair measure of consensus that in this overall scheme of "industry-transforming innovations" today in the banking sector, inclusive growth is an absolute must. With the economy currently being in a phase of rapidly rising rural and urban incomes, there is a burst of entrepreneurial activity. Households would be first time financial savers since they have higher disposable incomes. Declining poverty will add momentum to this. However, micro-credit and SHG movements are yet to realize their full potential in India. With greater liberalization underway, the role of banking sector is poised to increase. Banking must extend credit to new activities, rebalance their credit portfolios and emphasize more on segments, which have received inadequate credit. Deepening the financial system and widening its reach is crucial for both accelerating growth and for equitable distribution given the present stage of development of the country. This *inter alia*, requires efficient delivery of services with low cost of intermediation, shift from 'micro-credit' to 'microfinance' and resuscitation of rural branches by incentivised rural postings and attitudinal shift of staff members working in rural branches. Concerted attempts are also important to foster the growth of the SME sector, explore hybrid channels like NGOs-MFIs/post offices/RUDSETIs/educational institutions and achieve 100 per cent financial inclusion. There has to be a sharper focus on the entire wealth creation exercise in rural areas rather than merely disbursing crop loans with a stress on 'credit-plus approach', foster real sector linkages and leveraging technology to the maximum possible extent. In the ultimate analysis, bank branches should emerge as repositories of knowledge in rural areas. What is needed is better delivery methods and extension of timely and hassle-free credit facilitating the farmers' transition from non-formal sources to the formal banking-system.

Dr. C. Rangarajan, Chairman, Economic Advisory Council to the Prime Minister stressed that merely funding the rural households will not automatically result in inclusive growth. Dr. Rangarajan said that the banks have to reorient their rural branches by making them more proactive and flexible by fixing newer tasks of reaching the deprived households and helping them to improve their productivity. He maintained, "it is beyond credit that the banks have to shoulder the responsibility". Banks have to pay serious attention to attitudinal and empathy issues of its staff towards the rural folk; redraft procedures, products and systems and bring proper institutional changes in order to achieve the targeted financial inclusion.

ROLE OF INFRASTRUCTURE AND HUMAN RESOURCES

The role of human resources and infrastructure is critical in financial inclusion. To bring rural mass in the fold of banks, there has to be a widespread recognition of the need for educating them. Presently, bankers are required to complete 3 years rural posting in their lifetime for promotions. Public sector banks thus face the problem of both overstaffing in urban branches and understaffing in rural branches. Consequently, personnel policies could be moulded to make rural postings more attractive by giving incentives and rewards to staff. Banks can contribute to rural areas by imparting knowledge of cropping pattern, starting farmer training colleges, programmes like e-chaupal and e-seva, documenting existing materials and managing knowledge in rural areas.

Sustainable and balanced growth is possible only when it is contributed by all sectors of the economy. The growth benefits should be widespread. Inclusive growth is all about correcting the imbalances in the economy, which can be achieved only by financial empowerment and participation of rural masses.

India is an agricultural based economy with 70 per cent of the workforce living in the rural area. It is imperative to mainstream this section. Social banking has been the main area of operation for PSBs since nationalization and almost all banks achieved targeted 40 per cent priority sector lending. Microfinance and SHGs are few steps towards inclusive growth. Over time, Indian banks became stronger and can match international banks in terms of transparency, growth, products, technology, level of NPA and productivity and benefits should trickle down to the bottom line. In India, 31 per cent of the population uses banking services compared to 99 per cent in Denmark and 91 per cent in US. The recruitment of Agriculture graduates and Rural Development Officers would help in extending outreach of the services to the rural population.

The issue of right attitude and aptitude is of utmost importance. The focus of the banks should, therefore, be the common man. Bank's *dharma* should be to protect the depositor's money by rebalancing the credit portfolio to minimize the cost of operations. Many non-banking activities like NPA recovery may be outsourced to AMC and the focus should be on credit delivery. The market needs to have credit bureaus and borrowing centers for rural credit delivery. Two important Cs for banks relate to Capital and Customers.

Robust economic growth should not only be confined to the macro level but also distributed to the various sections of the society, particularly those living in rural areas. Financial inclusion can help in amelioration of poverty. Banks' staff should be sensitive about the need of rural credit growth. Agricultural Officers, Rural Development Officers, local staff well versed in local language may be recruited to meet the need of rural lending to overcome inadequate and unskilled manpower with lack of attitude to understand the rural market.

Growth is an inclusive concept and basic objective of the growth is reduction of poverty. Financial institutions are the vehicle for creation of awareness. RBI encourages schemes of reaching rural mass. The effectiveness of these schemes depends upon the infrastructure, initiatives, implementations and delivery. Financial awareness and innovative products are also required. Social schemes started are just statistical reporting with no indication of human development of rural population. Thrust on empowerment, NGOs and community based organizations are creating awareness for human development. SHGs through local participation have the ability for local penetration. Hence, rural masses should be brought into the mainstream.

INCLUSIVE GROWTH—SCOPE FOR REGULATION AND SUPERVISION

India has the best and the worst in the world with contrasts of high growth in the economy and the rising incomes levels of certain sections coexisting with extreme poverty. The question is of sustaining average 8 per cent growth with such contrasts and the organizational dilemma. There are now multiple channels of credit with multiple institutions. However, the existence of institutions like NABARD, RRBs, NBFCs, SHGs, etc., is a good sign. The best structure is the self-regulatory structure.

It must be obligatory to introduce insurance policies to cater to underprivileged sections of society. Bankers assume the pivotal role by extending long-term credit and working capital requirements. Banks must also extend consumption credit and pool risks. The role of the regulator is to balance the risks undertaken by lending and rising productivity and economic growth accruing due to lending efforts. The central banks must foster measures, such as, vigilance of financial institutions to avert crises, ensure transparency in guidelines and operations, policy consistency, flexible approach, continuous and efficient review and continuous interaction with the banking industry. Simultaneously while ensuring that there is no inconsistency with overall objectives, the central bank must refrain from activities, such as, intervention in day-to-day functioning of banks, rigid and inflexible policies, opaque policies, regulating individual institutions, applying policies across the board.

Despite the history of financial inclusion in India dating back to 1968 (nationalization of 14 banks), 48 per cent of population is yet to be covered by the banking system. SCBs, RRBs, co-operatives, MFIs, NGOs, SHGs, postal network, etc., are players in the financial system. Given the need for both growth and distributive equity, financial institutions must focus on inclusion and not only on profit. Rising incomes, consumer demand, etc., have led to greater financial activity. As banks have a crucial role, RBI has taken several steps to limit financial exclusion. Banking Regulation Act itself stresses lending and borrowing as important aspects of banks. This highlights the importance of financial inclusion. Countries like Sweden, Germany, France, Canada and US have achieved remarkable success in this regard. RBI has introduced schemes like the no frills account and liberalized the KYC norms for accounts falling in certain limits. Banks have also been allowed to utilize the services of NGOs. New private sector banks have also been asked to mandatorily open 5 per cent of their business in rural areas.

ROLE OF COOPERATIVES

Cooperative banks/cooperative society has major presence in rural India. These institutions need to be nurtured and developed with proper governmental support to increase the reach of banks in rural areas. It also requires political will and consensus. Many States have agreed to sign MoUs with State Governments in this regard. However, as of now, only one State, viz. Andhra Pradesh, has signed the MoU. Empowerment of primary cooperatives is a must. There should not be any compromise for uplifting the cooperatives. SHGs are a medium to reduce cost of banks. Therefore, there is a definite case to include SHGs in the banking net. Cooperatives must be free to work in their own way as they know the local pulse and are in constant touch with the borrowers. However, such freedom has to be coupled with required regulatory measures to greatly reduce the total cost of rural credit. Finally, all agencies involved in this process, i.e., banks, cooperatives, RBI, Government both Central and State, should coordinate towards the common goal of enhancing and strengthening cooperatives in promoting inclusive growth through rural credit.

RETHINKING WAYS AND MEANS OF INCLUSIVE GROWTH—ACCENT ON NGOs

Changes in socio-economic environment have led to concomitant changes in the identity, strategy and institutional structures within NGOs in India. NGOs are characterized by strong commitment to grassroots level work, training, flexible response to needs, advocacy work, ability to access wider networks and provide quality technical assistance, support of local initiatives. NGOs in India, as indeed elsewhere, helped funds reach marginalized groups both across functions and geographical regions.

NGOs work in providing succor to the poor, particularly vulnerable individuals through strengthened local capacity, skill acquisition, training, support to sustainable development model and local initiatives, building links with regional and international networks and addressing the needs of vulnerable groups. But the effectiveness of delivery system has been hampered by lack of a coordinated approach to capacity building, tendency to reinvent the wheel and undervalue local knowledge and skills and reluctance to lose control. There are also cases of failing to convert personal contacts into institutional linkages for policy dialogues, limited strategic perspectives, territorial competition between NGOs, insufficient attention to sustainability of projects, tendency to bypass Government institutions and underestimate the importance of linkages.

Given the clear absence of a plausible framework to ensure the accountability of NGOs, accountability and transparency are key issues in governance as stressed by the Draft National Policy on the Voluntary Sector 2003 and the Steering Committee Report of 10th Five-Year Plan on the Voluntary Sector. The surmounting of such difficulties requires information, openness, transparency, clear legal structure, within which the voluntary sector can operate with due recognition, accountability and credibility. It is, therefore, important to nurture policy and regulatory reform and develop the policy frame to improve conditions for sustainable inclusive development by devising mechanisms for verifiable outcomes.

While there continue to be areas of concern in planning, design, partnership, delivery, access, monitoring, NGOs are set to play an increasingly important role in inclusive growth and thus to discernibly improve the ground realities. But there is a manifest need to set quantifiable goals, build verifiable indicators, prepare transparent time table for action, stipulate details of costs and financing mechanisms and formulate goals, measures and strategies to check exclusion. There are difficulties in testing, measuring effectiveness of structural funds in combating exclusion, lack of a consensus of change indicators and good reporting systems, monitoring, etc.

MICROFINANCE (MF)

A recent World Bank-NCAER Survey on rural access to finance substantiates the thesis that despite about 40,000 bank branches across rural India, 70 per cent of the rural poor do not have a bank account and 87 per cent have no access to credit from a formal source. No wonder, then, that the poor are constrained to rely on informal sources for credit at exorbitant rates because of greater accessibility and flexibility in terms, size and purpose. Access to other financial services, such as, savings accounts, life, health and crop insurance also remains limited for the rural poor.

There are distinct signs of retooling rural financial institutions (RFIs) in designing financial services for the rural poor in India. The resources of the formal banking system can help overcome difficulties in mobilisation of financial resources for economic empowerment of India's about 60 million poor households. Economic empowerment is usually defined in terms of access to cheaper credit and other microfinance services, including savings and insurance. Considering the deposit resources of the formal banking system in India and the annual accretions to such deposits, the requirement of reaching the unreached in the country would perhaps constitute a small proportion of the resources of the formal financial sector. There are also several spin off effects of micro-credit for banks. These could *inter alia,* relate to increase in outreach measured by the number of new clients, volume of lending assessed on the basis of incremental increase in the flow of credit and loan recovery as indicated by the total volume of cash recoveries.

Micro-credit programmes, across countries, have been an effective tool of extricating people from 'vicious circle of poverty' and have helped to increase their participation in the economic and political processes of society. MF revolution is increasingly demand-led as contrasted to the supply-led, state sponsored rural credit and that microfinance is profitable with banks/Microfinance Institutions (MFIs) adopting a profit-centre approach with customer-friendly savings and loan products. Innovations by several institutions across countries reveal that the poor are bankable and that micro-enterprise activities themselves are sustainable.

Loans by MFIs move in the band of US $38 in case of BKD (Indonesia) to US $1,016 by Credit Union-AECP (Senegal). It has also been shown (Yaron 1992) that the average size of microfinance differed from US $26 in case of BKK (Indonesia) to US $18 in case of Grameen Bank (Bangladesh). In India, loans up to Rs. 25,000 are covered under microfinance. Since 36 per cent of the credit needs in the rural areas is still met by informal sources, viz. money lenders, land lords, friends and relatives, MF is a rational, relevant policy entirely in conformity with the interests of the banking system itself because of the efficacy of MF in credit dispensation, improved loan recovery and removal of poverty. Evidently, micro-credit not only provides the means for an alternative paradigm but also situates the terms of the quest for self-fulfillment in the poor and vulnerable sections of society by providing an appropriate institutional structure for rural banking in India.

MICROFINANCE / MFI FINANCE AND CREDIT LINKAGE

Reserve Bank of India had conducted a joint fact-finding study on microfinance along with some banks. The study made in one of the States revealed many areas of concern relating to MFI financing, which do not augur well for the development of best practices in the sector. The findings of the study are as under:

- Some of the MFIs financed / partnered by banks appear to be focusing on relatively better-banked areas, including areas covered by SHG Bank Linkage Programme. Competing MFIs were operating in the same area and trying to reach out to the same set of poor, resulting in multiple lending and over burdening of rural households.
- Many MFIs selected by banks were not engaging themselves in capacity building and empowerment of the groups to the desired extent. The MFIs were disbursing loans to the newly formed groups within 10-15 days of their formation in contrast to the practice of obtaining credit in the SHG Bank Linkage Programme which takes about 6-7 months for group formation/nurturing/handholding. As a result, cohesiveness and a sense of purpose were not being built up in the groups formed by these mFIs.
- Banks as principals of mFIs do not appear to be engaging them with regard to their systems, practices and lending policies with a view to ensuring better transparency and adherence to best practices. In many cases, no review of MFI operations is undertaken once having sanctioned credit facility.

Most banks have taken up microfinance through direct linkage of SHGs as well through NGOs/MFIs under their bulk lending programme for onward credit linkage of SHGs. Against the backdrop of the above findings while partnering with NGOs-MFIs /considering microfinance credit proposals of NGOs/MFIs, it is necessary to prioritise under-served and under-banked areas for their operations towards the greater goal of financial inclusion and accordingly advise the MFIs. The MFIs must be advised to lay emphasis on identification of disadvantaged and encourage group structure among them for eventual group formation and credit linkage and consciously desist from multiple/over financing individuals.

Branches/offices should look into homogeneity, group solidarity/culture by interacting with randomly chosen Self Help Groups formed by the MFI, while appraising the proposal. The business plan of the NGOs/MFIs should indicate measures for formation of new groups, sustaining group cohesion and member awareness, capacity building, pattern of activity of group members and graduating to economic activities. The credit appraisal should also look into the policies of the NGO/MFI with regard to the accounting system, interest rates and mode of application of interest, other service charges/fee charged to the groups, internal control, monitoring and follow-up action for recovery and methods of recovery.

Periodical post-sanction monitoring by the branches/offices should cover age/period of existence of SHGs credit linked during the period, proper maintenance of books of records and accounts by NGOs/MFIs, record of grading of SHGs on lent by NGO/MFI, submission of periodical MIS on lending and recovery and interaction with randomly selected SHGs credit linked by NGOs/MFIs at periodical intervals.

MICROFINANCE TRANSCENDS MICROFINANCE

MF, which is a broader concept than micro-credit, emerged as an innovative savings and loan mechanism. Microfinance is not entirely new or novel to India because of the IRDP for twenty years leading to cumulative financial assistance of around Rs. 250 billion to roughly 55 million families and an elaborate network of cooperatives, RRBs and 27 public sector banks (PSBs). Despite credit linkage of more than one million SHGs and mobilization of about Rs. 4,000 crore as credit from formal financial institutions, MF still forms a miniscule proportion of the total bank credit in India. Hence, there continues to be serious demand-supply imbalances.

STREAMLINING MF

Attempts need to be made to streamline MF by providing thrust and direction to the credit flow by identifying potential areas/activities, developing sub-sector approach based on potential refining and broad based existing credit packages, meeting the cost of promotion, training and nurturing of SHGs through convergence of resources emphasising modernisation, technology transfer, etc. Development of a sound data based information system and dissemination of information, self-financing of services by SHGs, such as, auditing, enterprise promotion, etc.; innovative/supplementary credit delivery models and conducive policy environment (Sharma, 2005) would also be useful.

A successful model of microfinance should mobilize its own resources through savings, repay their loans, cover their costs from their operational income and finance their expansion from their profits. "Sustainability" (Ledgerwood, 1999) requires offer of cost effective approaches to formal institutions for wider coverage of poor, testing other microfinance delivery innovations, synergise the tested alternative channel with the financial system, reduction in adverse selection in target groups, development of collateral substitutions, empowerment of poor and women. Institutions like the Grameen Bank, ACCION and the World Council of Credit Unions revolutionized micro-enterprise finance through repayment incentive structures, streamlined administration and market-based pricing. MFIs have developed poverty targeting strategies, which include components of ways of identifying and attracting the poor while excluding and discouraging the non-poor. Effective targeting necessitates careful consideration of various factors. Such factors include agent- related factors (type of MFIs, client needs, constraints); contextual factors (regulatory framework, infrastructure, etc.); outreach (number of people reached, poverty level of clients, in sectors of engagement, place of living, quality of services offered) and impact measurement methodologies.

HUGE MARKET AT THE "BOTTOM OF THE PYRAMID" (BOP)

A recent study of 11 major micro-entreprise finance programmes, viz. Agence de credit pour l'entreprise privee of Senegal, Asociacion Dominicana para el Desarrollo de la Mujer of the Dominican Republic, Banco Solidario of Bolivia, Badan Kredit Desa, Bank Rakyat Indonesia and Lembaga Perkreditan Desas of Indonesia, Bankin Raya Karkara of the Niger, Corporacion de Accion Solidaria of Colombia, Fondacion Integral Campesina of Costa Rica, Grameen Bank of Bangladesh, and the Kenya Rural Enterprise Programme showed that 10 of the programmes were operationally efficient. Five institutions were fully profitable, generating inflation-adjusted positive returns on assets.

As demonstrated by C.K. Prahlad in his classic book *The Fortune at the Bottom of the Pyramid*, there are teeming millions with little money. They, nevertheless, constitute a potentially profitable market estimated by the World Bank at US $225 billion a year and growing strongly. This market-led and synergy-driven thesis can easily be substantiated by the hugely successful experience of Bank Rakyat (Indonesia), Bank Pichincha's subsidiary CREDIFEC (Ecuador), ICICI (India), etc., in "building people's organisations to build people". It is, therefore, important to think out of the box and explore innovative mechanisms for reaching out to the poor, treating them as long-term investment. Professor Prahalad offers some solutions in eliminating global poverty. A large percentage of the world's population lives on a sustenance wage and millions can barely afford to get the basic goods needed for survival. It is this group that Prahalad refers to the BOP. Prahalad highlights three major points in this book. First, the BOP or those 4 billion people, who live on less than $2 a day, is a viable and profitable growth market. Secondly, to service the BOP, we need to find new and innovative approaches, world-class technologies, private enterprise, market based solutions to rise to the challenge of this vast untapped market. According to Professor Prahalad "What is needed is a better approach to help the poor, an approach that involves partnering with them to innovate and achieve sustainable win-win scenarios where the poor are actively engaged and, at the same time, the companies". Thirdly, all players especially the Government agencies, NGOs, large firms and the poor themselves must accept, to make this process work.

Rural markets are attractive because of substantial increase in purchasing power of rural communities, consumption of a large quantity of industrial and urban manufactured products post Green revolution and rural marketing initiatives are driving manufactured or processed inputs or services to rural producers or consumers. There are several examples of private companies successfully lifting people out of poverty. Jaipur Foot is tailored to the active lifestyles of the poor and it revolutionized the life of thousands of amputees around the world. Others in the health care industries are Annapurna Salt from Hindustan Lever Ltd, a company that helped to increase iodine intake and thus reduce the instance of Iodine Deficiency Disorder. Hindustan Lever Limited (HLL) an Indian subsidiary of Unilever, the largest soap producer in India, helped in combating health issue of diarrheal disease through innovative methods of marketing and the Aravind Eye Care Systems embarked on a series of innovations to bring world class eye care to the poorest people in rural and urban India.

Professor Prahalad also draws examples of some other successful companies that acted as major facilitators for poverty alleviation through their innovative ideas like ITC's e-choupal initiative began by developing technology to re-engineer procurement from rural India. The effort holds valuable lessons in rural engagement and demonstrates the magnitude of opportunity for private sector firms. In the Indian context, the BOP market is estimated at Rs. 8,27, 028 crore, of which the rural BOP market is estimated at Rs. 1, 74, 616 crore (Source: National Accounts , Statistics-projections for 2006-07, CSO, RCHS-2003-04, NDSSPI and NSSO-55th round).

Top 10 BOP Market	Size of the BOP Market (Rs. crore)	BOP Household Spend as per cent of Total Household Spend
Medinipur	6,138	65
South 24 Parganas	4,887	66
Murshidabad	4,057	63
Karimnagar	3,649	60
Dharmapuri	3,627	63
East Godavari	3,581	41
North 24 Parganas	3,293	56
Ahmadnagar	3,281	55
Solapur	3,273	70
Belgaum	3,222	69

BOP Household Annual Income Less Than Rs.1.5 lakh.

Analysis Source: Indian Analysis, Market Skyline of India 2006, District Profile.

According to a recent Assocham report, the per capita income of semi-urban Indians is Rs.15,000 per annum, whereas it is Rs. 7,000 per annum for rural populace. The per capita income of rural population is expected to double by 2012 and the rising per capita income will considerably enhance their consumption patterns. Further, the total number of rural households is expected to increase from 135 million in 2001-02 to 153 million in 2009-10. This makes it necessary to focus on the rural market. The successful model for rural business must incorporate local entrepreneurship, local distribution channels, local social networks as also a well-crafted delivery of public services-education, e-governance, health, commercial activities, such as, financial services, retailing and purchasing. This is why mega corporations like RIL, Field Fresh Foods (a joint venture between Bharati Enterprises and ELRO Holdings), ITC, etc., have justifiably identified the rural market as a potentially huge growth area.

The experience of ICICI Bank, the second largest banking institution in India, provides insights on how formal banking can improve the capacities of the poorest of the poor to participate in the larger economy. CEMEX—a giant cement manufacturer—is also featured in the form of its Patrimonio Hoy initiative to sell not only cement but complete home improvement solutions backed by convenient payment terms, support and the transfer of building skills to Mexico's poor. These examples clearly show how to innovate at the BOP and opportunities for innovation at the BOP. What is now needed is replication of such efforts on a macro scale to make a perceptible difference to the lives of the poor and deprived. The recent renewed emphasis on inclusive growth—both in India and abroad—is certainly welcome but clearly much more needs to be done in view of the enormous magnitude of the problem, the revolution of rising expectations and the blurring of geographical boundaries in an increasingly inter-linked world.

Micro-credit is profitable and indeed sustainable (Evers, et al. 2000). Global experiences show that micro-credit cannot reach the poor over the long haul at a rate of interest less than 25 per cent (funds-9-11 per cent, operations 12-15 per cent and bad debts-1-2 per cent). Not only is the interest rate lower than the informal lending rate of 48-120 per cent per annum but the poor also find these rates affordable. This is because of the high rates of return in activities, such as, petty trading, small livestock rearing and manufacturing ready-to-eat items. Consequently, there are several cases in India of corporates funding SHGs, directly or by partnerships and supporting NGOs, e.g., Citibank, ABN Amro, Hindustan Lever Ltd. (Stree-Shakti project), ITC (e-chaupal), Mahindra & Mahindra (Subha Labh), Tata Group (Kisan Sansar), HDFC, Max New Life Insurance, etc. Cashphor Financial & Technical Services (CFTS) is based on the model of Grameen Bank, where a group of 5-6 members is made and loans are given to individual members but the liability to repay is still collective. With financial help from NABARD, ICICI, UCO bank, UTI Bank, Deutsche Bank, Mumbai, Grameen Foundation USA etc., at 6 to 12 per cent interest, CFTS lends to villagers at 20 per cent interest.

Cross-country experiences (Moll, 1999) clearly reveal that innovative mechanism helps to expand and diversify local markets, boosts production of consumer goods, increases production through subcontracting and ancillary goods, e.g., toy-making, embroidery, candle-making, rearing cattle, making *papad,* pickles, automobiles, electronics, leather, textiles, furniture, electronic assemblies, handicrafts, etc. With some institutional support mechanisms in the form of credit, marketing, technology, infrastructure and training, such production can easily be upscaled while recovering almost the full cost. Large producers can use this success as a platform to penetrate new markets or consolidate the present position. Development of enterprise opportunity, growth of existing enterprises and jobs and strengthened sustainability of local communities requires restructuring and innovative approaches to streamline organizational, managerial and techno-financial capacities.

AGRICULTURAL MICROFINANCE

The Consultative Group to Assist the Poor (CGAP), supported by the International Fund for Agricultural Development (IFAD), examined over 80 providers of microfinance to identify "agricultural microfinance". CGAP stresses that successful agricultural microfinance rests on a judicious mix of 10 principal features, but it is not necessary for an effective model to incorporate all features.

ENTREPRENEURIAL PYRAMID—IMPROVING RURAL LIVELIHOODS ON A SUSTAINED BASIS

The poor are not a homogeneous mass with each group having its specific needs and absorption capacity for loans and other financial services. The target groups (markets) can be identified by the socio-economic characteristics of the clients the MFI wants to serve (including poverty level, gender, ethnicity, caste, religion) and the type and level of business activity (existing business, growth-oriented, or specific economic sectors). At the bottom of the entrepreneurial pyramid are the poor with subsistence income generating activities aimed at additional family income; at the middle level are micro-enterprises oriented towards stabilisation; and at the apex level are growth oriented small-scale enterprises. This requires a delicate balance between getting the poor eventually into the market economy and commercial lending rates and providing low-cost assistance to them at the initial stage of the entrepreneurship.

MF has distinct advantages in terms of increasing the outreach in rural areas, use of local informal organisations to deliver financial services and removal of economic constraints by strong cultural cohesion and social values and enable key innovations in the management of local MFI networks. Strong financial discipline, innovated institutional and management structures of local institutions and development of more effective savings and credit technologies are prerequisites to reduced transaction costs and enhanced sustainability. The prevailing discourses stress decentralisation of managerial functions to minimise credit delivery time, reduction of administrative costs by local employment and emphasis on training, simplified loan processing and collection, outsourcing, extension of outreach to remote areas, use of solidarity group lending methods to replace collateral and use of peer pressure for loan repayment, development of a method to replace collateral in individual lending products for the purchase of small machinery and development and diversification of products adapted to the needs and depth capacity of the clients groups in rural areas. This would significantly influence India's resurgent development process.

IMPACT ASSESSMENT

The very nature of MF makes it difficult to formulate uniform parameters of viable projects and systematic organisation of management information system (MIS) aimed at achieving the twin goals of sustainability and outreach. Such a streamlined MIS would help to reduce default and delinquency, optimize rotation of portfolio, help establish sustainable interest rates and improve operational efficiency programmes. Despite the serious theoretical, methodological and operational problems the issue is riddled with, there is a need for a continuum of objectives for impact assessment ranging from proving impacts for measuring the results of an investment to improving the practice of micro credit institutions (Hulme, 1991; Hulme and Mosley, 1996; Sebstad, et al. 1996).

Targeting the poor is saddled with controversies regarding the appropriation of benefit from micro-lending by the "better off poor" and resource crunch, which constrains a focus on the less well-off among the poor. Perceptible differences in the conditions of the poor require strengthened administrative structures, dynamic leadership, paid management staff and provision of information on available services to the poor.

SMEs IN INDIA—KEY GROWTH DRIVER

Small Scale Industries (SSIs) encompass a wide spectrum of more than 7,500 products. SSIs constitute 95 per cent of all industrial units in the country, 40 per cent of industrial output and about 35 per cent of exports. Post-reforms the growth of SSIs has almost always outperformed the growth of the industrial sector. The SSIs also act as a nursery for promoting entrepreneurial talent and as a catalyst in industrial growth through a wide network of about 3.6 million units. The role of SSIs in extricating less developed countries from the 'low-level equilibrium trap' and smashing the 'vicious circle of poverty' is congruent both with economic theory and historical experience of several countries. Hence, the growth of SSIs has continuously been stressed as an important instrument of achieving the avowed plan objective of 'growth with distributive equity'.

In the post-WTO world, however, there has been a heightened concern about the future of SMEs. The WTO prescribes the rules of the game based on non-discrimination. These relate to Most Favoured Nation Treatment (any trade concession offered to one member must be offered to all the members), National Treatment (imported goods should not be discriminated against in favour of the domestic goods—same treatment be accorded), freer trading system (with barriers coming down through negotiations) and predictable trading system (trade barriers would not be raised arbitrarily). These leading issues coalesce into the central theme of creating space for SMEs to co-exist and provide an enabling environment for a level playing field, providing SMEs with a reasonable period of time and pace for adjustment and adequate safeguards against unfair trade and investment.

The development of SSIs continues to be imperative for generation of productive employment on a sustainable basis with incremental creation of over 3 million jobs in the past five years alone and stagnant employment in the agriculture and large industry sector. SSIs also effectively check mass poverty, skewed pattern of distribution of income and wealth, low productivity and inefficiency across sectors and inter-regional disparities in growth. The sustained growth of the SSIs is, however, constrained by several structural and entrenched debilities, e.g., delayed payment of bills, technological obsolescence, inadequate working capital availability, marketing bottlenecks, weak infrastructure, lack of technological synergy between technology seekers (SSIs) and technology developers (R&D), high cost of patents and ineffective coordination between national level institutions involved in promoting fast-track development. This is why achievement of competitive advantage requires initiation and upscaling of technological upgradation and modernisation among SSIs on a much larger canvas to meet the pressing socio-economic requirements.

The growth dynamics require synchronization of the conflicting needs of allocative efficiency and equity by sectoral strategies with emphasis on investment and technology upgradation, infrastructure support, marketing credit facilities, testing, quality certification and training facilities for enhancing the inherent strength and resilience of SSIs. While technology plays an increasingly critical role in the competitive positioning of an environment, rapid proliferation of new technologies leads to rapid technological obsolescence. SSIs thus require identification of growth areas and technology requirements to meet the growing needs of growth, capacity building and equity on a much larger canvas.

A comprehensive study conducted by Swiss Development Corporation (SDC) and National Bank for Agriculture and Rural Development (NABARD) across eight states revealed that about one fourth of the rural population does not work in the agricultural sector but in the rural non-farm sector; the service sector (transportation, trading, etc.) has great potential for new jobs and agriculture and the non-farm sector are economically inter-dependent.

Employment expressed in terms of mono-dimensional measure like person hours, days, month or year is grossly inadequate. Hence, it needs to be supplemented by corresponding data/information on qualitative characteristics like earnings, productivity, regularity, stability, physical conditions of work, etc. (Papola, et al. 1999). Enhancement of the quality of employment and incomes in SSIs necessitates enabling Government policies, thrust on increased employment for unskilled workers and augmenting the incomes of the women by creating opportunities in the higher productivity sectors. Empirical evidence strongly suggests that identification of pro-poor growth engines at sub-sectoral level rather than at the level of broad sectors is of greater contemporary relevance.

WINDS OF CHANGE—BIG TRANSITION TRAVAILS FOR SMALL UNITS

The development of small industries significantly influences macro-economic parameters, such as, employment, industrial production and exports. However, in the post-reforms period, SSIs are confronted with an intensely competitive environment due to globalisation, domestic economic liberalisation and dilution of sector specific protective measures. Rural credit markets are characterised by high cost of legal enforcement, imperfect information, collateral security, underdevelopment in complimentary institutions and covariant risks. Consequently, a number of alternative strategies have to be devised to attract greater inward investment and unleash latent indigenous potential in the form of entrepreneurship and helping existing business to realise their expansion plans.

The development of entrepreneurship requires not just direct inputs but more importantly a broader framework characterised by stable economic conditions, relatively easy access to capital and an efficient physical infrastructure. This is necessary for the accentuation of a paradigm shift from the ethos of dependency and vulnerability to self-reliance and globally competitive capability. The spectrum of these promotional measures encompassing improved production methods, penetrative marketing strategies and modern scientific management capabilities would influence the determinants of growth by removing bottlenecks to business development. The introduction of innovative business models and financial technologies the world over received an impetus through (a) increasing integration of the productive process by outsourcing, licensing, subcontracting and other cooperative efforts, (b) rapid technological advances in the digital era, (c) the lowering or removal of the legal and institutional barriers to international trade and (d) a smoother and unhampered flow of international capital.

DEVELOPMENT OF SSIs—PARADIGM SHIFT FROM 'PROTECTION' TO 'PROMOTION'

In the context of developing countries like India preoccupied with the task of attaining higher growth rates, it is important not to be impervious to the concerns of development of SSIs. Despite the considerably reduced severity of the 'inspector raj' in the post liberalization era, the institutional procedures and formalities of managing an enterprise in India are still comparatively large, cumbersome and expensive in terms of both finance and time. In the present context, where the focus has shifted from 'protection' to 'promotion', SSIs should be calibrated to emerge from the environment of protection to face the emerging challenges of competition both within and outside the country. Leveraging of the dynamism, flexibility and innovativeness of SSIs increases manifold the financial and credit requirements of SSIs. Reduction of regional and sectoral imbalances by exploiting the available potential with appropriate development and credit packages, strengthening the system of planning, policy and operations to promote sustainable growth in SSIs for promotion of exports and employment, evolving credit support packages for diverse regions, development of common pool resources with appropriate technological, economic, legal and institutional measures, preferential treatment to the credit needs of SSIs could stimulate local economic development. Chadha (1986) forcefully stressed accessibility of RNFS as follows: "From the view point of employment and earnings of the rural household it hardly matters whether non-farm employment is available in the village itself or in a nearby village/town. In other words, all economic activities which display sufficient strong linkages with rural households irrespective of whether they are located in designated rural areas or not, should be a part and parcel of their employment-income matrix. After all, many of the rural households derive employment and income benefits from diverse varieties of non-farm activities, whether completely in the rural areas or partly in the rural areas or partly in the nearby urban areas or through any other arrangement. The sheer existence and the accessibility of the non-farm employment is the real question."

CREDIT DISPENSATION TO SSIs

Banks and financial institutions provide a range of modalities and terms for loans aimed at improving development performance of the SSIs, particularly output, employment and exports. These and other changes of far-reaching consequences were at least partly brought about by progressively larger doses of credit and the increasing availability of support mechanisms. The steady increase in the flow of bank credit to micro-enterprises in rural areas to help the vulnerable sections of society, including women (Sharma, 2001) influenced both the development of forces of production and the relations of production in a chain of 'cumulative causation'. The significance of adoption of modern technology to produce globally competitive goods and services increased manifold in the post-reforms period. But the rising globalisation of emerging economies, acceleration of capital flows and consolidation and convergence of financial markets cause concern. As business expands and practices evolve, management of change requires secular dynamic change and structural transformation. This requires transcending of the achievement of quantitative targets in terms of physical units and financial outlay and a thrust on various inter-related issues. These issues include those of speed, customer preference, quality certification, technology upgradation, cost reduction, professional learning, innovation promotion, marketing development and infrastructural support in a coordinated and concerted manner.

ROLE OF FIS AND BANKS IN FINANCING OF SSIs

Entrepreneurs need short-term, medium-term and long-term finance. Accordingly, the conventional mechanism for financing of SSIs in India stressed provision of term capital and working capital. Public and private sector banks, Small Industries Development Bank of India (SIDBI), NABARD, Regional Rural Banks (RRBs), urban co-operative banks (UCBs) and foreign banks meet the financial and credit needs of the sector. Public sector banks (PSBs) were conceived and functioned as instruments of social change and emancipation and also played a pivotal role in developing small industries. Banks have been involved in directed lending for a host of poverty alleviation/ self-employment programmes to enhance the standards of living of the downtrodden/neglected sections of society. Commercial banks (CBs) have been consistently directed by the RBI to allocate 40 per cent of their lending towards the priority sector, which includes agriculture, small scale industries, tiny sector, village and cottage industries, small traders, professionals and self-employed, etc. In view of the genuine difficulty of many SSIs, particularly the first generation entrepreneurs in accessing bank credit because of their inability to provide adequate collateral security, GoI launched a Credit Guarantee Fund Scheme. The Credit Guarantee Fund Trust for Small Industries (CGTSI), set up by the GoI and SIDBI, is the nodal agency for the scheme.

CONSTRAINTS AND CONCERNS

While the outstanding amount of credit to the SSI sector by PSBs steadily rose, the percentage share of SSIs in net bank credit (NBC) progressively declined. Such concern and consternation at least partly emanates from the difficulty of SSIs in surviving the screening of the credit mechanism set up by commercial banks, which pursue "reasonable risks and prudent stable returns". This causes a disconnect between SSIs' need for funds and their raising of finance. As SSIs continue to be an integral part of the blueprint of development, management of change requires not rhetoric but immediate and effective action as strongly urged by the recent Parliamentary Standing Committee on Industry (129th Report on Credit Flow to the SSI Sector). The Committee suggested relaxation of norms for banks in declaring SSI units as NPAs by considering factors such as delayed payments, blockage of credit flow and the enactment of the Securitisation Act.

INNOVATIVE FINANCING OF SSIs

A multi-agency credit structure evolved over the years in India to meet the financial needs of the sector. Traditionally, term capital required for creation of fixed assets like land, building, plant and machinery and other capital assets is raised from the market by way of issuing equity based and / or debt instruments of banks and other institutional sources. But SSIs meet working capital requirements by own funds, equity support, sundry creditors, bank borrowings and other short-term borrowings. Of late, a welcome process of convergence is discernible for both these type of funds. While the conventional instruments of financing the sector were successful to some extent, these are clearly inadequate. In view of the real and worrisome fault lines of the conventional process, nothing less than a fresh approach would serve to meaningfully redefine the parameters governing the SSIs. Questions such as how do various sub-sectors of the SSIs work together in development; whether there are alternative schemata being activated in simultaneously sequential or parallel development and the relationship between individual and societal expectations, frameworks and goals need to be explored and examined. Promotion of the SSIs with customer-centric strategies could thus work as a trigger mechanism in fostering faster development.

Timely and adequate credit is a basic pre-requisite of highly competitive global scenario. But, ultimately the SSIs have to improve their productivity and efficiency by adopting modern technology to produce globally competitive goods and services. Streamlining of the legal and institutional framework of the financial sector, application of market-oriented financing instruments, linking of the small enterprise sector to the formal capital markets, introduction of innovative financing techniques with simultaneous subsidisation of learning costs (e.g. revolving funds, leasing, factoring, securitisation) and introduction of new and variable techniques for securing loans (e.g. forms of joint liability) are called for. There is now also a need to specify guidelines relating to extension of credit by a financial institution to different categories of small enterprises, norms regarding quantum, proportion, method of computation, completion of formalities, revival packages, margins, collateral security, timely disposal and any other aspects that will ensure expeditious and easy flow of credit, both long term and working capital, to the small enterprises over the long haul. Different norms may be established for in respect of different categories of (a) small enterprises differentiated on rational criteria, (b) financial institutions and (a) credit facilities like term loans, working capital loans, etc.

The way ahead for SMEs is full of challenges. But the recently revised definition of SMEs is widely expected to give a big boost to the development of SMEs across the development spectrum.

Small & Medium Enterprises (SME) Sector—Revised Definitions and Enactment of MSMED Act, 2006

The Government of India has enacted Micro, Small and Medium Enterprises Development (MSMED) Act 2006 and the same has been notified in the Gazette vide Notification No S.O.1154 (E) dated 18.07.2006. This MSMED Act has come into effect from 2nd October 2006. The revised definitions in terms of MSMED Act, 2006 and reporting of data pertaining to SME sector are furnished here below:

Definitions:

	Manufacturing	Services
Micro-Enterprise	The investment in Plant and Machinery (original cost) does not exceed Rs. 25 lakhs.	The investment in equipment does not exceed Rs. 10 lakhs.
Small Enterprise	Investment in Plant & Machinery (original cost) is more than Rs. 25 lakhs but does not exceed Rs. 500 lakhs.	The investment in equipment is more than Rs. 10 lakhs but does not exceed Rs. 200 lakhs.
Medium Enterprise	Investment in Plant & Machinery (original cost) is more than Rs. 500 lakhs but does not exceed Rs. 1000 lakhs.	The investment in equipment is more than Rs. 200 lakhs but does not exceed Rs. 500 lakhs.

Notes:

1. Enterprise means an industrial undertaking or a business concern or any other establishment, by whatever name called, engaged in the manufacture or production of goods, in any manner pertaining to any industry specified in the First Schedule to the Industries (Development and Regulation) Act, 1951 or engaged in providing or rendering of any service or services.
2. In calculating the investment in plant & machinery, the cost of pollution control, research and development, industrial safety devices and such other items as may be specified, by notification, shall be excluded.
3. The word equipment is defined as "All instruments, office machines and such other electro mechanical or electronic appliances that are directly related to the service rendered but excluding furniture, fittings and other items not so related"

STRATEGIC OPTIONS AND CHOICES

Well-defined policy and procedures need include political will and determination, technological modernization, marketing with a focus on exports, adequate fulfillment of their credit needs by streamlined policy framework, provision of institutional and infrastructural support, promotion of appropriate linkages between large and small industries and coordinated action reflecting sectoral and regional differences by thrust on factoring and venture capital. Market segmentation through classifications based on (a) ownership, (b) operational stages, (c) geographical sources and (d) operational sectors would help to attain a sustainable growth trajectory. Classifications are also possible according to technology contents, industrial chain and bank-enterprise relations. In the emerging socio-economic milieu, the role of markets needs to be supplemented by Government support for enhancing the competitive edge. A deeper understanding of the market dynamics requires TQM, business process re-engineering (BPR) and financial restructuring. Appropriate repositioning, product and process innovation, increased activity given by learning curve across companies, benchmarking and other improvement-oriented programmes are important in the quest for multidimensional and multi-layered development of SSIs. All these make it necessary for SSIs, "to develop a global vision, respond to more demanding standards of customers, identify the patterns of shifting value and craft the key strategies that will leapfrog them ahead of competition" (Kapur Committee).

Things are not easy any more for SSIs with both the sector and all Development Financial Institutions (DFIs)—IDBI, SIDBI, IFCI, ICICI, IIBI and IDFC—being at the crossroads. Hence the developmental agenda must be implemented with alacrity. In sum, the background developmental processes need not be taken as exogenously given. What is needed is an action plan for defining strategic customer segments and value propositions, establishing enterprise wide customer guiding principles, identifying specific synergies, variations and gaps among business units and creating strategic customer initiatives.

GOING FORWARD

There are important elements of commonalities between financial inclusion, MF and SMEs. In the ultimate analysis, there is a need to graduate from MF to financial inclusion, which is far more comprehensive and encompassing than MF. Despite strong evidence thrown up by the steadily burgeoning literature on microfinance that the poor are creditworthy, the "poorest of the poor" may always not be creditworthy. These people must primarily have their basic needs fulfilled, such as health, education, and community development, services that they could not reasonably be expected to repay. Hence MF cannot be the panacea and would have to be supplemented by other services, especially training, information and access to land. Elisabeth Ryhne points out, that "important voices" outside of microfinance argue, "that the very poorest people are not reached by even the most poverty-oriented micro-credit programs, and that credit is not an appropriate service for people on the margin of survival". Clearly, then, the development of sustainable financing mechanisms needs to be dovetailed with holistic Government planning and budgetary procedures to qualitatively transform the lives of the poor.

There is no doubt that the reform of the national financial architecture must lead to early and sustained results to deal more effectively with future challenges and to raise general living standards. As President John F. Kennedy succinctly pointed out in his historic inaugural address delivered on January 20, 1961, "to those people in the huts and villages of half the globe struggling to break the bonds of mass misery, we pledge our best efforts to help them help themselves, for whatever period is required—not because ..., but because it is right. *If a free society cannot help the many who are poor, it cannot save the few who are rich*".

The dynamics of the underlying forces at work require an accelerated inclusive growth process. Financial inclusion is a win-win situation for the financially excluded, the corporate, the Government and the banks. An accent on financial inclusion and microfinance would, therefore, promote the avowed goal of growth with distributive equity, particularly at a time, when the greatest challenge is to unlock the potential of the people by providing them "skill for work". With one of the youngest populations in the world (the mean age of an Indian today is 24 years) and the only large country projected to have a declining age-dependency ratio till 2035, India is strategically positioned to be the "skill capital" of the world and leverage its demographic dividend. As Mr. Haruhiko Kuroda, President, Asian Development Bank, succinctly said in his closing address at 39th Annual Meeting of ADB held at Hyderabad in May 2006, "Pragmatic, sensible solutions for inclusive social development and sustained, equitable growth; a focus on good governance; and a commitment to environmental responsibility in the region will benefit everyone in the region, and they will certainly benefit the poor". These are powerful and inspiring thoughts and need to be fully implemented to create meaning and value in the lives of the poor, the vulnerable and the downtrodden sections of society. It is only then that India's 'tryst with destiny' and the vision of a 'brave new world' will be fully realized in India's journey from *swaraj* (self-rule) to *suraj* (good rule). The task ahead may be difficult; the road long and tortuous but coordinated and concerted measures with a sense of urgency are needed to meet the challenges of the present and the expectations of the future, to achieve the Millennium Development Goals (MDGs) of poverty reduction, gender balance, disease eradication, illiteracy, etc. Reduced exclusion from the growth process and improved social indicators require a paradigm shift from the conventional metrics based primarily on GDP growth rates, FDI, sensex, etc., to poverty ratio, infant and maternal mortality, nutrition levels, educational standards, employment, literacy, school enrolment and drop-out rates, etc. Promotion of labour-intensive manufacturing exports, changing from subsidy-based to productivity enhancing investments in agriculture, increasing women's agency and increasing public provision of essential services are also important elements of the overarching process of inclusive growth and realize the dream of a land free of the scourge of poverty.

REFERENCES

Agarwal, Bina (2000): "The Idea of Gender Equality: From Legislative Vision to Everyday Family Practices", *India: Another Millennium?* (ed.) Romilla Thapar, Viking, New Delhi.

Bardhan, Pranab (1995): "The New Institutional Economics and Development Theory", Reprinted in *Leading Issues in Economic Development*, Gerald M. Meier, OUP.

Besley, Timothy (1994): 'How Do Market Failures Justify Interventions in Rural Credit Markets', *The World Bank Research Observer*, Vol. 9, No. 1.

Chadha, G.K. (1986): "Non-farm Employment for Rural Households in India", *Indian Journal of Labour Economics*, No. 3.

Evers, J., Jack, S., Loeff, A and Siewertsen, H. (2000): *Reducing Cost and Managing Risk in Lending to Micro-enterprises: Handbook for Micro-lending in Europe*, FACET/IFF.

Harper, Malcolm (2002): "Promotion of Self Help Groups under the SHG Bank Linkage Program in India", Seminar on *SHG-bank Linkage Programme*, New Delhi, November 25-26.

Herath, Gamini (1996): "Rural Credit Markets: A New Perspective", *Savings and Development*, Vol. XX, No. 2.

Hulme, D. (1997): *Impact Assessment Methodologies for Microfinance: A Review*. Washington, D.C.: Management Systems International.

Hulme, D. and Mosley, P. (1996): *Finance against Poverty*, Volumes 1 and 2. Routledge, London.

Ledgerwood, J. (1999): "Sustainable Banking with the Poor", *Microfinance Handbook: An Institutional and Financial Perspective*, The World Bank, Washington.

Leeladhar, V. (2005): Commemorative Lecture on 'Financial Inclusion' at the Fedbank Hormis Memorial Foundation at Ernakulam on December 2.

Moll, H. (1999): *Microfinance and Development*, Selected articles, February.

Papola, T.S. and Sharma, Alakh N. (eds.)(1999): *Gender and Employment in India*, Indian Society of Labour Economics, Institute of Economic Growth and Vikas Publishing House Pvt. Ltd., New Delhi.

Patel, I.G. (1994): "Limits of Current Consensus on Development", *Proceedings of the World Bank Annual Conference on Development Economics*, World Bank.

Prahalad, C.K. (2004): *The Fortune at the Bottom of the Pyramid: Eradicating Poverty through Profits*, Watson School Publishing.

Reserve Bank of India: *Report on Trend & Progress of Banking in India* (various issues).

Report of the Committee on Informal Financial Sector Statistics (Summary) under Chairmanship of Dr. C. Rangarajan.

Role of Financial Intermediation Services in the Informal Sector. *Financial Inclusion Taskforce: Report on Progress towards the Shared Goal.*

Reserve Bank of India (2005): *Financial Inclusion*: RBI Circular No. RBI/ 2005-06/ 233 RPCD.RF.BC.54/ 07.38.01/2005-06 dated 13.12.2005.

Rhyne, Elisabeth (1998): "The Yin and Yan of Microfinance: Reaching the Poor and Sustainability", *MicroBanking Bulletin*, Vol. 2, No. 1, pp. 6-8.

Sebstad, J. and Chen, G. (1996): *Overview of Studies on the Impact of Microenterprise Credit*, AIMS, USAID, Washington.

Schumpeter, Joseph A. (1975): *Capitalism, Socialism and Democracy,* New York: Harper (originally published 1942).

Sengupta, Arjun (2006): Press Note dated 16.5.2006 on Report and Draft Bill on Social Security for Unorganised Workers—Government of India, National Commission for Enterprises in the Unorganised Sector under Chairmanship of Dr. Arjun Sengupta.

Sharma, Manoranjan (2005): "Rapidly Expanding Frontiers of Micro Finance: Assessment and Prospects", *Studies in Money, Finance and Banking*, Atlantic Publishers & Distributors (P) Ltd., New Delhi.

Stiglitz, Joseph E. and Hoff, Karla (1990): "Introduction: Imperfect Information and Rural Credit Markets: Puzzles and Policy Perspectives", *The World Bank Economic Review*, Vol. 4, No. 3.

Thorat, Usha (2006): Inaugural address on "Establishing Consumer Centric Financial Services Delivery Infrastructure" organized by the Financial Planning Standards Boards of India on May 29 at New Delhi.

Willamson, Oliver E. (1994): "The Institutions and Governance of Economic Development and Reform", *Proceedings of the World Bank Annual Conference on Development Economics.*

World Bank (1978): "Rural Enterprises and Non-farm Employment", *A World Bank Paper,* Washington, D.C.

—— (1978): "Employment and Development of Small Enterprises", *Sectoral Policy Paper*, World Bank, Washington, D.C.

—— (2003): *Microfinance in India: Issues, Challenges and Policy Option.* Washington DC: World Bank.

—— (2003a): *India: Development Policy Review—Sustaining Reform, Reducing Poverty*. Washington DC. World Bank.

—— (2006): *Inclusive Growth and Service Delivery: Building on India's Success,* Washington DC. World Bank.

Yaron, Jacob (1992): "Successful Rural Financial Institutions", *World Bank Discussion Paper,* No. 150.

Annexure: Coverage of Banking Services (Ratio of Demand Deposit Accounts to the Adult Population)

Region/State/Union Territory	Current Accounts	Savings Accounts	Total Population	Adult Population (Above 19 years)	Total No. of Accounts	No. of Acc. Per 100 of Population	No. of Acc. Per 100 of Adult Population
1	2	3	4	5	6	7	8
NORTHERN REGION	**4215701**	**52416125**	**132676462**	**67822312**	**56631826**	**43**	**84**
Haryana	572660	8031472	21082989	11308025	8604132	41	76
Himachal Pradesh	134285	2433595	6077248	3566886	2567880	42	72
Jammu & Kashmir	277529	3094790	10069917	5379594	3372319	33	63
Punjab	1156137	13742201	24289296	14185190	14898338	61	105
Rajasthan	689657	12139302	56473122	28473743	12828959	23	45
Chandigarh	80607	1126696	900914	546171	1207303	134	221
Delhi	1304826	11848069	13782976	7929589	13152895	95	166
NORTH-EASTERN REGION	**476603**	**6891081**	**38495089**	**19708982**	**7367684**	**19**	**37**
Arunachal Pradesh	10538	209073	1091117	544582	219611	20	40
Assam	378729	5071058	26638407	14074393	5449787	20	39
Manipur	12514	200593	2388634	1222107	213107	9	17
Meghalaya	24305	458779	2306069	1088165	483084	21	44
Mizoram	3441	117885	891058	476205	121326	14	25
Nagaland	13819	195452	1988636	995523	209271	11	21
Tripura	33257	638241	3191168	1784212	671498	21	38
EASTERN REGION	**1814219**	**47876140**	**227613073**	**122136133**	**49690359**	**22**	**41**
Bihar	464511	13225242	82878796	40934170	13689753	17	33
Jharkhand	166007	5834341	26909428	13737485	6000348	22	44
Orissa	228160	7030004	36706920	21065404	7258164	20	34

(Contd....)

1	2	3	4	5	6	7	8
Sikkim	4097	125365	540493	288500	129462	24	45
West Bengal	942733	21544753	80221171	45896914	22487486	28	49
Andaman & Nicobar Islands	8711	116435	356265	213660	125146	35	59
CENTRAL REGION	**2202217**	**64254189**	**255713495**	**129316677**	**66456406**	**26**	**51**
Chhattisgarh	192067	3346898	20795956	11209425	3538965	17	32
Madhya Pradesh	553381	11731918	60385118	31404990	12285299	20	39
Uttar Pradesh	1324509	45804350	166052859	82229748	47128859	28	57
Uttaranchal	132260	3371023	8479562	4472514	3503283	41	78
WESTERN REGION	**3178102**	**49525101**	**149071747**	**86182206**	**52703203**	**35**	**61**
Goa	81551	1584177	1343998	891411	1665728	124	187
Gujarat	955964	16220262	50596992	28863095	17176226	34	60
Maharashtra	2127240	31568184	96752247	56207604	33695424	35	60
Dadra & Nagar Haveli	6076	69308	220451	122765	75384	34	61
Daman & Diu	7271	83170	158059	97331	90441	57	93
SOUTHERN REGION	**4666014**	**83386898**	**223445381**	**135574225**	**88052912**	**39**	**65**
Andhra Pradesh	1156405	23974580	75727541	44231918	25130985	33	57
Karnataka	1086662	19147819	52733958	30623289	20234481	38	66
Kerala	600065	17669723	31838619	20560323	18269788	57	89
Tamil Nadu	1786514	22052812	62110839	39511038	23839326	38	60
Lakshadweep	491	22997	60595	33686	23488	39	70
Pondicherry	35877	518967	973829	613971	554844	57	90
ALL-INDIA	**16552856**	**304349534**	**1027015247**	**541031553**	**320902390**	**31**	**59**

Source: Reserve Bank of India.

Contributors

Y.V. Reddy, Governor, Reserve Bank of India, Mumbai.

M.B.N. Rao, Chairman and Managing Director, Canara Bank, Bangalore.

Rajesh Chakrabarti, Professor, College of Management, Georgia Tech, Atlanta, USA.

Y.S.P. Thorat, Chairman, National Bank for Agriculture and Rural Development, (NABARD), Mumbai.

Amitabh Kumar, IRS, Director-General, Competition Commission, Government of India, New Delhi.

Rakesh Mohan, Deputy Governor, Reserve Bank of India, Mumbai.

Ashima Goyal, Professor, Indira Gandhi Institute of Development Studies (IGIDR), Mumbai.

Ranjan Kumar Dash, Research Consultant, Institute of Economic Growth, Delhi.

Ashutosh Saxena, Institute for Development and Research in Banking Technology (IDRBT), Hyderabad.

Debesh Roy, Assistant General Manager, National Bank for Agriculture and Rural Development, (NABARD), Raebareli.

Golaka C. Nath, Advisor, Clearing Corporation of India Ltd. (CCIL), Mumbai.

Manoj Dalvi, Associate Professor, Long Island University, USA.

Amir Ullah Khan, Deputy Secretary General, Punjab, Haryana and Delhi Chamber of Commerce and Industry (PHDCCI), New Delhi.

Saleema Razvi, Researcher, Department of Community Health, Jawaharlal Nehru University, New Delhi.

Manoranjan Sharma, Chief Economist, Deputy General Manager, Canara Bank, Bangalore.